Roman Catholic/Pentecostal Dialogue (1977-1982):
A Study in Developing Ecumenism

STUDIEN ZUR INTERKULTURELLEN GESCHICHTE DES CHRISTENTUMS
ETUDES D'HISTOIRE INTERCULTURELLE DU CHRISTIANISME
STUDIES IN THE INTERCULTURAL HISTORY OF CHRISTIANITY

begründet von / fondé par / founded by
Hans Jochen Margull †, Hamburg

herausgegeben von / édité par / edited by

Richard Friedli
Université de Fribourg

Walter J. Hollenweger
University of Birmingham

Theo Sundermeier
Universität Heidelberg

J.A.B. Jongeneel
Rijksuniversiteit Utrecht

Band 44

Verlag Peter Lang
Frankfurt am Main · Bern · New York · Paris

Jerry L. Sandidge

ROMAN CATHOLIC/ PENTECOSTAL DIALOGUE (1977-1982): A STUDY IN DEVELOPING ECUMENISM

Volume II

Verlag Peter Lang

Frankfurt am Main · Bern · New York · Paris

CIP-Kurztitelaufnahme der Deutschen Bibliothek

Sandidge, Jerry L.:

Roman Catholic Pentecostal dialogue (1977 -
1982): a study in developing ecumenism /
Jerry L. Sandidge. — Frankfurt am Main ; Bern ;
New York ; Paris : Lang
  (Studies in the intercultural history of
  christianity ; Vol. 44)
  ISBN 3-8204-9877-X
NE: Studien zur interkulturellen Geschichte des
Christentums
Vol. 2 (1987).

BX
8764.2
.S26
1987
vol. 2

Library of Congress Cataloging-in-Publication Data

Sandige, Jerry L.
  Roman Catholic/Pentecostal dialogue (1977-1982)

  (Studien zur interkulturellen Geschichte des
Christentums = Etudes d'histoire interculturelle du
christianisme = Studies in the Intercultural history
of Christianity ; Bd. 44)
  Originally presented as the author's thesis (Ph. D.)
--Katholieke Universiteit Leuven, 1985.
  Bibliography: p.
  1. Catholic Church--Relations--Pentecostal churches
--History. 2. Pentecostal churches--Relations--Catholic
Church--History. I. Title. II. Series: Studien zur
interkulturellen Geschichte des Christentums ; Bd. 44.
BX8764.2.S26 1987   282   87-4221
ISBN 3-8204-9877-X

ISSN 0170-9240
ISBN 3-8204-9877-X

© Verlag Peter Lang GmbH, Frankfurt am Main 1987

TABLE OF CONTENTS

ROMAN CATHOLIC/PENTECOSTAL DIALOGUE 1977-1982

Dialogue Documents

This volume contains all of the documents prepared for and used in the quinquennial Dialogue sessions. The items are arranged in the same order for each year, with one exception, to be discussed later.

Photograph of Participants--including the full dialogue team, Roman Catholics, Pentecostals (both "participants" and "observers"), and various guests who were present at some time during the week of discussions.

Schedule-Agenda--though called by various names, i.e., "Proposed Agenda," "Proposed Schedule," "Daily Schedule," is the outline of the Dialogue week, including meal times, prayer time, and plenary sessions. The format changed from year to year, so they are not uniform but are presented just as they were in the Dialogue. Any significant information that is added is offset in brackets ([]).

Theological Papers--comprise the heart of the Dialogue week. Normal procedure was to present two papers, one from each side, on two different topics. Thus, a total of four theological papers are included for 1977, 1979, and 1980. In 1981 only two papers were the basis of discussion because the subject of Mary, the Mother of Jesus, consumed almost the whole week. So in 1982 the papers on ministry were re-read and discussed and the quinquennial report was drawn up.

Agreed Account--is the summary drawn up at the end of each Dialogue week. This document is intended to be the "expression-of-consensus" statement pointing out areas of agreement and divergence, as well as presenting a review of the subjects discussed.

Press Release--is always prepared at the end of the Dialogue week to share the major points of the Dialogue session with the secular and religious press. Material within brackets ([]) indicates additions to the original texts.

The only exception to this arrangement is for 1982. In this instance Agreed Account and Press Release reverse positions. The Agreed Account is renamed Final Report, which is the report covering all five Dialogue sessions. It is by necessity longer, and the report on the theological discussion on ministry (the 1982 theme) is included in the five-year Final Report.

There are several reasons why it was considered important to include all the Dialogue papers as Volume Two of this dissertation. 1) Only half of the papers are published and none of the consensus statements for 1977-1981 will be published. 2) All Dialogue papers from the first quinquennium (1972-1976) were not fully published, and they did not appear in Arnold Bittlinger's, Papst und Pfingstler, and consequently are not available for research purposes. 3) It was felt all the Dialogue documents would provide insight into the process and organization of the Dialogue, as well as having them at hand while reading Volume One.

4) Future research projects concerning bilateral dialogues might find here a helpful model.

Finally, a word needs to be said about the presentation of these documents, especially the <u>Theological</u> <u>Papers</u>. Except for evident spelling and/or grammatical errors, the papers are presented in the exact format as they were first given. Although, a similar order or outline of the material was used. They are not always uniform and some do not conform with standard dissertation procedure. However, it was felt that to "rearrange" them into a single style could prejudice the papers and bring criticism of "tampering" with the documents. The secretaries for both sides of the Dialogue have varified that this Appendix contains all and only the documents prepared for and in the second quinquennium of the Roman Catholic/Pentecostal Dialogue.

--PENTECOST 1987

ROMAN CATHOLIC/PENTECOSTAL DIALOGUE
3–7 October 1977—Rome

Dialogue Participants

1. Fr Joseph Lécuyer, CSSP
2. Rev Thomas Roberts
3. Msgr Basil Meeking
4. Rev Justus T. du Plessis
5. Rev James Lane
6. Fr Heribert Mühlen
7. Fr William J. Dalton, SJ
8. Rev Paul Finkenbinder
9. Rev David J. du Plessis
10. Rev James E. Worsfold
11. Rev F. P. Möller
12. Bsp W. Robert McAlister
13. Fr Pierre Duprey. WF
14. Rev John L. Meares
15. Fr Jan H. Walgrave, OP

ROMAN CATHOLIC/PENTECOSTAL DIALOGUE
3-7 October 1977 - Rome

Schedule - Agenda

3 October, Monday

4:00 p.m.   Tea

4:30   Session

    I.   i) Worship . . . . . . Msgr. B. Meeking
        ii) Welcome . . . . Father P. Duprey, WF,
                     Bishop R. McAlister
      iii) Introductions
      iv) The dialogue, its scope and
           orientation
       v) Practical details

    II. "Speaking in Tongues" - paper by
                 Dr. Vinson Synan

    Discussion

7:30   Supper

4 October, Tuesday

8:15 a.m.   Breakfast

9:30   "Speaking in Tongues" - paper by
               Fr. Kilian McDonnell, OSB

11:00   Coffee break

11:30 - 1:00   Plenary - Discussion

1:30 p.m.   Lunch

3:45   Tea

4:00 - 7:00   Plenary - Discussion

7:30   Supper

5 October, Wednesday

8:15 a.m.   Breakfast

9:30   "Faith and Experience" - paper by Dr. F. P.
               Möller

Dialogue Schedule - Agenda 1977

11:00 a.m.	Coffee break
11:30 - 1:00	"Faith and Experience" - paper by Fr. J. H. Walgrave, OP
1:30 p.m.	Lunch
3:45	Tea
4:00 - 7:00	Plenary - Discussion
7:30	Supper

6 October, Thursday

8:15 a.m.	Breakfast
9:30	Plenary - issues arising from the discussion
11:00	Coffee break
11:30 - 1:00	Plenary
1:30 p.m.	Lunch
3:45	Tea
4:00 - 7:00	Plenary
7:30	Supper

7 October, Friday

8:15 a.m.	Breakfast
9:30	Discussion and approval of draft
11:00	Coffee break
11:30 - 1:00	Discussion and approval of draft
1:30 p.m.	Lunch
3:45	Tea
4:00 - 7:00	Discussion and approval of draft
	Worship

Theological Paper

SPEAKING IN TONGUES
by
Rev Vinson Synan

Few religious movements have attracted the attention
of Christians in the twentieth century more than the Pentecostal and charismatic groups that have sprung up around
the world since the early beginnings in 1901. Likewise,
nothing taught and practiced by the Pentecostals has attracted more attention than the phenomenon of speaking in
tongues. Although glossolalia is not the essense of pentecostalism or of the "baptism in the Holy Spirit," it is
nonetheless the most spectacular and taked about practice
associated with pentecostal teachings.

The purpose of this paper will be to present a brief
survey of the teaching on speaking in tongues as commonly
believed and practiced by the traditional Pentecostals who
are now commonly known as the "classical Pentecostals."
(Including such groups as the Assemblies of God, the Church
of God, the Pentecostal Holiness Church, and the Church of
of God in Christ.) By its brevity, the paper will attempt
to be suggestive rather than comprehensive.

I. GLOSSOLALIA--PAST AND PRESENT

No serious student of the Scriptures maintains that the church was not charismatic in the book of Acts and that glossolalia was a common experience of the early Christians. Furthermore, no serious student of church history questions the fact that the early church retained its primitive pentecostal power in the decades of struggle before the triumph of Christianity in the west under Constantine. There is some controversy, however, as to when the church lost its apostolic power and as to the reasons why.

It is clear that the Montanist Movement of the second century A.D. represented an attempt to restore the charisms to the church that seemed to be dying out. Despite some early successes, Montanism was ultimately condemned as heretical by the Catholic Church--thus producing a legacy of fear of spectacular charismatic manifestations in the church.

The over-reaction to Montanism continued until modern times. Although a few special saints were said to speak with unknown tongues and produce miracles of healing through the centuries, the Church tended more and more to teach that the miracles of the Apostolic Age ended with the early church. Then followed the institutionalization of the Church with the less spectacular charisms of government, administration, and teaching remaining to the heirarchy.

Indeed, gifts such as glossolalia became so rare that the Church quite forgot their proper function in the Church. As the centuries rolled by, speaking in a language not learned by the speaker was seen as evidence of possession by an evil spirit rather than the Holy Spirit. By 1000 A.D. the Roman Ritual (*Rituale Romanorum*) defined glossolalia as *prima facia* evidence of demon possession. Thus the charismata fairly faded from the scene except in the lives of selected saints and mystics, primarily in monastic communities.

It might have been expected that the Reformation under Martin Luther and John Calvin would have restored the charismata to the Church as the common heritage of all believers. Yet this was not to be. One of the charges leveled against the reformers was that their movement lacked the miracles confirming their beginnings as did the founders of the Catholic Church in the New Testament. The apostolic miracles of healings, tongues, prophecies, etc., were seen as divine approval on the beginnings of the Church. Catholics pointed their finger at Luther and Calvin and demanded to be shown the signs and wonders which would attest to their authenticity as a true orthodox church.

Luther and Calvin simply replied to these charges by stating that the miraculous, charismatic, pentecostal gifts were only intended for the beginning of Christianity and had long since ceased to operate in the church. The reformers never tired of ridiculing miraculous claims of the Roman Church, along with the saints who were said to have performed them.

Thus, through the centuries, Christendom, in its Greek, Roman, and Protestant branches adopted the view that

6

the supernatural gifts of the Spirit had ended with the early Church and that with completion of the Canon of Scripture they would never be needed again. The Catholic mystical tradition allowed for a few saints possessed of "heroic holiness" to exersize some of the gifts--but such holiness was reserved for the clergy (bishops, priests, monks, and nuns) but not for the masses of ordinary Christians.

This view became the accepted "conventional wisdom" of the Church until the nineteenth century when historical and theological events caused the beginning of a dramatic change of view in various quarters--notably in England and the United States.

The incident that brought glossolalia to the attention of the modern world was the well-known experience of Agnes Ozman who spoke in tongues on 3 January 1901 in Charles Parham's Bethel Bible School in Topeka, Kansas [USA]. This "touch felt around the world" was the beginning of the modern classical Pentecostal movement with its emphasis on a separate and subsequent "baptism in the Holy Spirit" with the "initial evidence" of speaking in tongues.

The appearance of glossolalia in Topeka came during a time of heightened interest in the Holy Spirit due to the Holiness Movement in the USA and the Keswick "Higher Life" Movement in England. By the turn of the century, both movements taught that Christians should expect to be bap- tized in the Holy Spirit subsequent to conversion--water baptism, but there was much speculation and disagreement on the proper evidence that one had received the experience.

After the appearance of glossolalia, Charles Parham formulated the doctrine of "initial evidence" as the solution to the problem of evidences that existed at the time.

> Now all Christians credit the fact that we are to be recipients of the Holy Spirit, but each have their own private interpretations as to his visible manifestations; some claim shouting, leaping, jumping, and falling in trances, while others put stress upon inspiration, unction and divine revelation.... How much more reasonable it would be for modern Holy Ghost teachers to first receive a Bible Evidence, such as the Disciples, instead of trying to get the world to take their word for it. -- Vinson Synan, Holiness Pentecostal Movement (Grand Rapids, Michigan: Wm. B. Eerdmans, 1971), pp 121,122.

Thus was born the modern pentecostal movement with the "baptism in the Holy Spirit" accompanied by glossolalia as the centerpiece. Of course, tongues was not the only gift claimed, but the "initial" one. All the other charisms would follow and be encouraged, but tongues was, and remained, the most important.

This is not to say that all Pentecostals accepted the doctrine of initial evidence. Large and important groups accepted and practiced glossolalia without assenting to "initial evidence" since the phrase itself was not biblically based, (e.g., the Elim Pentecostal Church of Britian and the Methodist Pentecostal Church of Chile).

The vast majority of Pentecostals, however, adhere to the "initial evidence" view and have written the doctrine into their statements of faith. (See Walter J. Hollenweger, The Pentecostals (Minneapolis: Augsburg Pub. House, 1972), pp 515-517.) The following two examples would be considered typical:

Declaration of faith, Assemblies of God, USA

The Evidence of the Baptism in the Holy Ghost
    The Baptism of believers in the Holy Ghost is
witnessed by the initial physical sign of speaking
with other tongues as the Spirit of God gives them
utterance (Ac 2:4). The speaking in tongues in this
instance is the same in essence as the gift of tongues (1 Cor 12:4-10,28) but different in purpose
and use.

Declaration of faith of the Church of God (Cleveland)

    We believe in speaking with other tongues as the
Spirit gives utterance, and that it is the initial
evidence of the baptism of the Holy Ghost.

II. GLOSSOLALIA AND PENTECOSTAL DOCTRINE

While most traditional churches fear the manifestations of the charismata (including tongues) in regular
worship services, Pentecostals enjoy and encourage them as
part of normal New Testament Christian practice. Since
glossolalia plays such a prominent role in Pentecostal
faith and practice, the movement has often been called the
"tongues movement." This, of course, is a distortion, but
it does point up the impression that non-Pentecostals often
receive.

Traditional Pentecostal teaching concerning glossolalia might be summerized under the three headings of (A)
glossolalia as a sign, (B) glossolalia as initial evidence,
and (C) glossolalia as a continuing gift of the Spirit.

A. Glossolalia as a Sign

Since glossolalia is the only one of the charismata
not clearly seen in the Old Testament, its appearance on
the Day of Pentecost was intended as a sign that the age of

the Holy Spirit (or the Church age) had begun. Glossolalia thus became the Christian charism which hearlded a new age in God's dealing with His children. Glossolalia furthermore is listed as one of the "signs" that would "follow them that believe," in Mk 16:17. (Although this passage is disputed by some, in any case, it still points to the importance of glossolalia in the earliest apostolic church.)

As a sign, glossolalia is simply a way of stating that God is at work here. In fact, this is one of the more striking and eye-catching ways of making this point. Certainly this was the sign value of glossolalia on the Day of Pentecost. Although some mocked and attributed the phenomenon to the effects of "new wine," the majority were "confounded," "amazed," and "marvelled" at the phenomenon. After Peter's sermon, about 3,000 souls were added to the Church--the "sign" of tongues being central to the whole event.

Tongues as a sign is also alluded to by Paul in 1 Cor 14:22; "Wherefore tongues are for a sign, not to them that believe, but to them that believe not. . . ." This is perfectly logical since signs in Scripture are usually designed for unbelievers in an effort to have them repent. Believers do not need a sign to believe since they are already believers. Therefore, the major function of public utterances in glossolalia would be evangelistic in nature-- intended to bring unbelievers to Christ. (See Ralph Harris, Spoken by the Spirit (Springfield, Missouri: Gospel Publishing House, 1973), which relates many instances of tongues in a known language that led unbelievers to Christ.)

10

B. Glossolalia as Initial Evidence

Though Pentecostals recognize that the words "initial evidence" do not appear in Scripture, they base their doctrine on the data of Scripture which forms a pattern for the teaching. This is done much in the same way as the doctrines of the "Trinity" and the "Virgin Birth" which also do not appear in Scripture as such.

The doctrine is based on the historical accounts in the book of Acts where believers were "filled with the Holy Ghost" (or "baptized" or "received" the Holy Ghost.)

Of the five accounts, glossolalia accompanied the Holy Spirit's reception in three. In the other two accounts, there is an overwhelming implication that tongues were manifested. The five instances were as follows:

1. The Day of Pentecost--Ac 2:4; "And they were all filled with the Holy Ghost and began to speak with other tongues, as the Spirit gave them utterance."

Here there is no question that all 120 spoke in tongues at this time, including Peter, the other Apostles, and Mary the Mother of Jesus. It is also clear that the tongues (dialektos) was a form of xenoglossolalia, or speaking in a language unknown to the speaker but understood by the listener.

2. The Samaritan Revival--Ac 8:17; "Then laid they their hands on them, and they received the Holy Ghost." Undoubtedly the converts of Philip were already baptized believers in Christ. They had heard the Gospel preached (vv 5-11), they "believed" (v 12), "they were baptized"

in water (v 12), and "great joy filled that city" (v 8).

When Peter and John came to Samaria, they "laid their hands on them, and they received the Holy Ghost." (Subsequent to their conversion and water baptism.) It is not explicitly stated that these people spoke in tongues, but that probability is strongly implied. What Simon the sorcerer "saw" (and "heard" according to the Greek word) made him desire to buy the Power to confer the Holy Ghost (vv 18,19).

Many commentators clearly state that what Simon saw (and heard) was unquestionably glossolalia. (See F. F. Bruce, Commentary on the Book of Acts (Grand Rapids: Wm. B. Eerdmans, 1954), p. 181; Adam Clarke, Commentary (Vol 1, ed. 1837), p. 741; F. B. Meyer, Handbook on the Acts of the Apostles.)

3. The House of Cornelius—Ac 10:46; "For they heard them speak with tongues, and magnify God." Also Ac 11:15; "and as I began to speak, the Holy Ghost fell on them, as on us at the beginning."

In this event, known as the Gentile or Roman Pentecost, glossolalia accompanied the falling of the Holy Spirit on Cornelius and his household. This is the strongest case in the Scripture for initial evidence since the text reads: "and they of the circumcision which believed were astonished, as many as came with Peter, because that on the Gentiles also was poured out the gift of the Holy Ghost, for they heard them speak with tongues and magnify God" (vv 45,46).

The Gentile Pentecost illustrates a major point usually

overlooked by theologians--the fact that of all the charismata that were available, God chose glossolalia to prove
to a skeptical Jewish Church that the Gospel of Christ was
for the Gentiles--and the whole world. Were it not for the
strategic occurance of glossolalia at Cornelius' house,
it is possible that Christianity would have remained a
minor sect of Judaism rather than the universal faith it
became.

    4. The Ephesian Pentecost--Ac 19:6; "And when Paul had
laid his hands upon them, the Holy Ghost came upon them; and
they spoke with tongues and prophesied."

    The "Greek" Pentecost at Ephesus gives support to
the Pentecostal doctrines of subsequence and initial evidence. It is clear that the Ephesian Elders did not receive the Holy Spirit baptism at the time they "believed"
in the message of John the Baptist and were baptized in
water. It is also clear that Paul did not consider their
initiation complete until they were baptized in the name
of Jesus and had received the Holy Spirit.

    On this occasion all twelve elders spoke with ton-
gues after Paul laid hands on them. As Charles W. Conn
says:

> This recurrence of the glossolalia of pentecost oc-
> curred in the province of Asia, under the ministry
> of one (Paul) who had not even been present on the
> Day of Pentecost, to persons who could not have
> anticipated the experience, for the very reason that
> they had never heard of it.--Wade H. Horton, ed.,
> The Glossolalia Phenomenon (Cleveland, Tennessee:
> Pathway Press, 1966), p 51.

    And this took place some twenty years after the Day
of Pentecost.

5. Paul the Apostle--Ac 9:17; "Jesus, that appeared unto thee in the way as thou camest, hath sent me, that thou mightest receive thy sight, and be filled with the Holy Ghost."

At the conversion of Saul, there is no record that glossolalia accompanied his baptism in water or in the Holy Ghost. Of course, Paul later makes the claim that he spoke in tongues "more than ye all" to the Corinthian church (1 Cor 14:18). The only question remains--when did Paul begin to speak in tongues? The logical answer would be that he began when the other Christians did in the Acts record, i.e., at the time he received the baptism in the Holy Spirit. Thus one may infer that glossolalia accompanied Paul's pentecostal experience also.

From the foregoing instances one might conclude that the Scriptures do not conclusively teach the doctrine of initial evidence, but that the weight of scriptural data supports the theory, (although one could have room to argue against the doctrine using the same data).

C. Glossolalia as a Continuing Gift

1 Cor 12, 13, and 14 deal with glossolalia as a continuing gift in the life of the believer and in the congregational life of the church. Pentecostals have made a distinction between glossolalia as initial evidence and glossolalia as a gift. As initial evidence, this ability is given to all as the normative sign of the reception of the Spirit. Afterward one may or may not be blessed with a continuing gift of tongues or any of the other gifts of the Spirit.

14

J. H. King in _Passover to Pentecost_ (Franklin Springs, Georgia: Advocate Press, 1914), gave classic expression to the pentecostal view:

Tongues--"Sign or Gift?"

> The sign is an evidence of the incoming of the Spirit to dwell within us. The gift is that which the Spirit Himself bestows. This sign was universal; the gift was given individually. The sign was the Spirit speaking in praise to God the Father, and God the Son. The gift was used in addressing men for their edification. The sign was ecstatic speech, the person being lifted out of himself with great joy. While speaking, the gift was exercised soberly; the person having complete control of himself while speaking. The gift must always be interpreted; the sign was not accompanied with interpretation. When the Spirit bestowed a corresponding gift of interpretation; the one was essential to the other. In that form of speaking as associated with the outpouring of the Spirit, no corresponding interpretation was given; therefore we conclude that it was quite different from the gift of tongues, which always had its corresponding gift of interpretation.

It is in 1 Cor that the Apostle Paul deals with the uses and abuses of the gift of tongues and some simple rules for the regulation of the gift in the congregation.

First of all, one should list the positive values of glossolalia that are found in these passages, and then list the dangers that led to the regulation (but not abolition) of the gift in the corporate worship of the church.

1. The Value of Glossolalia--a) Profit, 1 Cor 12:7; "But the manifestation of the Spirit is given to every man to profit withal." All of the charisms, including glossolalia, are given for the profit of the believer who practices it.

b) Edification, 1 Cor 14:4; "He that speaketh in an unknown tongue edifieth himself. . . ." To edify means "to

build up" as in the contruction of a building. Tongues is
the only gift of which this is said.

c) Mystical Value , 1 Cor 14:2; ". . .in the Spirit
he speaketh mysteries." There is a mystical side to our
human nature and glossolalia satisfies this aspect of our
being.

d) Prayer, 1 Cor 14:14,15; "For if I pray in an unknown tongue. . .I will pray with the Spirit. . . ." Rom
8:26; "Likewise the Spirit also helpeth our infirmities;
for we know not what we should pray for as we ought: but
the Spirit itself maketh intercession for us with groan-
ings which cannot be uttered."

Prayer in tongues is biblically based and probably
the mode in which the Apostle Paul spoke his "ten thousand
words in an unknown tongue" (1 Cor 14:19).

e) Worship, 1 Cor 14:15; ". . .I will sing with the
Spirit, and I will sing with the understanding also." Many
of the elements of worship are ascribed to glossolalia in
the Scriptures. Men sing, pray, praise and magnify God,
bless, give thanks, etc., in tongues. All of these are
important aspects of worship.

f) Evangelism, Ac 1:8; "But ye shall receive power
after that the Holy Ghost is come upon you; and ye shall be
witnesses. . . ." 1 Cor 14:22; "Wherefore tongues are for
a sign, not to them that believe, but to them that believe
not. . . ."

It is the testimony of history that such evangelists
as St Francis Xavier and many others exercised the gift of

tongues to evangelize pagan peoples in many parts of the
world. This was the original effect of glossolalia on the
Day of Pentecost.

2. The Abuse and Regulation of Glossolalia--Because
some in the Corinthian church abused the gift of tongues,
Paul felt it necessary to correct these and lay down some
guidelines for the practice of glossolalia in the public
assemblies of the church.

From Paul's discussion in 1 Cor 14, we might list
the following abuses and correctives concerning the use
of glossolalia.

a) Public Glossolalia Without Interpretation. Paul
makes it abundantly clear that public utterances in glossolalia without accompanying interpretation is unedifying
and unprofitable, especially to unbelievers. "If therefore
the whole church be come together into one place, and all
speak with tongues, and there come in those that are un-
learned, or unbelievers, will they not say that ye are
mad?" (1 Cor 14:23).

In order to remedy this situation Paul suggests that:
"Let him that speaketh in an unknown tongue pray that he may
interpret" (v 13). The Pentecostal formula often used
(tongues and interpretation = prophecy) is given in v. 5:
"far greater is he that prophesieth than he that speaketh
in tongues, except he interpret, that the church may receive
edifying."

For the most part, prophesy is greater than tongues
and if a person is moved on to speak in tongues in public

without an interpreter present, it is better to "let him keep silence in the church; and let him speak to himself, and to God" (v 28).

b) Excessive Utterances in Tongues. As to the frequency of tongues and interpretations in a public meeting, the guidlines are "if any man speak in an unknown tongue, let it be by two, or at the most by three, and that by course; and let one interpret" (v 27).

At the end of his extensive corrective in chap. 14, Paul gives the last word on glossolalia to be found in the Bible--"wherefore, bretheren, covet to prophesy, and forbid not to speak with tongues" (v 39).

C. S. Lewis in a sermon on Ac 2:4 entitled "Transpositions" (ca. 1945) made the following comments: "Speaking in tongues is an embarrassment to us." Though he did say that there is one historic case of speaking in tongues which we must treat with reverence and respect--the original pentecostal outpouring which was all of one piece with the death and resurrection of Christ. But other than this glossolalia remained a continuing embarrassment to the church.

Embarrassing as it may be, glossolalia is the gift that God has chosen at strategic points in history to expand and renew the church. I agree with Larry Christenson who stated the following in the 1977 Conference on Charismatic Renewal in the Christian Churches in Kansas City, Missouri USA:

God has sovereignly chosen to use the gift of
tongues as a catalyst for renewal...it may not make
sense to our own reason...but He comes knocking
where He chooses....He has come in our day to a
church often puffed up with a sense of her own
wisdom and learning and said will you open to this
least of the gifts that has been boarded up so long?

BIBLIOGRAPHY

Two bibliographies have been published by the Society
for Pentecostal Studies which give excellent sources on
glossolalia.

Faupel, David, W. The American Pentecostal Movement--A
Bibliographical Essay. Wilmore, Kentucky: B. L.
Fisher Library, Asbury College, 1972.

Mills, Watson E. Speaking in Tongues--A Classified Bibliography. Franklin Springs,GA. Society for Pentecostal Studies, 1974.

The two best and most recent books on the subject
from the Catholic and pentecostal sides are:

Horton, Stanley M. What the Bible Says about the Holy Spirit.
Springfield, Missouri: Gospel Publishing House, 1976.

McDonnell, Kilian. Charismatic Renewal and the Churches.
New York: Seabury, 1976.

Theological Paper

THE FUNCTION OF TONGUES IN PENTECOSTALISM
by
Fr Kilian McDonnell, OSB

INTRODUCTION

In the body of the article I will not attempt to
define directly what tongues is in exegetical and theological
terms. That would be sufficient for an entire paper. The
definition of tongues will emerge indirectly in the section
on presuppositions and in the main part of the paper. Also,
some insight will be gained by the testimonies given in the
Appendix.

Since the paper is not really focused on the baptism
in the Holy Spirit, this will not be treated explicitly.
Some understanding of this is necessary if one is to understand what tongues is since the latter is, in one function,
the initial evidence of the form. For this reason, testimonies of those who have received the baptism are given in
the Appendix.

Attention has been given to tongues as initial evidence
more than to tongues as a gift of the Spirit exercised
throughout life. This makes for a heightened presentation

which may or may not correspond to many people's experience of the baptism in the Holy Spirit. The daily use of tongues, though it retains echoes of these mountain-top experiences, is in most cases no more and no less captivating than a morning meditation well made. Classical Pentecostals live in the valleys with the rest of Christians.

No attempt has been made to treat all of the functions of tongues in classical Pentecostalism. Some readers may be quite justified in saying that other functions than those treated are more important than those I have treated. To a large extent I have written of the functions of tongues as I see them. A classical Pentecostal may have quite different ideas.

I. PRESUPPOSITIONS

In treating the function of tongues one works with certain assumptions which are stated in this section. The research supporting these assumptions here given can be found in my Charismatic Renewal and the Churches, Seabury Press, New York, 1976.

1. Evidence exists which seems to indicate a persistent and widespread suspicion that glossolalics are psychologically deprived. This suspicion is to be found not only at the level of folk psychiatry but among persons trained professionally in the behavioral sciences.

2. To date the evidence would indicate that the practice of speaking in tongues is found among mature, normal, well-adjusted persons. Every social, economic, or educational class is to be found represented in the Pentecostal-charismatic renewal. At this point in the research it has not been demonstrated that glossolalia as a psychological phenomenon is related in any immediately direct manner to personality variables.

3. Psychological factors such as suggestion and trance may be present either at what is called baptism in the Holy Spirit, the first experience of tongues, or at subsequent exercise of tongues. A light trance is not unusual the first time a person begins to speak in tongues. Sometimes there is a deep trance.

4. The presence of trance does not deprive the experience of its religious meaning. The ability to enter a trance seems to be a common, normal faculty rather than an abnormal and unusual one.

5. There is insufficient evidence to indicate that trance is present in every exercise of tongues. The more likely position is that trance is not always present.

6. Suggestion is part of the total process of socialization and this must be considered when evaluating the role of suggestion in the onset of tongues. Susceptibility to suggestion is more likely a sign of normality than of the presence of most neurotic and psychotic states. Dissociative states (trances), which may or may not be present, seem to be found within the range of normal behavior.

7. A leader and a group may use suggestion and social pressures to such an extent that the religious quality of the experience of tongues may be greatly diminished.

8. The experience of tongues does not seem to be related in any necessary way to a leader or a group. There are sufficient instances to indicate that one can experience tongues without previous acquaintance with the phenomenon and without previous acquaintance with persons who speak in tongues. These experiences may take place either in the presence of a group or alone.

9. Cultural factors must be taken into consideration in evaluating psychological phenomenon. What might be considered deviant behavior in one culture may be considered normal in another. Even granting this principle, experiences in a religious context are more psychologically suspect of being neurotic or psychotic behavior the greater their emotional content. The more suspect they are psychologically, the less credence one gives to their religious content.

10. Convincing evidence that there is such a thing as a Pentecostal personality type has not yet been brought to light. All types seems to be found within the movement. There is no determined cultural pattern or social group out of which Pentecostals and charismatics recruit new adherents.

11. Glossolalia is very likely learned behavior. This does not mean that a glossolalic necessarily learns a pattern of glossolalic utterance from someone else,

though that is possible and happens in some Pentecostal-
charismatic groups. It is learned behavior in the much
more general sense namely that patterned vocalization is
learned behavior and sounds which are already in one's
language treasury are used. Some glossolalics come to the
practice of glossolalia spontaneously, without having heard
of the phenomenon, without having heard anyone speak in
tongues.

12. That speaking in tongues is learned behavior does
not militate against its being a gift of the Spirit. An
exaggerated supernatural view of the gifts should be avoided.
A gift of the Spirit is not necessarily a totally new endowment, a new faculty beyond those which belong to a full
humanity. A gift can be a natural capacity, exercised in
the power of the Spirit, and directed to the service of
Christ's kingdom. Tongues is very likely such a gift.

13. It is not true that what can be described in
psychological terms is therefore not a true exercise of a
charism, not of the Holy Spirit. This supposition would
relegate the Spirit to some Platonic ideal world as it
would presuppose that the Spirit operates in a psychological void. On the contrary, only what can be described in
psychological terms is a true charism, even though the
religious meaning and content is not adequately accounted
for in psychological terms.

14. Glossolalics do not understand the meaning of
what they are saying in the sense that one understands the
meaning of a grammatically structured sentence. This is

24

not an argument against their utterance being a gift of the
Spirit.

15. That tongues is a human capacity and experience
of which everyone is capable does not mean that it is not
supernatural. To be supernatural it does not need to be
miraculous and need not be a true language. To be supernatural, it is sufficient if the natural capacity is exercised under the power and inspiration of the Spirit,
directed toward the building up of the body of Christ (the
Church) and toward the kingdom of God.

16. From a phenomenological as well as from a psychological point of view, speaking in tongues is very likely
not a uniquely Christian event. It has yet to be demonstrated scientifically, however, that the phenomenon of
speaking in tongues as it appears in a non-Christian context
is, as a phenomenon, the same as is found among Pentecostals
and charismatics. From a theological perspective there is
no reason why such identity of phenomena in various religious
and cultural contexts should be denied or be a source of
embarrassment.

17. What gives speaking in tongues its meaning is not
the supposition, here not accepted, of its being a totally
new capacity, alien to man and given from above. Theologically the meaning of tongues is to be found in using this
phenomenon common to all men for the building up of Christ's
body and for the praise of the Father. The phenomenon in a
Christian context has both its human dynamics and its
religious content and meaning.

18. The difference of theological explanation is not to be found in the presence of God's power in one view and the absence of that power in another. Rather, the difference in theological views is to be found in the broader area of how one perceives the relation of nature and grace.

II. FUNCTIONS

A. Validation or Authentication of Baptism in the Holy Spirit.

1. Religious Validation - Doctrine of Initial Evidence-- More than any other doctrinal position tongues as the initial evidence has characterized the Pentecostal movement.[1] In brief, classical Pentecostals have believed that according to the scriptures, speaking in other tongues is the initial physical evidence that a person has in fact received the baptism in the Holy Spirit. Tongues validates or authenticates the experience of baptism. One must not take this in too juridical a sense. Though at the popular level many classical Pentecostals might treat tongues as the proof that one has been baptized, many reflective persons in the classical movement would say that evidence is not proof; it is evidence.

Doctrinally the teaching is based mostly on Lukan texts (e.g. Ac 1:3-5; 2:1-4; 10:44-47; 19:1-7). There is usually some emphasis on the word "initial." This is to say that following the initial evidence of tongues there should be further evidences of a Spirit-filled life, for instance, the fruits of the Spirit. Other manifestations and fruits of the Spirit are considered further "evidences" of a genuine baptism in the Spirit. David du Plessis, while retaining

26

the doctrine of initial evidence, gives it a different formulation. Tongues, he says, is the consequence of the
baptism.

Note should be made at this point of a distinction
common in classical Pentecostalism. Tongues is either considered as the initial sign of the baptism or is considered
as a gift of the Spirit which may be exercised subsequent
to baptism and possibly frequently. It is possible that
a person will speak in tongues when he or she received the
baptism but never again in his or her life. In this case
the person has received tongues as the initial evidence of
the baptism but has not received the gift of tongues.

Both Donald Gee and David du Plessis have said that
one cannot find the doctrine of initial evidence, as such,
in the Scriptures. This is not to suggest that it is therefore untrue. There are elements in the Lukan teaching
mentioned above which form a trajectory, that is, they impel
themselves (or are impelled) beyond the Scriptures where
they are further developed. What emerges is the doctrine
of initial evidence. This is to say two things. a) The doctrine of initial evidence is not found in Scriptures. b) It
is not without scriptural roots.

What should be noted here is that in true doctrinal
development the Scriptures (and for Catholics also the total
experience of the church as manifested in her teaching
authority) are controlling instruments. They insure that
where the development goes beyond Scripture, it does so in
a way which is consonant with the Scriptures. Catholics

and classical Pentecostals have not been able to agree on what constitutes legitimate development. In both traditions the development has scriptural roots but goes beyond Scripture. The disagreement lies in whether the doctrinal development is in fact consonant with Scriptures.

Pentecostals have problems with the Roman Catholic teaching on Mary, papacy, and the five other sacraments. Papacy, for instance, seems to them to institute claims which are contrary to the Scriptures.

Initial evidence is difficult for Catholics when it is tied to baptism in the Holy Spirit, which in turn is made normative for the Christian life. Roman Catholics would have less problems with baptism in the Holy Spirit, which can be an experience of those graces already received at initiation (Baptism, Confirmation, Eucharist). That tongues should be found frequently in the normal Christian community is not at all difficult to admit. But that tongues and tongues alone (through baptism in the Spirit) is normative for the Christian life seems to Roman Catholics not only to go beyond Scriptures, but to be contrary to the teaching of St Paul who says "Do all speak in tongues?" (1 Co 12:30). It does not seem cogent to say that at this point Paul is speaking about tongues as a gift but not about tongues as initial evidence. In the whole exegetical tradition, Catholic and Protestant, one would not find support for such a position.

One area in which the classical Pentecostals have given outstanding witness is in the specific character of

28

charisms. Many in the historic churches and in the more
evangelical of the free churches (some Holiness churches,
Baptists, etc.) have insisted that these "Pentecostal"
charisms belong to the church in her New Testament beginnings but not to the continuing life of the church.
Classical Pentecostals have demonstrated by a living witness
that tongues, prophecy, healing are not extraordinary gifts
but belong to the daily life of the ordinary congregation.
Not that every member prophesies or heals but that in the
normal congregation it would be unusual if one did not find
these gifts present in some member or members. The teaching
and practice of the classical Pentecostals in this area is
undoubtedly closer to the teaching of St Paul in chapters
12-14 of 1 Cor. Contemporary Roman Catholic exegesis (with
which I would want to identify myself as to its method, e.g.
historical-critical) is vastly different from the exegesis
of most members who have represented the classical Pentecostals in these dialogues. I would want to agree whole-
heartedly with the assertion that with the exception of
several points, the exegesis of 1 Cor 12-14 by the classical
Pentecostals has been nearer the truth than the exegesis of
most scholars in the historic churches.[2]

 2. Anthropological Validation: Bridge-burning--If we
turn to cultural anthropology we find another kind of
validation. Every movement has some kind of organization,
however fragmented it may be. It has a process by which
new members are recruited; it has a body of beliefs and
doctrine (ideology); and it has to have opposition, real or

imagined, in order to spread (as a kite needs wind to fly).
Beyond this, every movement, whether it be the labor movement, Viet Cong, Black Power or Pentecostal movement, needs
some experience of commitment, usually accompanied by a
commitment act.[3] What a social or behavioral scientist
will interpret as commitment to an organization or an
ideology, participants in the classical Pentecostal (and
also in the denominational charismatic movements) will consider commitment in the first instance as being to the person of Jesus Christ, who, as David du Plessis will never
let us forget, is the Baptizer in the Holy Spirit. The
commitment, say the classical Pentecostals, is the surrender
of self, of time and possessions, sometimes of life, to the
person of Jesus Christ. Participation in the organization,
and even acceptance of the ideology (doctrine) are of
secondary importance and flow from the primary commitment
to Jesus as Lord and Savior. Commitment, which takes place
after a decision has been reached, is accompanied by an
event or act which might be called the commitment act. In
some religious groups this might be going forward at the
altar call in the presence of friends and acquaintances.
For one joining the Black Power movement it might be the
burning of a grocery store owned by a white merchant. In
large areas of classical Pentecostalism (and in the
denominational charismatic movements) it is speaking in
tongues. This act means commitment first to Jesus, then to
His gospel, to the community of His followers, and to the
battle against the forces which oppose the coming of His
kingdom.

30

Even today speaking in tongues is the occasion of snickers in some quarters, and persons who engage in this strange manner of social behavior are given special labels (Pentecostals, tongue speakers, charismatics, or worse yet, the lunatic fringe, the emotionally unstable, the psychologically immature). It may be a bit over-dramatic to say that speaking in tongues constitutes a bridge-burning act, an act which in the social sense constitutes a point of no return, but there is a real sense in which that is true. Such an act validates the baptism in the Holy Spirit insofar as it says: "Paul Jones no longer belongs to that great unnumbered mass of Christians but now he belongs to this little group of so-called Christians who distinguish themselves in a number of ways, especially in speaking in tongues." Once that identification with the smaller group is known, one is tagged for life. Therefore, tongues as a sign of commitment to the movement, its goals, ideology and organization is a bridge-burning experience. You can't go back, in the social sense.[4]

One should note that even in Pentecostalism tongues does not always serve this function, only in those cases where Pentecostals do not engage in some other even more socially unacceptable behavior, or where speaking in tongues does not distinguish one from the general masses of people. I give two examples. Twenty or thirty years ago in Mexico the commitment act for entry into the movement was not tongues but the physical act of entering a Protestant classical Pentecostal church building. Mexicans who engaged in such behavior in the rural hill country were liable to be killed by stoning or hanging at the hands of other Mexicans, sometimes led by the local Catholic priest. These are not just horror stories dreamed up by fanatical classical Pentecostals. To enter a Protestant church was much more socially unacceptable (outrageously so) than to speak in tongues and was therefore enough for the individuals to burn their social and economic bridges in doing so. Research has noted that "glossolalia is much less common among Mexicans who have received the Baptism of the Holy Spirit than among American Pentecostals."[5] The reason: one is committed more radically to the movement by entering a Protestant church building than by speaking in tongues.

A somewhat similar case is found in Haiti where trance, spirit possession and what would appear to the scientific observer to be glossolalia are found in Haitian society. All of these are completely acceptable socially and constitute normal behavior in the dominant Voodoo culture. For a classical Pentecostal to speak in tongues in no way constitutes a bridge-burning event, passing the point of no return. In Haiti what cuts one off from the past one is rejecting is taking all of one's sacred objects used in voodoo ceremonies and publicly burning them, an act which arouses the hostility of the voodoo priest and other influential members of the convert's community. This and not tongues is the commitment act in Haiti. Such a public break with the voodoo society which permeates the land attaches the believer to the Pentecostal belief system, its organization, makes a recruiter of him, and pits him against

the forces of evil which would stop the growth of the
Pentecostal movement.

Even given these exceptions to the validating function
of tongues, both cultural anthropologists and classical
Pentecostals agree on one point: without tongues there would
have been no Pentecostal movement. This agreement in no way
cancels another consensus which the two groups enjoy,
namely that Pentecostalism is not just a tongues movement.
That this is so is seen from the curious fact that in Chile
half of the pastors of the Chilian classical Pentecostals
do not speak in tongues.[6]

B. Glossolalia as Prayer Event

For both Luke and Paul tongues is primarily a prayer
gift (Ac 2:11; 10:46; 1 Co 14:14,15). What concerns us
here is not to give a biblical teaching on tongues but
rather to describe what classical Pentecostals (and others)
experience when they pray in tongues. No attempt will be
made to describe all the various forms of glossolalic
prayer: adoration, thanksgiving, petition. Concentration
will be given to three dominant prayer functions which
tongues serve.

1. Experience of Presence--At the international level
classical Pentecostalism can be extremely diverse. One
theme which runs through the whole of the varied streams is
the category of presence. At the very beginning of the
classical movement Agnes Ozman knelt before Charles Parham
at a watchnight service on December 31, 1900, and asked him
to lay hands on her head and pray for her to be baptized in

the Holy Spirit with the evidence of speaking in tongues. Afterwards she said that she had "a depth of the presence of the Lord within" which she had never before experienced.[7] The presence of God pervades the whole of the classical movement.

Roman Catholics are easily misled by this terminology, thinking immediately of the exhortations in the older meditation books "that we now place ourselves in the presence of God." Presence in this sense is an act of the will, an effort by a person entering into prayer to set aside other thoughts and preoccupations, and to focus the mind of God. When classical Pentecostals and other charismatics speak of presence, they are speaking of something quite different. Here, too, there is presence in the sense of focus of attention, but the source is less the will and more the perception that someone is here and now, someone who makes claims. When it happens for the first time, classical Pentecostals tell us, it is like you are entering into a new territory which always belonged to you. The territory is not a tract of land but a person who is Jesus and one makes a voyage into Him and finds infinite spaces of love, care, tenderness, forgiveness, all of which are not ideas but the living personal reality of Jesus Himself. You are surprised that you can tour those personal spaces, surprised because you knew they always belonged to you (or you to them), and now you really see them for the first time. To your utter astonishment, the classical Pentecostals tell us, you find that those spaces are not words or talk. The spaces live. You move into them not as into the space of a room, which is exterior to yourself and embraces you from the outside. Here the spaces are both interior and beyond you. You can tour them from within and never come to the edge. You are in a primary closeness to Jesus to the point of touching from within.

In the same moment you know the infinite vastness which no voyage will exhaust. The immensity does not make the experience of Jesus less personal. It simply says to you that an infinity of journeys would not come near the first beginnings of that great interior space which is Jesus within you and beyond you.

All of this corresponds to what one meets often in classical Pentecostal testimonies, that is to say, the bewildering exclamation: "He is real; He lives; He is now, He loves me. It is true. He loves me."[8]

Some indication should be given to what life in the valley means for the person who prays in tongues. The ideal of the model to which classical Pentecostalism belongs is continual revival, and this lends itself to an exaggeration, which most classical Pentecostals would reject, namely that the Christian life is a progress from peak experience to peak experience. Classical Pentecostals know that this episodic pattern which moves from mountain top to mountain top does not correspond to the realities of the Christian life.

The experience of presence is an invitation to remain in a personal relationship with Jesus even when all that one feels is His absence. The dry, mechanical ritual of tongues is an invitation to the believer to sustain himself on the memory of Jesus who was almost perceptibly present, to nurture Himself in that dry but living faith which is our daily lot when Jesus manifests Himself as though He were the absent one. This, too, is a kind of intimacy. Dietrich Bonhoeffer was pointing to the same thing to which classical Pentecostals point when he wrote: "The God who is with us is the God who forsakes us. . . . Before God and with God we live without God."[9] The experience in tongues of presence gives meaning to the experience of absence. Without the experience of presence, the absence is only emptiness,[10] and has no memory to assure one that the absence is, in the last analysis, an illusion.

2. Experience of Praise--When a social scientist first meets the classical Pentecostal movement (and the other charismatic movements) he is liable to mistake the movement for a prayer movement. This is because prayer seems to be the most characteristic activity. A closer look will reveal that it is more than a prayer movement. What deceives one into thinking it is just prayer is the major role praise plays. Before all else tongues is used to tell of the mighty works of God (Ac 2:11). In classical Pentecostal prayer meetings one will hear interpretations of tongues which express the whole range of prayer. What is most striking is the primary orientation of this prayer. Personal needs and consequently the prayer of petition are of a minor concern. Even when classical Pentecostals gather

to pray for a specific need, or when they gather around
someone to pray over him, the tone and fabric of the prayer
is praise.

If presence is the primary modality in glossolalic
prayer it should not be surprising that praise follows
immediately. The immediate response to a presence which
reveals the Lordship of Jesus is praise. What is expressed
is awe and wonder; awe because His is a love without end,
because He draws near, because of the glory of creation,
because of the transformations which take place in the
lives of those whom He has touched.[11] Praise has a double
character. Though primarily concerned with the high transcendent Lord who reveal Himself as the unutterable, beyond
all praise, He reveals Himself also as the near Lord, who
walks among us and is that interior presence into which we
have entered. Here the transcendent and immanent are one.
The high Lord is in the forefront of Pentecostal consciousness but one of the most profound moments of glosso-
latic praise is when He reveals Himself as the completely
available and accessible one.

3. Experience of Power--There is scarcely a more
frequently quoted text in classical Pentecostal circles
than: "You shall receive power when the Holy Spirit has come
upon you" (Ac 1:8, cf. Lk 24:49). The Pentecost account
of the rush of a mighty wind filling the house where the
disciples were sitting (Ac 2:1-4) is cast in categories of
a mighty power from on high. Jesus of Nazareth, the
classical Pentecostals recall, was, according to Luke,

37

anointed "with the Holy Spirit and power" (Ac 10:38) and
this specifically for His ministry: "He went about doing
good and healing all that were oppressed by the devil."
(Ibid.) Both the baptism in the Holy Spirit and speaking
in tongues (since the latter is the evidence for the former)
are seen in relation to the reception of power. This is
intimately connected with the vocabulary of "more." Miss
Agnes Ozman, from whose experience the movement often dates
its beginning, found "the added joy and glory my heart
longed for."[12] In clearer terms one participant in the
Azusa street events in Los Angeles in 1906 spoke of the
first experience of tongues. He wrote: "I wanted to be
fully yielded to God. . . . I wanted more of him."[13] One
of the international patriarchs of the classical Pentecostal
movement, Lewi Pethrus of Sweden, uses the same terminology
of "more" to explain his baptism and experience of tongues.
"During the year 1905 God met me again, and made it very
clear that there was more than forgiveness and sonship to
be received from him. I not only understood that there
was more for me, but felt there must be more for me, or
otherwise my Christian life would be a failure."[14] In a
number of seekers after the baptism and therefore after
tongues the believer complains of "lack of power" in his or
her ministry.[15]

The "more" that the believer seeks in tongues is often
an upbuilding for service, an "empowerment" for the mission
to others as well as the strengthening of one's own spiritual
resources. Those who experience tongues witness to a new
dimension in their ministry. Sometimes this is seen as an

38

eagerness and boldness in ministry, sometimes as a new daring in prayer.

It is not unusual in classical Pentecostal circles for a person being assigned a task, especially if it entails difficulties, for the person to kneel, have his friends gather around him, and, with the laying on of hands, to pray for him. No request is usually made that the prayer be in tongues but the expectation of all concerned is that on such an occasion tongues will occur. When classical Pentecostals pray over others for the baptism in the Holy Spirit or for healing, or for some kind of deliverance the general expectation, even if never vocalized, is that there will be some prayer in tongues. These are "power situations" in which they expect the Spirit to act in a sovereign way. Quite naturally they turn to tongues. This expectation should not be given too much emphasis. In reality classical Pentecostals are surprised neither by the presence or absence of tongues.

Though the source of the power is beyond them it is also in them. They may speak as though the Spirit was coming from some place beyond space and time but they know that the Spirit also lives within. What is needed is not necessarily a new imparting of the Spirit but a stirring up of that power already present. In some cases their prayer in tongues is for a new imparting of the Spirit and a new endowment with power. The image of a surge of electric energy is sometimes used.

C. Knowledge Transformation

Tongues are said to be pre-cognitional and pre-conceptual, a primal experience giving expression to primal emotions, a crude, blunt pre-literary tool for articulating that in our archaeology (our deepest roots) which cannot be said with our more sophisticated literary tools of pre-thought and pre-written prayers.[15] When one brings to light root things one needs, on occasion, blunter, more elemental instruments. The primitive roughness of tongues allows one to say things one utters but scarcely ever hears because of their simplicity and familiarity, because they are daily before one's eyes.

There is here something akin to what some in linguistics call a primal innate universal grammar,[17] which makes it possible for persons to construct a language which is expressive of root emotions, emotions which are so primary that they have to be given different names from those we give to the other emotions. Though the names are clumsy and do not fit, they come as close as we can come to a proper naming. To name those emotions which can be felt and expressed in tongues we should start with the emotions of presence, praise and power. These are the original emotions of Pentecost and they form the matrix of all that is expressed in tongues; they determine and give character to all glossolalic utterance. Furthermore, these three receive one another, so that if one is present the others are necessarily there. We could go on and give rough unfinished names to those emotions, or movements of the soul, which cluster around the eternal, wholeness, identity, immersion, memory, recognition, brother-sister. These, too, receive their specificity from the fundamental categories of presence, praise and power.

Here we are up against the disparity between knowledge and experience which epistomology and psychology, to say nothing of the fine arts, have always had to deal with. Let me clarify.

Tongues is to prayer what abstract non-objective representations are to art. Praying in tongues, like abstract art, requires intelligence, discipline, form. The very abstract non-representational quality itself makes it possible for the artist and the person praying in tongues to move in close to one's archaeology, to those universal roots, to that which is embedded in the deepest source of our individual and collective selves.

Tongues has a memory function, a retrieval responsibility. It allows one to move in close and remember that which is the most primary in us. To remember in this way is a kind of anamnesis, a remembering which retrieves what was there in the past, in such a way as to render it living in the present.

To be more precise. St Thomas wrote that "the New Law consists principally in the grace of the Holy Spirit."[18] This central reality of the New Law, that is the gospel, is the object of remembering. The remembering in the Spirit is the recall of the realities of the gospel: Jesus is Lord, the love which the Father pours out, the Pentecost extravagance, the death and resurrection, the forgiveness of sins, the promise of eternal life. The experiences , which a person may have may be entirely new for the person and possibly for the community, but the gospel objects are not new. They are antecedent to our experiencing them. It is not as though God were making up brand new gospel realities at this moment, creating new gospels as we go along. Tongues is a modest sacramental act in which is brought forth that which was antecedent, which had already been bestowed.

The memory-experience of the Spirit may, in the intensity of feeling, be minimal, moderate, or considerable. In all degrees the remembering is a kind of knowing for the first time by special recall what was always possessed, a recall which is not the usual kind of learning. The remembering elicits presence, praise and power and through these "emotions" the believer reaches a new sphere of perception. These are new colors to his knowing. Knowledge is changed so it speaks with a new grammar. He who speaks in tongues remembers the Holy Spirit, already present these many years; remembers the absolute nearness of presence. He remembers from the depths of the gospel - past and present; he remembers with those root things that live in individuals and communities. But above all he remembers in the Holy Spirit who is antecedent to all remembering.

What occurs here an inadequate but real - if momentary - closing of the gap between knowledge and experience, between knowing and feeling. One feels the emotions

(in the usual sense) in such memory-experience as something
quite properly present and not merely an suffrance.

D. The Language Function--Demonstration of the Wondrous

In the presuppositions we touched briefly on tongues
as a true language. Something further should be said on
the topic if for no other reason than that tongues is often
used to demonstrate the wondrous, to show that the age of
miracles is not past.

The ancient writers generally held that glossolalia
is a true language, a view held today by some exegetes, by
conservatives, fundamentalists, denominational charismatics,
and classical Pentecostals. Most modern exegetes hold to
the view that tongues in both Luke and Paul were not real
languages but rather a language-like utterance to express
deep religious sentiments.[19] This is also the view of
William Samarin, the student of anthropological linguistics.
He concludes: "In spite of superficial similarities,
glossolalia is fundamentally not language."[20] From a
strictly scientific point of view it is not gibberish. Not
every non-language sound uttered is tongues. It takes
intelligence to speak in tongues. It is a derivative
phenomenon which depends on the linguistic ability and knowledge of each speaker.[21] Each uses the treasury of vocali-
zations already at his or her disposal. The syllables are
not created in that instant and given from above.
Nonetheless, the belief that tongues represents a true but
unknown language is very widespread in classical Pentecostalism, indeed, in all the charismatic denominational movements.

Or it is supposed to be, in some literal sense, the language of angels (1 Co 13:1).

Some fear that were one to deny that tongues is a true but unknown language one would thereby be denying its supernatural character. This is clearly not so. Even if it is not a true language but rather, as Arnold Bittlinger has declared, a natural phenomenon of which everyone is capable, it can still be filled with the power of the Spirit and be supernaturally transformed.[22] It is equally dangerous to equate the miraculous with the supernatural as many classical Pentecostals do. In this framework the supernatural would include the miraculous but would extend far beyond it and would embrace those non-miraculous, ordinary, unremarkable aspects of daily spiritual striving.

In a theological perspective it is essentially irrelevant whether or not it is a true language, though scientifically, the true language question is a valid object of research. What is relevant theologically is that God is praised in freedom, spontaneously and joyously in the Spirit.

One must distinguish between scientific statements and faith statements. "Jesus is Lord and Savior" is a faith statement which cannot be verified scientifically. "Greta is speaking Greek" is a statement of fact which could be verified scientifically, with all the laboratory controls which scientific verification implies. Such a statement cannot be verified "spiritually." To my knowledge no instance of tongue speaking has been verified by

the methods proper to science. In no sense is this a
depreciation of tongues. Having said this I would also
want to agree with the Swiss psychiatrist, Th. Spoerri:
"The solemn assertion of people who are of themselves
trustworthy, that they have heard someone who speaks in
tongues speaking in Italian, Hebrew or Latin, cannot simply
be rejected as an invention."[23] Though I can find no case
in which tongues has been scientifically verified, I know
persons, whose judgment I trust, who have asserted that a
true language was recognized in given cases. This gives
me pause and suggests that I do not close the door too
quickly nor with too great assurance. At very least I have
to put the instances testified to by a considerable number
of trustworthy witnesses into a special category which I
label "Things I do not understand and cannot account for,
which need further investigation."

If it is not a true language, what is it? It is, I
think, a language of the heart as distinguished from a
language of the mind (*nous* in Greek), an art-language[24]
which allows one spontaneous prayer in a pre-conceptual
way. Though pre-literary it is not mindless prayer because
the believer knows he is praying and usually know what kind
of prayer it is (e.g. praise, petition, thanksgiving). It
is one way of praying (not the only one) with those root
realities which lie deep in the individual and collective
unconscious; it dares in this pre-conceptual freedom to pray
by the Spirit (1 Co 14:15), to sing hymns by the Spirit
(ibid.),[25] to bless by the Spirit (1 Co 14:16), to speak
to God (1 Co 14:2).

Even if it is not a true language and is not a
miraculous event it is still a free gift of the Spirit,
using those powers and that equipment which all possess.
It is a non-rational (not anti-rational) expression of
mountain-top experiences, but much more often of those
valley experiences which make up the larger portion of the
Christian life. In no sense is it deprived of worth or
meaning when one has said that it is not a true language
or that it is a human competency within the reach of all.

Every religious system has its occupational hazards.
In Catholicism, with its hierarchical structure and sacramental system, the hazards are legalism and mechanism or
ritualism. In classical Pentecostalism it is a preoccupation with the demonstration of power, with the miraculous.
Out of this come those individuals who build their ministries
around the wondrous, sometimes called "miracle ministries."
Classical Pentecostals have themselves recognized the
danger to the gospel when a ministry becomes miracle-
oriented. For one thing people are drawn for the wrong
reason, and they are not nurtured. Real pastoral care is
neglected and people do not get fed. All of this is well
known to classical Pentecostals who also know it does not
characterize their ministry in general.

The sense of the wondrous so strong in classical
Pentecostalism has also its very positive side. In the gift
of tongues it witnesses to an aspect of religious experience which belongs to the fullness of the gospel. Tongues,
the lowest of the gifts, is still a gift of the Spirit. It

46

belongs to that complete spectrum of Christian experience and pertains to the realm of the ordinary Christian life, not to the extraordinary. Anyone who knows classical Pentecostals well enough to know the patterns and rhythms of their life, will know that in practice they have not taken one gift of the Spirit and built "a special little chapel around it."[26] For instance, classical Pentecostals might gather to pray together; they do not gather specifically to pray in tongues. They have demonstrated, not that the tongue-speaker is a special kind of Christian, but that this lowly gift belongs to the full complement of gifts which build up the body.

* * * * * * * * * * * * * * * * * * * *

There are a number of important functions of glossolalia not treated in this paper, including tongues as a function of private prayer and public "liturgical" prayer (and classical Pentecostals have a real if unperceived liturgy); as a daily actualization of conversion; as consolation; as a prophetic utterance in conjunction with the gift of interpretation; as an expression of the collective psyche; and as a therapeutic instrument liberating from psychological repressions, blocks and alienations.

FOOTNOTES

[1] There are some exceptions but the doctrine of initial evidence is sufficiently widespread to merit the generalization.

[2] In this matter I would agree substantially with Dunn. In a monograph in which the author, James D. G. Dunn, severely criticizes the classical Pentecostal exegesis (as well as the Roman Catholic exegetical schools) he closes with these words: "And in case it should be thought that I have been less than just to the Pentecostals let me simply add in reference to these questions that Pentecostal teaching on spiritual gifts, including glossolalia, while still unbalanced, is much more soundly based on the New Testament than is generally recognized."--Baptism in the Holy Spirit. Studies in Biblical Theology, second series, no 15 (London: 1970), p 229.

[3] Luther P. Gerlach and Virginia H. Hine, People, Power, Change (New York: 1970), pp 99-158.

[4] Ibid., pp 124-126.

[5] Ibid., pp 125,126.

[6] Christian Lalive d'Epinay, Haven of the Masses: A Study of the Pentecostal Movement in Chile (London: 1969), pp 197, 198. "May one say that the Chileans, at this point, are more faithful to the spirit of the Acts of the Apostles, while the North Americans cling to the letter of it, since, as has been shown, the consequence of Pentecost is essentially evangelization, not glossolalia" (p 198).

[7] Klaude Kendrick, The Promise Fulfilled: A History of the Modern Pentecostal Movement (Springfield: 1961), pp 48,49. Cf. also Stanley Howard Frodsham, Smith Wigglesworth: Apostle of Faith, (Springfield, 1948), p 44.

[8] Kilian McDonnell, "Ideology of Pentecostal Conversion," Journal of Ecumenical Studies 5 (1968), pp 105-126.

[9] Eberhard Bethge (ed.), Letters and Papers from Prison (New York: 1972), p 360.

[10] Henri Nouwen, The Living Reminder (New York: 1977), p 45.

[11] The behavioral changes are clearly set forth in the idology and are witnessed to in that period following the commitment act. Cf. Gerlach and Hine, People, Power, Change, pp 99-182.

[12] Kendrick, The Promise Fulfilled, pp 48,49.

[13] Frank Bartleman, How Pentecost Came to Los Angeles: As it Was in the Beginning (Los Angeles: 1925), p 73.

[14] Lewi Pethrus, The Wind Bloweth Where it Listeth (Minneapolis: 1945), p 20.

[15] Cf. John H. Osteen, "Pentecost is not a Denomination: It is an Experience," Full Gospel Business Men's Voice, 8 (June 1960), pp 4-9; Aimee Semple McPherson, "In the Service of the King" (New York: 1927); Thomas Ball Barratt, When the Fire Fell and an Outline of My Life (Oslo: 1927), passim; Pethrus, The Wind Bloweth, pp 31,32.

[16] A good liturgy also allows one to express one's archaeology. The root vocabulary here is that of Paul Ricoeur.

[17] Cf. Noam Chamsky, "Language and Mind," (New York: 1968), pp. 24,67; Cecil H. Brown, Wittgensteinian Linguistics Approaches to Semiotics, no 12 (The Hague: 1974), pp 17,18.

[18] *Principalitas legis novae est gratia Spiritus Sancti.* Summa Theologica, I-II, q. 180, al.

[19] George T. Montague, The Spirit and His Gifts (New York: 1974), pp 18,19.

[20] Tongues of Men and Angels (New York: 1972), p 227.

[21] Ibid., p 127.

[22] Arnold Bittlinger, Glossolalia (Schloss Craheim, 1969).

[23] "Ekstatische Rede und Glossolalie," Beitrage zur Ekstase (Basel: 1968), p 151.

[24] Bittlinger, Glossolalia, p 24.

[25] There seems to be a play on meanings in 1 Cor 14:15. The spirit here is both the human spirit and the Holy Spirit. "It is self-understood that the human spirit is not envisaged here in its natural isolation from the divine Spirit, but in its complete union with it."--Frédéric Godet, Commentaire sur la Première Épitre aux Corinthiens vol 2 (Neuchatel: 1965), p 283.

[26] Krister Stendahl, Paul Among Jews and Gentiles (Philadelphia: 1976), p 121.

APPENDIX

I give here some testimonies to baptism in the Holy
Spirit and tongues. Some of the earlier testimonies are
cast in a vocabulary which would be as strange to classical
Pentecostals today as they are to Roman Catholics who also
no longer speak today as they did in 1900 or 1906.

1. The first recipient: Miss Agnes Ozman (1901)

One of the students who was to occupy a unique place
in the beginning of Modern Pentecost was Agnes N. Ozman. . . .
Though she had been raised in the Methodist Church, Agnes had
become associated. . .with the Holiness movement. . . .She
attended for one year A. B. Simpson's Bible school in New
York. . . . She attended John Alexander Dowie's services
in Zion City, Illinois. These experiences fired her with
evangelical enthusiasm, so that she continued mission work
in Nebraska and then in Kansas City. At this latter place
she heard of the opening of Bethel Bible College and decided
to join the student body. . . . About 7:00 p.m. January 1,
1901 when meditating in her devotions, Agnes Ozman was
reminded that believers in the New Testament church were
"baptized in the Spirit" on several occasions when hands
were laid on them. Acting on an impulse when Charles Parham
returned from the mission, she asked Parham to lay hands
upon her in biblical fashion. Refusing the request at first,
he finally relented and said a short prayer as he laid his
hands on her. According to Miss Ozman's own testimony: "It
was as his hands were laid upon my head that the Holy
Spirit fell upon me and I began to speak in tongues,
glorifying God. I talked several languages, and it was
clearly manifest when a new dialect was spoken. I had the
added joy and glory my heart longed for and a depth of the
presence of the Lord within that I had never known before.
It was as if rivers of living waters were proceeding from
my innermost being. . . .I was the first one to speak in
tongues in the Bible school. . . . I told them not to seek
for tongues but to seek for the Holy Ghost." Although Agnes
Ozman was not the first person in modern times to speak in
"tongues," she was the first known person to have received
such an experience as a result of specifically seeking a
baptism in the Holy Spirit with the expectation of speaking
in tongues. From this time Pentecostal believers were to
teach that the "baptism in the Holy Spirit" should be sought
and that it would be received with the evidence of "tongues."
For this reason the experience of Agnes Ozman is designated
as the beginning of the Modern Pentecostal Revival. --Klaude
Kendrick, The Promise Fulfilled: A History of the Modern
Pentecostal Movement (Springfield: 1961), pp 48,49,52,53.

2. <u>A Los Angeles Recipient</u>: <u>Mr Frank Bartleman</u> (1906)

On the afternoon of August 16, at Eighth and Maple, the Spirit manifested Himself through me in "tongues." There were seven of us present at the time. It was a week day. After a time of testimony and praise, with everything quiet, I was softly walking the floor, praising God in my spirit. All at once I seemed to hear in my soul (not with my natural ears), a rich voice speaking in a language I did not know. I have later heard something similar to it in India. It seemed to ravish and fully satisfy the pent up praises in my being. In a few moments I found myself, seemingly without volition on my part, enunciating the same sounds with my own vocal organs. It was an exact continuation of the same expression that I had heard in my soul a few moments before. It seemed a perfect language. I was almost like an outside listener. I was fully yielded to God, and simply carried by His will, as on a divine stream. I could have hindered the expression but would not have done so for worlds. A Heaven of conscious bliss accompanied it. It is impossible to describe the experience accurately. It must be experienced to be appreciated. There was no effort made to speak on my part, and not the least possible struggle. The experience was most sacred, the Holy Spirit playing on my vocal cords, as on an Aeolian harp. The whole utterance was a complete surprise to me. I had never really been solicitous to speak in "tongues." Because I could not understand it with my natural mind, I had rather feared it.--Frank Bartleman, <u>How Pentecost Came to Los Angeles</u> (Privately published, Los Angeles: 1925), p 71.

3. <u>The reception by the European father of the Pentecostal movement</u>: <u>Pastor T. B. Barratt</u> (1906)

When praying I constantly felt the need of a <u>still greater blessing over my own soul</u>! I stood and had from youth been standing, for holiness and the baptism of the Holy Ghost, and had no doubt often felt somewhat of the fire burning within, a touch of the unseen hand, but I knew there must be a <u>still deeper work and a constant victory</u>. All the trials I had passed through during the last year. . .brought me down - deeper down, before the Lord, seeking, praying, weeping in His presence, thirsting for a full baptism of the Holy Ghost - <u>the experience itself</u>, and not only the intense longing for it. . . . I had noticed, at times on Sunday, a remarkable warmth in my breast, but it left me. Whilst weeping Sunday afternoon, a little before 5 p.m., the fire came back to my breast. I had my face in a towel, so as not to disturb the inmates next door, but it did not last long ere I shouted so loudly, that they must have heard me afar off, had it not been for the noise in the street. I was bathed a while in perspiration. (They no doubt shouted aloud in the house of Cornelius - "loudly magnified God," Norwegian translation - Acts 10:46) I could not help it; <u>I was seized by the Holy Power of God throughout my whole</u>

being, and it swept through my whole body as well. . . . I
did not expect tongues as a definite sign of the Pentecostal
blessing, but the friends at Los Angeles wrote and said I
must press on to get the gift of tongues. . . . I want the
finished work. In one sense never finished on earth, but
the Pentecostal testimony or seal (gift of tongues) to the
power, and still more power! . . . Former letters told of
persecution, even from the Methodists, but I was told that
"the Holy Ghost only comes in when you come to an end of
yourself." - They were delighted to hear of my experinece.
I quote a few lines of a letter: . . . "The speaking in
tongues should follow the baptism. If you had remained under
the power, until the Lord had finished, you undoubtedly
would have spoken in tongues, not necessarily for use in a
foreign field, but as a sign to you of Pentecost, the same
as at the house of Cornelius and at Ephesus. . . . I had not
received any teaching concerning the tongues as a special
sign of Pentecost before, in the circles where I had
hitherto been. . . . The Lord showed me nevertheless,
through this break in my experience, that it is possible to
receive great anointings of the Spirit, without speaking in
tongues, but that if we receive the full Pentecostal Baptism,
as they "at the beginning," it will be a greater infilling,
accompanied with tongues, prophetic language (Acts 19:6),
loud praises (Acts 10:46). In the Norwegian version:
"høilig prise Gud," that is: praising God loudly, but
especially tongues, which was to be the special sign of the
new dispensation, all other signs having been found among
the believers before Pentecost (Mark 16:16). . . . I possibly
made a mistake on the 7th of October, and disturbed the
workings of the Spirit, by expecting help from others. At
any rate I had to wait more than a month before the Power
was turned on again, as it were, in an ever increasing
degree, until I burst forth in tongues and loudly magnified
God, in the Power of the Holy Spirit. This time nothing
interferred with the workings of the Divine Spirit, and as
a result, the outward sign of the Spirit's presence
was seen and heard as on the Day of Pentecost in Jerusalem,
Halleujah! I learnt also, that the change wrought in our
lives, by the Holy Spirit, when we become the children of
God (regenerated), was a different experience to the Baptism
in the Holy Ghost, when He fills us, and immerses us into
His own being - body, soul and spirit. . . . I asked the
leader of the meeting, a little before 12 o'clock to lay
hands on me and pray for me. Immediately the power of God
began to work in my body, as well as in my spirit. . . .
When they were praying, the doctor's wife saw a crown of
fire over my head and a cloven tongue as of fire in front
of the crown. Compare Acts 2:3-4. The brother from Norway,
and others, saw this supernatural highly red light. - The
very same moment, my being was filled with light and an
indescribable power, and I began to speak in a foreign
language as loudly as I could. For a long time I was lying
upon my back on the floor, speaking - afterwards I was
moving about on my knees with my eyes shut. For some time
this went on; then at last I sat on a chair, and the whole

time I spoke in "diverse kinds of tongues" (1 Corinthians
12:10) with a short interval between. --Thomas Ball Barratt,
When the Fire Fell and an Outline of my Life (Oslo:1927),
pp 103,108,109, 112-116, 120-130. (Emphases given as found
in the original text, but some emphases omitted to facili-
tate reading).

   4. A contemporary Neo-Pentecostal recipient: The
Rev Mr John Osteen (1960)

   I stand as one of the group of pastors who are desper-
ately concerned and deeply disturbed and confused over the
lack of power. . .there has been a growing concern in my
heart, for I knew that something ought to be there which was
not there, and could not be found. . . . I read in the
Bible about the early church and its supernatural power and
I so longed for such as that. . . . Men and women are tired
of deadness and failure. - My subject was in the form of a
question. "When did Jesus baptize you in the Holy Ghost and
Fire?" If we know when we are baptized in water, we should
certainly know when and if we had been baptized in fire. I
confessed to them that I had not had this experience, but
was setting my heart and soul toward God to have it! - I
discovered that even though Jesus was the Son of God, nothing
was ever heard of His supernatural ministry on earth until
the Holy Ghost came upon Him. . . . Directly, there came
into my hands a strange feeling, and it came on down to the
middle of my arms and began to surge! It was like a
thousand - like ten thousand - then a million volts of
electricity. . . . In an air-conditioned room, with my hands
lifted. . .and my heart reaching up for my God, there came
the hot, molten lava of His love. It poured in like a
stream from Heaven and I was lifted up out of myself. I
spoke in a language I could not understand for about two
hours. My body perspired as though I was in a steambath:
the Baptism of Fire! - This was about two years ago. Between
seventy and eighty of our people have received this glorious
experience. Men and women who wearily trudged to prayer
meeting and drove themselves to be faithful have become
flaming evangels for Jesus!--John H. Osteen, "Pentecost is
not a Denomination: It is an Experience," Full Gospel Business
Men's Voice 8 (June 1960), pp 4-9.

   5. A convert to Pentecostalism from a Southern Baptist
background during World War II.

   I had to lay aside my own ideas in order to receive
the infilling of the Holy Spirit. I had to accept it on
God's terms. And God's terms for me were that I go back
there with that group of loud-praying Christians. I had to
humble myself and let them pray for me.

   I didn't know much about the Holy Spirit. I had heard
one of my buddies tell of one of the boys who was slain

under the power of God and he had fallen to the deck under the power of the Spirit. I knew how hard that flight deck was, so when I finally went back to the prayer meeting that night I said, "Lord you won't have to knock me down; I am going to lie down on the deck to start with!" And I did. I may seem humorous now, but I was completely serious. In my hunger for God I did the simple act of lying down on the deck and lifting my heart and hands to the Lord Jesus.

I wasn't there long until a boy whom I had won to Christ a few months before but had received the Baptism before I did, he came over and put his hands on me. The Lord began to pour forth His Spirit in great torrents of blessing. If I had the vocabulary of Webster it would be insufficient to explain the joy, the blessing, the new dimension of praise in worship, the new comprehension of divine truth, the new appreciation of the Cross, the increased devotion to the Christ who died for my salvation which came as a result of my infilling.

Hour after hour, it was as if a waterfall was falling on me in Spirit; it was as if liquid love penetrated me all the way through as I praised in the Spirit. I worshipped Him in a language I never learned. I felt this great liberty to praise Jesus as I'd always wanted to but never could. I felt the Holy Spirit flow through me in a divine electricity, or a divine energy current - current after current until I didn't feel like I could stand any more and yet there was no desire at all that it would stop. It was a glorious meeting - a glorious revelation that He did to my heart until about two o'clock in the morning. That was the beginning of the Spirit walk.

When we receive the Baptism, we don't jump from a buck private to a four star general overnight, but we do become officer material. The Baptism of the Spirit isn't a goal, it's only a gateway. If we walk in obedience to the captain of our salvation, He will lead us into the deep things of God.--Luther P. Gerlach and Virginia H. Hine, People, Power, Change (New York: 1970), pp 120,121.

6. A Presbyterian minister, an African missionary, receives the baptism and tongues during the 1960's under the ministry of a classical Pentecostal pastor whom he considered his intellectual inferior.

I made it very clear to him at the beginning that I was interested in the Baptism of the Holy Spirit to give me the power for the job I wanted to do as a disciple of Jesus Christ, but that I wanted nothing to do with tongue speaking. He very wisely said, "All right, then, let's just forget about it."

54

So then we went over the scriptures again together and then we began to pray. He laid his hands on me and suggested that I just relax and think, not about my sins and worriedness, but about the promises of God and my rights as a son of God. There was no question in my mind that I felt a physical warmness, a mellowness of heart, a certain relaxation and more and more I was enjoying praising God. Now this sounds strange, but as a Presbyterian, I had never had a freedom in worship. People had told me that I was a good preacher, but this was a result of hard work and following my manuscript. I had never had a real sense of liberty in the pulpit or in prayer - maybe the best way to put it is I'd desired a sense of intimacy with God.

So I was enjoying praising and just praying without thinking what I was going to pray. This was all in English of course. And then he (the Pentecostal) suggested that I stop speaking in English and start letting the Holy Spirit motivate a divine language. Well, I remember thinking, "Ah, well now he's caught me." But I guess I decided, "Well, Lord, I have to accept those things on your terms and I know from scriptures that tongues did come with this for the early disciples, so I'm willing to be a little bit more foolish here and see what comes of it."

I was aware of what was going on around us. His wife was preparing a meal. I was not caught up in an ecstatic experience nor was I emotionally beside myself. I just sort of opened my mouth as if I were going to speak and tried to let go and sure enough, this language came out of me. There was no stuttering or stammering. It just came out as a language. I remember my first thought was that it sounded sort of oriental or Indian or something although I know no languages except English and Swahili and of course some Hebrew and Greek. When this language began to come it was to me a tremendously releasing experience. I really felt like I was being given the power to express my joy and worship of the Lord without any limitations in having to think about what I was going to say, so that I was really not praying. The Holy Spirit was praying in cooperation with me, taking my voice and my body - in order to formulate the words, using my muscles, but the Spirit was animating it. The language was divine, but there was nothing divine about the speaking itself.

I'm told this lasted about forty-five minutes. I had my arms up, which is most un-Presbyterian, during this whole period. Another physical manifestation which took place, which also was most un-Presbyterian, and completely new to me, was that I became aware of the muscles of my arms quivering - a sort of spasmodic quivering. My first thought was that I'd been holding them up too long and the blood had drained out. So I lowered my arms and realized that this didn't help at all, but as a result it began to pass into the other muscles of my body, even till it got down to

55

my stomach muscles. I remember I opened my eyes to make
sure I wasn't imagining it. The other thing which is very
common with many people but very unusual for me was weeping. I had never wept, either in confessing my sins or
with joy, being taught all my life that men don't cry.
But the release manifested itself in tears. I didn't want
to stop the tongues. I was enjoying it too much.

The joy remained with me for a whole week even though
I was not able to tell anyone about this experience for
something like a month afterward, except to my wife who did
not accept it at all. However, three months later she did
seek the experience for herself and received it in our
home.--Gerlach and Hine, People, Power, Change, pp 122,123

ROMAN CATHOLIC/PENTECOSTAL DIALOGUE
3 - 7 October 1977 - Rome

Theological Paper

Faith and Experience
by
Rev F. P. Möller

Faith and experience are two subjects with special
interest, on the one hand, for the orthodox, and on the
other hand for the evangelical practical Christian. The
ways of many theologians would part over the difference
of emphasis in regard to these concepts. Yet these two
facts must be seen in unity if one wants to come to a
scriptural and balanced view of both.

I. DEFINING THE SUBJECT

Before entering this discussion, we have to limit
our scope extensively. Both faith and experience have so
many aspects that it will be practically impossible to
deal with all of them. In the process of our discussion
we shall have to limit the scope even more. We endeavour
to say one thing clearly rather than to launch into too
many discussions and consequently be vague on all of
them.

Firstly, we want to point out that we are not
referring to faith in its objective sense as we find it

in Jd 3 ("the faith which was once delivered unto the
saints"), but rather in its subjective sense, as in
Heb 11:1 where the following definition is found: "Now
faith is the substance of things hoped for, the evidence
of things not seen." This faith is an expression of the
spirit of man, energised by the Holy Spirit, by which he
puts his trust in God and in all that He has revealed to
man.

Experience denotes some happening in which one is
involved, and by which one becomes aware of, and tires,
proves or tests the nature and extent of that happening.

Seen in the biblical context, we can bring the two
concepts in relation to each other by stating: through
faith one enters into an obedient relationship with God
and subjects oneself to the working of his Word and
Spirit: whereas experience is the effect which the appropriation of these facts has in his life.

It also needs to be said that the awareness of
faith in one's life is in itself already an effect, an
experience. If we consider the noetic qualities of
faith as put forth in Heb 11:1, we discover two vital
truths. First of all faith is described as consisting
of a substructure (*hupostasis*), a firm conviction, a
solid foundation for the realisation of the things we
hope will take place. At the same time it bears within
it also the evidence (*elekchos*) of that something by
which a thing is proved, of those facts of which we do

not yet see the realisation. Faith, in other words, is an enablement by which one can see the unseen (Heb 11:27).

This type of faith is not merely a matter of human thought and volition (though they are vital parts of it), but it finds its substructure and evidence in an act of grace, worked by the Holy Spirit through the revelation of God's Word in man. For that reason one's faith is to some great extent a reaction, an effect, an experience of this working of the Spirit (Eph 2:8; Rom 10:8-17). Even God's injunction: "Believe", "Have Faith", is accompanied by some creative power which comes into operation when one yields to the word, and thus faith is created.

True faith has not only a noetic quality, but manifests itself also as a power in man. Real faith gains control over one's whole being, becoming in one a directive, normative and motivating force. To this Paul alludes in 1 Cor 2:4,5:

> And my speech and my preaching was not with entic-
> ing words of man's wisdom, but in demonstration of
> the Spirit and of power: that your faith should not
> stand in the wisdom of men, but in the power of
> God.

At this juncture we quote Rudolf Bultman:

> . . . for pistis can frequently denote the living
> and dynamic aspect of faith rather than the mere
> fact. This applies when there is reference to the
> metron pisteôs (Rom 12:3), to the weakness of faith
> (Rom 14:1), to its strength, to its growth
> (2 Cor 10:15), to enduring in faith, to its fulness,
> to its superabundance (2 Cor 8:7), to its practice
> (1 Thes 1:3), or to its unity, and all the verses
> where pistis and agape are combined,--Theological
> Dictionary of the New Testament Vol VI pp 212,213.

All these instances prove that faith has an experiential side which is an integral part of it.

We also have to note that faith is not a means in
itself, but that it always leads to some recognizable
happening, to some works, as James puts it. He declares
that "faith without works is dead," and that "faith
wrought (lit. worked together) with his works, and by
works was faith made perfect (complete)" Jas 2:20,22.
The type of faith which we are referring to must be
described in terms of works or happenings. Only through
a knowable experience can this faith be made manifest.
Bringing faith and experience under the ambit of one
concept, we may speak of faith-experience or even better:
spiritual experience. This brings us to the actual topic
of our discussion, namely: what is spiritual experience?
By elucidating this matter we answer at the same time the
question: what is the relationship between faith and
experience?

II. SPIRITUAL LIFE

Before we can discuss spiritual experience per se,
we first have to consider spiritual life, the source from
which all spiritual manifestations originate. This in
turn brings us to regeneration or rebirth (Jn 3:3-6).
We receive spiritual life by appropriating through faith
that which Christ did for us, and by receiving His Spirit.
This appropriation takes place at our identification with
Christ's death and resurrection of which water baptism
gives the expression (Rom 6:3,4). The Spirit of Christ
in us constitutes our spiritual life. This life exists

in and in relationship with God--the human subject (I
am), in a conscious and loving relationship with the
Subject (the great I AM). The unregenerate or natural
man is a spirit who has not yet come to life; it is
actually a dying spirit (dead in sin and trespasses).
Unless this new dimension of life has opened up to man,
all matters pertaining to God and spiritual things are
strange and even foolish to him. Of this Paul speaks in
1 Cor 2:14: "But the natural man receiveth not the things
of the Spirit of God: for they are foolishness unto him:
neither can he know them, because they are spiritually
discerned." The moment man receives real life (the
Spirit of Christ), his own spirit comes alive and thus he
discovers his real existence. "For what man knoweth the
things of a man, save the spirit of man which is in him
(1 Cor 2:11)?"

III. BAPTISM IN THE HOLY SPIRIT

Inseparably linked together with regeneration and
yet distinctive from it, is the baptism in the Holy
Spirit. This peak spiritual experience is a major
contributary to the manifestation of spiritual things.
If we have to describe the baptism in the Holy Spirit, we
venture into the following definition: the baptism in the
Holy Spirit is that act of grace, based on the promise
of Ac 1:5,8, whereby God reveals Himself to the believer
in a personal, direct, intimate and continuous fashion,
by bringing man under the control of and into the fulness

of the Holy Spirit, through which the believer becomes, in a distinctive way, aware of the resurrected and glorified Christ in his life, and as a result of which he is equipped with power to lead a life in which he can be more an effective witness for Christ and enjoy a fuller dimension of worship.

By this we do not mean to speak of the Holy Spirit in a quantitative sense, as though one receives a small measure of the Spirit at new birth, and an abundance of the same Spirit at the baptism. What we do say however, is that there are various dimensions in the operation or revelation of the Holy Spirit--dimensions which correspond with the different ministries of Christ. The Spirit of God convicts of sin, regenerates, acts as *parakletos* (comforter), equips with power, sanctifies, glorifies, etc. At regeneration the Spirit applies Christ's re- demptive work in man, and thus he comes to know Him as the Saviour. At the baptism in the Holy Spirit man is made aware of the presence and empowerment of the risen Christ in his life, and thus he knows Him as the Baptizer in the Holy Spirit. What is quantitative, is the measure in which one comes to the knowledge and experience of all the riches in Christ (Eph 4:7). We can assume that Old Testament believers and Christians prior to the day of Pentecost had the experience of redemption (salvation) in their lives, but the baptism in the Holy Spirit is only for believers subsequent to the outpouring as described in Ac 2. Christ Himself indicated this in Jn 7:37-39;

14; 16; Lk 24:49; Ac 1:8, etc. The baptism in the Spirit is referred to as the coming of the Spirit as Comforter (the One to be at the side of the believer) to take as it were the place of the visible Christ on earth (Jn 14:16-20; 16:7). "Receiving the Spirit" became a terminus technicus for the revelation of the Spirit in the sense of Pentecost. Of this experience one can give witness as to the time and place when and where it happened as the various references in the book of Acts prove (Ac 2:1-4; 4:31; 8:14-17; 10:44-47; 19:1-6). This baptism experience is subsequent to regeneration, although in the case of Cornelius and his people there is no indication of any lapse of time between their coming to faith and their baptism in the Holy Spirit. Whether one considers this baptism simply as a fuller revelation of the Spirit in oneself, a greater release of the Spirit whereby His manifestation, influence and power is enhanced in one's life, or whether one sees it as a special coming of the Spirit from the outside upon and in one, is not of great importance. It is not for man to know all the mysteries of divine actions. What does matter is the fact that he has received the fulness of the Spirit by which both he and others can testify to what they "now see and hear" (Ac 2:33).

IV. SPIRITUAL MANIFESTATIONS

Experiencing regeneration as well as the enduement of power by the Holy Spirit does not mean that whatever

spiritual manifestation man produces will be totally
divine and perfect. Although we have received divine
nature in us the "the Spirit of life in Christ Jesus"
(Rom 8:2), we still have "this treasure in earthen
vessels" (2 Cor 4:7). Although we are partakers of divine nature and have within us incorruptible and eternal
life, we are still part of this world and of fallen
nature. This often causes conflict between the "Flesh"
and the "Spirit" in man (Rom 7:18-25). It is only by the
continuous mortifying (literally: rendering powerless,
Rom 6:6) of the sinful nature that we can live in the
victory of the Spirit.

Any manifestations of the Spirit or any spiritual
experience still bears the mark of both the divine and of
the fallen human nature. For that reason we can have
spiritual manifestations which are useless (1 Cor 13:1-3),
unedifying and disorderly (1 Cor 14:9-25, 40), hence the
necessity of judging of all such manifestations
(1 Cor 14:29; 12:3; 1 Jn 4, etc). We may compare it with
photography. Perfect rays of light bring the image of
the object to be photographed through the camera's lens
to the sensitive film. If the lens be defective, and if
the film has any weakness, the camera will produce a
distorted image, sometimes even beyond recognition of the
object photographed. The working of God's Spirit in man
is divine and perfect, but man's reaction to this working
or prompting, and his experssion of it, will always to
some extent obscure or warp the spiritual manifestation.

In order to live and walk in the Spirit, to be a means
through which the Spirit of God can reveal something of
the glory of the risen Christ, man must constantly die as
far as his carnal nature is concerned and yield himself
(all physical and mental faculties), to God (Rom 6:6-13).
Christ's death on the cross was not only an historic
conciliative act for man to appropriate his salvation,
but it is also a working, a mortifying power in him,
through the Holy Spirit by which "the old man is crucified
with Him, that the body of sin might be destroyed"
(Rom 6:6). There must be a constant dying, a constant
applying of the cross in man's life, for the liberation
of spiritual and resurrection life in him. This under-
lines the inseparable unity between Easter and Pentecost,
between the cross and fiery tongue (of Pentecost). "For
if we be dead with Christ, we shall also live with Him"
(2 Tim 2:11).

Though man is part of fallen nature, and will only
be liberated from it at his glorification in the hereafter, yet nature and this world is still the field of
labour for both God and man. Incorruptible seed (Christ)
is brought into fallen and cursed mankind to redeem it,
to grow in it, until "this corruptible must put on
incorruption, and this mortal must put on immortality"
(1 Cor 15:42-53).

V. THE MIRACULOUS ELEMENT IN SPIRITUAL EXPERIENCE

When mention is made of the "miraculous" element in spiritual experiences, it is not because they are void of any natural explanation or are contrary to the laws of nature, but because they are manifestations of the Spirit, of an order beyond the natural, though working in and making use of the natural. Being spiritual in its origin, a miracle cannot be established on scientific grounds. The most science can say is that it has no explanation for a certain happening or phenomenon, but it can never adduce proofs that these originate from the world beyond. Neither God nor His dealings with man can ever be reduced to an object of scientific investigation. This is the elusive quality of divine truth. It is only accessible to those who open up their hearts to the Spirit of God. A miracle can only be discerned as such on spiritual grounds, through the knowledge which faith furnishes. Only on these grounds can one know and judge that a certain occurrence or experience is a working of God. Such revelations serve as signs of the presence and revelation of God and are aids in preparing the way for and extending the kingdom of God on earth. They must be seen as acts of divine grace.

VI. SPIRITUAL AND NATURAL EXPERIENCE

At this juncture the following questions are revelant: What are the differences between a spiritual and a natural experience? Can spiritual experiences not,

for instance, be explained in terms of known psychological processes and mechanisms? What about psychological
correlates of the charism or spiritual manifestations
such as those mentioned in 1 Cor 12:8-10? In order to
get a fuller and clearer concept of what a spiritual
experience is, it is important to discuss the above
questions.

Firstly, we have to reiterate that from the biblical
viewpoint man is also spirit, which means he exists in a
relationship to God, and that he becomes aware of this
relationship when his own spirit becomes alive through
the working of the Holy Spirit. For that reason the
unregenerated person can have no knowledge of spiritual
realities and can only be limited to those contents which
he can apprehend through his senses and by means of
scientific methods. Not accepting spiritual realities
one tends to explain any spiritual experience in terms of
science, especially in terms of psychological knowledge
and deduction. By way of example we may mention the
following psychological explanations which are propounded
for the baptism in the Holy Spirit and related charisms:
a dependency syndrome where one leans heavily on some
external and fictitious authority, hypnagogic states
where there is an overflow of preconscious contents into
the conscious mind, mild forms of neuroses, motor dis-
association causing some split in the personality, the
emergence of repressed contents from the subconscious
into the conscious mind in the Freudian sense, the

influence of the collective subconscious mind with its
embedded archetypes in the Jungian sense, psychologically
induced states of mind like suggestion, trance conditions,
mass hysteria, etc.

In a study of various scientific researches on the
phenomena of glossalalia we discovered that science
cannot offer any acceptable and conclusive explanation
for this charism. The most that could be established is
that there are certain psychological mechanisms which may
be employed in the manifestation of such charisms. In
this connection the following statement of Kevin and
Dorothy Ranaghan is very apt:

> Without the acceptance of God in Christ, analysis
> of religious experience can lead one to say 'it is
> nothing but this or that.' Karl Stern in his book
> dealing with psychiatry and religion (The Third
> Revolution) shows the pitfall in this line of
> reasoning most clearly: 'If there were nothing
> beyond the psychological, all the saints from
> Simeon Stylites to the Poverello, to Benedict
> Joseph Labre, to Therese of Lisieux, would indeed
> make up a fool's parade. Yet there is no area in
> which the 'nothing but', the reductive principle,
> is more absurd than the life of the spirit.--
> Catholic Pentecostals, p 204.

To this we also want to add the following remarks
of a subcommittee of the United Presbyterian Church in
the USA:

> The subcommittee warns that it will be a dark and
> tragic day in the life of Christianity if psycho-
> logical norms are to become the criteria by which
> the truth or the untruth of religious experience is
> judged. Psychological insight has enriched, deep-
> ened and humbled our knowledge of ourselves beyond
> measure; but, when it is asked for a decisive
> answer to the question of whether a man has or has
> not experienced the living Christ it is an aborted
> and inappropriate use of the science.--Report of the
> special Committee on the Work of the Holy Spirit,
> p 15.

In comparing spiritual experience with natural (scientific controlable and determinable) experience, we submit the following observations. (Here we have in mind those manifestations which accord with the biblical norms and patterns, excluding the spurious and the obvious merely psychological phenomena.)

A. Source

The source of the spiritual manifestation, like the spiritual gifts (1 Cor 12:8-10), is an urge or prompting within someone which coincides with the awareness of a measure of faith for the manifestation of a specific gift. This prompting usually arises in one's communion with God in the spirit, but often it may come very suddenly and unexpectedly. Let us take prophecy as an example. First of all one becomes aware of the prompting of the Spirit in one to speak forth. When one starts to speak, unpremeditated words and thoughts flow from one's lips as though given to one from some other source (". . .and they began to speak. . .as the Spirit gave them utterance" Ac 2:4). The speaker's words then become a revelation to himself as well.

In all this however, the subject is in full control of himself and well disposed to those present. He has an awareness of God's presence and love, and his conscious mind is enlightened.

B. Quality

Natural experience is determined firstly by personal factors, like mental and emotional states, motives, needs, prejudices, past experience, etc., and secondly by environmental factors, like outside stimuli, interaction of the group in which you are, mass suggestion, prevailing customs and usages, etc. All the characteristics of natural experience can be analyzed and described in terms of the above mentioned factors.

With spiritual experience we have a different picture. Although the above mentioned factors will also have some bearing and influence, they do not determine the dominant characteristics of such an experience. All true spiritual experiences (like the spiritual gifts in 1 Cor 12:8-10) are predominantly revelationary by nature. They reveal something of Christ and our relationship with Him. They bear witness, in other words, of a world beyond this world and yet in this world. The nature of the charism transcends the natural ability of the subject through whom it is manifested and often causes a reaction of amazement from others witnessing it. That is what happened on the day of Pentecost (Ac 2:7,12). Even the fashion in which a charism is manifested bears some characteristic which differentiates it from a natural experience. It usually carries with it such awareness of authority that those to whom a charism is directed sense that they are being addressed by an authority, superceding the subject through whom the charism is manifested. All these and other distinctive features of spiritual experience can only be properly discerned if there is an openness of mind, and faith in divine truth.

70

C. Means

In order to do anything in the natural field, one has to employ natural means. These means could either be the actions of certain parts of one's body or the use of certain external objects as instruments or tools. If a medical doctor for instance, wants to perform a pendectomy to relieve a patient he has to apply surgical instruments and techniques.

With a spiritual manifestation like a charism of healing, no such means or skilled techniques are necessary. The means through which a charism works are spiritual. They pertain to faith in divine truths. They are things such as trust in the promises of God, prayer, exorcism, confession of sin, and the like. In saying this we do not exclude the possibility that such a work of grace or spiritual manifestation may also work through or in conjunction with some known medical or psychotherapeutic means. This, however can only be known by a revelation, a witness within one's own spirit. Be it as it may, spiritual means are of an altogether different nature from those of the natural. In terms of natural judgment there is, for instance, no casual link between prayer and the healing of appendicitis nor even a contribution to such a cure. When such a healing is affected through spiritual means, it is from a source, and according to laws, outside the scope of scientific knowledge and research.

D. Dynamics

In order to accomplish anything there must be some kind of energy expended. In the case of natural experiences we have energies and the laws by which they operate inherent in nature, such as electricity, chemical reactions (fire), nuclear power, neuro-physical power in man's body, etc. We also have personality-dynamics such as willpower, emotion, drives, aspirations, etc. In terms of these dynamics natural behaviour and experience can be understood and explained.

When we come to a spiritual manifestation we also have the working of the Holy Spirit as part of it. Granted the Holy Spirit usually employs natural dynamics, but we can never equate Him with these forces inherent in nature, otherwise we lower Him to the level of a creature where He becomes part of nature or at least becomes enmeshed in the structures and laws of nature. For the working of the Holy Spirit one needs to pray to God and then He will work as He wills. Natural energy is at the disposal of mankind to explore, to harness and to use according to his will. The Holy Spirit may employ natural energy, but under no circumstances can a natural or psychological process employ the Holy Spirit.

We can also explain it by the following illustration. An atheistic psychologist can hypnotize an unbeliever, and in his trance state give him some post hypnotic suggestions whereby he would perform (in a way) similar to a genuine expression of a charism such as prophecy. The subject may then indeed manifest some behaviour which stimulates a believer who prophesies, but we cannot at any time claim that this is a manifestation of the Holy Spirit. The mere fact that God sustains the whole creation with all its dynamics, affords no grounds to equate spiritual and natural manifestation.

The outcome of a natural process is in accordance with a fixed law of causality, inherent in nature. Because man applies certain methods and means according to certain principles the effect will be in accordance with its causal link to the process. A spiritual manifestation, on the other hand, can never be performed merely by physical and psychological processes. There is always present some elusive "factor" actually causing, directing and using the manifestation to effect some specific result.

E. Meaning and Purpose

Natural happenings and experiences have meaning and purpose for this world and this life. Spiritual manifestations have meaning and purpose, not only for this life. They are primarily aimed at the edification of man's spiritual life and his preparation for life hereafter. A spiritual manifestation also serves as a sign to make us conscious of the presence of God. It acts as an appeal to the minds and hearts of people and helps believers to make a fuller commitment to God. It strengthens faith, increases love, helps to overcome sin, creates greater liberty to worship, etc.

The following illustration will elucidate the point. A natural experience such as a psychotherapeutic process, can lead to mental health and better adjustments, but it does not change an atheist into a believer nor reveal God's truths to an unbeliever. On the other hand however, a spiritual experience can make a believer out of an infidel and can increase the faith of the believer. We can even have the situation where a person is, psychologically speaking, ill, and yet can be a staunch believer and a true witness for Christ. A psychotherapeutic process has, in other words, a humanitarian meaning, whereas a spiritual experience has a soteriological meaning. At the same time, however, we can have an interaction between a psychological process and a spiritual experience. Psychological healing may help to pave the way for spiritual experience, whilst spiritual experience helps towards better personality-integration, and social and personal adjustments.

Through insight into the real nature of spiritual experience we are better enabled to discern the true from the false: we gain a fuller picture of the relationship between faith and experience; and becoming more open to the working of the Holy Spirit, are thus of greater use in the hands of our Master.

In summerising, we may say that the ideal relationship between faith and experience exists when the Word (that in which we believe) becomes, as it were, flesh in our own lives (experience) and thus we beomce co-witnesses of what Paul says in Rom 1:16: "For I am not ashamed of the gospel of Christ: for it is the power of God unto salvation to every one that believeth."

Theological Paper

EXPERIENCE AND FAITH
by
Fr Jan H. Walgrave, OP

I. GENERAL THEOLOGICAL BACKGROUND

1.   The Holy Spirit is the Spirit of the Father and the
   Son, sent by both the Father and the Son after the ascension
   (Jn 14:16,25; 15:26) in order to govern the Church from
   within, guiding her to accomplish in her the aims for which
   Christ died on the Cross: the salvation and sanctification
   of God's elected people.

2.   One of the essential aspects of the Church is that
   she is a visible social body with various offices. Those
   offices are instrumental functions, aiming at the realization
   of the spiritual goods for which the Spirit was sent.

3.   The Church being the "congregation of the faithful"
   (St Augustine), the Spirit directly operates in and through
   individual members and indirectly in the social body of the
   Church, disposing it for a more efficacious exercise of its
   offices.

4.   This does not mean that the effects, worked in the
   Church by those individuals in and through which the Spirit
   operates, are only meliorations in the exercise of her

permanent essential offices. The Spirit also works in the Church new independent movements (prophetical movements) which are related to the numerous structures in a way characterized by "polarity". The Spirit who is the antecedent unity of the Church's life manifests Himself in two opposite forces: on the one hand essential organizations which by their very nature tend to static self-conservation and formalism; on the other hand free spiritual movements tending to change and renovation. In a certain sense, those tendencies are opposite and their coexistence creates tensions and struggles. Both together influencing, correcting and counteracting each other, lead to a historical process characterized by creative adaptive power in substantial continuity and identity. Thus understood the two opposites are equally necessary in the Church and precisely in their relation of polarity or conflictive unity.

5.   The effects worked by the Spirit in the faithful are specifically given either for the sanctification of the received *(gratia gratum faciens)* or for the edification of the Church *(gratia gratis data)*. However, they cannot entirely be separated. For, on the one hand, there is an invisible *communio sanctorum* united in the Spirit of Christ, in which the holiness of the individual members invisibly works for the spiritual good of the others and of the Church, while on the other hand, the gifts specifically given for the edification of the Church are ultimately directed to the essential aim of the Church: the sanctification of the elect.

6.   I see no reason to maintain that such gifts only as
are specifically given for the edification of the Church
are charisms. On the other hand it seems equally difficult
to call all the effects of the Holy Spirit's working in the
Church charismatic. For the meaning of the word "charismatic" seems to imply the idea of "something exceptional,"
not occuring according to an ordinary rule. Different
people receive different charisms and in different degrees.
Hence not all Christians have them in virtue of their being
baptized and having true faith as if they were regularly
connected with them.

For the sake of systematic theological clarity I
tentatively propose to reduce the distinction between what
is charismatic and what is not to the basic distinction,
made by St Augustine and St Thomas Aquinas, between *gratia
operans* and *gratia cooperans*. In the former God (the
Spirit) alone is working in sovereign freedom. In the
second we are operating by ourselves but not without God's
graceful cooperation. By baptism and faith we are endowed
with abiding powers to accomplish some acts. We call those
powers "infused virtues": powers to act, infused in us by
the Spirit and hence not acquired by our efforts. Yet we
have received them as perfections of our substantial being.
Therefore it is natural or according to rule that--with the
assistance of the Spirit of course--we accomplish the acts,
corresponding to those powers, at will according to our own
judgment. But the gift of miracles for example is not a
perfection of our own substantial being which we exercise

at will, but a gift that makes a person an elected instrument of the Spirit's working miracles by Himself alone (2a 2ae, q. 178, 1. ad 4).

II. EXPERIENCE

The very situation of dialogue in which we find ourselves here imposes upon me the duty of dealing with my subject as a Catholic theologian. Catholic theology however is not a repetition from age to age of traditional propositions. It is something living and does not shrink from using insights of contemporary philosophy in order to unfold and present in a new way the position of the Church. This is what I will try to do.

Now, the most important notion of contemporary philosophy is the notion of experience. I shall maintain that faith enters into what William James calls the stream of consciousness or Edmund Husserl the *Erlebnisstrom* (stream of experience) as a particular experience: that it modifies the stream's course that it develops there in a way similar to the way in which all experiences live in the stream of experience and that in the course of its progress it may be enriched by new experiences some of which are charismatic.

But first I have to explain my notion of experience. The general notion of experience is: "coming to know" something in immediate cognitional contact with the thing known.

There are two qualified notions of experience in contemporary thought: according to the older classical empiricism experience is reduced to sense-experience; a

coming to know objects in immediate sense-contact with
these objects. Experience, thus understood, provides us
with the data which experimental science has to explain.

In contemporary philosophy there is a growing opposition against this idea of experience. Sense experience,
it is said, is only a part of what we consciously grasp in
immediate cognitional contact, and even as a part it is so
closely connected and intertwined with other facts we are
conscious of that there is no pure sense-experience. Pure
sense-experience does not exist. Hence this notion is an
abstraction from a concrete whole to which it originally
belongs. Therefore, being obtained by abstraction, it is
only secondary. For the concrete whole from which an aspect is abstrated is more primitive than the abstracted
aspect.

It is logical then to say that "Experience" is the
sum total or series and the structuralization of all our
doings and undergoings as far as they are immediately had
by the self-witnessing subject. A feeling of uneasiness is
no less something we come to know in immediate cognitional
contact with it as a tree we observe. It is no less objective: an object perceived by a subject.

[Here are] some theses about experience.

1.   "Experience" (with majuscule) presents itself as a
process in continous change. Hence the image of a stream.

2.   It is made of let us say--millions of elements or
"experiences" (with minuscule).

3.   It is not a chaos but a structured process in which

80

the elements (James' "substantive moments") coalesce and succeed to one another according to definite rules (James' "transitive moments") which may be phenomenologically described.

4.   Each momentary stage in the process forms a definite pattern.

5.   The elements are not only cognitive, but also emotional and conative: all in one. There is no pure cognition, pure emotion, or pure conation. They are all co-inherent one in the other, so that an element of experience which presents itself to consciousness as an emotion or an impetus to action has in itself also a moment of cognition of which perhaps one is not explicitly aware. An experience of emotion may precede the cognitive experience of what causes it.

6.   The stream of Experience is cumulative. What from moment to moment we are conscious of accumulates in the mysterious sack of the past which is no longer under the spotlight of our attention yet from which memory can draw its materials (Husserl's "retention").

7.   This unconscious realm of the past is no less a real part of our Experience as that which at this present moment we are aware of.

8.   The unconscious results of the past process are a structured whole with permanent or strongly fixed states: habits of thought and action, emotional sensibilities, inclinations, etc., which taken together constitute our character or personality. At each stage of our life our character or personality can as it were be defined in terms of

the structuralized sum total of what we have done or under-
gone in the past, now fixed in mental traits.

9.   The character determines in a certain measure our
future experiences (Husserl's "protention").

10.   Being situated in the context of the stream between
its "retentions" and "protentions" is the condition of
possibility and meaning of each present experience.

11.   The stream of experience does not go on in the
isolated sphere of the individual but in the multiple social
interchanges that are the public side of its life. But what
those interchanges and communications put into the stream
are assimilated in the individual's experience and only as
such they are part of experience. This social input of
experience is of utmost importance for the formation of
the individual's stream of experience.

12.   Whether the experiences which enter into the stream
of Experience and modify it have their origin in social
influence or in personal deeds or invisible influences,
such as the action of the Holy Spirit, does not make any
difference for their being experiences in the same general
sense.

III.   RELIGIOUS EXPERIENCE

1.   Catholics generally hold that there is a natural
knowledge of God, previous to the knowledge by faith in the
strict sense.

2.   Whether such a knowledge can be attained by logical
reason I leave aside. If it can be done, it is in itself

only a notional knowledge of God.

3.   But in the stream of Experience there are some deep
general and directive experiences which, when fully clarified naturally issue in a "real apprehension" of God
(John Nenry Newman).

4.   The first of those general directive experiences is
that of self-transcendence, strongly stressed in contemporary philosophy, and even in the philosophy of the sciences:
"l'homme passe infiniment l'homme" (Blaise Pascal). This
self-transcendence is not infinite in the sense of not being
directed towards a final state in which it comes to rest,
but, as Søren Kierkegaard argued against the young Friedrich
Schlegel, it is directed towards a definite ideal realization
of personality which is inherently obligatory for man as
such, and is somehow related to an existing infinite. As
Thomas Aquinas and Maurice Blondel maintain, this infinite
object is not clearly known from the start, but, as the cause
of an emotion may be implicitly and unconsciously known in
the experience of the emotion itself (cfr. II. 5), so the
cause of the infinite self-transcending thinking and acting
is a being in search of the true knowledge of its object.

5.   Connected with this is the experience of conscience,
so strongly stressed, described and analysed by Samuel Tay-
lor Coleridge, Newman, Kierkegaard, Count Leo N. Tolstoy
and so many others. Conscience is the immediate experience
of discernment between what is good and bad, that is, of
what agrees or does not agree with the true object of our
essential self-transcendence. It is specifically characterized by an accompanying experience of unconditional duty

to do the good and to avoid the bad (Immanuel Kant:
"kategorische Imperativ" ; Newman: "sense of duty").

6.   As Newman beautifully describes, when we are faithful to the imperatives of our true being or to the dictates
of conscience, this experience naturally issues by the
way of self-clarification into an experience or "real
apphehension" of God.

IV. EXPERIENCE IN FAITH

1.   According to Christianity there are two essential
inducements to faith: the exterior hearing of the Word and
the inner movement of God's Grace. Miracles are not necessary (Thomas Aquinas, Quodlibetum 2. art. 6). The definitive inducement is the inner movement of Grace (id. Summa
Theologiae, 2a 2ae 2,9 ad 3).

2.   The inner inducement is called by Aquinas "The instinct of the inviting God". Instinct is not a disposition
but an occurence: an actually being moved. The movement,
as worked by God is described in biblical terms as "invitation", "vocation", "attraction". As happening in man it
is described by the term "instinct". Why? "Instinct"
means a being moved from within by a higher power. The
term unites in its meaning a discernment of value and a
being moved toward it or a discernment of menace combined
with a movement of flight. So, in the "instinct of the
inviting God" we discern His ultimate value of salvation
and are attracted by it. In Thomas' theology this is an
experience because, as he says, it is morally bad to resist

it. We cannot resist a movement which we do not experience at all.

3. As a divine initiating of a new life, the instinct of faith is a work of God's "operating grace" and therefore it may be called charismatic (I. 6).

4. As man is by nature a willing, free being, the initiating experience of faith cannot become active in his personal life except on the condition that he does not resist it but freely accepts it and integrates it in his life-pattern as the supreme leading conviction of his conduct. By so doing the experience of faith, entering in the stream, engenders in it the infused habit or virtue of faith (II. 8).

V. EXPERIENCE IN THE LIFE OF FAITH

1. Enriched by faith the stream of experience is profoundly modified by it. Imperfect in the beginning, its influence on life has to increase as to its scope and to its intensity, tending to become the all-pervasive motive of the faithful's conduct.

2. This process naturally (in accordance with the general laws of experience) engenders within the stream new experiences which confirm and strenghten faith. Those experiences are worked with the aid of God's cooperating grace. They are not charismatic.

3. Such experiences are no additions of new elements of faith. Through such experiences faith grows, like all virtues not by the way of addition, as Aquinas says, but by

the way of greater participation in the perfection of the
habitual disposition, or by a deeper rooting of it in the
subject or a greater command in scope and intensity over
the life of the believer.

4.   According to Aquinas there are other kinds of experiences connected with the gifts of the Holy Spirit. As
he sees it, those gifts are infused by God together with
the theological virtues, yet do not consist in man's being
thus moved by the Spirit according to His divine will and
judgment. Those actual movements are worked by operating
grace: "The wind (Spirit) blows where it wills". Therefore
these movements are charismatic. It is very significant
that Aquinas, in dealing with the gifts of the Holy Spirit
in general (1a 2ae, 68) soon replaces the biblical term
"inspiration" by "instinct" which then becomes his habitual
designation; just as, in dealing with the beginning of the
basic change through faith he translates as we have seen
(cfr. IV. 2) the biblical terms "invitation" and so on with
the term "instinct" in as far as those divine actions are
considered as occurences in man.

5.   There are two kinds of motions which the Spirit freely
works in man. The first properly operated by the gifts of
the Spirit, we may call "general" because they take place
in the life of all true believers who have received the Spirit
as the first inner principle of this life. They are specifically directed to the sanctification of the individual
believer. The second, worked by the same Spirit, yet not
through the gifts connected with the virtues, might be called "special" because they are only given, different in nature

86

and degree, to some particular persons in the Church. They are specifically directed to the edification of the community: prophecy, miracles, healing, tongues, teaching, government, exorcism, etc.

6. The "general motions" are at work in all the activities which spring from faith and from divine love. All the exercises of the infused virtues, while being really ours, freely operated by us according to our free disposition and "prudence", are at the same time supervised and "super-directed" by immediate motions of the Holy Spirit, acting according to His divine good pleasure and "prudence" (judgment or wisdom). This "spiritual" aspect may be more or less penetrating or overpowering. The process of spiritual life precisely consists in that our own "prudence" is more and more penetrated by, assumed into, spontaneously conform to, identical with the inner superior, immediate guidance of the Spirit. According to our spiritual progress we are more and more right in saying: "Not I live but Christ (through His Spirit) lives in me".

7. All those motions or instincts by which the Holy Spirit personally directs us are in our inner life "experiences", ordinarily not so clear and distinct as for instance an experience of bodily pain or pleasure, but often the more powerful as they are unheeded. The highest mystical experience belonging to the aspect of union with God, which Jan Ruysbroeck calls "with gifts" (in which the proper consciousness of the I is preserved) are called by Ruysbroeck and St John of the Cross "touches" (Ruysbroeck: *"rueren"* or *"gherinen"*; St John of the Cross: *"toque"* - *"o toque*

delicado" as he says in the poem of the "<u>Llama</u> <u>de</u> <u>amor</u> <u>viva</u>") and St John emphasizes that they are so delicate and deep that mostly those who receive them are not explicitly aware of the fact.

8.   The "gifts of the Spirit," combined with the infused virtues, emanating from the *gratia gratum faciens* and hence directed to the sanctification of the individual receiver, form together an order distinct from the order of the *gratiae gratis datae,* given for the good of the others or the "common good of the Church which is in the ecclesiactical order" (Thomas Aquinas 1a 2ae, 111, 5, ad 1). The works of those ecclesiastical graces are all exterior and in principle independent of the personal holiness of the receiver.

There is however an analogy between the working of those graces and the working of the gifts properly called so. For in both cases the form of the grace is not an habitual perfection of the substantial person but a disposition for being moved by an instinct of the Holy Spirit. Hence they are charismatic, their exercise being worked by God alone (operating grace) according to His good pleasure and divine judgment. This analogy justifies our calling both of them <u>gifts</u> <u>of</u> <u>the</u> <u>Holy</u> <u>Spirit</u>.

ROMAN CATHOLIC/PENTECOSTAL DIALOGUE
3-7 October 1977   -   Rome

Agreed Account

1.   Introduction

This dialogue session, the first of a second five-year series, is unique from those previous, in that the pentecostal position was represented by classical Pentecostals only, without the inclusion of those who share the pentecostal experience from the Protestant and Anglican Churches.

2.   Papers

On this occasion two subjects were presented in four papers and discussed:

Speaking in tongues as a characteristic aspect of of the experience in the Pentecostal Movement; and

The relationship between faith and experience. (Final Report 1972-1976, para 45 (a) and (d).) (See One in Christ 12, 4 (1976), p 318.)

3.1.   SPEAKING IN TONGUES

Neither of the authors of the papers were present throughout the full period of the discussions. This posed a problem in that it was impossible for participants to question them on their papers in order to get clarity on certain issues. However, a fruitful discussion did ensue. (Fr Kilian McDonnell was absent as a consequence of illness and Dr Vinson Synan had to leave early.)

3.2.   The question was raised whether speaking in tongues was essential to salvation. Participants were referred to the Final Report 1972-1976, para 17. [See One in Christ 12, 4 (1976), pp 312,313.]

The pentecostal position was once again stated that at no time was it accepted or taught that a person could not be a Christian unless he spoke in tongues.

3.3.   To become a Christian necessitates a vital personal encounter and personal relationship with Jesus Christ.

3.4.   The speaking in tongues was never entirely absent in the history of the Church.

3.5.   In the course of the discussion several Scriptural reasons for Christians to speak in tongues were enumerated (Mk 16:17; Ac 2:4; 10:46; 19:6; 1 Cor 12:4,10,18; 14:2,15, 22; Rom 8:26).

3.6.   Roman Catholics acknowledge the spiritual value of speaking in tongues. It is currently practiced in approved Catholic charismatic groups.

It is also the view of both Roman Catholic and Pentecostal participants that the final evidence of the validity of spiritual gifts is to be found in a transformed life of faith and love (Gal 5:22).

3.7.   The point was well made in both papers that were it not for tongues there would be no Pentecostal Churches.

3.8.   It was also agreed that every discussion about Christian *glossolalia* should be founded on Scripture.

Roman Catholic exegetes accept basically the historical-critical method of interpretation: e.g., the need first to understand an ancient author in his own idiom, scope of

90

writing, cultural and religious background.

This interpretation does not exclude but goes in harmony with a spiritual interpretation. There is clearly a great difference between the style of interpretation of a modern Roman Catholic exegete and that favoured by many Pentecostals. Further discussion is needed on this apparent diversity of opinion.

3.9. In Fr Kilian McDonnell's paper the reference to a *glossolalic* being in a lighter or deeper "trance" gave rise to some misgivings. In any case it was pointed out that speaking in tongues does not diminish either self-awareness or responsibility.

3.10. It was agreed that the teaching of the classical Pentecostals on the *charismata* are in general faithful to the picture of the Church as reflected in 1 Cor 12-14 and that they have rendered service to the Church in that they encouraged it to be open to and receptive of those spiritual gifts to which they have been faithful.

4.1. FAITH AND EXPERIENCE

Experience in the context of the two papers means that a person comes to a personal awareness of God. The experience of God's "presence" or God's "absence" can be felt in the mind, but at the same time at a deeper level there remains the constant abiding assurance of God's loving presence as revealed in the person of His Son.

4.2.   At some stages of our lives the experience of absence
can leave the Christian with a feeling of desertion--as
experienced by Jesus on the Cross. Therefore at the very
heart of our Christian experience is to be found the death
of Christ and therefore the experience of one's own death
(Gal 2:20; Rom 6:6). (Final Report 1972-1976, para 44.)
[See One in Christ 12, 4 (1976), pp 317,318.]

A Christian is one who not only experiences Pentecost
but also the Cross. In this context it was noted that the
experience of speaking with tongues involves a denial of
self and a kind of death.

4.3.   It was agreed that whatever we receive in the way of
experience, must, if it is truly from God, lead us back to
the Word of God and not rest at the level of experience.

.4.   The question arose where a spiritual life in the
Holy Spirit can be found. A literal reading of Scripture
insists on salvation and grace within the Church and seems
to exclude non-Christians.

According to modern Roman Catholic theology (as
expressed in Vatican II) all men without exception are called
by God to faith in Christ and salvation; it remains mysterious how this precisely occurs. This theology is seen as a
legitimate development of the total New Testament presentation of God's saving love in Christ.

The Pentecostal participants declared that they would
hold to their understanding of the dictum of God's Word (Jn
3:16; Ac 4:12; Rom 10:9; Tim 2:4; 2 Pe 3:9) and would refrain from further elaboration.

92

4.5.   The question of the immediacy of God's action in man
was discussed and it was agreed that the Holy Spirit usually
employs natural faculties but that we can never equate them
with these forces inherent in nature, otherwise we lower
Him to the level of a creature where He becomes part of
nature or becomes ensnared in the structures and laws of
nature.

In the exercise of *charisms* the human faculty is
not disregarded--rather it is used.

4.6.   The importance of individual spiritual experience is
unquestioned, but there is also another dimension in spiritual experience, viz., the social dimension. Men live in
community, particularly in the Church. This community has
a rich history, for example, the experience of previous
spiritual movements and outstanding spiritual Christians
in the Church.

No matter how vivid and powerful a spiritual
experience may be, it needs to be approved in some way by
the community. In any case, the final criterion of all the
gifts is that of love, the communitarian direction of life.

Press Release

A meeting was held at the Convent fo Trinità dei
Monti in Rome, 3-7 October to take up the second phase of
a dialogue between the Roman Catholic Church and some
Pentecostal Churches. A series of five meetings of study
and discussion had ended in 1976 and this 1977 meeting
began another five-year cycle.

On this occasion there were two themes.

Dr Vinson Synan, General Secretary of the Pentecostal
Holiness Church and Father Kilian McDonnell, OSB, President
of the Institute for Ecumenical and Cultural Research, St
John's Abbey, Collegeville, Minnesota USA, had prepared
papers on "Speaking in tongues as a characteristic aspect
of the experience in the Pentecostal movement".

Father J. H. Walgrave, OP, Professor of Dogmatic
theology, University of Louvain, Belgium and Dr F. P.
Möller, President of the Apostolic Faith Mission Church,
South Africa, presented papers on "The relationship between
faith and experience."

Aspects of these topics had been touched on frequently in the previous cycle of meetings but were now
treated at greater depth. The outcome of the discussions
will be incorporated in a general report which will be
presented at the end of the five-year period.

One of the main problems to emerge from the discussion and one which calls for immediate attention is the

interpretation of the Scripture. This will be taken up
as the main theme for the meeting in 1978.

Other participants were:

Classical Pentecostals:

Dr   David J. du Plessis, USA, Co-Chairman
Dr   Robert McAlister, Brazil, Co-Secretary
Dr   Justus T. du Plessis, Republic South Africa
Dr   John Meares, USA
Dr   Thomas Roberts, France

[Pentecostal] Observers:

Dr   Paul Finkenbinder, USA
Dr   James Lane, USA
Dr   J.E. Worsfold, New Zealand

Roman Catholics:

Fr   Pierre Duprey, WF, Italy, Co-Chairman
Msgr Basil Meeking, Italy, Co-Secretary
Fr   W. Dalton, SJ, Italy
Fr   J. Lécuyer, CSSP, Italy
Fr   Heribert Mühlen, Germany

ROMAN CATHOLIC/PENTECOSTAL DIALOGUE
8–12 October 1979—Rome

Dialogue Participants

1. Fr William J. Dalton, SJ
2. Rev William L. Carmichael
3. Rev F. P. Möller
4. Msgr Basil Meeking
5. Fr Charles W. Gusmer
6. Rev Howard M. Ervin
7. Fr Pierre Duprey, WF
8. Bsp W. Robert McAlister
9. Rev Justus T. du Plessis
10. Rev John L. Meares
11. Rev Elias Malki
12. Rev David J. du Plessis
13. Fr Jerome Vereb, CP
14. Fr Kilian McDonnell, OSB
15. Fr Barnabas Ahern, CP
16. Rev Paul Schoch

ROMAN CATHOLIC/PENTECOSTAL DIALOGUE
8-12 October 1979 - Rome

Schedule - Agenda

8 October, Monday

9:30 a.m.   Plenary

                i)   Worship
                ii) Welcome (co-chairman)
                iii) Introductions
                iv) Practical details

11:00   Coffee break

11:30   Plenary

                "Hermeneutics: A Pentecostal Option"
                  paper by Dr H. M. Ervin

                Discussion

1:00 p.m.   Lunch

4:00   Tea

4:30   Plenary

                "The Composition, Inspiration and
                  Interpretation of the Bible"
                  paper by Fr W. J. Dalton, SJ

8:30   Supper

9 October, Tuesday

8:00 a.m.   Breakfast

9:00   Plenary

                "The Ministry of Healing in the Church"
                    paper by Fr C. W. Gusmer

                Discussion

10:30   Coffee break

11:00   Plenary

                "The Ministry of Healing in the Church"
                  paper by Bp W. R. McAlister

                Discussion

1:00 p. m.   Lunch

Dialogue Schedule - Agenda 1979

4:00 p.m.	Tea
4:30	Groups
	"Hard Questions"
8:30	Supper

10 October, Wednesday

8:00 a.m.	Breakfast
9:00	Plenary
	Discussion
10:30	Coffee break
	<u>Audience with His Holiness Pope John Paul II</u>
4:00	Tea
4:30	Plenary
	Discussion
8:30	Supper

11 October, Thursday

8:00 a.m.	Breakfast
9:00	Plenary
	Discussion Drafting
10:30	Coffee break
11:00	Plenary
	Discussion Drafting
1:00 p.m.	Lunch
4:00	Tea
4:30	Plenary
	Discussion of Draft
8:30	Supper

Dialogue Schedule - Agenda 1979

12 October, Friday

8:00	Breakfast
9:00	Plenary
	Discussion of Draft
10:30	Coffee break
11:00	Plenary
	Future plans Press Release Closing Worship
1:00 p.m.	Lunch

Theological Paper

HERMENEUTICS: A PENTECOSTAL OPTION
by
Rev Howard M. Ervin

Epistemology is a question fundamental to any discussion of hermeneutics. Simply put, what is the basis of
knowledge? What are the criteria for determining the limits
and validity of knowledge in any academic discipline? In
the ensuing discussion our purpose is to note basic assumptions which affect ones approach to hermeneutics. A
detailed discussion of the subject is not within the purview
of our present concerns.

In our western culture there are two ways of knowing
that are accepted as axiomatic, namely, reason and sensory
experience. However, a theology that limits itself to
reason and sensory experience inevitably finds itself faced
with an unresolved dichotomy between faith and reason. It
is to this dichotomy that the so-called New Hermeneutic[1]
seeks to speak, with what success the individual must judge
for himself.

The resolution of the dichotomy between faith and
reason by traditional hermeneutics has been no less unsatis-
factory. With its strong commitment to a critical-historical

exegesis, traditional hermeneutics has opted for an epistemology that either abdicated faith for reason, or conversely
sought to validate faith epistemologically by a category
of special pleading in the interests of a propositional
theology. Pietism, as a logical extension of *sola fidei* has
tended to abdicate the role of reason in favor of faith in
terms of the immediacy of subjective personal experience.[2]

The consequence for hermeneutics has been in some
quarters a destructive rationalism, in others a dogmatic
intransigence, and in yet others a non-rational mysticism.
What is needed is an epistemology firmly rooted in the
Biblical faith with a phenomenology that meets the criteria
of empirically verifiable sensory experience (healing,
miracles, etc.) and does not violate the coherence of
rational categories. A pneumatic epistemology meets these
criteria, and provides a resolution of (a) the dichotomy
between faith and reason that existentialism consciously
seeks to bridge; (b) the antidote to a destructive rationalism
that often accompanies a critical-historical exegesis;
(c) and a rational accountability for the mysticism fostered
by a piety grounded in *sola fidei*. To this we shall return
later.

The English noun "hermeneutics" is derived from the
Greek *hermeneia* meaning "interpretation." Something of the
scope of meaning is indicated by the verbal cognate *hermeneuo*,
(1) "to explain in words, expound," and (2) "to interpret,
e.g., to translate what has been spoken or written in a
foreign language into the vernacular." The numinous quality

of interpretation as speech is instanced by the spiritual
charism of *hermeneia glosson*, "interpretation of tongues"
in 1 Cor 12:10.

The range of meaning of the Greek is conveniently
summarized by James M. Robinson thus:

> The Greek noun *hermeneia* thus embraced the whole broad
> scope of "interpretation," from "speech" that brings
> the obscure into the clarity of linguistic expression,
> to "translation" from an obscure foreign language into
> the clarity of one's own language, and to "commentary"
> that explicates the meaning of obscure language by
> means of clearer language.[3]

Apart from etymological considerations the methodology
of hermeneutics as both translation and commentary can be
illustrated by the episode of Ezra reading "the law of God"
in Hebrew, while the Levites "gave the sense" in Aramaic
"so that the people understood the reading."[4]

What is especially significant in interpretation as
"translation" and "commentary" is that both are endemic to
the understanding of a written text. While interpretation
as "speech" is germane to the elucidation of the oral
tradition, it cannot be gainsaid that the oral tradition,
e.g., behind prophecy and kerygma, is mediated in a literary
text. Scholars have recognized that oral tradition and
textual transmission are not merely sequential but coter-
minous during the early stages of the textual tradition.
The presence of the oral tradition contemporaneously with
the textual tradition can therefore be mutually interpretive.
Where the oral tradition is no longer alive, the task of
hermeneutics is confined to the written text.

The numinous influence of "speech" upon meaning can scarcely be gainsaid. Certainly anyone who has edited an "oral" presentation for publication is acutely aware of the difficulty in capturing the nuances of the human voice that affect meaning. A critical question raised by the New Hermeneutic is whether or not the numinous effect of "speech" upon meaning can be reconstructed from the written text. The repeated contention one encounters in the literature on the New Hermeneutic that the words may or may not reflect the intentionality of the text is an ambiguous response to the question. This introduces a subjectivity into hermeneutics that if pressed could negate objective criteria such as critical-contextual exegesis for the determination of meaning.

Inescapably, biblical hermeneutics is textual interpretation, which provides justification, if justification is needed, for the critical role of exegesis in a sound hermeneutical methodology. Inasmuch as biblical hermeneutics commits us to the task of translating and clarifying the sacred textual tradition, there can be no hermeneutical integrity apart from a critical, contextual exegesis.

It is not entirely accurate to write, as Robinson has, that "The profound implication that these three functions--speech, translation, commentary--belong together as interrelated aspects of a single hermeneutic was lost in traditional hermeneutics, which was the theory of but one aspects of *hermeneia*, exegesis."[5] To subsume the whole of traditional hermeneutics under the single rubric of

exegesis is to ignore the fact that traditional hermeneutics
clearly accepted the responsibility for "translation" and
"commentary," and furthermore, distinguished textual
criticism (e.g., translation) and exposition (commentary)
from exegesis. The question is best addressed by an expo-
nent of an older and traditional hermeneutics whose book has
been a school-text for generations of American theological
students.

> Hermeneutics properly begins "where textual criticism
> leaves off" and aims to establish the principles,
> methods, and rules which are needed to unfold the
> sense of what is written. Its object is to elucidate
> whatever may be obscure or ill-defined, so that every
> reader may be able, by an intelligent process, to
> obtain the exact ideas intended by the author.
> Exegesis is the application of these principles and
> laws, the actual bringing out into formal statement,
> and by other terms, the meaning of the author's words.
> Exegesis is related to hermeneutics as preaching is
> to homiletics, or, in general, as practice is to
> theory.[6]

The intuition of traditional hermeneutics that exegesis
is indispensable to hermeneutical integrity is sound, where
it has erred, if indeed it has erred, was in placing the
hermeneutical enterprise at the service of textual and propositional theology. In this, hermeneutics has been but
responsive to the polemic and apologetic exegencies of
various currents both within and without the Church. A
sound grammatico-historical exegetical tradition has therefore been indispensable to hermeneutical methodology. This
has been both a strength and a weakness. A strength in
that it gave priority to the scriptual text, but a weakness
in that it placed the text at the service of rationalistic
and propositional theology. From an existential perspective

an equally notable weakness of traditional hermeneutics is its relative insensitivity to the numinous in the ethos mediated by the biblical text. And from a charismatic or Pentecostal perspective, the present writer is inclined to agree.

On the other hand, the New Hermeneutic, rooted as it is in an existential theological mood, while it is respon- sive to the numinous none the less threatens the hermeneu- tical enterprise by its subjectivity in its efforts to reconstruct the numinous intentionality of the text. Its demythologizing of Scripture because of its dis-ease with the biblical world view robs exegesis of its critical- contextual historicity and facticity. Hermeneutics is then an exercise in private reconstruction of the intentionality of the text.

This is aided and abetted by the existenalist obliter- ation of the boundaries between sacred and secular hermeneu- tics.[7] This is particularly true of the approach of Rudolf Bultmann who categorically affirmed: "The interpretation of the Biblical Scriptures is not subject to any different conditions of understanding from any other literature."[8] Does this not suppose an optomistic view of humanity at odds both with the biblical view of man, and the empirical evidence of man's fallenness furnished by the twentieth century. Whether then one says with orthodoxy that the Scriptures are the word of God, or with neo-orthodoxy that they bear witness to the word of God, the result is the same. Scriptures are subjected to an anthropological reductionism that denies their character as the word of God.

The psycho-socio-cultural dimensions of this anthropology make the demythologizing of the Scriptures essential
to an existentialist hermeneutic, for only thus is it com-
mensurable with the pre-understanding of the modern mind.
But one may well ask do the results of this process of
demythologizing contribute to *hermēneia*, and if so, how?
Within the context of an anthropological reductionism, it
is a moot question whether one really encounters the word
of God, or words about God; and horror of horrors to an
existentialist theology, the latter has a propositional
ring to it.

This leads one to suspect that the demythologizing of
Scripture is simply an exercise in futility. On the one
hand, the notable growth of evangelical churches, with their
ready espousal of biblical miracles, and on the other the
proliferation of all forms of psychic-occult mysticism, even
among the intelligentsia, make it clear that the biblical
world view is not what inhibits the modern mind from understanding the Scriptures. The modern mind has proven itself
to be far more amenable to the miraculous or even the
pseudo-miraculous than either liberal or existentialist
theology has been willing to admit. For this reason, though
not for this reason alone, the demythologizing enterprise
indeed emerges as an exercise in futility.

If then it is not an "archaic" world view that pre-
cludes the modern mind from understanding the Scriptures and
their message, what is it?

Let it be said that one must applaud the

existentialist's concern to make the Scriptures intelligible
to the modern mind. However, from the perspective of the
last quarter of the twentieth century, it becomes increasingly difficult to identify this "modern mind." In the
final analysis, it is the absolute transcendence of the word
of God that renders it incomprehensible to the modern
temper. In Pauline language it is the scandal of the cross.
"Christ crucified, a stumbling block to Jews and folly to
Gentiles" (1 Cor 1:23). As a matter of fact modern man is
a better than reasonable facsimile of his ante-diluvian
ancestor. One indeed might ask whether or not the cause of
a biblical hermeneutic would be better served by "demythologizing" the concept of a "modern" man.

Having spoken of God's word as absolute and transcendent in itself poses a problem in hermeneutics. Within
the cultural pluralism of our day there are no ethical,
moral or spiritual absolutes. Even as in our methaphysical
systems transcendence is but a surd.

The Scriptures affirm, however, that the word of God
is the ultimate word. It is the transcendent word. It is
the word beyond all human words, for it is spoken by God
(revelation). It is indeed the word that contradicts all
human words, for it speaks absolutely "of sin and of
righteousness and of judgment" (Jn 16:8). It is both an
eschatological and an apocalyptic word that judges all human
gnosis. It is a word for which there are no categories
endemic to human understanding. It is a word for which, in
fact, there is no hermeneutic unless and until the divine
hermenēutēs (the Holy Spirit) mediates an understanding.

The insight of an existential hermeneutic that we encounter language itself as hermeneutic is salutary. However, failure to distinguish the nature of the speaking subject in the word-event leads to confusion. It seems clear that on the human level, we encounter each other as willing, thinking, feeling subjects in the word-as-event. It is our common humanity in all its cultural, social, existential commonality that makes understanding possible. When, however, we encounter the word of God there are no egalitarian predicates in common, for the word is the divine Logos before whom we stand in the finiteness of our creature-hood. There is in fact, from the human standpoint at least an incommensurable gulf between the Creator and the creature. The word of God is fundamentally an ontological reality (the incarnation). The biblical precondition for understanding that Word is man's ontological re-creation by the Holy Spirit (the new birth). It is as "partakers of the divine nature" (2 Pe 1:4) that the Holy Spirit "guides...into all truth" (Jn 16:13). However, even the new birth does not erase the boundary between the Creator and the creature. However, the conditions for hearing and understanding the Word are now present for we become by grace what He is by nature. But, and it is a large but, we can never transgress the limits of our creaturehood. Even though the conditions for hearing and understanding are now present, that does not automatically insure our understanding the divine address. The qualitative distance between the Creator and the creature, although it is bridged is not erased. This distance renders the word ambiguous until the Holy Spirit, who "searches even the depth of God" (1 Cor 2:10), interprets it to the hearer. Thus the hearing and understanding of the word is qualitatively more than an exercise in semantics. It is theological *theos-logos* communication in its deepest ontological context. The incarnation makes truth personal--"I am the truth." It is not simply grasping the kerygma cognitively. It is being apprehended by Jesus Christ, not simply in the letter-word but the divine-human word. Herein lies the ground for a pneumatic hermeneutic.

Before, however, proceeding to a discussion of a pneumatic hermeneutic, there are several other concerns that must at least be noted. Preeminent among these is the question of the relationship between the word of God, as the spoken existential word (2 Pe 1:21) and the Scriptures, as the written word. Let it be said then, that the word of God is indivisible from a sacred literature, the Bible, or the Holy Scriptures (2 Tim 3:15). It is as George Florovsky has so trenchantly observed:

> The Scriptures are "inspired," they are the Word of God. What is the inspiration can never be properly defined--there is a mystery therein. It is a mystery of the divine-human encounter. We cannot fully understand in what manner "God's holy men" heard the Word of their Lord and how they could articulate it in the words of their own dialect. Yet, even in their human transmission it was the voice of God. Therein lies the miracle and the mystery of the Bible, that it is the Word of God in human idiom. And in whatever the manner we understand the inspiration, one factor must not be overlooked. The Scriptures transmit and preserve the Word of God precisely in the idiom of man.... The human idiom does not betray or belittle the splendour

of revelation, it does not bind the power of God's Word. The Word of God may be adequately and rightly expressed in human words.[9]

Linguistic, literary and historical analysis are indispensable as a first step to an understanding of the Scriptures. This is the province of exegesis. But rationality by itself is inadequate for the task of interpreting the words of Scripture. It is only as human rationality joined in ontological union with "the mind of Christ" (1 Cor 2:16) is quickened by the Holy Spirit that the divine mystery is understood by man for: "What no eye has seen nor ear heard nor the heart of man conceived what God has prepared for those who love him, God has revealed to us through the Spirit" (1 Cor 2:9,10).

It is the testimony of Scripture that it is not possible to penetrate to the heart of its message apart from the Holy Spirit.[10] This is the fundamental inadequacy of the New Hermeneutic, it lacks a clearly articulated pneumatic dimension. Since the Bible spells out quite clearly the initiative of the Holy Spirit in the miracles, neglect of a clearly enunciated pneumatic dimension in the New Hermeneutic leads to a demythologizing of miracles and conversely the demythologizing of miracles renders the Holy Spirit irrelevant. They are opposite sides of the same coin. Consequently the problem of hermeneutic according to Bultmann is the problem of "demythologizing the New Testament message," only within a Bultmannian anthropology.

But precisely what is to be demythologized? Ernest Fuchs responds:

> The problem applies to the mythical statements
> in the New Testament. No one can deny that there are
> such statements: Jesus is conceived of as a pre-
> existent heavenly being. After his resurrection he
> rules together with God at God's right hand. During
> his lifetime he can walk on the water like a spirit.
> He was conceived by the Holy Spirit without male
> participation. And so forth.[11]

While the events specified may bear an analogical

relationship to similar categories in the Gnostic literature,[12]

from the orthodox perspective the analogies are semantic not

substantive. What is myth to the demythologizers is mystery

to the orthodox, and the difference is due to the role

ascribed to the Holy Spirit--or not ascribed to the Holy

Spirit as the case may be.

The cogency of argument for demythologizing may appeal

to the "modern mind" because it fits readily into the frame

of reference of an eighteenth or nineteenth century scien-

tific world view. But such a scientific world view is

neither self-evident nor self-authenticating today. True

the world view forged from the postulates of Newtowian

physics, Copernican celestial mechanics and Lyellian uni-

formitarianism may have provided a congenial frame of refer-

ence for such speculations. But does the modern scientific

mind think in these categories any longer? With the advent

of nuclear physics, science has made a quantum leap forward

and the older scientific materialism is obsolete. As one

physicist friend remarked to the writer: "From a rational

standpoint, the theory of quantum mechanics makes it

easier to understand from a scientific viewpoint the post-

resurrection appearances of Jesus."[13]

Morton Kelsey is but echoing a growing concensus when he writes:

> In field after field scientists have discovered
> that man's knowledge of the world is simply not final
> or static in the way nineteenth century science
> believed. The tight, confining box of materialism,
> held together by precise natural laws, has come apart
> at the seams. And still the revolution is continuing
> and men have begun to realize the magnitude and
> scope of the change.[14]

Lest anyone judge these conclusions too sweeping, Kelsey quotes the trenchant observation of Robert Oppenheimer in an address to the American Psychological Association. "It is futile, he warned the psychologists to model their science 'after a physics which is not there any more, which has been quite outdated.' "[15]

The scientific phenomenology of the last half of the twentieth century is suggesting radically different ways of understanding time and space, energy and matter and a host of related categories. Does not the existentialist hermeneutic address itself to a fossilized mind-set of the nineteenth century? The question is neither rhetorical nor polemical, but nonetheless presses for an answer.

Once again George Florovsky has something pertinent to contribute to the discussion.

> Most of us have lost the integrity of the scrip-
> tural mind, even if some bits of biblical phraseology
> are retained. The modern man often complains that
> the truth of God is offered to him in an "archaic
> idiom"--e.g., in the language of the Bible--which is
> no more his own and cannot be used spontaneously.
> It has recently been suggested that we should
> radically "demythologize" Scripture, meaning to
> replace the antiquated categories of the Holy Writ
> by something more modern. Yet the question cannot
> be evaded: Is the language of Scripture really nothing
> else than an accidental and external wrapping out of

which some "eternal idea" is to be extricated and disentangled, or is it rather a perennial vehicle of the divine message, which was once delivered for all time?[16]

The question may be phrased in another way. Is the dichotomy between a biblical faith and the rationality of the modern mind truly substantive or merely circumstantial? From the writer's perspective, it is more apparent than real. Its cogency is dependent upon the viability of a nineteenth century mind-set conditioned by a materialistic world view. Sensory experience and reason may supply knowledge adequate for one to function within such a world view. Alone they are inadequate to account for the new insights into the nature of reality. More and more this reality takes on the character not only of a time-space continuum, but of a "natural"-"supernatural" continuum that predicates a revised epistemology. It is in this new intellectual climate that a pneumatic epistemology offers a new synthesis.

Hermeneutically, this raises the question in a new context of an intuitive, non-verbal communication between God and man namely, miracles. The reality of a direct encounter between God and man is precisely what the biblical record of dreams, visions, theophanies, miracles, etc., is saying to us. Seen in this perspective, the Scriptures are the ikon of God's self-revelation. Morton Kelsey, from the standpoint of a Jungian psychologist has developed in some detail the validity of dreams and visions in the process of revelation, and their contemporary value for a direct encounter with God.[17] Since in existential theology there is no provision for knowledge mediated by direct encounter

with God, the only sources of knowledge within this system
are sense experience and reason. However, these assumptions
are being challenged from another direction. For instance,
the startling research findings of a medical doctor,
Raymond A. Moody, Jr., and a psychiatrist, Elisabeth
Kubler-Ross, on death and dying with patients who have
experienced a "clinical death",[18] and been revived, must
give pause to all except the most intransigent skeptics.
Despite the preoccupation of existential theology with
ontological analysis, its anthropology arbitrarily excludes
consideration of the epistemological consequences of a large
area of non-verbal communication.

Symptomatic of the epistemological myopia that excludes
direct encounters with a spiritual or non-material realm of
reality is the hypothesis that "Paul was converted via the
kerygmatic Christ, i.e., the Christ known to him in the
kerygma"[19] learned before he became a Christian. But one
might ask: What is the difference between the kerygmatic
Christ and the Christ of the Damascus Road? The biblical
record makes it clear that if Paul did know the kerygma
before his conversion, it did not produce his conversion.
If anything it seems to have intensified his hostility. It
was not until his encounter with Christ on the Damascus
Road that his conversion resulted.

The repudiation of a concept of a direct (i.e.,
miraculous therefore "mythological"?) encounter with God
exposes another weakness in a hermeneutic derived from such
a theology. The Word, or kerygma, upon which existential

theology lays great stress in its hermeneutic, is conceived as spoken cognitively not experientially in direct encounter with God. Have we therefore come full circle again so that the kerygma is simply a propositional word about God (merely "God talk") rather than the Word of God? The question is further compounded by categorical statements like the following. "Paul's hermeneutic requires that the saving event be understood as word and word only, as the word spoken by God in Christ."[20] At the risk of belaboring the point, it must be objected that _Word_ apart from the Holy Spirit cannot produce faith. Recall again the witness of Paul. "And my message and my preaching...were in _demonstration_ _of_ _the_ _Spirit_ _and_ _of_ _Power_" (1 Cor 2:4).[21] Since the "_demonstration(s)_ of the Spirit and of power" are by definition miraculous therefore "mythological" for the New Hermeneutic, they receive short shrift in the hermeneutical enterprise. The question then recurs in another form. If the saving event is "word and word only," is the New Hermeneutic equating Word and Spirit in a crypto-Sabellianism?[22]

A pneumatic epistemology posits an awareness that the Scriptures are the product of an experience with the Holy Spirit which the biblical writers describe in phenomenological language. From the standpoint of a pneumatic epistemology, the interpretation of this phenomenological language is much more than an exercise in semantics or descriptive linguistics. When one encounters the Holy Spirit in the same apostolic experience, with the same charismatic

phenomenology accompanying it, one is in a better position
to come to terms with the apostolic witness in a truly
existential manner. One then stands in "pneumatic" continuity with the faith community that birthed the Scriptures.

There are at least two immediate consequences for
hermeneutics resulting from a Pentecostal encounter with the
Holy Spirit. First, there is a deepening respect for the
witness of the Scriptures to themselves. A recurrent theme
among colleagues who have experienced the Pentecostal reality
is this: "The Bible is a new Book." At the risk of a
tautology, one might ask, "but why"? The answer is self-
evident in the context of the present discussion. They are
now reading it "from within," accepting its own idiom and
categories, not imposing the alien categories of a nineteenth century mind-set upon them.

The second is a corrolary to the first, the Scriptures
are now read within the pneumatic continuity of the faith
community, and that community is much larger than the post-
Reformation communities of the West. There is a growing
sense of accountability to and for the cumulative consensus
of the Church to the deposit of the faith once for all
delivered. Part of Jesus' promise of the Holy Spirit to
the Church is that "he will teach you all things and bring
to your remembrance all that I have said unto you...he will
guide you into all the truth" (Jn 14:27; 16:13). Thus it
seems at least to this writer, that the hermeneutical enterprise must entertain seriously the insight of the Eastern
church that, "tradition is the life of the Spirit in the

116

Church."[23] The creeds are not Scripture, but neither are they the memorabilia of a dead past. They are warp and woof of a living hermeneutical tradition.

Hermeneutics needs to relate its insights to this historical "succession" in the understanding and proclamation of the gospel, lest it become "another gospel". Care must be taken to relate hermeneutics to the whole of the Church's understanding. Loyalty to the credo's of individual sects and denominations cannot be taken for the whole counsel of God. A viable hermeneutic must deal responsibly with the apostolic witness of Scripture in terms of an apostolic experience, and in continuity with the Church's apostolic traditions.

It is the testimony of Scripture that understanding of its words is not possible apart from the agency of the Holy Spirit who first breathed them. The ambiguity of an existential hermeneutic with regard to the Scripture's pneumatic ethos is its great weakness. In fact given the anthropological presuppostions of existential theology, the miracles, e.g., the supernatural manifestations of the Holy Spirit, must appear as mythological. A programmatic demythologization of the biblical words and categories relating to the miraculous is ancillary to a denigration of the centrality of the Holy Spirit in the hermeneutical task. The former is simply the logical consequence of the latter.

The contribution to hermeneutics of the present charismatic, or Pentecostal renewal of the Church is its insistence upon the experiential immediacy of the Holy Spirit.

There are direct contacts with non-material reality that inform a Pentecostal epistemology hence its hermeneutics. This must not be construed as a plea for a spiritualizing (allegorical) interpretation. Rather it is a truly existential and phenomenological response to the Holy Spirit's initiative in historical continuity with the life of the Spirit in the Church.

In conclusion, there are at least four factors that must influence any programmatic development of a Pentecostal hermeneutic:

1. Respect for the facticity of the biblical record as the testimony of the Church "following the traditions handed down to us by the original eyewitnesses and servants of the Gospel" (Lk 1:2 NEB). This involves pneumatic continuity in experience, faith and doctrine with the Church's historic understanding of these elements in its corporate and individual life.

2. An acknowledgement that although we may never be able to reconstruct a "biography" of the historical Jesus, primarily because of the episodic and theological nature of the gospels, nevertheless, the reminisences of the words and deeds of Jesus constitute historical data indispensable to Christian faith. The Christ of faith is the Jesus of history.

3. Acceptance of both the methodology and substantive contributions of grammatico-historical, critical-contextual exegesis. However, a Pentecostal hermeneutic has no other recourse than to mistrust the extrapolation of circumstantial

differences in the narratives into pluriformity of theological sources and contradictory doctrines. Its hermeneutical
stance is predicated upon the evidence of an apostolic
colleguim in Jerusalem (Gal 1:18; 2:1 ff). The normalizing
influence of such a colleguim upon doctrine is made explicit
in the Jerusalem council--if the suggestion of F. F. Bruce
is accepted, Christian Sanhedrin--in Ac 15:6 ff.

4. Pentecostal experience with the Holy Spirit gives
existential awareness of the miraculous in the Biblical
world view. These events as recorded are no longer
"mythological", but "objectively" real. Contemporary
experiences of divine healing, prophecy, miracles, tongues
and exorcism are empirical evidence of the impingement of
a sphere of non-material reality upon our time-space
existence with which one can and does have immediate
contact. Awareness of and interaction with the presence of
this spiritual continuum is axiomatic in a Pentecostal
epistemology that affects decisively its hermeneutic.

FOOTNOTES

[1] James McConkey Robinson and John B. Cobb, Jr (eds.) The New Hermeneutic (New York: Harper & Row, 1964).

[2] A colleague, Dr Steven O'Malley has pointed out that this would be especially applicable to the more mystical varieties of Pietism, e.g., Moravianism; while others, such as the Reformed Pietists Cocceius and Lampe, worked out a precisely ordered plan of salvation (Heilsordnung) for personal appropriation.

[3] Robinson, The New Hermeneutic, p 6.

[4] Neh 8:8.

[5] Robinson, The New Hermeneutic, p 6.

[6] George R. Brooks and John F. Hurst, (eds.) Biblical Hermeneutics, Library of Biblical and Theological Literature Vol 2 (New York: The Methodist Book Concern, 1911).

[7] Ebling, "Word of God and Hermeneutics," Word and Faith, Translated by James W. Leitch (Philadelphia: Fortress Press, 1963), pp 310,311.

[8] Ibid., p 311, fn 1.

[9] George Florovsky, Bible, Church, Tradition: An Eastern Orthodox View (Belmont, MA: Nordland Pub. Co., 1972), p 27.

[10] It is also the testimony of the Apostolic tradition. The definitions of the councils express the harmony of the human will with the Divine will in the Church; cf. Ac 15:28 --"It seemed good to the Holy Spirit and to us. . . ."

[11] Robinson and Cobb (Ernest Fuchs), The New Hermeneutic, p 115.

[12] Ibid., pp 115,116.

[13] This does not imply that scientific theory can adequately explain the mystery of our salvation as revealed in the Christian faith. Some may provide more appropriate analogies to illumine our understanding. The preoccupation of the Church with such theories may exert detrimental effects. As Dr O'Malley points out, such a preoccupation with Copernicianism by the Protestant "Enlightenment" theologians shifted the attention of theology from the central concerns of soteriology to cosmology.

[14] Morton Kelsey, Encounters with God (Minneapolis: Bethany Fellowship, 1972), p 92.

[15] Ibid., p 93.

[16] Florovsky, _Eastern Orthodox View_, p 10.

[17] Kelsey, _Encounters_, p 92.

[18] Raymond A. Moody, _Life After Life_ and _Reflections on Life After Life_, two in one vol (Carmel, NY: Guideposts, 1975).

[19] Robert W. Funk, "The Hermeneutical Problem and Historical Criticism," _The New Hermeneutic_, p 171.

[20] Ibid., pp 172,173.

[21] Italics supplied.

[22] I am indebted to a colleague, Dr Ted Williams, for this insight.

[23] Timothy Ware, _The Orthodox Church_ (Baltimore: Penquin Books, 1972), pp 253,254.

Theological Paper

THE COMPOSITION, INSPIRATION AND INTERPRETATION
OF THE BIBLE
by
Fr William J. Dalton, SJ

I. THE COMPOSITION OF THE BIBLE

The Bible is the sacred book of Christians. From a
human point of view, it has had a long and complicated
history. Originally written in Hebrew, Aramaic and Greek,
it is read now in various translations, none of which transmit fully its original meaning. At the beginning of the
Christian Church, the Bible consisted in what Christians
came to call the "Old Testament". Because the predominant
culture of the early Church was Greek, the Old Testament
was normally read and cited in its Greek translation, the
so-called Septuagint; this translation was already an
interpretation of the original semitic scriptures. These
scriptures themselves had a long history. They start with
oral traditions going back to the second millenium before
Christ, and bit by bit the various books were composed.
The Old Testament received its present definitive form in
the late period preceding the Christian era after the
return from the Jewish exile.

The continuous flow of the text in the modern print-
ing of the Bible conceals an immense activity throughout the
centuries. The presence of various sources behind the text
is an accepted fact which must be taken into account if the
books are to be fully understood. This is evident in the
Pentateuch, the five "books of Moses", where the so-called
J, E, D and P traditions can be discerned. In other words,
there was a continuous process of literary composition from
about 1000 B.C. to about 400 B.C. in which the original
traditions were sometimes preserved intact, sometimes fused
with later sources, and regularly commented on and edited.
While this is particularly evident in the Pentateuch, it
is true, to a greater or less degree, of every book of the
Old Testament. For example, the book which goes under the
name of Isaiah is really a collection of prophecies, which
start with Isaiah in the eighth century (B.C.) which includes a great section due to a nameless prophet of the
exile conveniently called second Isaiah, and which are
completed by later prophets and editors.

Before we leave the Old Testament, we could raise at
this point a number of questions which bear on our interpretation of these ancient scriptures. Allowing for the special
guidance of God throughout the whole process, we may well
ask: Who is the human author, or who are the authors of the
various books? We have to answer that the authorship is
composite; perhaps the most adequate answer is that the
people of Israel itself is the author. In its various
communities, at different stages and needs of its history,

through various individuals called to the task, the long process of composition went on until it was completed. And the work of translating these scriptures into Greek to form the accepted Christian Old Testament might well be included in this process. The second question is even more important: Is all this discussion relevant for our understanding of the Old Testament? Can we not read the text as it stands, in our English translation, and forget about the long story of its composition and translation?

To start with, if we have some understanding of the literary composition, we shall be saved from some obvious errors of interpretation. For example, we shall not be tempted to attribute to the original Isaiah a miraculous knowledge of the future, of the exile and beyond, a knowledge for which there is no warrant. If indeed we accept the ancient Jewish tradition, preserved in the pages of the New Testament itself, that Moses himself wrote the five books ascribed to him, then we are in a still more miraculous situation: he would have been gifted with an extraordinary foreknowledge of his people's history. It is not a question whether God could give such knowledge, but simply whether there is any real basis for such an assumption. So it is fairly evident that our knowledge of the process of composition bears directly on our interpretation of the text.

But going beyond this, we have to deal with a more fundamental aspect of the question. In all human writings, language and literature reflect the historical situation, the culture, the accepted conventions of the times to which

they belong. We are bound to misunderstand them, at least
partially, if we know nothing of this background. If this
is true of an author like Shakespeare, separated from us
by a few centuries and belonging to our general European
culture, how much more true must it be of writings so
ancient and different in background as those of the Old
Testament.

One could reply that the Bible is a law unto itself,
that God can guide us to its meaning without any need on our
part to understand the human culture, the historical situations, the literary conventions of the authors. But such a
view is altogether too simple. The writers of the Old
Testament belonged to the greater world of their time; God
did not directly give them their language and culture.
Ancient pagan literature, political and social customs,
throw a flood of light on the meaning of biblical language
and thought. The interpretation of the Bible requires human
investigation as well as spiritual insight. God has given
us a mind to work with, He calls scholars to discover the
past, and with their help we can come ever closer to what
the ancient writers were thinking and feeling when the
biblical texts were being composed.

When we come to the New Testament, we find ourselves
in a situation essentially the same as that of the Old
Testament. Most of us have a far greater familiarity with
the New Testament; we tend to domesticate it, to read it
solely through the eyes of a modern Christian. Thus it is
instructive to recall also its origins and the historical
process of its composition.

As we have already seen, the first Christians shared the faith of the Jews that the Old Testament Scriptures were sacred books. For them the profoundly new element was their faith that Jesus, crucified and risen, was the Messiah and Son of God, and that with His coming the last times were inaugurated. It was only gradually that Christian writings were admitted to the rank of sacred Scriptures. In any case, with the lively expectation of the imminent end of human history, the need for a new set of Scriptures was hardly felt. For the first Christians, the person of Jesus, proclaimed, believed in, active through His Spirit in their communities, was enough. And the first Christian theology was a meditation on the meaning of Jesus in the setting of the Old Testament, of the religious experience of the Church, of the general culture and needs of the time.

As in the case of the Old Testament, the origins of the New Testament are to be found in oral tradition, a tradition of preaching, teaching, exhortation, and liturgy. The Acts of the Apostles refers to "the teaching of the apostles" and to "the breaking of bread" (2:42), and gives us example of the sort of missionary sermons that were preached (2:14-36; 10:34-43, etc.). The faith of the communities needed to be given expression by the beginnings of a Christian theology as described above. And the gospel had to be presented to the world, first to the Jews and then to the Gentiles, respecting, in each case, their background and needs.

By-passing, for the moment, the special direction taken by Paul in his preaching and teaching, let us consider the origins of the Gospels. This step involved a return, not merely to the death and resurrection of Jesus, but to the deeds and words of Jesus during His earthly life. Traditions about Him were recalled to give power and point to missionary preaching; that Jesus could bring salvation was seen in the saving power of His miracles (cf. Ac 10:38). Collections of miracle narratives were made to help the wandering missionary. And, above all for the instruction of the Christian communities, the sayings and parables of Jesus were recalled and collected. The study which has come to be called Form Criticism has helped us to see this process at work.

There are two things to note in this process. First, the collection and ordering in oral tradition of the deeds and words of Jesus were due primarily to the missionary and catechetical needs of the Christian communities. While there is no reasonable ground to doubt that they represent substantially what Jesus actually said and did, their arrangement is not historical but geared to the needs of preaching and teaching. Secondly, above all with regard to the words of Jesus, this recall already represented an interpretation. Jesus proclaimed the Kingdom of God and its demands to His Jewish contemporaries: as yet there was no resurrection, no Christian Church. It is a fact of language that words receive meaning not merely from the mind of the speaker but from the audience to which they are

addressed. A Christian community which listens to a parable of Jesus believes that He is the risen Lord, the Son of
God and is committed to Him by baptism; they find in His
words an answer to the needs of their actual life. Even
the term "God" has a new meaning for Christians: He is more
than the God of Abraham and Isaac: He is the God who raised
Jesus from the dead and sent His Spirit on those who believe.
And Christian teachers who selected the words of Jesus to
suit their needs, did not hestiate, to adapt them. For
example, Jesus was not primarily concerned with the problem
of the refusal of the Jews to accept the gospel and the
rapid entry of pagans into the Church; but, after the first
Jewish converts, this became a major issue in the early
Church. Thus, if, for example, we compare two versions of
a parable of Jesus (Lk 14:16-24 and Mt 22:1-14) we can see
the hand of tradition at work developing an original parable
to suit the later situation. This sort of development is
made more understandable if we recall the belief of the
early Christians that Jesus was present by His Spirit in the
Church and that He could speak just as really through His
prophets and teachers as He could through the traditions of
His words handed on from the past. This is not to deny
the special value given to the words of the earthly Jesus,
but it warns us not to be too wooden in requiring that every
word put into His mouth in the gospel narrative was actually
spoken, exactly in that form, by Jesus in His earthly life.

Thus, for a period of about 35 years, in a scattered
and unsystematic way, oral tradition was at work before the

128

writing of the first gospel; and we have every reason to believe that oral tradition still remained important even when this writing began. Almost all scholars agree that the first gospel was that of Mark. It is of the greatest importance to realize that this gospel, as well as the others, is in no sense a biography of Jesus in the modern sense. A good modern commentary, such as that of Eduard Schweizer, brings out clearly that Mark used the traditions available to him for a catechetical and theological purpose. In the general framework of a year of Jesus' missionary work, he portrays Jesus as the Son of God, who, despite His miracles and teaching was rejected by the Jewish leaders (3:6), by His own family (6:1-6), misunderstood by His own disciples (8:27-38), and who insisted that discipleship which refused to accept Him as the crucified Son of God could not be genuine (9:30-37; 10:32-45). Hence the importance for Mark of the centurions's confession at the moment of Jesus's death that "this man was really the Son of God" (15:39). The area of research which shows precisely how Mark used his materials to bring out his message is called "redaction (or better "composition") criticism".

If we accept the common view that the authors of Matthew and Luke used Mark in composing their gospels, we have an even clearer idea of the composition process involved. They did not reject Mark's gospel, but found it insufficient for their purpose. The bulk of the first gospel is incorporated in their work, but set in a new structure, with a new and different theological and pastoral purpose. On occasion, Mark's text is adapted and modified (for example, Mk 4:35-41 and Mt 8:18, 23-27; Mk 10:11,12 and Mt 19:9, Mk 10:18, and Mt 19:17).

In the preceding sketch of the formation of the Gospels, we have not referred to the gospel of John. Scholars see behind this gospel the same sort of development, traditions about Jesus recalled and molded, in various editions, to suit the needs of a particular community. This gospel, too, would seem to be the corporate work of a "school" inspired by the spirituality and theological insight of the "beloved disciple". It is not clear what contact this tradition had with the synoptic tradition. But in any case, the process of interpretation has gone much further. Again, there is no reason to doubt the general background of history; but here, much more than in the synoptics, the tradition has been deeply modified to bring out the divinity of Jesus. C. H. Dodd's great work is rightly entitled: "The Interpretation of the Fourth Gospel".

Meanwhile, during the process which was forming the Gospels, the great figure of Paul appeared. Actually his letters provide the first written documents of the Christian Church. Paul gives no indication that he regards his letters as inspired Scripture: they are for him merely pastoral means of recalling and reinforcing his oral teaching. He almost certainly wrote other letters which have not been preserved. Thus, in his extant letters, we cannot claim to have a full account of his teaching. In addition, it is difficult to know how much of his doctrine is original, since he himself received a great deal from the common Christian tradition (cf. 1 Cor 11:23; 15:3; Phil 2: 6-11, etc.). It is interesting to note how much he can take for granted in a letter such as that to the Romans, which was directed to Christians who had never heard his teaching.

Paul, despite his developed theology, represents the earlier stage of the New Testament: he is concerned about seeing the meaning of Jesus, crucified and risen, in the light of the Jewish Scriptures, of Christian experience, and of the Greek secular culture in which he lived. The last element should not be neglected or underrated. Paul can, in his argument, use the methods of the Greek diatribe common in the Stoic tradition of philosophy. He is a man of his day in the Hellenistic world. And when he comes to   . Christian behaviour, he can utilize an accepted code of good human life found in popular philosophy, which he enlivens with a new Christian meaning and motivation (for example, Col 3:18-4:1). He has remarkable little reference to the tradition of Jesus's words and deeds. While there are a number of obscurities in his writings, due to our ignorance of the circumstances and to his rabbinical way of thinking, his letters, in general, do not present special difficulties of interpretation: the letter is, after all, one of the simplest and most direct forms of communication. It is true that a number of letters ascribed to him are not accepted by many scholars as authentic, notably Ephesians and the Pastoral Letters (some would also

include 2 Thes and Col). Such a view does not remove these
letters from the canon of inspired Scripture, but it does
involve a new element of interpretation; but it is beyond
the scope of this paper to enter into this question.

The Acts of the Apostles and the other letters do not
raise problems beyond those already discussed. But the book
of Revelation, a favorite quarry for Christian enthusiasts,
demands a special effort at interpretation. Written in the
form of apocalyptic literature, it is full of symbolic
imagery. Unless one goes to the trouble of understanding
its background, literary conventions and symbolism, one has
no chance of reading it aright.

Revelation is the only book in the New Testament
which claims a special revelation (1:1-3; cf. 22:18,19),
although the author says nothing about the special divine
guidance in the writing of it. In 2 Pe 3:16, Paul's letters
are mentioned side by side with "other scriptures". We have
no clear information as to how the New Testament writings,
as a body, came to be regarded as sacred Scripture, or why
these particular books were chosen. The story of the formation of the canon is a complicated one. Probably as these
writings were read at Christian meetings together with those
of the Old Testament, they began to receive the same dignity;
and, little by little the Church was guided by the Holy
Spirit to see in these books, rather than in others, an
essential element in its ongoing life.

One last word on the composition of the New Testament.
Its real human author is the primitive Christian Church.

This is clear enough in the formation of the Gospels, where
nameless Christian preachers and teachers gradually assembled
the matter later incorporated into the recognized Gospels.
But even the other writers did not act solely as individuals.
They drew on the common faith they themselves received from
Christian communities and they were conscious that they wrote
both in the name of the Church and for the good of the Church.

II. THE INSPIRATION OF THE BIBLE

This long account of the composition of the Bible has
been given out of the conviction that, as well as being
sacred, the inspired Scriptures are thoroughly human books.
We have in them a reality similar to that of Jesus Himself:
He is no less human because He is the Son of God. If, in
the interests of affirming the divinity of Jesus, one
doubts or denies His real humanity, one is already at
variance with the essential common tradition of Christian
faith. One faces the same danger if one by-passes the human
composition of the Bible.

But, for all that, it is part of the common Christian
faith that the Bible is not merely a human book. The New
Testament takes it for granted that the Jewish Scriptures
are inspired by God (expressly stated in 2 Tim 3:16,17, but
implied throughout). In Christian theology various expressions have been used to indicate the sacred character of
the Scriptures: they are inspired by God, they are the word
of God, God is their author. Let us briefly discuss these
descriptions.

It would be a mistake to think that divine inspiration means that the authors were conscious of being lifted above the human level and of writing in a sort of ecstatic condition (which is the meaning of the word found in some non-Christian texts). It is equally a mistake to think of biblical inspiration as being the same as divine revelation. It is true that we have examples in the Bible, notably in some of the Old Testament prophets and in the book of Revelation, where God communicates in a direct and extra-ordinary way with the believer. But, as a rule, the writers, in presenting their work to their readers, reveal no such experience (cf. Lk 1:1-4). And in any case we are dealing with the process of _writing_, not with the way by which the writer came by his information. In most of the biblical writings, the author was conscious of using his own natural powers, but as a believer with something important to say to the community; and he used the literary forms which suited his purpose, poetry, teaching, exhortation, apocalyptic, and various forms of narrative.

If we use the expression "word of God", we cannot mean that the Bible is strictly divine, that it is the word of God just as Jesus is the Word of God: this would be surely idolatry. The condition for the Bible's influence as the word of God is that of faith. Thus it would be more exact to say that the Bible contains God's message or word for those who believe. For others it is just a human religious phenomenon.

In the theology of inspiration, God is often called

the author of Scripture. But this term is ambiguous. It can retain its primitive Latin meaning of *"auctor"*, that is, "cause" or "founder". This would indicate God's special influence in the whole process of Scripture writing. On the other hand, the word can have the modern meaning of "literary author". Some would thus understand God as the actual writer of the Scriptures, dictating verbally to the human writers the words He wished to be used.

For a number of reasons this last meaning, though often proposed in the theology of the past, cannot be sustained. Writing, like eating, is a human activity. The great variety of language, style, literary forms, all conditioned by the culture and historical background of the biblical writers, indicates with the utmost clarity that there were really human writers, not merely passive scribes under God's dictation. We have already said that it is a mistake to understand biblical inspiration as a form of prophecy. Even if in some way the prophet heard words spoken to him by God, it does not follow that biblical writers simply wrote down words dictated by them to God.

And finally we have the problem of the original text. If the Bible is literally the result of God's dictation, then this inspiration falls only on the original Hebrew, Aramaic and Greek texts. Although textual criticism has done magnificent work in restoring the original text, noone would claim that the text has been fully restored. While we can be confident that we have at our disposal the substance of the Bible's meaning, one can see, in a

critical edition of the biblical books, almost on every
page variant readings which have a greater or less probability.
If then biblical inspiration means dictation by God, this
design has been partly frustrated by the simple fact of manuscript corruption. And, what is even more important, in the
translations of the Bible we commonly use, we would have to
admit that we are not dealing with the inspired text.
Every translation is necessarily an interpretation, which
by its very nature cannot fully represent the meaning of the
original. This is generally true apart from those special
texts containing obscure or ambiguous expressions which are
the despair of the human translator.

Despite these problems, we must firmly hold that the
Bible is not merely a human book, not even a human religious
book like those written by Christian believers of a later
age. But in our earlier discussion we have neglected one
aspect of the Bible which is of fundamental importance, that
is its ecclesial aspect. The Bible comes to us as part of
a greater Christian tradition. God was quite aware that
manuscripts could become corrupted and He provided no
miraculous means of preserving the original copies. But He
did provide us with a living Church. This total Christian
tradition implies the presence and guidance of the Holy
Spirit; it includes the sacraments, the creative reaction
in faith and practice of Christian believers to the words
of the Bible as they are read in numerous translations
throughout the Church's history, the guidance of those called
to be teachers in the Church as they discern what is the

genuine meaning of the Scriptures in moments of doubt or
crisis.

Thus the inspiration of the Bible should not be
divorced from God's activity by which He founded and guided
the people of Israel, by which He constituted the Christian
Church and enlivened it through its history by His Spirit.
The original writers were conscious that they wrote within
their communities for their communities. In fact, there is
no clear Scriptural warrant for determining what books
actually belong to the biblical canon. It was the guidance
of the Holy Spirit which led the Church to accept some
books and to reject others. And it could do this because
it recognized in these books an element constitutive of its
own full reality, destined by God to be an essential part
of its life through the ages.

And because of the ecclesial nature of the Scriptures,
it is the Spirit of God in the Church which guides it
through its history to interpret these Scriptures according
to the Spirit. It belongs to the scholar to understand
these ancient documents as human writings; and the individual
believer has the right to read them and find in them God's
message to him personally. But the final word about interpretation lies with the discernment of the whole Church,
expressed by those who are called to be its pastors and
teachers.

III.   THE INTERPRETATION OF THE BIBLE

And so we come to deal more expressly with the problem

of interpretation. This involves a process which has many
aspects, a process which has developed with the ongoing life
of the Church, a process guided by faith, responding to the
real questions raised by believers from age to age. In many
ways the time in which we live provides a far better understanding of the past and possibilities of interpretation
than were available in pre-critical days. For example, the
great task of reestablishing the original biblical text
still goes on. While the medieval scholar could be excused
for taking his Latin Bible simply as the Word of God, an
educated believer of today is not justified in having the
same attitude towards, for example, the Authorized English
version. An earlier age knew little of form or redaction
criticism, and yet these Christians could find God's word
in their reading of the Bible. But we, in our day, have
new knowledge and responsibilities; we can appreciate and
feel the original message in all its strangeness, and be
thus less tempted to domesticate this message to suit our
own ideas. Thus the work of the scholars is part of the
Church's life. Their established findings, after testing
and discussion, enter into the general thought of the
Church and find expression in preaching, teaching and more
popular writings.

It is important to insist that critical studies do
not undermine the Bible, but, on the contrary, clarify it.
From the beginning, even in the New Testament itself, there
was never an opposition between faith and human intelligence.
If Paul rejects "philosophy" (1 Cor 1:18-2:16), it is only a

wisdom which would be a substitute for the gospel. He himself used his powerful intelligence in the ways available
to him to clarify the Christian message for the people of
his day.

Thus the first step of the interpreter is to understand the various books of the Bible in their original
ancient setting. This involves a serious study of their
process of composition as outlined above. Such an approach
to interpretation requires a considerable effort of mind
and imagination. Thus, despite its narrative style, biblical
history writing, whether it be found in the Old Testament,
the Gospels or the Acts, cannot be read as a modern historical production. While ancient writers were interested
in what actually happened, often they had no way of knowing
this exactly: they narrate traditions which can be factual
or legendary. And in any case they wrote with a moral or
religious purpose: we would be inclined to call much of
their writing "propaganda". Thus the Gospels are religious
messages about Jesus and His importance, messages which
utilize recollections of His sayings and deeds in an
uncritical way. There is nothing unworthy about this. If
one were to compare this presentation with a film of the
total life of Jesus, there would be little difficulty about
choosing. Nor should it come as a surprise or a shock that
often we do not know exactly what Jesus said or did. We
must be content with our ignorance and not demand from God
or His Scriptures things He did not see fit to communicate.

There may be some sincere Christians who feel nervous

about such an open approach to interpretation: they would
insist rather on what they call "the truth of the Bible".
This means a literal understanding of whatever is narrative
or descriptive in form, whether it is the creation of the
world in six days, the life-span of the patriarchs, the
canticle of Jonah in the belly of the great fish, the last
trumpet, the messianic banquet, etc. But this sort of
"biblical truth" is a sheerly human assumption, which has
no warrant in the Bible itself or in reasonable principles
of interpretation. The Bible is wonderfully human in its
great variety of literary forms: in it God respected the
imagination of man, his poetic and symbolic gifts, as well
as his interest in facts. Jesus himself told marvellous
stories in His parables and used vigorous imaginative
language about hating father and mother and cutting off
one's right hand.

But when the Christian scholar in the service of the
Church has done his best to understand the Bible as a human
work, the task of interpretation has only begun. His work
is always within the context of Christian faith. As we
have seen, the Scriptures are an integral part of the Church
itself. Towards the end of the first century, the Church
was complete with its Scriptures and ready for its journey
through history. This Church was a live Church and it
brought with it a living Bible. Merely to repeat mechanical-
ly the words of the Bible was not enough. They had to be
interpreted to face new knowledge, new experiences and
problems. We have seen that the very translations of the

140

Scriptures into other languages was an effort at interpretation. Paul had himself reacted creatively to the culture of his day by using the popular philosophy of his Greek world to keep the faith pure from corruption. The Church was only being faithful to his example in its more developed doctrinal expositions, found in the early Councils, which took into account the actual questions of the day, the Bible and the accepted philosophy of the time. The Arians, who knew the New Testament as well as their orthodox opponents, thought they could deny the real divinity of Christ and still be faithful to the Bible. But the leaders of the Church, interpreting the faith of the whole Christian people, made it clear in terms borrowed from the current philosophy that the absolute divinity of Jesus was an essential part of Christian tradition.

It should be clear that this task of interpretation has to go on as the Church continues through history. A thorough and even profound knowledge of the text of the Bible combined with personal religious experience is not enough. What are we to say to a sincere Christian who maintains that, in his understanding of the New Testament, Jesus did not personally rise from the dead, that the resurrection is merely a myth to show that the memory of Jesus is strong enough to inspire the believer? What do we say to another who does not accept a life after death, but hopes merely for a future limited to the corporate life of the earthly Church? Or again, what is our answer to the modern theological movement which goes further than the Arians in seeing in Jesus only an outstanding prophet? An intellectual debate is inevitably frustrating and fruitless. Within the resources of the Church there must surely be some voice which can speak with authority in discerning the genuine Christian tradition, otherwise we are destined to become a group of quarreling sects, with each of us claiming to be guided by the Spirit in our understanding of the Scriptures.

Finally, the very nature of all human writing demands that, in our search for meaning, we go beyond the thought and understanding of the original writer. Once a book leaves its author's hands and moves out into human society to be read and pondered by future generations with their developing cultures and new human problems, it takes on a life partly derived from the world around it. For example, a play of Shakespeare means something different to a modern audience from that which it meant to the audience of his day, to Shakespeare himself. Meaning arises from the dialogue between book and reader. There is a continuity with the past, but there is also a necessary development. Whether it is admitted formally or not, all Christian groups re-read the Bible in the light of their own tradition, their situation and special interests; and, from this background, they partly create the meaning they experience in reading it. Meaning is not to be found simply in the printed page: meaning occurs when the printed page is read by a live human being, and in this process the dead text becomes alive.

In the case of the Bible, the context in which meaning
develops is not simply human society, it is the living
community of the Church. Since the Bible is essentially
ecclesial, it is in this context that it must be interpreted. The Bible becomes alive in the faith of the Church
which believes that it will always be guided by the Spirit
in discerning the essential elements of God's message of
salvation.

Before we leave the task of interpretation, it would
be well to consider for a while the limitations of the
Bible. While this remains a delicate topic, such a discussion seems useful if we are to use the Bible aright in
our search for God's truth. Let us take a few examples
from the New Testament--the limitations of the Old Testament,
belonging as it does to the preparatory stage of God's
message, are obvious enough. The New Testament, as a human
writing, is bound by the limitations of its time and background, not merely in the aspects of its human culture, but
even in its religious and moral teaching. Thus the early
writers of the New Testament including Paul took it for
granted that the end of the world was imminent. As human
life continued on this earth, it was seen that such a view
was unfounded; and the later writers of the New Testament
adapted their message to suit this fact. But it is not a
service to biblical interpretation simply, in the interests
of a theory of inspiration, to deny this early expectation
of the end. Again, Paul thought that the whole of the human
race was to be found in the world he knew, and that it could

be reached, at least in a general way, by his preaching;
he had no knowledge or appreciation of other ancient
religious cultures. He and the other early Christian
preachers were so involved in their great missionary endeavour,
that they seemed to take it for granted that salvation could
be found only within the Christian Church. Except in a few
obscure texts (for example, Rom 1:19-21; 2:14-16), they had
no time or inclination to reflect on the situation of those
who would never have a chance of hearing the gospel; they,
of course, had no idea that the vast majority of men
belonged to this category. But we, in our time, on the
basis of Jn 3:16 or 1 Tim 2:3-6, can hardly avoid the issue.
In other words, guided by the Spirit, we can find ourselves
called to go beyond the letter of Scripture to express its
basic insight into the nature of God and His relationship
with men.

Further, Paul accepted without criticism aspects of
social life which later Christians were bound, in fidelity
to his own principles, to challenge. One outstanding
example is the institution of slavery. The Church of today
has been considering another assumption of Paul: the social
inequality of men and women. Here too new developments may
be needed.

In the delicate task of interpreting the Bible for
our times it is necessary, above all, to be open to the
central message of the whole of the Bible, particularly
that of the New Testament. This has to deal essentially
with who God is, what He has done and is doing in Christ,

His incredible love for men. We need the help of the Spirit
to receive this message and not to be distracted from it
by marginal or partial statements, even those found in the
Bible itself. We need to be able to discern the Bible's
degrees of affirmation. Paul, for example, is more concerned
with the resurrection of Jesus than with baptism for the
dead (1 Cor 15:29), about the importance of love than the
veiling of women (1 Cor 11:5-10), about the preaching of the
cross than powers and principalities (Rom 8:38, etc.). And
if our human judgment is too weak to discern what is essential, then we must believe that "our sufficiency is from
God, who has qualified us to be ministers of a new covenant,
not in a written code but in the Spirit; for the written
code kills, but the Spirit gives life" (2 Cor 3:6).

NOTE: Attached to this paper as an Appendix was a photo-
        copy of the "Dogmatic Constitution on Divine
        Revelation" as translated by Austin P. Flannery,
        ed., Documents of Vatican II (Grand Rapids: Wm. B.
        Eerdmans, 1975) pp. 750-765.

Theological Paper

THE MINISTRY OF HEALING IN THE CHURCH
by
Fr Charles W. Gusmer

It is difficult to conceive of a more contemporary
and controversial topic among Christians than that of
spiritual healing. The subject is contemporary, because
of the current concern of the churches for healing,
especially among Pentecostal-charismatic groups, as also
the interest generated by the revised Roman Catholic Rite
of Anointing and Pastoral Care of the Sick (7 Dec 1972).
The theme of healing is also controversial, because of the
many attendant and theologically disputed areas such as
the mystery of suffering and evil (theodicy), the meaning
of the healing activity of Christ (biblical exegesis), the
abiding place of healing in the overall mission of the
Christian Church (ecclesiology), the relationship between
Nature and grace (Christian anthropology), religion and
behavioral science (e.g., methods of psychotherapy
employed--consciously or unconsciously in healing), and the
relationship between sacramental and charismatic healing.
This paper will begin with a consideration of human sickness in the light of faith. It will then consider the

the significance of Jesus' ministry to the sick. The
conclusion will explore how this ministry is continued in
the Church today in a ministry which is pre-eminently
pastoral, as well as charismatic and sacramental. No
exhaustive claim is made towards providing all the answers.
The writer of this paper will rest content if at least the
proper questions are posed.

I. THE PHENOMENON OF HUMAN SICKNESS

A wise physician once asserted that there is no such
thing as sickness in itself, only people who are sick.
This remark should serve as a safeguard against the danger
of abstractionism in theologizing about human illness.
Sickness is very real indeed.

A. The Human Person in His/Her Totality

Rather than resort to a kind of unconscious dualism
which neglects the essential unity of the human person as
a composite of body and soul, we might do well to return
to a biblical anthropology which views the human person as
an animated body, or to adopt a more contemporary theological approach towards the human person as a spirit-in-the-
world, an incarnate spirit. Applied experientially to the
phenomenon of human sickness, illness profoundly touches
and influences the total person. In addition to the
physical pain, the sick person endures psychic stress:
isolation from family and profession; the impersonalism
which even the best of hospitals can seldom avoid; the
anxiety about "tests" and what the future may hold. When

a person is seriously ill, the whole person suffers a
disruption from the experience of life as it is normally
lived. Serious illness also presents a temptation to
one's faith in God: it is an ambivalent occasion for either
human growth and holiness, or regression and possible despair. The book of Psalms, the prayer book of the Bible,
vividly depicts this torturous and ambiguous plight of the
sick (Ps 6, 32, 38, 39, 88, 102). As the revised <u>Rite</u> <u>of</u>
<u>Anointing</u> succinctly puts it: "The man who is seriously
ill needs the special help of God's grace in time of
anxiety, lest he be broken in spirit and subject to temptations and the weakening of faith" (para 5).

B.   <u>Human</u> <u>Sickness</u> <u>and</u> <u>the</u> <u>Mystery</u> <u>of</u> <u>Evil</u>

      Although Jesus is careful to avoid too direct a
casual relationship between illness and personal sin (Jn
9:2,3), it is nonetheless a biblical insight that some
intangible relationship exists between cosmic sin and sickness, especially as illness is experienced today. The
acute pain and often unrelieved anguish is the result of
the sin of the world, a sinful disharmony in a creation
which "groans and is in agony" (Rom 8:22) awaiting its
deliverance. For example, Jesus frequently uses the word
sozein in his healing works ("Your faith has saved you),
which may refer either to salvation from sin, or from
sickness and disease, or both! Or again, the prescription
in Jas 5:14,15a on anointing the sick is concluded with an
admonition to repentance: "If he has committed sins,
forgiveness will be his. Hence declare your sins to one

148

another, and pray for one another, that you may find healing" (5:15b,16). Witness also the numerous exorcisms of the sick in the New Testament and primitive church. Contemporary data from psychosomatic medicine seems to substantiate the claim that an intimate and inseparable connection exists between the human psyche and the body. In sum, the relationship between sin and sickness should not be misconstrued in a simplistic sense that personal sin caused a given illness, or that sickness is the vindication of divine providence by an angry deity who rains down chastisement upon disobedient children. Rather, the human person is an historical whole who suffers sickness as a consequence of sin in the world, traditionally referred to as "original sin." Two important conclusions follow. First, we should be careful not to blame God directly for sickness, as if God were its author. Rather, God reacts to and respects humankind's use--and lamentable misuse-- of its freedom. There is a misunderstanding still deeply lodged in the hearts of many good people, who somehow revert to a "god of the ambush" instead of the New Testament revelation of a God of love called Father. Secondly and very positively, the promised salvation in Jesus Christ is going to touch the total person, for its goal is none other than the resurrection of all humankind (1 Cor 15). In this holistic vision of humankind, Jesus has come to free us, to heal us, from sin and evil and all its manifestations so that we can grow to full stature as children of God.

II. JESUS' MINISTRY TO THE SICK

Jesus' ministry to the sick is one of healing in the widest sense of the word. He is presented at the outset of Mark's Gospel as a doctor come to cure an ailing human race (Mk 2:17). In its mission to the nations, the Church very early recognized--and quickly rejected--a parallelism between Christ and Askleipius, the god of healing in the ancient world. This broad based ministry of healing is evident in the account of the woman caught in adultery (Jn 8:1-11): a ministry of listening, for Jesus utters not a word until the end; a ministry of affirming ("Nor do I condemn you."). Together with other scriptural images such as reconciliation, justification, recapitulation, redemption (Redeemer), salvation (Saviour)--healing (Healer) is synonymous with Jesus' life and ministry. If, therefore, human sickness is derivative from our alienation for God, healing is a divine reality which aims primarily at a wholeness before a transcendent God, a restoration or reconciliation which can bring about secondarily a temporal healing.

A. Jesus' Healing Works as Eschatological Signs of the Kingdom

On the other hand we often labor under the inherited notion of miracle from the age of enlightenment, whereby a miracle is perceived as a supernatural act contrary to the laws of nature and hence an apologetic proof of divine intervention. To this must be contrasted the scriptural viewpoint that just as word and action go together in the

revelation of God, so also do creation and salvation form
as unity. Thus there exists a close similarity between
nature miracles (e.g., calming the sea, etc.) and healing
miracles. A characteristic of the reign of Satan is Satan's
hostility to creation! Lest Jesus be taken simply as a
thaumaturgical wonder man, the Gospels generally avoid the
terms miracle or wonder in preference for the more modest
"acts of power" *dynameis* in the synoptics, "works" *terata*
and "signs" *semeia* in John's Gospel.

On the other hand, the existence of the healing
activity of Jesus of Nazareth is central to the New Testament. Mark's Gospel alone records over twenty individual
acts of healing, so that roughly one-half of his Gospel is
given over to healing narratives. In the Acts of the
Apostles the witness of healing activity is likewise
integral to Peter's kerygma on Pentecost Sunday (Ac 2:22)
and elsewhere. In other words, the key question is not
whether the healing works took place (which is assumed) or
how they happened (possibly psychological suggestion in some
instances) but rather what is their meaning.

The disciples of John the Baptizer approach Jesus to
ask if He is the long-awaited Messias who is to come (Mt
11:2-5). Jesus' response, invoking the imagery of Isaiah 35,
contains an imagery which goes beyond physical healing:
the "blind" are able to see the glory of God, "cripples"
can walk in the paths of God, "lepers" are cleansed of their
sins, "deaf" people hear the good news, the "dead" are
raised to true life in Christ, and the "poor" become rich

through the preaching of the Gospel. Similarly the seven
signs of the Fourth Gospel, three of which are healing
miracles, have a deeper underlying meaning. For example,
the man born blind (Jn 9:1-34) shows us that Jesus is the
light of the world; the raising of Lazarus (Jn 11:1-44)
points to Jesus as the resurrection and the life.

The healing works of Jesus are thus signs of the
kingdom of God, that central message of the New Testament
that a new reign of peace and justice was at hand whereby
God would put an end to the ancient enemies of the human
race, sin and evil, sickness and death. The healing works
of Jesus are eschatological signs in the sense of the
"already" and the "not yet." The miracles foreshadow the
ultimate transformation of humankind and the universe on
the day of Jesus' second coming, the resurrection of all
flesh, an event not yet come to pass. The blind man and
Lazarus will eventually die, but the healing works on their
behalf indicate, however briefly, something of the healing
transformation which will take place on the last day. At
the same time the healing miracles are eschatological signs
of the "already" dimension of the kingdom at work in the
world through the present offer of eternal life and communion
with God which begins already now in this life. Such appears
to have been the understanding of the first Christians who
transposed the healing gestures of Jesus into the rites of
Christian initiation: exorcisms, profession of faith *ephpheta*
(Mk 7:34), anointing with oil (Mk 6:13), bathing in water
(Jn 9), and the laying on of hands. In other words, the

the Risen Lord touches and heals us now in baptism.

In passing, further similarities between the healing
works of Jesus and the Christian sacraments may be observed.
First of all, both bring about what they signify: the
healing miracles are signs which announce the Kingdom and
usher it in; so sacraments signify the saving presence of
God and also effect what they signify. And secondly, in
both the healing experiences and the sacraments the response
of faith and conversion is paramount. Neither is magic or
automatic: the beneficiaries--the individual recipients
and the witnessing community--are expected to behave as
persons whose lives have been radically changed.

B. Paschal Mystery: The Healing Death and Resurrection of
    Jesus Christ

To all this must be quickly added that human wholeness
is always a relative concept in this life. The ultimate
healing transformation comes from suffering and death borne
out of love. This is how the kingdom of God advances.
This is how Jesus became Risen Lord and how we too personally share in the Easter victory of Christ. This is what
the Paschal Mystery is about and scripture could not be
more explicit on this point.

The Risen Lord confronts and consoles the distraught
disciples at Emmaus: "Did not the Messias have to undergo
all this so as to enter into his glory?" (Lk 24:26). He
tells the doubting Thomas: "Take your finger and examine
my hands. Put your hand into my side" (Jn 20:27). Even
in His glorified condition the risen Christ still bears
the marks of His crucifixion.

An authentic Pauline mysticism strives for union with the crucified and risen one: a union which begins at Baptism (Rom 6:3-11) and glories on the cross (Gal 6:14) as the only way towards full communion with the beloved. And while Paul graphically depicts the sufferings which came with his apostolate, the celebrated "thorn in the flesh" (2 Cor 12:7) would seem not to exclude the misery which comes from ill health. Far from a misguided spirituality which seeks to justify suffering for suffering's sake, and equally distanced from the opposite extreme which fails to see that Easter Sunday issues forth from Good Friday, Saint Paul captures the dynamic tension of sharing in Jesus' life-giving death and resurrection: "I wish to know Christ and the power flowing from his resurrection; likewise to know how to share in his sufferings by being formed into the pattern of his death. Thus do I hope that I may arrive at the resurrection from the dead" (Phil 3: 10,11).

The message of the Fourth Gospel is similar: "Unless the grain of wheat falls to the earth and dies, it remains just a grain of wheat. But if it dies, it produces much fruit" (Jn 12:24). The driving force behind this ultimate healing through suffering and death is love. As John begins his account of the last supper and passion: "Before the feast of Passover, Jesus realized that the hour had come for him to pass from this world to the Father. He had loved his own in the world, and would show his love for them to the end" (Jn 13:1). The cross theology of John's

Gospel further reveals that Jesus' "lifting up" on the cross--a turn of phrase which refers to the cross both as an instrument of torture and a way to exaltation--is the manner whereby Jesus will draw all men to himself (Jn 12:32). Finally, the blood and water flowing from the pierced side of the Lord are an indication that the crucifixion, resurrection and outpouring of the Spirit are intimately bound up together (Jn 19:34).

The introductory paragraphs to the revised Rite of Anointing (paras 1-4) on human sickness and its meaning in the mystery of salvation sum up this paradoxical predicament of Christian existence. On the one hand we are challenged to struggle against sickness and seek the blessing of good health in the name of Jesus. And yet on the other hand there is a clear realization that the ultimate healing is not found in this life, but comes rather from loving communion in the Lord's dying and rising. To deny this would be to fall inadvertently into the hands of the very death-denying culture we are trying to evangelize.

III. CHURCH'S MINISTRY TO THE SICK

Jesus' ministry to the sick is continued in his Body, the Church. The Good Samaritan is the model of Christian compassion towards our suffering brothers and sisters (Lk 10:25-37). Jesus goes so far as to identify himself with the sick: "I was ill and you comforted me" (Mt 25:36). The Church's mission in the world is to be a loving, healing, reconciling presence with special concern and affection for

155

the helpless, the sick, the infirm, the aging. This overall healing ministry encompasses unpleasant social issues
so easily glossed over in our Gospel preaching such as
better housing for the poor, more equitable distribution of
food to the hungry, the critical need for energy conserva-
tion, nuclear disarmament amid a spiraling arms race, etc.
The Church's ministry of healing should not be isolated or
viewed apart from the rest of its mission to be a sign of
Christ's continued presence in the world.

A. Pastoral Ministry to the Sick

"Every scientific effort to prolong life and every
act of heartfelt love for the sick may be considered a
preparation for the gospel and a participation in Christ's
healing ministry" Rite of Anointing (para 32). More
specifically, the Church's pastoral ministry to the sick is
practiced by all who care for the sick and dying at home,
in the parish and in hospitals. Through the ages this
ministry has led to the foundation of Christian hospitals
as well as religious communities dedicated to caring for
the sick. This pastoral ministry is also concerned about
the spirituality and motivation of those involved in this
work: the doctors, nurses, families should know that they
participate in the ministry of Christ to the sick continued
in His Church. Today especially there are hopeful signs of
a rapprochement with the medical profession. In particular,
certain psychologists (C. G. Jung, Viktor Frankl) have been
warmly disposed towards religion as providing a meaning to
human existence so necessary in an often disturbed world.

The pastoral ministry to the sick is unexpendable and undergirds any further charismatic or sacramental ministrations.

B. Charismatic Ministry to the Sick

The Acts of the Apostles abounds with instances of charismatic healing (Ac 6:8; 8:5-11; 10:38; 13:9-12; 14:8-12; 15:12; 19:11-16). There is also strong evidence of a flourishing charismatic ministry in the early church as attested to by Quadratus (c. 125), Justin Martyr (d.c. 165), Tatian (c. 160), Irenaeus of Lyon (d.c. 202), Tertullian (d.c. 220) and Origin (d.c. 320). Some have attributed the waning of explicit charismatic healing activity to the rejection of the enthusiastic Montanist movement of the Spirit already in the second century; others locate the slackening of charisms to a loss of spiritual vitality resulting from the conversion of Constantine and the advent of the cultural synthesis known as "Christendom." Nonetheless, traces of charismatic healing continued in the lives of saints and worthies such as Martin Luther (d. 1546), Philip Neri (d. 1595), George Fox (d. 1691), John Wesley (d. 1791), Pastor Blumhardt (d. 1880) and Father John of Cronstadt (d. 1908). In the Roman communion charismatic healing figures in shrines dedicated to the memory of the saints, e.g., Mary at Lourdes, and in the provision for verifiable healings required in the canonization process. Although charismatic healing has therefore theoretically, at least, always been recognized, it is only in this century through the efforts of Pentecostal and neo-Pentecostals

communities that this gift of the Spirit has been more
fully restored to the Church.

C. Sacramental Ministry to the Sick

Just as the charismatic ministry to the sick is to be
situated within the context of the Church's overall pastoral
concern for the sick, so also the sacramental ministry.
The Eucharist as action (Lord's Supper) is a representation
of the healing power of the Paschal Mystery; as sacrament
(communion) it is a pledge of the ultimate resurrection of
the whole person (Jn 6). As charismatic communities may
practice some form of exorcism or deliverance, a more common
Roman approach would be the sacrament of penance, the
healing sacrament directed per se towards the forgiveness
of sins.

What is generally called the sacrament of the sick,
however, is the anointing of the sick. In its recent
revision it is no longer referred to as extreme unction,
nor is it any longer a rite for the dying as such. Four
reasons have prompted the Roman communion to revise the
rite of anointing as a sacrament for those seriously ill
from sickness or old age: scriptural evidence (Jas 5:14,15),
the tradition of the anointing for the first 800 years,
ecumenical convergence (practice of the Eastern Church and
the Anglican communion regarding anointing), and the dis-
appointing pastoral experience of a ministration people
would postpone until their dying moments when they would no
longer be capable of entering into the action of prayer.

The Rite of Anointing is described in these terms from its introduction:

> The celebration of this sacrament consists especially in the laying on of hands by the presbyters of the Church, their offering the prayer of faith, and the anointing of the sick with oil made holy by God's blessing. This rite signifies the grace of the sacrament and confers it (para 5).

As is readily apparent, the sacrament is not without its epicletic moments when the power of the Holy Spirit is invoked both for the blessing of the oil and during its application upon the forehead and hands of the sick person:

> Through this holy anointing
> may the Lord in his love and mercy help you
> with the grace of the Holy Spirit. Amen.
>
> May the Lord who frees you from sin
> save you and raise you up. Amen.

Indeed, the very efficacy of the sacrament is attributed to the sanctifying Spirit from which various spiritual, psychological, and even physical benefits could proceed:

> This sacrament provides the sick person with the grace of the Holy Spirit by which the whole man is brought to health, trust in God is encouraged, and the strength is given to resist the temptation of the Evil One and anxiety about death. Thus the sick person is able not only to bear his suffering bravely, but also to fight against it. A return to physical health may even follow the reception of this sacrament if it will be beneficial to the sick person's salvation. If necessary, the sacrament also provides the sick person with the forgiveness of sins and the competion of Christian penance (para 6).

IV. DISTINCTION AND DISCERNMEN.

Charismatic and sacramental healing have many similarities. They are situated within the community of the Church, although a healer with a special charism or a presiding

liturgical celebrant may play a greater role in the service. They employ similar gestures, namely the laying on
of hands, the sense of touch conceived particularly as a
way of bestowing or releasing the power of the Holy Spirit.
They are both--charismatic and liturgical--first and foremost prayer: prayer of petition (charismatic "soaking
prayer," sacramental "litany of intercession") and prayer
of praise and thanksgiving.

Why then a distinction between the two? This distinction, in the opinion of this writer, is made on the basis
of different modalities of prayer rooted in scriptural
origin, their respective place in the Church, and the
expected results. Scripturally, charismatic healing takes
its origin especially from the charismata listed by Paul in
1 Cor 12: a gift within the community to be used to build
up the Body of Christ. Anointing of the sick finds its
scriptural precedent in Js 5:14,15, where the elders or
presbyters appear to be not simply men of advanced years
or wisdom, but rather office holders or ministers in the
primitive Church. As Paul's description of the charismata
is to be located within the total picture of his message to
the Corinthians, so likewise it is helpful to recognize the
background of James' letter. The author is advocating
prayer as a response to various situations in which a
Christian finds himself, be this hardship, good spirit or
sickness--in which case the presbyters are to be summoned.

Regarding their respective place in the Church, the
Church embraces both charism and institution, gifts and

structure. The institutional may appear to mirror more the visible, tangible, incarnational side of the Church, whereas the charism reflects more the invisible, intangible, pneumatological aspect of the Church. (Too great a split or cleavage should be avoided, for both come from God and should be animated by the Spirit of Jesus.) It follows that charismatic healing partakes of the charismatic dimension just as sacramental healing--in particular the anointing of the sick--is related to the Church as its official liturgy on behalf of the sick.

Finally, concerning expectations which are sought from charismatic and sacramental healing, there seems to be a marked disinclination to predict results. Charismatic healing is often not instantaneous, and the grace of anointing the sick is described with a necessary ambiguity. Both involve expectant faith, although discernment of the Spirit should be undertaken as to what the praying community and the sick person can realistically expect. For this reason, for example, several optional prayers are provided in the anointing rite depending on the condition of the sick Christian. In general, however, one could say that charismatic healing intends a cure, be this physical, psychological ("healing of the memories"), or spiritual (healing from sinful habits such as drugs, alcoholism, sexual abuse). Sacramental healing would appear to be less directly concerned with physical or emotional cures and aims at a deeper conformation with Christ through the healing power of the Paschal Mystery.

Some suggested principles of discernment, applicable to any Christian service of healing, conclude this paper:

1. Does the service flow out of the local Christian community's ongoing pastoral care of the sick?

2. Is the prayer service pastorally responsible in terms of prior preparation and follow-up care?

3. Is there a sense of cooperation with the medical profession?

4. Is there a proper emphasis on the worship of God and service of neighbor rather than a narrowly selfish therapeutic attitude which delights in the "miraculous"?

5. Are healings, whenever and wherever they occur, signs pointing to a deepened faith and conversion in which the beneficiaries are changed or transformed persons?

6. Is the approach imbued with the central mystery of the Christian faith, the passion, death and resurrection of Jesus Christ and our participation in this saving paschal event?

Theological Paper

THE MINISTRY OF HEALING IN THE CHURCH
by
Bp W. Robert McAlister

In this paper I will deal with the healing of the physically and emotionally sick through prayer and faith. No attempt will be made to discuss healing through the science of medicine or the practice of psychology, both of which play an important role in the total healing process.

I. PRESUPPOSITIONS

The ministry of spiritual healing practiced by the Pentecostal Churches is based on certain assumptions, four of which I will mention.

A. The Word of God

Our understanding of God is not based on reason, sense-knowledge or philosophy, but rather on the manner in which God has revealed Himself in the Scriptures. Without apology we accept the Bible in its entirety to be the inerrant Word of God. The word used to describe the Pentecostals in Brazil is "*crentes*", that is, "believers". We believe what the Bible says and base our faith and practice on its teachings.

B. **The Early Church**

Jesus established the pattern for the Church's ministry
to all generations. "And Jesus went about all Galilee,
teaching in their synagogues, and preaching the gospel of
the kingdom, and healing all manner of sickness and disease
among the people" (Mt 4:23). Jesus defined what the gospel
ministry would be: teaching, preaching, and healing.

The evangelist, Philip, went to Samaria to preach
Christ and the people were astounded and filled with great
joy "seeing the miracles which he did, for unclean spirits,
crying with loud voices, came out of many that were possessed
with them; and many taken with palsies, and that were lame,
were healed" (Ac 8:5-7). Pentecostal evangelism follows
this Bible pattern. Our preaching declares Jesus to be the
divine healer.

C. **The Unchangeable Christ**

One of the favorite Bible verses of Pentecostals is:
"Jesus Christ the same yesterday, and today, and forever"
(Heb 13:8). We interpret these words to mean that what
Jesus was, He remains today: loving and compassionate.
What He did during His earthly ministry, He continues to do
today through His annointed servants: minister eternal life,
physical health, and mental soundness to the sinful and
suffering.

D. **The Supernatural**

We believe that a loving and sovereign God, in
response to faith and petition, invades our world in ways
that we cannot understand. He acts beyond our knowledge of

science. He communicates with us through the "divine
madness of prophecy". He touches our lives and transforms
us in ways that reason rejects. When the distraught father
came to Jesus with his demonized child, Jesus said, "If thou
canst believe, all things are possible to him that believeth"
(Mk 9:23). All things, including the miracle of healing,
are still possible to those who believe.

II. THE MINISTRY OF HEALING IN THE PROTESTANT TRADITIONS

A. The Reformed Churches

The general feeling among the majority of Protestant
Evangelical churches seems to be that the days of miracles
are past and that healing was merely a device to certify
the credentials of Jesus and the apostles, but has no rele-
vance to the message of the gospel for men today. Whether
it is the greater or lesser Catechisms of Martin Luther,
the Sixty-Seven Articles of Ulrich Zwingli, John Calvin's
Institutes, or The Westminster Confession or the Thirty-Nine
Articles of the Church of England, one does not find
affirmations of faith in a miracle-working God that accompanied apostolic teaching and ministry. When challenged to
show themselves to be the true followers of the apostles by
means of the miraculous, the reformers affirmed that the
mark of the true Church was true preaching on right sacraments, and rejected supernatural manifestations as necessary to authenticate their position. Consequently, the
ministry of divine healing is not a part of the reform
tradition.

B. The Anglican Tradition

Only recently has the Church of England begun to recognize divine healing as part of its ministry. The Order of St Luke in the American Episcopal Church conducts regular healing missions. But this is a recent development and is a part of the charismatic renewal in the Anglican Church.

C. The Methodist Tradition

The Methodist Church was born in a revival of spiritual experience, rather than a conceptual understanding of God. One finds in the journals of John Wesley over two hundred references to examples of divine healing. In his Commentary on James, Wesley wrote that the gifts of healing were meant to be a part of the Church's ministry in every generation, but that they had been lost through neglect and unbelief.

In recent years, the Methodist Church has departed from its early convictions. When, at the beginning of this century, it took a position against the baptism in the Holy Spirit with speaking in other tongues, it also rejected other manifestations of the Holy Spirit, including the gifts of divine healing. Consequently, the Methodist tradition of healing is not being carried on by the Methodist Church, but rather by those churches which were born out of the Methodist revival, including the Pentecostal Church.

D. The Pentecostal Tradition

The distinctive characteristic of pentecostalism has been the outward evidence of the gifts of the Holy Spirit, among which the gifts of healing have always been prominent. It is no exaggeration to say that every Pentecostal

church in the world is a Lourdes or Fatima where miraculous
physical healings are a common occurance. So much so that
Pentecostalism is in danger of treating this invasion of
grace into nature with indifference.

Without exception, the founders of the Pentecostal
movements were men who prayed for the sick. The name of
Smith Wigglesworth is synonymous with miracles of healing.
Dr A. G. Garr became known as "the man who prayed sick
people well". The biography of George Jeffreys of England
is entitled, A Ministry of the Miraculous. The lives of
the "grand old men" of pentecostalism testify to the fact
that the Pentecostal witness to the Church and the world
has always included the evidence of the supernatural power
of God through the ministry of divine healing.

III. HEALING IN THE ATONEMENT

It is a cornerstone of the Pentecostal theology of
divine healing that provision was made for the healing of
the body through the atoning work of Jesus on the cross.
In Isaiah's prophecy of the suffering savior there are three
references to the healing of the body (Is 53:4,5).

A. Jesus Bore Our Sicknesses

The King James Version is alone in translating Is 53:4
to read, "Surely he hath borne our griefs". The Hebrew text
uses the word *kholee*, which is translated, sickness. The
King James Version correctly translates Dt 7:15 to read,
"The Lord will take away from thee all sickness (*kholee*)."

The Douay Version of this verse reads, "Surely he hath borne our infirmities." Robert Young (of concordance fame) translates Is 53:4 to read, "Surely our sicknesses he hath borne". St Matthew's reference to this prophecy uses the Greek word *astheneia*, which is translated, infirmities.

Although there are fourteen New Testament references to this prophecy of Isaiah, it is Matthew's quotation, united with the healing ministry of Jesus, that creates the solid link between the two.

"When the even was come, they brought unto him many that were possessed with devils, and he cast out the spirits with his word, and healed all that were sick, that it might be fulfilled which was spoken by Isaiah the prophet, saying, Himself took our infirmities and bare our sicknesses" (Mt 8:16,17).

Matthew wrote his gospel to the Jews who were familiar with Isaiah's prophecy concerning the Messiah. The apostle witnessed Jesus healing the sick and casting out demons, and declared that these things happened in fulfillment of that prophecy.

B. Jesus Bore Our Pain

The King James Version reads that Jesus "...carried our sorrows". The Hebrew word used here is *makob*, which means pain. Job 33:19 reads, "He is chastened also with *makob* (pains)". Robert Young agrees with this translation and says, "...and our pains He carried them". There is nothing to indicate that these pains are other than physical suffering, which Jesus bore for us on the cross of Calvary.

C. We Are Healed Through His Stripes

Isaiah wrote, "...and with his stripes we are healed" (Is 53:5). The apostle Peter makes reference to this prophecy and writes, "Who his own self bare our sins in his own body on the tree, that we, being dead to sin, should be alive to righteousness; by whose stripes ye were healed" (1 Pe 2:24).

The Greek word *iaomai* is used twenty-two times in the New Testament to mean physical healing.

There exists, therefore, a *prima facie* case that the healing of sickness as well as the forgiveness of sins flows from the sacrifice of Jesus.

It is a conviction of the Pentecostal Church that Jesus came to save both the soul and the body. Having taken upon Himself sickness as well as sin, He is in a position to set us free from the one as well as the other. So, just as we get the first fruits of our eternal salvation in the life that now is, so we get the first fruits of our physical salvation in the life that now is. The atoning death of Jesus secured for us not only physical healing, but also the resurrecting and perfecting and glorifying of our bodies.

We therefore rejoice with the psalmist David who sang, "Bless the Lord, O my soul, and forget not all his benefits: Who forgiveth all thine iniquities; who healeth all thy diseases" (Ps 103:2,3).

IV. THE GOSPEL OF HEALING

The healing of the body is part of the gospel message

for all generations. It is as correct to say "the gospel
of healing", as to say "the gospel of forgiveness" or, "the
gospel of peace". Whatever grace man receives through the
merits of Jesus Christ is part of the good news which, when
accepted in faith, brings health and wholeness to body,
soul, and spirit.

While there were instances of healing under the old
covenant, both individual (Miriam's leprosy) and collective
(the healing of Israel's sick through the symbol of the
bronze serpent), it was not until the ministry of Jesus that
the good news of healing through faith became an integral
part of God's offer of grace to all who would believe.

The narratives of healing in Jesus' ministry are
merely representative of the vast number of people who received deliverance from all manner of sickness and disease.
Two quotes will suffice to indicate the extent of Jesus'
ministry of healing.

"And everywhere he went, into villages, towns or
countryside, they placed the sick in the marketplaces. They
begged him to let them touch even the edge of his cloak,
and all who touched him were healed" (Mk 6:56, NIV).

"When the sun was setting, the people brought to Jesus
all who had various kinds of sicknesses, and laying his
hands on each one, he healed them. Moreover, demons came
out of many people, shouting, You are the Son of God"
(Lk 4:40, NIV).

It is important to note the manner in which Jesus performed these healings. He did so through His anointed

humanity, and in obedience to the will of the Father. "How God anointed Jesus of Nazareth with the Holy Spirit and power, and how he went around doing good and healing all who were under the power of the devil, because God was with him" (Ac 10:38, NIV).

It is obvious from the gospel texts that Jesus' ministry of healing was not meant to simply establish his credentials as the anointed of God, but was a part of the good news of redemption for sinful and suffering mankind. When Jesus sent out the twelve (Lk 9) and the seventy (Lk 10) their instructions were clear. "When Jesus had called the twelve together, he gave them power and authority to drive out all demons and to cure diseases, and he sent them out to preach the kingdom of God and to heal the sick" (Lk 9:1). And also, "When you enter a town and are welcomed, eat what is set before you. Heal the sick who are there and tell them the kingdom of God is near you" (Lk 10:8).

It is the conviction of every Pentecostal minister that part of his job is to bring divine healing to sick people. We take very seriously the great commission which says:

> Go into all the world and preach the good news to all
> creation. Whoever believes and is baptized will be
> saved, but whosoever does not believe will be condemned.
> And these signs will accompany those who believe: In
> my name they will drive out demons; they will speak
> in new tongues; they will pick up snakes with their
> hands; and when they drink deadly poison, it will not
> hurt them at all; they will place their hands on sick
> people, and they will get well (Mk 16:15-18, NIV).

In the New Life Pentecostal Church in Rio de Janeiro, there is a special weekly service, attended by an average of 600 people, where the sick are ministered to. Almost without exception, there is a prayer for healing in every public service.

The practice of healing in pentecostalism is based on four facts: (1) the provision for physical healing through the atonement; (2) the ministry of our Lord and the Apostles; (3) the great commission; and (4) the gifts of the Holy Spirit.

The "spiritual gifts" of 1 Cor 12 are considered by Pentecostals to be the power tools for ministry. These manifestations given "for the common good" include the gifts of healing. These gifts of the Spirit were not given merely to establish the Church, but for its ongoing life.

"Now you are the body of Christ, and each one of you is a part of it. And in the church God has appointed first of all apostles, second prophets, third teachers, then workers of miracles, also those having gifts of healing" (1 Cor 12:27,28, NIV).

The early church understood its responsibility, and James wrote, "Is any one of you sick? He should call the elders of the church to pray over him and anoint him with oil in the name of the Lord. And the prayer offered in faith will make the sick person well; the Lord will raise him up" (Jas 5:14,15, NIV).

V. HEALING AND THE MISSION OF THE CHURCH

It is the mission of the church in all generations to declare the good news of redemption; to make disciples; to baptize those who would follow Jesus as Lord and to teach

172

obedience to those who are converted to Christ. This evangelizing of those who are lost in their sins has, since the days of the early church, included the full scope of gospel ministry. An example of this missionary activity is found in the story of Philip in Samaria.

This first evangelistic mission outside of Jerusalem, conducted by a deacon who quickly became an evangelist, stirred the entire population until there was "great joy in that city". Philip "proclaimed Christ" (Ac 8:5), and "preached the good news of the kingdom of God and the name of Jesus Christ" (v 12).

Here is a description of a Pentecostal missionary evangelistic campaign: "When the crowds heard Philip and saw the miraculous signs he did, they all paid close attention to what he said. With shrieks, evil spirits came out of many, and many paralytics and cripples were healed" (vv 6,7).

When a theologian of the Baptist Church asked me the reason for the unusual success of Pentecostal missionary activity in Latin America, my immediate reply was, "the healing of the sick, and the baptism in the Holy Spirit of the new converts."

We can find no reason to believe that the preaching of the gospel today is any different from its proclamation by Jesus and the Apostles. To say that medical science has replaced, or made unnecessary, the ministry of the gospel of healing is to deny the gifts and graces that God has established in the church for its edification. As ministers of the gospel, we proclaim redemption for the whole man in body, soul, and spirit.

VI.   HEALING AND THE KINGDOM OF GOD

In spite of its dispensational theology, there is a growing awareness in pentecostalism of the present reality of the Kingdom of God. The ministry of healing is a part of that reality; a demonstration in the here and now of "the powers of the coming age" (Heb 6:5).

The gospel of Jesus Christ is the gospel of the Kingdom of God. Jesus went about Galilee preaching "the gospel of the kingdom" (Mt 4:23). When instructing the seventy to heal the sick, He told them to inform the people that "the kingdom of God is near you" (Lk 10:9).

The "coming of the Kingdom" was to be evidenced by the healing of the demonized. Jesus said to the Pharisees, "But if I drive out demons by the Spirit of God, then the kingdom of God has come upon you" (Mt 12:28, NIV). With these and many other references, Jesus relates the ministry of healing to the coming of the Kingdom.

Since divine healing restores the sick person to a situation of temporary health, and does not guarantee him perpetual human life, the question is raised as to its merits. Why spend so much time ministering healing to people who are going to die, no matter what miracle is bestowed?

The answer to this very good question is to be found in the nature of the Kingdom of God. Before the fall, Adam

and Eve lived in perfect obedience and enjoyed perfect
health. One of the consequences of their rebellion was
pain and sickness. Suffering has always been part of the
human condition. In speaking of his affliction, Job said
that "man is born unto trouble as the sparks fly upward".

We are told that in the coming Kingdom, "God shall
wipe away all tears from their eyes; and there shall be no
more death, neither sorrow, nor crying, neither shall there
be any more pain: for the former things are passed away"
(Ap 21:4, KJV).

Does God not wipe tears from our eyes even now? Has
He not removed the "sting of death" through the promise of
the resurrection? Does He not give us the "oil of joy for
mourning?" Does He not remove our pains through the sufferings of His cross? Are we not healed by His stripes?

Healing is not an isolated phenomenon. It is not an
invasion of nature by God's grace, without justification.
It is a manifestation of the Kingdom of God. It is the
down-payment on the promise of divine health that we will
enjoy for eternity. It is a present proof of the new covenant, and an earnest of the inheritance of our glorified
bodies.

While temporary, even as human life is as grass that
fades, divine healing is a manifestation of God's grace, an
evidence of His mercy, and a promise of eternal life.

We are messengers of the good news of the Kingdom of
God. Just as the gift of repentance does not isolate the
child of God from temptations and failures, even so, the

gift of healing does not guarantee him freedom from future
pain and suffering. As we walk in the Spirit we grow in
grace unto perfection. And as we experience the grace of
healing we learn to put our trust in the One who is able to
deliver us from all of the works of the enemy.

VII. THE MINISTRY OF DELIVERANCE

One important, and misunderstood, aspect of the ministry of healing is the deliverance of the demon-possessed.
For the past 24 years I have been involved in this ministry
and offer a brief synopsis of my conclusions.

1. Demon-possession is a real problem, and is most
prevalant in countries like Brazil, France, England, Haiti,
India, Italy, etc. where spiritism (and spiritualism) is
practiced by vast numbers of people.

2. Most demonized people are considered to be either
epileptics, schizophrenics, or "just plain crazy". Medical
science has yet to acknowledge the reality of what is so
clearly described in the Gospels as the possession of the
human body by evil spirits.

3. In order to effectively minister to the demonized,
it is necessary to correctly define the problem. Many
emotional disturbances, aberrant behavior, satanic attacks
in the form of temptation, involvement in the occult, etc.,
has no relation whatever to what the Bible describes as
possession by evil spirits.

4. Jesus gave power and authority to the twelve disciples to drive out all demons (Lk 9:1). While there is no

specific gift of exorcism, the ministry to the demonized is part of the preaching of the good news to every creature. "And these signs will accompany those who believe: In my name they will drive out demons" (Mk 16:17, NIV).

5. In spite of some popular teaching to the contrary, it is not possible for a born-again believer to be demon-possessed. "Do you not know that your body is a temple of the Holy Spirit, who is in you, whom you have received from God" (1 Cor 6:19)?

6. In the light of recent appeals to sensationalism, and a lack of teaching in some areas of the charismatic renewal, I would call for a renewed examination of the position of the believer in Christ, the nature of satanic attack in the areas of carnal temptations, and a better understanding of demonic activity.

CONCLUSION

Relative to the mystery of suffering and the ministry of healing, there are certain facts that become apparent as we read and ponder the Scriptures.

1. The human body is important to God. The importance of the human body was highlighted when the Word became flesh. The body is sacred because our Lord took human flesh and glorified it. We are told that our body is the temple of the Holy Spirit.

2. Man is a unity. He cannot be split up into separate parts of body, soul, and spirit to function independently one of the other. Jesus treated sickness and sin as different expressions of the same principle of evil.

177

When Jesus "forgave" the paralytic (Mk 2) He revealed that the body and soul are interdependent. James taught that the prayer of faith would heal the sick, and if he had sinned, he would be forgiven (Jas 5:15). The gospel is good news for the whole man, bringing forgiveness and restoration of health.

3. Jesus regarded His ministry of divine healing as a sign that the Kingdom of God had come. He invites us to recognize the signs of the Kingdom and enter into it.

4. Jesus looked for faith in the hearts of those who came to Him. He did not blame the sick person for a lack of faith when healing was not the immediate result of prayer. Where there was no faith, Jesus inspired it.

5. Jesus made no attempt to hide His healing ministry, although there were times when He told the healed person to go and tell no man. He always acted in accordance with the situation. It seems that Jesus wanted to avoid the sensationalism of being considered a "healer", preferring to make healing a normal part of His total ministry: a part of salvation to mankind.

6. In New Testament times, the power of the healing Church was the name of Jesus. It remains so until this day.

ROMAN CATHOLIC/PENTECOSTAL DIALOGUE
8-12 October 1979 - Rome

Agreed Account

I. THE COMPOSITION, INSPIRATION, AND INTERPRETATION OF THE BIBLE

1. Scripture and Tradition

A. Both Pentecostals and Roman Catholics hold that the books of the Old Testament were accepted by the early Church as inspired, that the primitive Church existed for a period without its own Christian Scriptures, that after the writing of a number of books by Christians, a certain number were accepted by the Church in the light of the Holy Spirit as inspired.

B. However, Roman Catholics believe that these Scriptures have been handed down through the centuries in the context of a living faith, experienced by the whole Church, guided by Church leaders, operative in all aspects of Christian life, and on occasion expressed in written form in creeds, councils, etc.

These are not two seperate sources. Rather there is only one source, the revelation which is transmitted in Scripture and responded to and actualized in the living tradition of the Church.

C. Pentecostals maintain that there are not two authorities (e.g., Scripture plus Church tradition) but one authority, that of Scripture. However, Scripture must be read and understood with the illumination of the Holy Spirit. Pentecostals believe that the interpretation of Scripture

can only be truly discerned through the Holy Spirit. Also,
overall in Pentecostal movements there is a broad consensus
of elements fundamental to the Christian faith. On the
other hand, Pentecostals feel that some religious
traditions can operate against the gospel.

D. Further dialogue will be needed to discuss how the
Roman Catholic Church can propose, as a matter of faith,
doctrines such as the Assumption of Mary, which go beyond
the letter of Scripture, and which seem to Pentecostals to
be unacceptable tradition.

2. Exegesis

A. Pentecostals completely reject the philosophical
and theological principles of form criticism and redaction
criticism. They insist on the necessity of the light given
by the Holy Spirit if the reader is to respond with faith
and understanding to the Word of God. This insistence was
a valuable contribution to our dialogue.

B. Roman Catholics equally reject these principles.
However, they are encouraged to use some of the methods used
by the New Hermeneutics, but always and only when this is
compatible with the traditional faith: thus form criticism
and redaction criticism are commonly used. Such methods
are regarded as useful means to a better understanding of
the text, to be adapted or put aside according to their
helpfulness.

C. The Pentecostal form of exegesis, while having its
roots in fundamentalism, is not specifically defined. It

is admittedly in a formative stage. However, current exegesis would tend to be a pneumatic, literal interpretation, though moving away from strict fundamentalism.

3. Discernment of Meaning

A. In the event of conflicting interpretation of Scripture texts, Roman Catholics accept the guidance of the Spirit as manifested in tradition. While the teaching of the Church stands under the Word of God, this same teaching serves the communication of the Word of God to the people. (Cf. Vatican II, "Dogmatic Constitution on Divine Revelation," para 10.) While Catholics believe both Scripture and Tradition cohere in each other and, thus, transmit the Word of God, Catholics do accord a certain priority to Scripture.

B. In the event of conflicting interpretation of Scripture texts, Pentecostals rely on the Holy Spirit's guidance, but without the more developed structure found in the Roman Catholic Church. While there may be some danger of subjectivism, God is trusted to provide the guidance of the Spirit.

4. Faith and Reason

In a biblical epistemology (the determination of the limits and validation of knowledge), it was agreed that faith and reason cannot be polarized, just as the supernatural and the natural cannot be polarized. However, the Pentecostals place a greater emphasis on supernatural manifestations, while both Catholics and Pentecostals agree that the supernatural is not in opposition to the natural, but work in harmony.

5. Points of Agreement and Clarification

A. Points of agreement:

1) The basic content of Christian faith (e.g., deity of Christ, virgin birth, resurrection of Jesus).

2) The inspiration of Scripture.

3) The preaching of the Gospel is an integral part of the ministry of the Church.

4) Corporate guidance by the Holy Spirit.

B. Points needing clarification:

1) The relation between Scripture and Tradition as this has been described by the Second Vatican Council Decree (DV, paras 9,10):

"Sacred Tradition and sacred Scripture make up a single sacred deposit of the Word of God."

"Hence both Scripture and Tradition must be accepted and honoured with equal feelings of devotion and reverence."

2) To what degree various methods of exegesis (e.g., form criticism as used in the Catholic Church) are compatible with Pentecostal principles.

II. THE HEALING MINISTRY IN THE CHURCH

1.   The ministry of healing in the Church is practiced in both the Roman Catholic Church and the Pentecostal Churches as part of their total ministry to the needs of the people. The means of ministering healing is the same in both. Both Pentecostals and Roman Catholics likewise agree that through prayerful petition they seek the healing of the whole man in his physical, spiritual, and emotional needs. Catholics consider the anointing rite a sacrament, whereas Pentecostals accept this as a part of the commission to minister healing with the preaching of the Gospel.

2.   In the life of the Roman Catholic Church there have
been, and are, those who dedicate their lives to the care
of and ministry to the sick, and not just to the ministry
of physical healing. Pentecostals are becoming increasingly
involved in this important aspect of ministry to the sick
and suffering.

3.   The "expectation of being healed" is looked at from
a different perspective. The Roman Catholic practice places
healing of the body as one outcome of the ministry to the
sick in the Church. Pentecostals place more emphasis on
seeking actively to arouse expectation of healing in the
afflicted through preaching and praying. There is a basic
difference in each one's approach to healing, e.g., the
Catholics have places where healings have taken place, such
as Fatima and Lourdes and healing is often sought in Novena
services and in similar forms of devotion. Pentecostals
teach people to expect healing anywhere at anytime. Both
recognize and accept that Jesus is the Healer and that faith
looks to Jesus for this grace. There is an admitted new
awareness of the reality of healing in the Catholic Church
both within and without the sacramental order.

There is a difference in expectation--that of the
Catholics being more passive while that of the Pentecostals
is more agressive.

4.   The place of suffering in this life was looked upon
by both Catholics and Pentecostals as a means of grace, a
purifying of the soul, and a means of receiving God's
spiritual provision in our lives that sustains us and causes
us to rejoice in affliction.

We both believe that suffering may lead one to understand and be conformed (Phil 3:10) to the redemptive suffering of Jesus. Pentecostals continue to expect healing unless there is a special revelation that God has some other purpose, such as Paul's "thorn in the flesh", that brings a new provision of God into ones life. Both Catholics and Pentecostals accept that the will of God is preeminent in the whole matter of healing.

5.   Both the Roman Catholics and Pentecostals are aware of the existence of a "folk religion" that often lacks sophisticated theological understanding. This aspect of healing within the Church is recognized.

6.   Pentecostals do not accept the concept of going to a shrine for healing as it seems to them to promote superstition rather than faith in Jesus the Healer. Catholics exercise considerable reserve in making judgements about miraculous manifestations and healings. The greatest miracles taking place at shrines such as Lourdes and Fatima seem to be miracles of conversion rather than of physical healing.

7.   Although there appears to be some similarity in lay participation in the ministry of healing, it was confessed that there is still a wide gap between Catholics and Pentecostals. A baptized member of the Catholic Church can pray for the sick, be they in his own household or that of another believer, and it is done in the "whole Christ, Head and members". He may also pray with a sick person in the context of the ministry of a priest but he may not anoint

with oil, as Rite of Anointing is a sacrament, an act of
the Church through its priests in a special and solemn way.

Pentecostals anoint with oil (Ja 5:14,15) but do not
confine the rite of anointing to the ordained ministry.
The ministry to the sick, with the laying on of hands by
all believers (Mk 16:17,18) is commonly practiced.

8.   There is wide divergence of position between the
Catholics and the Pentecostals concerning the reference to
social injustice in the area of the healing ministry. Catholics would feel that many illnesses arise from unjust social
conditions. Therefore they see it as a mandate to rectify
social conditions to bring about a healthy environment. The
Pentecostals do not accept that Divine healing should embrace such a broad range of matters as social injustice.
Pentecostals do believe that social injustice should be rectified, but emphasize the priority of the preaching of the
Gospel to "heal" the sinner and when the sinner is "healed"
of his sin, then there is a change in his way of life, in
his relationship to others, and to his environment.

9.   There were a number of areas where there was agreement
among the Catholics and Pentecostals. Among them were the
following: suffering; healing as a sign of the Kingdom,
healing and wholeness, the involvement of the laity in prayer for healing; the expectation of healing through the
Eucharist (Communion); Christ as the healer and anointer.

12 October 1979

Press Release

The 1979 session of the Pentecostal/Roman Catholic
dialogue was held in Rome 8-12 October at the Sts John
and Paul Retreat House of the Passionist Fathers. The
composition, inspiration and interpretation of the
Scriptures was one of the main themes, the other being the
Church's ministry of healing.

Papers on the Scripture topic were presented by Dr
Howard Ervin of the Oral Roberts University, Tulsa,
Oklahoma [USA] and by Fr William Dalton SJ of the
Pontifical Biblical Institute, Rome. Bishop Robert
McAlister of the New Life Pentecostal Church, Rio de
Janeiro, Brazil and Fr Charles Gusmer of Immaculate
Conception Seminary, Darlington, New Jersey, gave papers
on healing.

After the themes had been presented they were
developed by means of a series of "hard questions" which
each side addressed to the other. One of these was the
relation of Scripture and tradition where some new understandings emerged while important divergences remain.
The Catholic use of critical methods in the exegesis of
Scripture was described by exegetical practice is diverse
in the two traditions. To discern the meaning of
Scripture, Catholics and Pentecostals invoke the guidance

of the Holy Spirit but the role of the Church in communicating the Word of God is seen in different ways. Both
sides agreed in emphasizing the supernatural but noted
considerable differences in the respective emphasis placed
on the way it is manifested. It was possible to note a
number of substantial points of doctrinal agreement
including the inspiration of Scripture, the preaching of
the Gospel as an integral part of the ministry of the
Church, and the acknowledgement of corporate guidance by
the Holy Spirit.

It was noted that both Catholics and Pentecostals
practice a ministry of healing although it is exercised in
different ways. In both traditions there is also an
expectation of healing but this is emphasized in a more
striking manner in the Pentecostal tradition. A surprising number of areas of agreement were noted including
healing as a sign of God's Kingdom, healing as a means of
wholeness, Jesus Christ as the healer and anointer, the
Eucharist as a source of healing. Divergences had arisen
on social justice as part of the work of healing, the
participation of laity in the ministry of healing, and the
attitude to suffering.

The participants in the dialogue took part in a
public audience with His Holiness Pope John Paul II when
he welcomed them saying:

> For seven years now this effort of mutual under-
> standing and reconciliation has been going on,
> and I wish to assure you that it has my fullest
> interest and prayerful support. If we Christians
> are to attain the unity willed by our Lord, we are
> called to "shared investigation of the truth in

the full evangelical and Christian sense"
(Redemptor Hominis, 6). You are contributing
to that by your work this week. May God support
you in it and by the light of his Holy Spirit
enable you to know and experience his truth, his
grace and his love.

The Holy Father greeted all participants personally

at the conclusion of the audience. The following took part

in the meeting:

Pentecostals:

Dr David du Plessis (Chairman) - Oakland
    (California) USA
Bishop W. Robert McAlister (Secretary) - Rio de
    Janeiro (Brazil)
Dr John L. Meares - Washington D.C. (USA)
Pastor Justus T. du Plessis - Lyndhurst (R. South
    Africa)
Dr Howard Ervin - Tulsa (Oklahoma) USA
Dr F. P. Möller - Lyndhurst (R. South Africa)
Rev William Carmichael - Salem, (Oregon) USA
Rev Elias Malki - Walnut (California) USA

Roman Catholics:

Fr Kilian McDonnell, OSB (Chairman) - Institute
    for Ecumenical and Cultural Research -
    Collegeville (MN) [USA]
Msgr Basil Meeking (Secretary) - Secretariat for
    Promoting Christian Unity - Vatican
Fr Pierre Duprey, WF - Secretariat for Promoting
    Christian Unity - Vatican
Fr Jerome Vereb, CP - Secretariat for Promoting
    Christian Unity - Vatican
Fr Bill Dalton, SJ - Pontifical Biblical Institute -
    Rome
Fr Charles Gusmer - Immaculate Conception Seminary -
    Darlington (New Jersey) USA
Fr Barnabas Ahern, CP - Passionist Monastery -
    Rome

ROMAN CATHOLIC/PENTECOSTAL DIALOGUE
13–17 October 1980—Venice

Dialogue Participants

1. The Very Rev Liam G. Walsh, OP
2. Rev Richard B. Foth
3. Rev Ronald C. Haus
4. Mrs Ronald Haus (Connie)
5. Rev Jerry L. Sandidge
6. Fr Jerome Vereb, CP
7. Mrs David du Plessis (Anna)
8. Fr Pierre Duprey, WF
9. Rev William L. Carmichael
10. Miss Paola Fabrizi
    (devoted secretary)
11. Rev Ronald McConnell
12. Mrs Ronald McConnell
    (Marge)
13. Rev Desmond Evans
14. Fr Barnabas Ahern, CP
15. Fr Robert J. Wister
16. Rev Terry Law
17. Fr Anthony Meredith, SJ
18. Fr Rino Cozza
    (parish priest of Madonna
    dell'Orto, Venice)

19. Rev Justus T. du Plessis
20. Rev Howard M. Ervin
21. Rev John L. Meares

22. Mrs John Meares (Mary Lee)
23. Rev David J. du Plessis
24. Fr Kilian McDonnell, OSB

ROMAN CATHOLIC/PENTECOSTAL DIALOGUE
13-17 October 1980 - Venice

Schedule - Agenda

8:30 a.m.	Breakfast
9:00	Morning Prayer
9:15	Plenary
10:45	Coffee Break
11:00	Plenary
12:30 p.m.	Conclusion of the Session
1:00	Lunch
3:45	Tea
4:00	Plenary
5:45	Break
6:00	Plenary
7:30	Evening Prayer
8:00	Supper

Reminders:

Thursday afternoon is an excursion to a monastery.
Thursday night is a concert in the Basilica di San
Marco.

Dialogue concludes 9:00 a.m. Saturday morning,
17 October.

ROMAN CATHOLIC/PENTECOSTAL DIALOGUE
13-17 October 1980 - Venice

Theological Paper

THE CHURCH AS A WORSHIPING COMMUNITY
by
Rev Richard B. Foth

In a description of classical pentecostalism,
worship mode and orientation are central. The elements
of worship--e.g., praise, prayer, music, sacraments, Holy
Scripture, spiritual gifts--are, obviously, not unique to
Pentecostals. The synergism and results of worship
experiences, however, do distinguish this group within the
Church. The existential quality of New Testament church
life is captured in the Pentecostal worship service.

Traditionally, the emphasis on the worship service
as a primary form of spiritual experience and expression
has been paramount. Detractors have, until recent years,
juxtaposed this focus with lack of involvement in more
socially-oriented forms of Christian service. Indeed,
often the most vocal, gift-oriented persons in a local
congregation have been seen as the more "spiritual."
Within the last fifteen years, however, more balance has
been evidenced within the Pentecostal community in
evaluating spirituality according to the fruit of the
Spirit and not just the gifts.

I. WORSHIP AS COMMUNITY

The Pentecostal movement could be described as a community created by worship. To the extent that the baptism of the Holy Spirit is a worship experience, they are initiated into a methodology and quality of worship which is often very personal and exuberant. The desire for verbal and physical expression in the early part of this century was one of the things which caused rejection by church bodies practicing more formal worship styles.

The emphasis in a given service revolves around God's ability to accomplish anything and everything-- immediately. This understanding is centered in God's character and couched in Biblical language (e.g., "our helper," "a very present help in time of trouble," "our healer," and "provider"). Responsibility is placed upon the worshiper to seek the God who desires to do things for His people. Phrases to encourage this process, such as "laying hold on God," "praying through," and "causing the blessings to fall," are not uncommon. The vertical nature of church life, therefore, dominates Pentecostalism with horizontal relationships seen as subsidiary. Biblical injunctions to worship "in Spirit and in truth" (Jn 4:24) or "ye shall seek Me, and find Me, when ye shall search for Me with all your heart" (Jr 29:13) are axiomatic.

Much basis for style-in-worship is found in the Old Testament. Expressions as diverse as a person who ". . . fell prostrate before the Lord. . ." (Dt 9:18) and David "dancing before the Lord" (2 Sm 6:16) would be taken literally and no doubt seen as high points of God's expression through the beliver. It must be noted that such expressions are extremes characterized by spontaneity and not particularly thought to be acts of the human will. Although currently there is solid Biblical instruction in many Pentecostal churches regarding one's ability and responsibility to control his own actions in a worship context for the sake of the whole (e.g., "spirit of the prophet is subject to the prophet" 1 Cor 14:32), it has not always been so. This reflects the idea of God's ability to move dramatically in persons and circumstances.

The clapping of hands (Ps 47:1), lifting of the hands (Ps 134:2), shouting of praises (Is 12:6), weeping (Jl 2:17; Rom 12:15), and other physical mannerisms are common in congregational worship. Passages oft-quoted from the New Testament would reflect other participatory experiences such as 1 Cor 12:7-11:

> Now to each one the manifestation of the Spirit is given for the common good. To one there is given through the Spirit the message of wisdom, to another the message of knowledge by means of the same Spirit, to another faith by the same Spirit, to another gifts of healing by that one Spirit, to another miraculous powers, to another prophecy, to another the ability to distinguish between spirits, to another the ability to speak in different kinds of tongues, and to still another the interpretation of tongues. All these are the work of one and the same Spirit, and he gives them to each man, just as he determines.

A Pentecostal reading this passage would greatly appreciate the concept "to each man."

Therefore, a kind of God-centered individualism permeates the church. Although not usually stated so,

the idea of "God is real because He's at work in me"
characterizes the Pentecostal experience. Again, God's
Spirit moved in the Old Testament, in the New Testament,
and He's at work now.

II. ELEMENTS OF THE WORSHIP SERVICE

A. Music

As a matter of course, music often provides the
thread within the elements of worship. From the prelude
to a concluding time of prayer, music serves as a foil.
Although not dictating the course of a service, it certainly reflects the "soul" of the proceedings. Exhortations from the Psalms are often given as encouragement to
the worshiper and as biblical premise for events-at-hand.

It has been well said that one's songs reveal his
theology. Pentecostals are no different. Many of the
songs have come out of revival movements around the world
within the past century. Much emphasis is placed on the
grace of God, His shed blood, His power to save and heal,
and His imminent return for the saints. In recent years
more old hymns of the Church--from the 16th century on--
have gained popularity once again. Indeed, even more
recently, scripture songs and "the psalter" with new
melodies have surfaced. These modes of praise and exul-
tation would no doubt conform to the injunction of Col 3:16:

> Let the word of Christ dwell in you richly as you
> teach and admonish one another with all wisdom, and
> as you sing psalms, hymns, and spiritual songs with
> gratitude in your hearts to God.

B. Prayer and Praise

Since these subjects have been spoken to in previous
Dialogues, suffice it to say that such activities are
central to worship. In fact, many opportunities are
afforded in a normal service for spontaneous praise
punctuated often with prayer for specific circumstances
and individuals. Prayer is commonly accompanied by laying
on of hands and annointing with oil in the manner described
in Jas 5:13-18:

> Is any one of you in trouble? He should pray. Is
> anyone happy? Let him sing songs of praise. Is
> any one of you sick? He should call the elders of
> the church to pray over him and annoint him with oil
> in the name of the Lord. And the prayer offered in
> faith will make the sick person well; the Lord will
> raise him up. If he has sinned, he will be forgiven.
> Therefore confess your sins to each other and pray
> for each other so that you may be healed. The
> prayer of a righteous man is powerful and effective.
>
> Elijah was a man just like us. He prayed
> earnestly that it would not rain and it did not
> rain on the land for three and a half years. Again
> he prayed, and the heavens gave rain, and the earth
> produced its crops.

C. Personal Testimony

The value of the individual is focused once again
when accountings of "God's work in your life" are called
for. This event is obviously designed to encourage faith,
edify the church, and honor God as noted in 1 Cor 14:26:

> What then shall we say, brothers? When you come
> together, everyone has a hymn or a word of instruc-
> tion, a revelation, a tongue or an interpretation.
> All of these must be done for the strengthening
> of the church.

"Victory" and "overcoming" are classic themes here, possibly stemming from persecution experiences in the early days of this century, as well as a strong eschatological bent.

D. Spiritual Gifts

1 Corinthians 12-14 is a basis and guideline for the manifestation of "spirituals" in the local assembly. Although a range of interpretations exists regarding the mechanics of encouraging and controlling manifestations, their validity and necessity are accepted a priori.

A visitor entering a Pentecostal service often raises questions of understanding about glossalalia ("speaking in tongues" or "messages in tongues"). Explanation is given about the Biblical validity of this experience indicating that most Pentecostals understand such a manifestation as "God speaking to the congregation through an individual" which must necessarily be followed by an "interpretation" by the same individual or another congregational member.[1]

1 Cor 14:13-17:

> For this reason the man who speaks in a tongue should pray that he may interpret what he says. For if I pray in a tongue, my spirit prays, but my mind is unfruitful. So what shall I do? I will pray with my spirit, but I will also pray with my mind; I will sing with my spirit but I will also sing with my mind. If you are praising God with your spirit, how can one who finds himself among those who do not understand say "Amen" to your thanksgiving, since he does not know what you are

---

[1]Another view--growing today--is that a "message in tongues" is often a praise or prayer to God still needing interpretation 1 Cor 14:2.

saying? You may be giving thanks well enough, but the other man is not edified.

1 Cor 14:27,28:

If anyone speaks in a tongue, two--or at the most three--should speak, one at a time, and someone must interpret. If there is no interpreter, the speaker should keep quiet in the church and speak to himself and God.

An interpretation is not equated with translation. Therefore, the "message" can be lengthy and the "interpretation" short and vice-versa. Perhaps a model would be the difference between social dance and interpretive dance. In social dance the motions and movements are planned, learned, accepted--only modified by the individual dancer. The movements may or may not have meaning, as opposed to just a way of expressing a person's feelings at a given moment. On the contrary, in interpretive dance no one generally knows the pattern of the dance or the meaning of the dance until it is explained by the dancer or some other enlightened party. What is known is that these movements are a creative expression of the inner person. In the case of the Pentecostal that inner person is the Holy Spirit expressing Himself through human personality in a supernatural manifestation. The combination of message and interpretation can be general in focus or quite specific; usually the total expression is understood to be the equivalence of prophecy in content. In other words, "here is another way in which God is speaking to us."

1 Cor 14:5:

> I would like every one of you to speak in tongues, but I would rather have you prophesy. He who prophesies is greater than one who speaks in tongues, unless he interprets, so that the church may be edified.

Biblically, one must evaluate prophetic manifestations.

1 Cor 14:29:

> Two or three prophets should speak, and the others should weigh carefully what is said.

It is at this point that many Pentecostal churches struggle. Usually, the pastor is left with this responsibility, and understandably so as a leader in the fellowship. However, with the advent of the charismatic movement in the 1960's a fresh flow of creative worship developed, and other alternatives for methods of evaluation were generated. Some church leaders have noted this and are "experimenting" in methods of evaluation.

Prophecy is more clearly-defined, less awkward, and better understood in Pentecostal circles. This is an obvious instance of God speaking to the congregation through a person in the language of the people. The purpose may be timely exhortation or explanation; it may be futuristic in thrust. Each occurrence needs evaluation and validation by whatever method is generally accepted.

Some congregations make opportunity in worship services for the verbal gifts; others take them "as they come." Traditionally, among American Pentecostals at least, structuring the timing of manifestations would be seen as control or even "quenching the Spirit." Strong biblical teaching has modified that view in some instances.

Other spiritual manifestations are less clearly defined in the average Pentecostal church. However, these gifts are spoken of consistently in a variety of settings and are somewhat less obvious in the normal flow of a service and church life.

E. Instruction

Pentecostal assemblies appreciate preaching. The proclamation of the Word is key to the service as a whole. It usually follows a period of prayer requests, singing and receiving of the tithes and offerings. The emphases would traditionally fall into four categories: 1) personal redemption; 2) the empowering work of the Holy Spirit in Spirit-baptism; 3) divine healing; and 4) the second coming of Christ. Depending on the particular subject matter, an action on the part of the hearer is usually called for at the closing. Often the congregation as a whole will gather at the front of the sanctuary to pray personally or for each other. Extended times of prayer in which Spirit-baptism is the object have been called "tarrying meetings," in reference to Jesus' words in Ac 1:4,5:

> On one occasion, while he was eating with them, he gave them this command: "Do not leave Jerusalem, but wait for the gift my Father promised, which you have heard me speak about. For John baptized with water, but in a few days you will be baptized with the Holy Spirit.

Although enthusiasm and vocal expression is common during the course of a given meeting, the greatest interaction and fellowship usually takes place following

the core of the service--spiritually, in the altar area
at the front of the sanctuary, and socially, in the
narthex.

F. Christian Initiation

When a person makes a confession of faith in Jesus
Christ, it is most often public and verbal. Water
baptism by immersion follows, but is not necessarily
concurrent with the confession itself. In this century
the American evangelical church has not always connected
the two acts closely and, in my opinion, many Pentecostals
have absorbed by osmosis that mentality. Biblically,
public confession and believer's baptism coincide; in
practice, significant numbers of Pentecostal churches are
reemphasizing that stance.

G. The Sacraments

Since the Pentecostal church at large is essentially
non-sacramental, water baptism and the eucharist are
observed as ordinances. Let us deal here only with the
eucharist.

Indications are that the early church observed the
eucharist once a week on the Lord's Day, if not every
time they met. The American Pentecostals would be more
prone to a once-a-month communion service, which is an
addition to the regular worship time rather than a
substitution for it. Interestingly enough, with the bilateral dialogues of the last few years and persons from
sacramental backgrounds frequenting Pentecostal assemblies,
certain churches are reexamining both the theological and

pragmatic purposes for the eucharist being observed more often.[1]

III. "OPEN" VERSUS "CLOSED" COMMUNION

In most of the literature connected with major Pentecostal groups early in this century, the eucharist, its meaning and form did not seem to be an issue of great consequence. Discussions on water baptism, however, developed into serious controversy culminating in some fragmentation around 1916.

The subject of participation in the communion service was not a dilemma apparently. Written in 1914 the Preamble to the Constitution of the largest Pentecostal body in the United States reads as follows:

> We . . . do not believe in identifying ourselves or establishing ourselves into a sect, that is a human organization that legislates or forms laws . . . and creates unscriptural lines of fellowship and disfellowship and which separates itself from other members of the General Assembly (Church) of the first born, which is contrary to Christ's prayer.

Similarly, the Statement of Fundamental Truths of 1916 in the article entitled, "The Lord's Supper," states:

> The Lord's Supper, consisting of the elements, bread and the fruit of the vine, is the symbol expressing our sharing the divine nature of our Lord Jesus Christ, 2 Pe 1:4; a memorial of his suffering and death 1 Cor 11:26; and a prophecy of His second coming, 1 Cor 11:26; and is enjoined on all believers 'until He comes.'

---

[1]This observation is limited to the writer's travels in a variety of geographic areas within the United States.

In a denominational publication of the same year,
one of the leaders of the movement writes; "It (the
Lord's Supper) should be open to all believers."

In evaluating this stance, one finds a case built
on the analogy of faith, the tenor of Scripture, if you
will. To view the New Testament church is to see a
delicate balance between the power and harmony of the
corporate entity over against the preciousness of the
Spirit at work in the individual. To put it another way,
the individual act is made harmonious by the acceptance
of the whole. Passages such as 1 Cor 11-14; Eph 4; and
Rom 12 speak significantly to that point.

To understand why Pentecostals accepted this practice, it is necessary to capture the historical setting
out of which the movement was born. Many of the earliest
Pentecostals in this century were involved in churches of
Baptistic and Zwinglian persuasion. When they experienced
what they called the baptism of the Holy Spirit, they
were rejected by their traditional churches and formed
independent assemblies primarily for fellowship and,
ultimately, missionary effectiveness. In making the
change, they brought with them theological and traditional understandings which, in their minds apparently
had little relationship to their new found experience in
Jesus. In the words of a Pentecostal historian and
theologian:

> We have inherited a cluster of things imported
> without theological judgment, reflection or
> examination . . . such as, open communion and

dispensational eschatology. We are uncritical
recipients of large packages of tradition . . ."[1]
In another sense, the practice of open communion may be
connected to a rather unstructured approach to local
church discipline. Reaction in recent years to external
codes of holiness may have brought some Pentecostals into
an anti-authoritarian position. Closed communion could
serve as a disciplinary approach within the fellowship,
but without the larger disciplinary framework, it is not
seen as "part of the fabric."

In summary, classical Pentecostals as a worshiping
community are unique in at least three aspects:

1) They stress individualism in worship, but with
great appreciation for the participation of the
whole body.

2) They emphasize the God-of-the-now.

3) They desire and have a Biblical basis for their
worship and sacramental practices, but in the main
are unaware of the numerous traditions which affect
their approaches to worship.

---

[1]William Menzies, Professor of Historical Theology,
Assemblies of God Graduate School, Springfield, MO, USA.

Theological Paper

THE CHURCH AS COMMUNION
by
Fr Pierre Duprey, WF

In these personal reflections, I base myself on the utterance of Popes Paul VI and John Paul II and make much use
of a speech by Cardinal Willebrands on this matter ("The
Future of Ecumenism" in One in Christ, 11, 4 (1975),
pp 310-323).

To present the Church as Communion, I should begin
with the opening verses of the first epistle of St John:

> That which was from the beginning, which we have
> heard, which we have seen with our eyes, which we
> have looked upon, and touched with our hands, con-
> cerning the word of life - and life was made manifest,
> and we saw it, and testify to it, and proclaim to you
> the eternal life which was with the Father and was
> made manifest to us - that which we have seen and heard
> we proclaim also to you, so that you may have fellow-
> ship with us: and our fellowship is with the Father
> and with his Son Jesus Christ.[1]

I cannot attempt here to explain all the richness of
this passage. I confine myself to some aspects of it, and

---

[1] I have kept in this translation the word "fellowship".
Behind it there is the greek word *"koinõnia"* that I translate by "communion".

first to the word "communion." What is its meaning? I
shall try to expound it as participating together in the
same good. This participation together sets up a relationship between the participants: because they share in this
good they are part of a group· they form a community. The
quality of the communion is determined by the nature of
the good they share and the manner in which they share it.
Passing from this general description to the Christian
communion of which St John speaks in the text quoted, the
latter is clearly a sharing in the light of God, in the
eternal life which is God's own life. Throughout the
epistle communion with God is described in terms of sonship.
Eternal life, that of the Word, who is centered on the Father,
we share because in the Son we are become sons. We live
because we are now centered on the Father. But to have part
in that communion it is necessary to receive witness of the
apostles, to be in communion with the apostolic community.

If we look in St Paul we find the same reality, e.g.,
in 1 Cor 1:9, "God is faithful, by whom you were called into
the fellowship of his Son, Jesus Christ our Lord." We are
tempted to recall here the great texts of Romans and Galatians where Paul describes the actions of the Spirit, filling
us with the mind of the Son, turning us towards the Father.

The second epistle of Peter must also be cited (1:4)
which affirms that Christians become partakers of the divine
nature, are put into communion with the divine nature.

The reality with which Christians enter into participation is, in a certain way, God himself. They have all received the Spirit of God and between them and God a new mysterious relationship is set up. They are sons in the Son by the gift of the Spirit of the Son. This too is the whole reality which Paul expresses when he speaks of life in Christ Jesus or of life in the Spirit. Here is a spiritual relationship—that is to say an eminently real relationship because the Holy Spirit is the final eschatological reality.

Here we must mention all the preparation which the Bible gives for the theme of communion, and give a brief outline of the similar theme of inheritance and that of covenant, so closely linked with it. Israel is the inheritance of Yahweh (cf. Ex 34:9) His particular possession. These statements are intended to show the intimacy of the relationship which exists between God and His chosen people. Here we see the close link with the theme of the covenant: You will be my people and I will be your God (cf. Jr 24:7). But to this His own people God has promised to give as heritage a land in which they can live. Here again the theme of inheritance is linked with the covenant (cf. Gn 15). The notion of heritage like that of covenant, was to be progressively deepened and made more spiritual. For the Levite, whose tribe had no land of its own, the heritage was Yahweh (Dt 10:9), but this was also a characteristic of the whole people: Yahweh is its inherited portion (cf. Jr 10:16; Ps 16:5). To possess the land: this became the conventional expression for perfect happiness (Ps 37:11). In the third beatitude (Mt 5:4), the land is the equivalent of the kingdom. In the New Testament, the new covenant, the inheritance, becomes the totality of the divine gifts, the Kingdom (Mt 23:34), eternal life (Mt 19:29). The members of the new people of God are the heirs of God and coheirs with Christ (Rom 8:17). The Father gives all He has to His Son, risen from the dead, and through Him to the faithful. The inheritance is participation in the life of the risen Christ (cf. 1 Cor 15:49,50). Even now we live by the promised Spirit who has been given us and we hope from Him to reach the fullness of possession (cf. Eph 1:14).

To explain what Scripture means by the inheritance of the new people of God, we have been obliged to use the same vocabulary as when we explain communion. Is this another indication that the theme of communion is the fulfilment, and in a way the synthesis, of what is progressively and ever more explicitly expressed through the themes of inheritance and covenant? In the new covenant, the promised inheritance is already given: it is communion with the Father through the Son in the Spirit.

Let us go back now to our analysis of the idea of communion, which brings the Christian into a new relationship with God and at the same time puts the faithful in a new and mysterious relationship among themselves. The relationship among the faithful is as real and as mysterious as that between the faithful and God: "so that you may have fellowship with us, and our fellowship is with the Father and with his Son Jesus Christ". We are brothers as really and as mysteriously as we are sons.

I think this is the meaning we now give to the expression "communions of saints". It is the communion established between those who have been made holy by their union with the Father through the Son in the Holy Spirit; it is the eschatological reality already present in human history and growing until the moment when Christ shall attain the fulness of His stature or, in the language of the Apocalypse, until the moment when the number of the elect shall be complete. At that moment the Church will reach its full realization and, to paraphrase a well-known passage of St Augustine, there will henceforward be only one Christ loving the Father for all eternity. That will be the moment in which Church and Kingdom will be identified: the full realization of which St Cyprian speaks; *De Unitate Patris et Filii et Spiritus Sancti plebs adunata*; a people united in the unity of the Father, the Son, and the Holy Spirit.

While we await that time when Christ will reappear in glory and when we too shall appear in glory, during the time that separates us from Christ's return, all those who are in communion with God and mysteriously in communion with each other should make a community, and this is just our present problem. That communion which is by its nature invisible because it lies at the level of faith, of mystery, should none the less manifest itself visibly in and through a community; and that community is moreover the milieu in and through which communion may be established with God.

The community of Christ's faithful, through the unity it has from communion with the Father through the Son in the Holy Spirit, must witness before the world that the Father has really sent the Son; that through the Son who gave Himself for us we have really become sons in the Son by the gift of the Holy Spirit, and so brothers of one another; that the Father has sent the Son to gather the children of God who were dispersed. Here we are at another level of communion.

What are the components of this communion on the level of the Christian community? St Luke answers the question in the Acts of Apostles when after his account of the descent of the Holy Spirit at Pentecost, the renewal and transformation worked by the Spirit, he wants to give us a picture of a Christian community perfectly faithful to the teachings of Christ and the promptings of the Holy Spirit: "they devoted themselves to the Apostles' teaching and fellowship, to the breaking of bread and the prayers" (Ac 2:42). Those who, renewed by the gift of the Spirit, form one community, unite in the acceptance of the apostles' teaching, that is in the shared profession of the same apostolic faith: they make up a community united in fraternal charity in which the multitude of believers have but one heart and one mind and hold all things in common. They form a community gathered into one in and through the eucharistic celebration which is at once the source and the highest expression of the

community's life and of every dimension of its communion.
Here I think we must stress the normally inseparable components of the communion which makes the Christian community. Fidelity to the teaching of the apostles is not
merely the hearing of the word; it is also, inseparably,
the celebration of the same worship received from the Lord,
whatever the diversity of forms it may take; a worship which
progressively identifies each of the members of the community
with the Lord, and thus builds the community from within.
Here the decisive importance of baptism in establishing
communion with Christ in the Spirit must be clearly
emphasized. Evidently, when we speak of a eucharistic
community this supposes baptism which is the means to entry
into it (cf. Gal 3:26,27; Rom 6:9-11; Col 19:9).

We might recall here the old word used for a eucharistic
community: synaxis. Eucharistic synaxis is not only the
gathering together in unity of the assembly of the faithful
participating in the eternal life of the triune God through
the body and blood of Christ: it is also the identification,
in and through the Spirit of that celebrating community
with the community contemplated by the seer of the Apocalypse,
that of the believers of all times jointed with the apostles
around God and Christ for the eternal heavenly liturgy. The
eucharistic synaxis is thus the contemplation of a future
already present: it is also the present anticipating the
future. But this contemplation of the future already present
in the privileged moment of the eucharistic celebration must
not distract us from the requirements of daily fraternal

life; on the contrary it must be the source of a life of
love in which the gifts of the Spirit stimulate a holy
rivalry in the service of the Godpel (Phil 1; 5:2) and in
the service of the brethren, particularly of the poorest
(Rom 15:26; 2 Cor 8:4; 9:13).

The Christian community then is gathered for a life
of holiness by and around those who within it continue to
exercise the ministry which the apostles received from the
Lord (Jn 20:21-23; Ac 1:8; 2:4), insofar as that mission
must continue, though in a different manner and degree,
throughout the ages. It seems certain even that this
sharing in the faith and in the sacrament of faith was
what was meant from the beginning by the phrase *communio
sanctorum*. It meant first communion in and of holy things,
before it conveyed the present sense of communion of saints.

Sharing in these holy things creates among the faithful
a visible communion, an ecclesial communion. Professing
together the same faith, celebrating together the same
sacraments served and held together by ministries established
as such by the same sacrament, striving together after a
growing holiness of life in the service of their brethren
after the model of Jesus (cf. Phil 2:5), these faithful are
united not only by a spiritual relationship on the plane of
mystery and of the invisible, but also on the visible plane
of human realities transformed by the Spirit.

In a local church (cf. Christus Dominus, para 11) this
visible communion is shown forth above all in the assembly

of the faithful participating actively in a single prayer at the celebration of the Eucharist, in which the word of God is proclaimed and explained, before the single altar at which the bishop presides, surrounded by his priests and his ministers (cf. Sacrosanctum Concilium, no 41).

This conception of the local church is already strongly and clearly expressed in the letters of St Ignatius at the beginning of the second century (cf. among others, Trall. 3, and Smyrn. 8). It is also this same idea which is expressed in the ancient custom of describing the Eucharist by the word "synaxis", the act which gathers together, which puts together.

Each local church participates in the same realities with which Christ willed to establish His Church; in this way a visible ecclesial communion is formed between them.

The bishops, whose task is to witness to the faithfulness of their church and of the churches to the apostolic faith, are the bond of this communion. It is essential for the local church to be in communion, with the other local churches, with the universal Church which exists in every place. The bishop must open his church to this communion; he must represent within his church the universal communion; at the same time he must open the universal communion to his church; he must represent his church within the universal communion. The bishop knit together (cf. Col 2:19) the communion of the churches in its unity and its catholicity both on the local level and on the universal level.

This is the foundation of what the eastern tradition

212

calls the conciliarity of the Church. Certain languages,
notably English, have only a single word for two very different realities: council (concile), council (conseil).
This leads to many ambiguous expressions in certain ecumenical circles in which English is almost the only theological
language. Conciliarity is not the establishing and assemb-
ling of councils (conseils) which are entrusted with tasks
for which authority is delegated to them. Conciliarity is
quite a different kind of reality. It results from the
fact that the Church is a communion. At the sign level,
it is the expression and the manifestation of the communion
necessary between the local churches, at the same time as
it is one of the chief means of maintaining and deepening
that communion. Conciliarity belongs to the sacramental
order. The Second Vatican Council, approaching this question in a perspective which saw the Church first of all as
universal, used the category of collegiality to express the
bond which exists between the bishops because of their
ordination, thus setting in relief the sacramental aspect
of this reality. But the approach we have followed, which
starts from the local church and sees the universal Church
as the universal communion of the local churches, and seeing that communion expressed and maintained by conciliarity,
is just as sacramental, if not more so. One view is based
directly on the sacrament of Order, the other is based on
the whole sacramentality of the Church, ensuring communion
as we have tried to expound it. We are very far here from
a simple arrangements of councils (conseils).

This conciliarity can structure the Catholic communion at different levels: regional, national, continental. There is a very ancient juridical text which witness to this function of the episcopate; I refer to canon 34 of the canonical collection called the Apostolic Constitutions. It is agreed today that this canon--I do not say the whole collection, but this thirty-fourth canon--is certainly to be dated before 340, probably from the end of the third century, possibly even earlier, for the historian Eusebius already speaks of the bishops who gather by "province" when referring to the synods for the paschal quarrel (E.H. V,XXIII, 2,3). It probably comes from Syria. However this may be, canon 34 states:

> The bishops of each nation must know which of them is the first and which they consider their chief (note that Greek word used is képhali. They should do nothing important without his assent, even though it belongs to each one to handle the affairs of his own diocese and the territory belonging to it. But neither should he (i.e., the one who is the first) do anything without the assent of all the others. Thus harmony will prevail and God will be glorified through Christ in the Holy Spirit. (cf. C. Kirch, Enchiridion Fontium Historiae Ecclesiasticae Antiquae, (Barcelona, 1947) n. 694.)

It is not my intention to draw out all the theological riches of this text here. I wanted to quote it to show how ancient is this functional reality which is called conciliarity. I would simply point out that to describe the role of the first of the bishops in a region the word "head" képhali is used. So one must not be surprised to find it again as a description of the role of him who is first in the universal communion. For conciliarity can structure the communion right up to the universal level, that of the

214

Church "which presides within the fellowship of charity" (Ignatius' Letter to the Romans); "that Church, very great and very ancient and known to you all, that the two most glorious apostles Peter and Paul founded and established in Rome, that Church with which, because of its more excellent origin (*propter potentiorem principalitatem*) every Church--i.e., the faithful everywhere--must necessarily be in accord; that Church in which, for the benefit of people everywhere, the tradition which comes from the apostles has always been preserved" (Adv. aer. 3.3.2--translation: Sources Chrétiennes).

I have just quoted one after the other two famous texts, that of Ignatius of Antioch's letter to the Romans and that of Irenaeus in his work against heresies. I do not want to go into a precise exegesis; this is not necessary for our purpose here. It is enough, for our purpose here, to express in this way and with two non-roman witnesses, the function which throughout the first millenium, without major objection, was acknowledged as that of the Church of Rome and its bishop within the universal communion. This function must always be exercised for the keeping of all within the faith of the apostles (Lk 22:32) and in the spirit of the true apostolic fraternity (the *homothymadon* of Acts), in which also the first does nothing important without the first, as it was said in the thirty-fourth canon of the Apostolic Constitutions which we have just quoted.

To come back to Ignatius' letter to Romans, let us simply note, since it is directly on our subject, that

Fr Hertling thinks, and I am in agreement with him, that
agapi here is the equivalent of "communion"; we should
understand, therefore, the Church "which has the task of
presidency in the communion" (L. Hertling, SJ, <u>Communio</u>,
<u>Chiesa</u> <u>e</u> <u>Papato</u> <u>nell'antichita</u> <u>cristiana</u>, Rome, 1961,
p 10, which refers to Smyrn. 12 and Philad. 11).

The communion just described is called "full communion".
This expression, which has become common among Catholics,
often occasions ambiguity elsewhere. To say that churches
are in full communion means that, according to the Catholic
faith, those churches share in all the good things, all the
elements which the Lord has given through and in the Spirit
to His Church to maintain it in unity and make it grow in
holiness. This alone is what full communion means. It
does not at all mean that those churches live in full
communion with the Father through the Son in the Holy Spirit
and achieve fully that communion of holiness for which they
are designed. This is not what we are talking about: in
this sense communion in the Church and communion between the
Churches must go on growing and deepening until the moment
when God will be all in all. This is always a dynamic
reality, a reality in progress, a reality never achieved, a
reality for which we must struggle, fight, as we must for
the personal communion of each one of the faithful with his
Lord and with his brethren.

Reference to this mystery of Christ and His gifts to
men for the building up of His Church is also the right way
of understanding the communion which exists between the

churches. This is an unequivocally Christocentric approach to our relationships with the churches or ecclesial communities with which we are not in full communion. We do not judge them with reference to ourselves; we judge them and we judge ourselves in relation to Christ and to His mystery.

I have just used the expression "the churches with which we are not in full communion," for within this perspective which we have sketched, we speak of partial or imperfect communion between the divided churches according to the way in which they participate in these gifts of the Spirit, in these realities which are the gifts of the Spirit; the way in which they are in agreement as to the content of their profession of faith; the way in which they celebrate the sacraments and the eucharistic liturgy; the way in which they benefit from the apostolic ministry and His holding together of catholic unity. We have to be careful here of thinking of spiritual realities in a quantitative way, because they cannot as such be quantified. They are visible realities which, on the one hand, belong to our human world, but which are transformed by the Spirit and thus in this sense transcend any possible measurements.

Before ending, we must note that one also speaks of hierarchical communion, or of canonical communions, when one wants to express the full communion which exists among the Churches and shows itself in the ordered relationships between their hierarchies. Must we not think here of Gal 2:9, and see in it the beginnings of this reality? Paul went up to Jerusalem with Barnabas and Titus to expound his gospel to James, Peter and John, who to express their

agreement, gave them "the right hand of communion", that
is to say, gave them the right hand as a sign of communion.

One could also point out here the etymology of the
Latin word *communio*, which comes from the adjective *communis*,
com-munus, those who have the same task.

Finally, we must note two things before concluding:

1.   In the description of Catholic communion as I gave
it earlier, two very different elements have of necessity
been mixed up.   One, which Catholics believe to be necessary
and which is central in the ecumenical debate, is the ministry
of unity of the bishop in his church and between the churches,
and, among them and between them, the ministry of the Bishop
of Rome in his church and within Catholic communion as a
whole.

The other is the way in which these ministries are
exercised; councils (conciles) at different levels, or
organization into provinces, patriarchates, etc.; the style
of the relationships of the bishops between themselves and
of the bishops with the Bishop of Rome.   These manners or
forms of organization are historical and ecclesiastical in
origin, and however venerable and beneficial they are, they
leave room for a liberty all the greater the more profoundly
one is in agreement on the essential reality of these
ministries.

2.   All that has been said about visible ecclesiastical
communion, about full communion or imperfect communion, must
not make us forget, nor relegate to second place, what was
said first of all about communion in the mystery,

communion of faith, of love, of hope, with the Father, through the Son, in the Spirit, which is the ultimate and definitive reality in relation towards which all the other aspects are directed as means to their end and which transcends all the limitations of visible communion. What we already are, the reality of our communion, will only be manifested when Christ appears in glory (cf. 1 Jn 3:2; Col 3:4).

ROMAN CATHOLIC/PENTECOSTAL DIALOGUE
13-17 October 1980 - Venice

Theological Paper

THE PLACE OF TRADITION IN SCRIPTURE
AND IN THE EARLY FATHERS
by
Fr Anthony Meredith, SJ

INTRODUCTION

At the outset it will be wise for the sake of the
future discussion to distinguish two senses of tradition.
The first is basically the active sense of *paradosis*, the
actual handing down of something. There is nothing very
special in this sense and it could be applied also to the
handing over of a message or of a present or gift. The
second sense refers to the thing handed over, the content
of the message, the gift, the instruments of office. Tradition in the ecclesiastical sense of the word is of the
second kind. It refers to the truths, books, practices
that have been handed down to us and are now part of the
church's treasure. Two points should be made:

1) The basic content of the tradition handed down is
the revelation of God made in Jesus Christ. He is the basic
object of faith and source of revelation. All tradition
somehow relates to Him. 2) The actual process of trans-
mitting this mystery ought not to be thought of in too
simplistic terms, as though it were simply a question of

handing on, or of trying to hand on, material that remains independent of the agents of transmission. Tradition in this context is not like the handing on of a family heirloom or a manuscript, where the duty of the transmitters is to hand on the object intact. In the tradition of the church, on the other hand, tradition and interpretation are inextricably intertwined. It is impossible to get at the primary object of the tradition, Christ Himself, without going through the various media that channel Him to us, the Bible, especially the New Testament, the Church and the creeds of the believing community. Christ, as John Henry Newman observes in the _Apologia_, chap 3, is not to be thought of as "entirely objective and detached. . .but lying hid in the bosom of the church as if one with her and clinging to and (as it were) lost in her embrace."

I. THE NEW TESTAMENT IS ESSENTIALLY AN ECCLESIAL DOCUMENT

This entails three separate elements. The New Testament expresses a tradition that derives from the existing and believing community of the church; it was composed by members of that same community and it was written primarily for the benefit of that community, in other words it was written from faith to faith. That it presupposes an already existing church follows from the simple and generally agreed fact that however early the composition of the New Testament is placed--and few critics would place the bulk of the writings in it before the year 60--there was a lapse of a quarter of a century between the death of Christ and

the records of His life and teaching in the form of gospel
narrative. It follows from this that these narratives record and pattern existing traditions about Jesus; and, if
it be correct to date the birth of the church from the first
great outpouring of the Spirit at Pentecost, then the church
predates the gospel accounts as we now have them by about
30 years. The authors of these accounts, the four evangelists, were themselves drawn from the believing communities
whose traditions they organized under the names of Matthew,
Mark, Luke, and John. It is surely significant in this
connexion that whatever view is taken of the _real_ as distinct from the putative authors of the Gospels, Papias, the
early second century bishop of Hierapolis in Phrygia, is
recorded by Eusebius (H. E., iii. 39.15) as making Mark the
interpreter of Peter. If, in addition, Luke's connexion
with St Paul may be reasonably inferred from the reference
to the "beloved physician" in Col 4:14, then all four evangelists have strong links with the apostles, or at least so it
pleased the early church to suppose. Their ecclesial character is beyond question. The church is the author of the
New Testament, not the other way around. Finally the ecclesial function of the whole of the New Testament is clear.
The Acts narrates the early growth of the church in Palestine
and the Near East; St Paul's letters are all or nearly all
addressed to various groups of Christians in Greece, Asia
Minor, and Italy. Revelation is heavily ecclesial in its
interests, and the Gospels in their different ways are meant
to strengthen rather than create faith in their readers.

Matthew does this by providing Old Testament evidence of the
"fulfilled" character of the mission of Jesus, John by offering evidence on the basis of which the reader might be able
to deepen his faith and so find life in the name of Jesus
(cf. Jn 20:31). So far, I have argued that the particular
traditions that are embodied in the New Testament were derived from the church, were written by members of the church,
and were designed for the benefit of the church. Neither
the authors nor the content of the books is self-generated.
Both act under the influence of the Spirit to provide for
the needs of the Spirit-filled community of believers.

II. TRADITION AS INTERPRETATION IS OF THE VERY STUFF OF THE N T

In their attempt to present and recommend Christ to
their different audiences the evangelists and St Paul and
the author of the book of Revelation portray Him as the one
in whom the Messianic hopes of the Jewish nation had found
fulfillment. This is clear both in the typology that they
employ and in their use of Old Testament proof-texts, though
it is important to note at this stage that the sense that
the New Testament gives to the proof-texts from the Old Testament is not the sense that the original context requires or
supports. So especially in St Matthew, Christ is presented
as the antitype of the patriarchs and prophets of the Old
Law. So, for example, He delivers a sermon on a mountain
in the fifth chapter much as Moses had done, or rather had
received in the book of Exodus. Nor is the Moses typology
restricted to the Sermon on the Mount. Further, in the

Fourth Gospel Christ is the Passover Lamb, pointed out by
St John in the first chapter and hanging on the cross in
the nineteenth. Alongside such typologies Christ is often
related to various Old Testament prophecies, the literal
exegesis of which may not support the particular sense
placed on them. So, for example, Mt 1:22 quotes Is 7:14;
"A virgin shall conceive and bear a son", where the Hebrew
original, as Justin's adversary in the Dialogue with Trypho
(43; 67; 71; 84) was quick to point out, would be better
rendered by "young woman". Again it is hardly likely, that
the use of Jr 31:15 at Mt 2:15 is the exact exegesis of the
original passage. Examples could be multiplied, but the
point remains, the New Testament use of the Old is not such
as to inspire confidence in the view that the inspired
authors were simply or indeed primarily interested in the
literal meaning of the Bible. For them the whole of the
Old Testament spoke of Christ, and it was in Him that it
found its truest meaning.

The New Testament does not only portray Christ as the
antitype of certain Old Testament figures and fulfiller of
prophecies. It also bears witness to the existence of
tradition that antedates it. This is above all true of St
Paul, who on several occasions either overtly or by implication refers to traditions he has received--a fact which
is a strong warning against the tendency to split up Scripture and tradition as belonging to two different categories.
So in Rom 6 he writes, as though he expected his readers to
be well aware of the point he is making; "Do you not know

that all of us who have been baptised into Christ Jesus
have been baptised into his death?" Again in 1 Cor 11 he
writes with reference to the eucharist, "For I received
from the Lord what I also delivered to you, that the Lord
Jesus on the night when he was betrayed..." There is a
further appeal to received tradition in the beginning of
the fifteenth chapter of the same letter. "For I delivered
to you as of first importance what I also received, that
Christ died for our sins in accordance with the scriptures."
Here we have an added motif. Not only is Christ's expiatory
death part of an already existing tradition, it is also
linked at a relatively early stage to an appeal to the Old
Testament.

So far I have suggested that in our attempts to arrive
at and to begin to understand the person and mission of
Jesus we are necessarily involved in a dialogue with the
written word of the New Testament, and that even if we
confine ourselves to the word of Scripture we are brought
in it face to face with two other logically separable
realities, tradition and the church. Scripture does not
stand alone by itself. It is part of a continuous process.
It records the tradition and the interpretation of the time
and it proceeds from the believing community of the church.
Important though it is and normative though it was to
become, it is not primary in the sense that the church
that produced it is and that the traditions it records are.
Nor is it all-sufficient or self-explanatory, as we shall
shortly see. The all-sufficiency of Scripture is not a

scriptural doctrine, and the attempt to make "*scriptura sola*", as distinct from the church and tradition, the only criterion for the belief of Christians, in practice has never really worked out.

III. THE FORMATION OF THE CANON, THE MEANING OF SCRIPTURE AND THE TEACHING OF THE CHURCH

The date and the manner of the formation of the canon of the New Testament are alike unclear. Several things, however, are clear enough. There was an abundance of material in the first three centuries of the history of the church, whose uncanonical character is now recognized by all Christians, but which enjoyed both popularity and importance in the earliest, pre-canonical days. Such were the Apocryphal Gospels, conveniently collected by M. R. James in The Apocryphal New Testament, which contains the gospels of Peter and Thomas and such romances as the Acts of Pilate and the Acts of Paul. Allied to these were the Gnostic Gospels, the bulk of which became partially known to the world after their discovery at Nag Hammadi in 1945. The contents of these works is more esoteric and gnostic and has been the subject of recent work by James M. Robinson and others. Side by side with the tendency on the part of some gnostic sects to produce their own versions of Jesus' teaching, embodied for example in The Gospel of Truth from the school of Valentinus, there existed a quite different tendency, viz., to curtail the contents of the New Testament to a minimum by removing from it everything that

depended on the Old Testament and which suggested that
there was any connection between the natural order of the
world and the work of salvation effected by Jesus. The
heresy of Marcion proposed the Draconian measure of reducing the New Testament to the gospel of St Luke without the
infancy narratives and ten epistles of St Paul. It was
partly, if not entirely, in response to this challenge that
the church was encouraged or compelled to make up its mind
as to what books it proposed to regard as authentic records
of the life and teaching of Jesus.

It would, however, be wrong to suppose that this
decision was simply declaratory, universal, and immediate.
On the first point it would be a mistake to suppose that all
that needed to be done was either merely to endorse what was
already clear to the majority of believers or to erect out
of a heterogeneous collection of texts a purely arbitrary
canon. Unfortunately our knowledge of the actual methods
employed in the, at that time, not very centralized church
is very slight. In the early church the term "scripture"
refers to the Old and not to the New Testament. Justin
Martyr writing in the middle of the second century says that
at the eucharist the memoirs of the apostles or the writings
of the prophets were read out (i Apol. 67.); but there is
nothing to indicate that he thought there were only four,
or that he thought they enjoyed a canonical status. It is
not till thirty years later, that we find Irenaeus arguing
against the Gnostics that there could be only four gospels
because there were only four winds and only four beasts in

Ezekiel, both to our minds somewhat bizarre arguments (cf. Adv. H. iii. 11). How this conclusion that there were only four gospels was arrived at we have no means of discovering. The process must lie someway between recognizing on the one hand and deciding on the other. Nor have we any means of knowing how widely accepted was the view that Irenaeus expresses. That other gospels continued to be used is certain from the date of the Nag Hammadi find (c. 360 A.D.). Neither is there any indication that the early church thought that its canon was either self sufficient or self explanatory.

Even after the brave words of Irenaeus, although there seems to have been no attempt to add or to subtract from the number of the gospel, there did exist considerable doubt as to the rest of the New Testament corpus. Aside from the fact that certain canonical lists seem to have been drawn up with a definitively polemical purpose, like the famous Muratorian canon (late second or perhaps fourth century), there were those, for example in the east who found the book of Revelation hard to take and the letter to the Hebrews fared hardly better in the west. Again some lists quite late on added 1 Clement, Barnabas and the Shepherd of Herman. It is only with St Athanasius in the fourth century that we have for the first time a list of the twenty-seven books of the New Testament. In his letter 39 for Easter, 367 not only does he list the books that are considered canonical but he also goes on to add that "the Teaching of the Apostles and the Shepherd" are merely read; nor is there in any place a mention of apocryphal writings.

228

Evidently there were some who treated the aforementioned books as canonical--proof, surely, that even as late as 367, at least in Alexandria, there was no universal consensus as to the composition of the canon. Even here there is no reason why we should regard Athanasius' ruling as binding for the whole church. The same may be said for the council that met at Carthage in 397 and promulgated its own canon, identical in content with that of 367 and doubtless possessing more authority, but scarcely definitive. Rather are these two pieces of evidence witnesses to the fact that, although there was a fairly general agreement about what belonged in the canon and what was foreign to it, the decisions were slow and partial, partly declaratory, partly definitive. Even if Oscar Cullmann were correct in his view that the establishment of the canon placed Scripture over the church, at least he should admit that the process by which this occurred was long and drawn out. If his view is taken to mean that before 397 (or 367) non-scriptural traditions and ecclesiastical interpretation and decisions of doctrine were permissible, but that afterwards they were illegitimate, he seems to be left with the odd position that with the establishing of the canon a radical change overtook the church, and that from then onwards, councils and the rest if they failed to be controlled by scripture, were in some way unfaithful to the work of the spirit. Even on this hypothesis it is not all clear what can be meant by the "bible standing over the church". The formation of the canon was in some ways beneficial, in some ways a disaster

for the church, for, while inhibiting the unhealthy proliferation of apocryphal gospels, by the same token it turned
Christianity slowly but surely into the religion of a book,
and in doing so posed questions (at Trent for example)
about the relationship between the Bible, the teaching and
tradition of the church and the magisterium. These questions
are still with us and because of the way they are asked any
answer is bound to appear either one-sided or a compromise
solution.

BUT if the content of the New Testament took at least
three centuries to be fixed neither was its sense abundantly
clear. Ignatius of Antioch and Clement of Rome quote the
gospels, not as some inspired source, but simply as witnesses to the life and teaching of Christ. One would hardly
conclude simply from reading 1 Clement that the quotations
from the words of Jesus that abound in it, presuppose an
attitude to the canonical Gospels as in any sense a book
apart. We know too little about the date and the mode of
the mysterious process of their reception by the church to
be able to say at what date the gospels are quoted with the
sort of authority that later ages have given to them. By
the last quarter of the second century, as we have seen, a
certain consensus was beginning to emerge and the first
commentaries on the New Testament by orthodox writers that
survive, from the genius of Origen, date from shortly
before the middle of the third century.

But even this mark of reverence for the text did not
originate within the orthodox community. We know from the

great commentary of Origen on St John that he was not the
first on the scene. He quotes, largely, it must be admitted, for hostile purposes, an earlier (c. 160) commentary
on the same gospel by Heracleon the disciple of the
archnostic Valentinus. But though officially hostile to
the methods and views of Heracleon, Origen allowed himself
to be influenced by the very same method of interpretation
whose results he deplored, the allegorical method. Starting from the negative conviction that nothing in Scripture
is unworthy of God and the positive one that everything
speaks to us of Christ, he proceeded to give an interpretation of the gospel, which, unless we quite misread the nature
of the early third century church, must have been at the
same time both stimulating and profoundly disturbing. The
simple message of the gospel became in his capable hands a
cryptogram for profound doctrinal and spiritual truths. But
what must be emphasised about the whole of his work is this:
He thought of himself as being in all respects the interpreter of the inspired Word of God. His profound love for
Scripture is manifest in the vast amount of his scriptural
writings that survive. Only his Contra Celsum and a few
minor dialogues cannot be described as profoundly scriptural.
We may be inclined to feel that his overt love for the Word
of God masks in reality a radically philosophical spirit;
but it should be remembered in the first place that even
our ability to disagree with him is itself a proof that the
words of Scripture do not easily render up a clear and
obvious sense. Again, some of the issues on which we feel

that he has erred are not issues on which Scripture has an answer to offer.

Finally the creeds were creations of the future and were regarded by some contemporaries (and by later writers) as having expressed themselves in language, at any rate, that could not be paralleled in the New Testament, e.g., *homousios*. In other words, it is not really because Scripture is self-sufficient or self-explanatory that we feel unhappy with Origen's approach. It may be that his whole method of interpreting Scripture allegorically is misconceived. Yet such a conclusion assumes that more modern techniques are superior, and this latter proposition is certainly not one for which the New Testament provides a shred of evidence.

The gradual reception of the canon within the church did not lead to the consensus on doctrinal issues that might have been expected. This is hardly surprising. The New Testament is neither in fact nor in intention a doctrinal handbook. It embodies indeed certain views about the person and work of Jesus, but it is too diffuse in manner and too moral in tone to adapt itself easily to a purpose for which its authors had never intended it, a short summary of the main tenets of the faith. The search for a creation of short and compendious summaries of the faith is a natural, and as far as our evidence allows us to decide, an ancient practice. That from earliest times there did exist clear and simple summaries of *"credenda"* is evident from the New Testament itself (e.g., Phil 2:5-11; 1 Cor 15). Nor did this process stop with the death of the last apostle. Simple summaries of doctrine, *regulae fidei* as they came to be called, are found in the Demonstration of Irenaeus. Chapter 6 of this seems to presuppose an already existing credal structure.

> And this is the drawing up of the faith, the foundation of the building, and the consolidation of a way of life. God the Father, uncreated, beyond grasp, invisible, one God the maker of all; this is the first and foremost article of faith. But the second article is the word of God, the Son of God, Christ Jesus our Lord. . .and the third article is the Holy Spirit, through whom the prophets prophesied.

The elaboration and philosophical character of the passage mark it out from the simpler formulations of the New Testament, but as a key to the basic teaching of the New Testament about the threefold name and nature of God, that it implies it is accurate; and at the same time it stands as an invaluable witness to the desire of the church in pre-canonical days to sum up in a convenient form the central message of the faith.

By the end of the third century and the beginning of the fourth a consensus had been arrived at about the central texts of the New Testament, but unfortunately this "canonical" consensus did not bring with it any consensus about the nature of the central articles of the Christian faith, above all, the relation of the Son to the Father. Sabellians, Origenists, Adoptionists, and Arians fought among themselves on this crucial question. All of them appealed to Scripture, but in this matter Scripture did not appear to speak with a clear and undivided voice. Scripture was neither all sufficient nor self explanatory. This is not the place to attempt

an analysis of the various motives, soteriological, theological or philosophical, which may have led to the first
ecumenical council at Nicaea in 325. What is quite clear
from our surviving documents is that both Arius and his
opponents regarded the canon of the New Testament as their
ally and to it they appealed. The same story is true of
the next three ecumenical councils. The councils themselves
and the quarrels they intended, alas often unsuccessfully,
to reconcile quoted Scripture and claimed to depend on it,
but the fact remains that their own deliberations were not
only necessary for the settling of the disputes but also
themselves entered into the fabric of the Christian faith.
So, for example, the Council of Chalcedon (451) begins its
acts by quoting the creed of the 150 fathers of Constantinople and then proposes its own formula for solving the
Christological debate about the nature of the person of
Christ. The year 451 is over half a century after the
Council of Carthage of 397, yet there is still no suggestion
that the canon, uninterpreted by the church, was of itself
adequate to resolve the dogmatic debate. This is not, of
course, to say that the tradition of the church as it appears in conciliar decrees acts independently of or over
against the word of Scripture. I hardly think that the
interrelation of the two was to the early church a problem.
Both were important and inseparable moments in the stream
of revelation that came from and referred to Christ. As in
Irenaeus (compare Adv. Haer. iii. 1; 3) so too in the later
fathers Scripture, tradition (that is either Scripture

234

interpreted by exegesis or creed, or independent facts) and the authority of the church all taken together formed a sort of triple cord. It was only with Martin Luther's appeal to *scriptura sola* as the criterion for belief that its relation to tradition had to be clarified. Our present embarrassment is a direct result of the appeal of the Reformers to this principle.

CONCLUSION

1. In a large sense tradition includes all that has been handed down to us about the life and meaning of Jesus. In this understanding of the word, it includes Scripture and is not something over against it. In a narrow sense, as distinct, that is, from Scripture, it is limited to all the explanations, the definitions of the church and other information that has been handed down. It is in this latter sense unfortunately that the term is usually understood and has appeared to some to denote a separate source of information about the *credenda* of the church. I have tried to suggest that the attempt to keep the two components in watertight compartments is historically unsound and theologically undesirable.

2. The existence of the New Testament presupposes both the existence of the church and of antecedent tradition about Christ. To put the matter in a slightly different light, the church created the New Testament, the New Testament did not create the church. Furthermore the establishment of the canon took some considerable time and was the result of

a number of factors, above all, the growth of gnosticism.
It was never ever a question of the church simply endorsing
certain books which were of self evident authenticity,
though it was partly that. Rather it was a process, a
combined one, of both accepting and establishing at the
same time. It was the act of recognition conferred on already worthwhile books, the stamp of genuineness. They
became canonical not solely because they were accepted, nor
solely because of some inherent quality that they possessed,
but for both reasons.

3. If the New Testament canon is not totally self-
justifying, neither is it totally self-explanatory. The
meaning of the text whether in its entirety or in its
separate parts is not clear and has been the subject of
considerable debate from earliest dates. For example,
which of the following apparently contradictory texts is
to be regarded as normative for Christian belief about the
person of Jesus? "Why do you call me good? No one is good
but God alone" (Mk 10:18 and parallels); or, "I and the
Father are one" (Jn 10:30). Both purport to be dominical
sayings. The former suggests what the latter denies, the
inferiority of the Son to the Father. The Scripture itself
does not present us with a principle of decision; the scope,
drift or sense of Scripture needs to be filled out by a
quasi-external supplement, the tradition and authority of
the church. Difficulties such as these bring home a truth
that scarcely needs reiterating, that the all sufficiency
of Scripture is not a scriptural doctrine, and on most

occasions Scripture is incapable of supplying an answer to

the question it is asked. While on this subject it seems

appropriate to conclude with some words of Newman from the

first chapter of the Apologia.

> He (the Provost of Oriel, Dr Hawkins) lays down a
> proposition, self-evident as soon as stated, to those
> who have at all examined the structure of Scripture,
> viz. that the sacred text was never intended to teach
> doctrine, but only to prove it, and that, if we would
> learn doctrine, we must have recourse to the formu-
> laries of the Church; for instance to the Cathechism,
> and to the Creeds.

The creeds and non-scriptural traditions of the church,

far from being a rival to the Bible, are rather its

complement and backbone.

Theological Paper

THE TIES THAT DIVIDE
by
Rev Howard M. Ervin

In this gathering where community relationships are
so frequently stressed, this word of introduction may well
be in order, for it will but underscore the paradox of my
own position. If God has called you to community, let it
be said that I honor that calling. Some however are not
called to community but to a solitary pilgrimage. Nor
should the word solitary as I intend it here be construed
to mean isolation, or worse an egocentric individualism.
I have no kingdom to build, save His kingdom.

The Church historically has recognized the validity
of the calling of both the anchorite and the cenobite, the
solitariness of the dessert and the concord of community.
I speak metaphorically of course, Both are valid as they
serve the Kingdom of God. Despite fruitful human relationships over the years, my own interior, spiritual pilgrimage
has been and still remains essentially a solitary one, and
I choose to see in this a divine calling, not an expression
of self-sufficiency. I shrink from identifying with the
metaphore, but the voice in the wilderness announced the
community of the New Covenant, and subsequently lost his head.

Paradoxically, however, it was in this interior solitariness that I heard and responded to another calling, viz., the urgency of the high priestly prayer of our Lord Jesus "that (we) may become perfectly one" (Jn 17:23). These words are the sole justification, if there is need for justification, for this presentation. Because of an ecstatic confrontation with the Holy Spirit in the St Louis airport a number of years ago - an experience already related at another time - my commitment to the Great High Priestly prayer of Jesus is both a theological commitment and an existential imperative. I repeat, it is theological and existential in the patristic understanding that theology is more than the manipulation of intellectual constructs for, it is not theology until it is prayed.

It is an abiding conviction that the Holy Spirit will implement the four-fold petition of Jesus, (Jn 17) to the degree that we are willing to face the hard questions that divide us. Divine initiative is conditioned by human response to implement His purposes. I am pragmatic enough to believe that there are no answers to unasked questions. If then we truly seek answers, we must accept the risk of asking hard questions, abrasive questions, even explosive questions. Unless we are prepared to face without defensiveness and hostility the questions posed by the brokenness of Christ's body the Church, the most we can hope for is a concord based upon the lowest common denominator of pious intention.

Since we cannot escape our history I purpose to surface

several of the substantive questions that historically constitute serious stumbling blocks in ecumenism. The treatment will be summary though I trust not superficial. It
is my intention to surface them as topics for more discursive reflection, and as representative of a number of other
equally thorny problems.

The first of these questions relates to the intra-mural
triumphalism that has characterized the Church since its
inception. Which one of our various communions is the one
true New Testament Church? If we are loyal to our denominational distinctives, we must respond in chorus: "Mine, of
course." In its beginnings, the rule of faith developed in
conflict with the gnostic sects within the Catholic and
Orthodox fold. Each schism since within the body politic
and ecclesiological has justified its existence as the one
authentic alternative in the conflict between truth and
error, that is to say the one true expression of the Church.
Thus the true source of our arrogant and self-righteous pretensions, in the corrupted ego of fallen man, is legitimized
as "contending for the faith once for all delivered." My
remarks are not intended to gloss the reality of the subversion of the faith by error, rather they are intended
to show that in reality much of our contending is simply a
carnal contentiousness that further fragments the body of
Christ. Are not the rival contentions that each communion
constitutes the one true church simply an expression of
carnality rather than spirituality? Thus indeed does the
apostle Paul characterize the end (1 Cor 3:1).

One lamentable consequence of this malaise that afflicts all of our denominations is the perversion of evangelism into proselytism. Is it too sweeping a judgment to say that most of the statistics on church growth result from the shuffling of denominational labels rather than evangelism? Is there perhaps an echo of our Lord's judgment that we, like the Pharisees, compass land and sea to make one Methodist a Baptist, or one Episcopalian a Presbyterian, or.... I well remember the casual remark of a Jewish professor before a mixed group of Jewish and Christian scholars. In response to a question about Christian evangelism, he said quite simply: "Christians do not evangelize, they proselytize one another."

Is it not time to repent of our carnal sense of superiority that predicates authentic identity upon a selective use of history, dogma, culture or usage, rather than upon an incarnational encounter with Jesus Christ? If I understand what Paul is saying (1 Cor 12:13), we do not join the Church, rather "in the Spirit we are baptized into one body," the Church.

The second question, I propose that we address is the question of the source and exercise of authority. At the risk of over simplification, I offer this schematic.

The sources of authority, at least since the Reformation are commonly regarded as (1) papal authority, (2) conciliar authority, (3) *sola scriptura*. There are strengths in each that, emphasized to the exclusion or near exclusion of the others in popular understanding, contribute to the fragmentation of the Church.

For the average Protestant who thinks about it, papal authority is the apex of a monolithic structure that is administratively effective but at the expense of private conscience and individual freedom. Negatively concentration of power brings unconscionable abuses of authority. Correct me if my memory fails me. Was it not Lord Acton who reported to have said that "power corrupts, and absolute power corrupts absolutely?" Whether true or false, such is the understanding of papal authority entertained as law and gospel by many Protestants. Perhaps mutual trust and love will enable this generation to face the accumulated debris of past conflicts, and together ask whether Jesus ever intended a _primacy_ of _love_. Only the miracle of _mutual_ repentance, forgiveness and trust can provide a context in which this question can be asked without the acrimonious recriminations of past encounters.

Conciliar authority is more readily entertained over a wider spectrum of Protestants than papal authority, though not all councils are regarded as of equal authority. For some only the council of Nicaea is binding (Nestorians). For others Chalcedon marks a water shed in the history of the Church (Monophysites), while for others the seven so-called ecumenical councils are binding for faith and practice. Even those groups who stem from the Radical Reformers will accept the Christological and Trinitarian formulae of the councils while rejecting their pretensions to bind faith and practice to a creedal rule of faith. For these latter, conciliar authority is suspect as pre-

242

empting the right of private judgment where matters of faith
and life are at issue. They are seen as introducing rigor
mortis into the theological task confronted by each new
generation. For such the pneumatic takes precedence over
the conciliar. The danger in denigrating the past wisdom
of the Church, however, is that old heresies, weighted and
found wanting in the past, are resurrected as new revelation.
How else can one explain the subversion of charismatic
groups by Arain and adoptionist Christologies and Sabellian
Modalism?

The question here that presses for an answer is simply
whether or not truth collegially, affirmed in the past, can
form the basis for mutual faith and practice today. And
furthermore, whether the ephemeral social, political
ecclesiastic and ethnic concerns of the past even though
collegially sanctioned, can be re-evaluated and detached
from the irreducible deposit of faith.

The question of authority that pressed upon the
Reformers was resolved by the principle of *sola scriptura*.
This is understood and affirmed in my own Baptist communion
under the following rubric: "The Bible in the Old Testament our only and sufficient rule of faith and practice."
The strength of this position is it's unqualified endorsement of Scripture as the fountain of Christian faith and
practice. The power of Scripture, thus released in the
lives of individuals, to reform and transform individuals
and society bears witness to its vitality at the grass
roots level. But as so frequently happens, its strength

is also its weakness. For the right of private judgment
coupled with the ultimate and absolute authority of the
Scriptures has accelerated the fragmentation of the Church
to an alarming degree. In the final analysis, however, it
is not Scripture that possesses final authority, but the
"private interpretations" of the individual that are
authoritative.

Perhaps the most serious weakness here is the failure
to recognize that Scripture's own history is essential to
an understanding of Scripture. When we detach the Scriptures
from their own history, we inevitably impose our personal
histories upon them. In turn these private histories impose
new social, cultural, political and ecclesiological criteria
for the interpretation of Scripture. Lacking an exegetical
and hermeneutical consenses further fragmentation of the
"one body" results.

The questions then of authority is one referred to by
our Catholic brethren under the rubric Magisterium. Who then
determines ultimate questions of faith and practice? May I
hazard a suggestion as to a starting point for a discussion
of this question. I refer to your attention Ac 15:28,22.
A perusal of the context will make clear why I choose to
invert the literary sequence in favor of what I conceive to
be their spiritual sequence. These verses represent the
summation of the deliverations of the first Jerusalem
council viz., "For it has seemed good to the Holy Spirit
and to us..." (v 28). Then it seemed good to the apostles
and the elders with the whole church..." (v 22). The

244

church then is neither an autocracy nor a democracy, it is a _pneumatocracy_. The authenticity of the Spirit's guidance is validated by the twin principles of collegiality and consensus.

Collegial consultation among responsible leaders ratified by the consensus of the whole community are twin principles for discerning the direction of the Spirit's inspiration. They provide the checks and balances conducive to wholesome Church relationships. Collegiality without consensus may all too easily degenerate into a despotism, while consensus without collegiality is constantly threatened by the irrationality of anarchism.

At no other time and place is the brokenness of Christ's Body, His Church, more evident than at "the Lord's table." Even in our ecumenical gatherings, when it seems in order to celebrate the Christian mysteries--the death, the resurrection, and the return of Jesus Christ--we gather at separate altar-tables while paradoxically affirming our unity in Christ. I venture to say that most Christians would stoutly affirm that our divergent views of the Holy Communion views that in themselves preclude inter-communion--are sanctioned by inerrant Scripture and tradition, but are they?

For the purpose of this discussion, I shall reduce to two, the divergent views of the Communion Service, and at the same time by-pass the nuances that these evoke. The two may be described historically as (1) trans-substantiation, the Catholic view, and (2) symbolic, in general a Protestant view. Remember that I relegate to more discursive discussions

the various nuances these may imply. It is of the essence
of the question to inquire into the origins of these views.
Again our discussion must needs be summary although I trust
not inaccurate for that reason.

Perhaps a case may be made for the origin of the view
of transubstantiation in the folk religious expression or
earlier centuries as a literal understanding of the words
of our Lord, viz., "this is my body, this is my blood."
One may wonder to what degree, if any, the literalism
associated with a folk religious expression of the words of
institution provided polemic ammunition for the pagan ad-
versaries of the early Church who accused the Christians of
cannibalism. However, what does seem clear is that the
scholastic formulation of this dogma at the Council of
Trent was phrased in Aristolian categories. In an
Aristotelian metaphsic, there is no super-sensory realm of
metaphysical ideas as there is in Platonism. The Aristotelian philosopher worked with the two categories of substance and accidents. That is to say, each object consisted
of two elements, a universal category that defined its
identity--e.g., chairness, bookness, etc.; and the physical
components, i.e., its accidents, that made it concrete.
Applied to the communion, or eucharist, this implied that
the metaphysical substance--i.e., breadness and wineness
must have visible accidents, i.e., color, weight, smell
hence transubstantiation.

The symbolic view of the communion elements proceeds
from a different philosophical premise, viz., the Platonic.

Here the _reality_ subsists in a non-sensory realm of ideas. It is concretized through an infinite series of gradations, in each gradually acquiring a greater degree of concreteness until it is finally concretized in the object itself. The reality then is seen as super-sensory and its concretized representation only as a symbol of this metaphysical reality.

Historically the Platonic affinites of the symbolic view of the communion elements were both recognized and condemned wherever in antiquity a symbolic view emerged, e.g., the repeated condemnation of the Messalian's--an anti-sacramental monastic sect of the early centuries of Christianity.

The symbolic or Platonic view of the communion seems to have emerged again in the 16th century in the writings of a Dutch lawyer Cornelius Hone (or Honius). According to one account he wrote a letter to Martin Luther at some time either before or during the Markburg colloquies between Luther and Ulrich Zwingli, the Swiss reformer. In it he set forth a symbolic interpretation of the words of institution at the Last Supper. The letter is reported to have fallen into the hands of the Swiss reformer, Zwingli, who was in addition a Renaissance rationalist, and seems to have been the catalyst that disposed him in favor of the symbolic view. Ever since the Reformation, at any rate, the symbolic view is closely identified with the name of Zwingli.

At issue here is whether Christ is mystically present in the Eucharistic meal (Real Presence), or whether it is a memorial of the Last Supper symbolically re-enacted. Just in passing is it amiss to ask whether He who changed water into wine, still has power, in a manner not described, to change wine into His blood and bread into His body? Or does the symbolic view demythologize the miracle of Real Presence? Perhaps an older tradition can be of help here when it affirms that Christ is truly present in the eucharistic elements, but it is a mystery that defies definition or interpretation, a view that is more consistent with Scripture than the philosophical views discussed above.

The point that we raise here is whether our divisions over the nature of the communion rite are biblical or philosophical.

The most controversial stumbling block to ecumenism may yet prove to be a christological question: Who is Jesus? The angel Gabriel declared him to be "the Son of God" (Lk 1:35). Paradoxically, the thorniest question the Annunciation raises for us is not the divine paternity of Jesus, but the human maternity of the Son of God. Thus the former question has unsuspected nuances, e.g., Whose mother is Mary? For the identity of the Son is as much contingent upon His human maternity as upon His divine paternity.

To raise the question is to draw again ancient battle lines, and to marshall antiquated theological artillery. To the average Protestant, nurtured on Reformation and post Reformation polemics, the popular Catholic cult of Mary is an idolatrous worship of the creature rather than the Creator. Nor is the charge entirely without substance. To

248

the popular mind even the florid titles ascribed to Mary, e.g., co-Redemptrix etc., undoubtedly have so compounded the mystery of the Incarnation that in popular devotion the veneration offered to the mother has transgressed the worship due to the Son. When this occurs the authenticity of the Incarnation itself is prejudiced.

On the other hand, to his Catholic counterpart, steeped in the apologetics of the counter Reformation, the Protestant is at best guilty of gross insensitivity to the incarnational significance of Mary's role, and at worst vulnerable to the charge of Nestorianism. As the Protestant sees the authenticity of the Incarnation prejudiced by what he perceives as divine prerogatives attributed to Mary, so too his Catholic counterpart also sees the Incarnation denigrated by what he interprets as a cyrpo-Nestorianism, i.e., the rejection of the divine maternity of the mother. The catch phrase here is the title "Mother of God." The phrase itself has been controversial since the fourth century, and is misleading depending upon one's prior biases. However, all disputants must reckon with this fact that the Scriptures do not even imply, nor could they, that Mary is God, the Mother. Such a claim would also destroy the authenticity of the Incarnation, for then Jesus would no longer be bone of our bone, and flesh of our flesh. A demi-god, perhaps. Our Divine-human redeemer, never, for the gulf between God and man would remain an unbridgable chasm.

At no point does one despair of rational and objective consideration of problems cited as of this one. No issue is calculated to generate more heat than light than the Christological implications in the Virgin Birth, perhaps one ought to add also Virgin Conception of Jesus Christ. If I may be pardoned a personal reminiscence. A certain sense of futility still grips me as I recall one such encounter before a substantial assembly of charismatics. Perhaps unwisely, albeit honestly, in that setting the question was addressed to the speaker from the participants: "How does one understand Mary's role?" The answer can only be understood as a rebuttal to what the speaker must have sensed was a theological time-bomb. The answer came like a verbal bludgeon: "Mary bore the humanity of Jesus." And on that crypto-Nestorian note further discussion was foreclosed. Naive and lacking in theological sophistication though this rebuttal may be, it is a moot question to what degree a crypto-Nestorianism has contributed to the secular humanism that has dominated liberal/modernistic christologies, a secularized humanism that denies deity to Jesus Christ.

The conflict is an old one. Nestorius, patriarch of Constantinople in the fifth century, took issue with the term *Theotokos* by which the patristic Church sought to safeguard the unity of person in face of the duality of natures in Jesus Christ. What Nestorius objected to, and which still continues as a common misunderstanding, is the idea that a mere mortal could be the mother of the imcommensurable, the eternal Father. But apparently that is not what

was meant by the term. What apparently was intended was a
definition of Mary's role as mother of God in His incarnation. Luke 1:35 says clearly that she is the mother of "the
Son of God." What the term *Theotokos* affirms is that the
Son of God is also God, the Son. Within the historical context this is more clearly refined, for the patristic tradition held firmly to a distinction between *latreia* and
proskunēsis. The former is worship offered only to God,
while the latter represents the homage which may be offered
even to another Christian who through divine grace becomes
a channel of grace to others.

The issues at stake in the clash between the Alexan-
drian and Antiochian christologies (of which Nestorius was
representative in the fifth century) are summarized by John
Meyendorff. He notes that the Antiochian theologians

> ...emphasize the full humanity of the historical
> Jesus, they understand this humanity not merely as
> distinct from the divinity, but as "autonomous" and
> personalized. If "defied," Jesus could no longer be
> truly man; he must simply be the son of Mary if he is
> to be ignorant, to suffer and die. It is precisely
> this understanding of humanity as autonomous which
> has attracted the sympathies of modern Western
> theologians toward the Antiochians, but which provoked
> the emergence of Nestorianism and the clash with
> Alexandria (<u>Byzantine</u> Theology, pp. 32,33).

In other words, to insist on the autonomous, person-
alized humanity of Jesus is to divide the person of Jesus.
It is then not a matter of distinguishing a divine nature
and a human nature in one hypostatic union, rather the very
person of Jesus is sundered His diety from His humanity.

While the problem is a serious one for Protestant/
Catholic ecumenical dialogue, it is especially acute for

the charismatic/Pentecostal movement. Ancient heresies
under the guise of new revelation have arisen to plague the
charismatic movement. With Nestorian, Arian and Gnostic
christologies, not to mention Pelagianism and Sabellian
modalism, claiming pneumatic authentication among charismatic groups, the whole question of the Incarnation becomes
an urgent agenda item. The term *Theotokos* was a powerful
weapon against heresies in the theological arsenal of the
patristic Church. The renaissance of ancient heresies in
our midst argues for a reassessment of its theological
significance as a defense against heresies, and a reaffirma-
tion of the integrity of the Incarnation.

One final item remains for the present agenda. This
perhaps should have been included under the section on
authority since it concerns the relative authority of
Scripture and tradition. However, the ramifications of the
problem involved, biblically, theologically, and historically
prompt a separate notice. We have already observed that the
question of ultimate authority in faith and life which
pressed upon the sixteenth century Reformers was resolved
by the principle of *sola scriptura*. In the context of
Reformation and Counter-Reformation polemics, the relation
of Scripture and tradition was polarized. The both/and of
the Catholic apologetic, i.e., Scripture and tradition, was
countered by the Reformation principle of Scripture and
Scripture alone as the ultimate authority in the rule of
faith.

It may be an oversimplification of complex theological

issues, but the following series of Reformation antitheses serves to highlight the serious consequences of this polarization. Scripture alone, not tradition. Faith alone, not sacraments. Christ alone, not the Church. Grace alone, not works. Whether or not this is a generalization that distorts the complexities of the issues involved is not our immediate concern. What is of practical consequence for the ecumenical dialogue is the mutual intransigence coupled with the bitter animosities that have marred the life and witness of the Church to the world in the intervening centuries. What must be apparent to all is that a revival of the acrimonious debates the past are both counter productive and an exercise in futility.

In addressing a subject so exhaustively debated in the past, I am not naive enough to think that I have anything to say that has not already been said. However, perhaps it is not too much to hope for that, in an irenic context, one may hope to contribute to fresh initiatives at reconciliation.

It is commonly recognized that oral tradition is prior to written tradition, i.e., Scripture, and is quantitatively larger than the written tradition (cf. Jn 20:30; 21:25). However, what is not commonly recognized is that a process of selection at work in editing and reducing the oral tradition to the written tradition necessarily involves evaluative judgments on the part of the author. The value judgments which dictate the selection of one part over another also implies some relative precedence of the written portions over the oral. If furthermore, the author is an apostle, as is the case with the New Testament documents, this invests the written tradition with an apostolic precedence over the oral tradition. This is not to denigrate the role and importance of the oral tradition in the formation of the apostolic community, but it does suggest that the relative importance of the written tradition to the oral tradition is implied in the apostolic editing of the oral tradition. Granted that the written tradition was a response to the day to day needs of the various Christian communities, the fact remains that a process of selection involving value judgments is at work in the committing of the oral tradition to writing. Although the local, time conditioned concerns of the early Church did affect the selection process, the universal themes of the Gospel are the primary concerns dictating the content of the written tradition. What we are at pains to point out here, lest it be overlooked in the general discussion, is that both the oral tradition and the written tradition, i.e., Scripture, are indivisible parts of an organic whole, Tradition. The question at issue is their relative importance for the rule of faith.

The subsequent development of patristic tradition, the second stage in the development of tradition, relies upon both oral and written tradition, but in the process of development increasing emphasis is placed on the interpretation and application of the written tradition. There is a precedent for this in the development of the *misvoth*

zeqēnim, the "tradition of the elders" among the Jews.
Thus the development of patristic traditions among both
Jews and Christians tends to identify tradition with the
hermeneutical and exegetical efforts of each.

If, however, the subsequent development of tradition
is a result of reflection on, and application of the written tradition to questions of faith and practice, this does
not negate the importance of the oral tradition. The continuity with the past of a living ecclesial tradition is
critical for the exposition of the Scriptures. The importance of this living ecclesial tradition for the development of patristic tradition can be illustrated from the
Christological controversies of the early centuries. If,
for example, the Gnostics had succeeded in subverting the
Church to a docetic Christ, the whole moral stance of
Christianity in the world would have been drastically
altered either in the direction of unbridled libertinism,
or of a metaphysical asceticism. The illustration is all the
more germane to the present subject, since both sides
appealed to written tradition. The fact that the Gnostics
had produced their own corpus of written tradition is *de
facto* evidence of the recognized importance of the written
tradition. On the side of the orthodox, however, was the
added consciousness of its identity with a living ecclesial
tradition of apostolic ministry. As I have written elsewhere, "A viable hermeneutic must deal responsibly with the
apostolic witness of Scripture in terms of apostolic experience, and in continuity with the Church's apostolic

traditions" ("Hermeneutics: A Pentecostal Option," presented at the Roman Catholic/Pentecostal Dialogue, Rome,
1979).

Nowhere is the importance of a living ecclesial
tradition more painfully evident by its absence than in
the numerous sectarian interpretations of Scripture, many
of which are not only contradictory but mutally exclusive.
Failure to recognize the organic relationship of Scripture
and tradition has contributed to this sorrowful fragmentation of the Christian community.

The debate over the role of Scripture and tradition
is, as we have suggested, endemic to the very process of
reducing the oral tradition to a written corpus. The word
"tradition" *(Paradosis)* is used some thirteen times in the
New Testament.[1] It is used in three senses. First, it is
used of the oral teaching of the Jewish elders from Moses
on, i.e., the *misovt zeqēnim*, "the tradition of the elders."
It was against the externalism and formalism fostered by
these "traditions of the elders" that Jesus leveled His
strongest condemnations. In this case the oral Torah had
taken precedence over the written.

Secondly, the term "tradition" is used by Paul of his
Christian teaching which he shared with the churches of
Corinth and Thessalonica (1 Cor 11:2; 2 Thes 2:15; 3:6).
It is interesting to note that though conscious of his own
inspiration, he equated his instruction with tradition

---

[1]Mt 15:2,3,6; Mk 7:3,5,8,9,13; 1 Cor 11:2; Gal 1:14;
Col 2:8; 2 Thes 2:15; 3:6.

(paradosis) rather than Torah (Scripture). Within the
Jewish consciousness of the "tradition of the elders," this
must say something to us of his sense of apostolic
authority with which he delivered his Christian "traditions."
Used in the singular (2 Thes 3:6), "tradition" refers to a
corpus of instruction delivered to the Thessalonian Christians. In the plural (1 Cor 11:2; 2 Thes 2:15), it refers
to the instruction given separately to these same churches.

The third use, "the traditions of men" (Col 2:8),
refers to merely human tradition that is apparently more
than just Jewish tradition. Contextually, Paul inveighs
against "philosophy and empty deceit" as human tradition,
apparently the human wisdom both philosophical and religious
that pervaded the whole of Graeco-Roman culture.

It is use of tradition in the second sense that bears
more directly upon the question of Scripture and tradition
in the rule of faith. The development of both Jewish and
Christian traditions bear a marked resemblance. Both derive
from truth revealed orally and subsequently committed to
writing. Historically, the *Torah sebaal peh*, "the Torah
that came by mouth," developed out of the forensic study of
the Scriptures. The forces of custom and the changing needs
of daily life required new definitions, interpretations and
applications of the written Torah. These in time became
the *halakot*, i.e., rules governing the normal walk (Hebrew:
Halak, walk) of life. These were later compiled in the
Mishnah and Gemara, a supplement to the Mishnah. Paren-
thetically, Paul's use of the expression "walk" used several

times in his epistle to the Ephesians suggests the possibility of an incipient corpus of Christian *halakot*.

Another category, the *haggadot*, (Hebrew: *higid*, show,
tell) paralleled the *halakot* in their concern for a life
conformed to both the oral and the written Torah. In the
case of the later, however, the substance of instruction
was drawn from the narratives of Scripture. The lessons of
life were taught by way of principle and examples related
in the story-teller's art.

In time the *halakot* acquired an authority and influence equal to, if not surpassing, the written Torah. The
development of post-apostolic tradition in the Church shows
a close affinity to the method by which the Jewish tradition developed. The common denominator in the development
of both Jewish and Christian tradition is a response to the
felt needs of the community to interpret and to apply the
written tradition to changing life situations. Both pass
from an oral to a written stage that gradually acquires by
force of custom the authority and influence of the written
tradition from which they derive.

Although there are similarities between the processes
of development in Jewish and Christian tradition, including
the force of an ecclesial tradition, there are significant
differences. In Judaism the oral Torah is essentially the
memory of past words formulated with great dialectical
skill, while, according to the promise of Jesus, tradition
is the life of the Spirit in the Church illuminating and
communicating truth anew. "But the Counselor, the Holy

Spirit, whom the Father will send in my name, he will teach you all things, and bring to your remembrance all that I have said to you.... When the Spirit of truth comes, he will guide you into all the truth" (Jn 14:26; 16:13).

In summation, if tradition is viewed only as the memory of past words, there seems little hope of resolving the deadlock inherited from the Reformation. On the other hand, if tradition is viewed dynamically as the life of the Spirit in the Church, as Jesus promised, new possibilities and new questions arise. It is possible then to see tradition in its several levels, oral and written, apostolic and ecclesiastical as the ongoing ministry of the Spirit to the Church. However, the written tradition (i.e., Scripture) does take precedence by virtue of its apostolic origins, while tradition as hermeneutic must yield primacy to the very Scriptures it expounds. Both Scripture and tradition as integral facets of one organic Tradition, in turn co-inhere in a living ecclesial tradition, otherwise every sectarian, even cultic, aberration in the interpretation of Scripture is equally authentic. In speaking of a living ecclesial tradition, we do not equate this with a single ecclesiastical structure, but see it rather as an acknowledgment of the pneumatic dimension to Tradition in which the entire Christian *ekklēsia* participates. This is broad enough to include the sectarian but not the cultic.

In relation to the written tradition (i.e., Scripture), apostolicity is critical for the authority of the written tradition vis a vis the oral tradition. It is at this

point in the discussion, that apostolicity in relationship
to a living ecclesial tradition becomes the issue. For
example, Paul could say to the Thessalonians, fully conscious
of his apostolic authority, "stand firm and hold to the
traditions which you were taught by us, either by word of
mouth or by letter" (2:15). In a modern context, the question that presents itself is this: To what degree, if any,
can apostolic authority be claimed for subsequent formulations of traditions? Is apostolic succession ecclesiastical,
or pneumatic, or both? Regardless of how it is defined, can
apostolic tradition be formulated and expressed apart from
collegiality and consensus as these are inspired by the
Holy Spirit? In fine, is the apostolicity of a living
ecclesial tradition possible apart from an ecumenical consensus? It is upon the answers to these questions that the
question of the authority of tradition rests.

ROMAN CATHOLIC/PENTECOSTAL DIALOGUE
13-17 October 1980 - Venice

Agreed Account

Introduction

At the 1980 meeting of the Roman Catholic/Pentecostal
Dialogue, October 13-17 in Venice, special attention was
given to two broad subjects, community and tradition.

Representing the Pentecostals, the Rev Richard B.
Foth gave a paper entitled "The Church as a Worshiping
Community." This paper described the classical Pentecostal
community at worship. On the Roman Catholic side, the
Rev Pierre Duprey followed with a paper on "The Church
as Communion." This contained a discussion on the essential components of the Roman Catholic church on the level
of Christian community. Dr Howard M. Ervin, representing
the Pentecostals, presented a paper entitled "The Ties
that Divide" dealing primarily with tradition as understood
by the Pentecostals. Fr Anthony Meredith, SJ, representing the Roman Catholics, presented a paper on the subject,
"The Place of Tradition in Scripture and in the Early
Fathers." The paper articulated the Roman Catholic understanding of the role of tradition in shaping the faith of
the Roman Catholic church.

I. THE CHURCH AS A WORSHIPING COMMUNITY

A. Ordinance and Sacrament

Both Pentecostals and Roman Catholics celebrate the Lord's Table, but with notable differences in doctrine and practice. Roman Catholics regard the Eucharist as a sacramental memorial, in the biblical sense of the word *anamnesis*, which, by God's power, makes Jesus present in His death and resurrection and becomes for the Christian life a privileged means of grace. The Eucharist, therefore, is central to Roman Catholic worship and is celebrated frequently, even daily. Among Pentecostals the Lord's Table does not hold an equally predominat place in their life of worship. All Pentecostals celebrate the Lord's Table as an ordinance in obedience to the command of the Lord, but many experience this memorial to be more than a reminder of Jesus' death and resurrection considering it also a means of grace.

B. Open and Closed Communion

The Lord's Table occasions another difference between Pentecostals and Roman Catholics. Generally Pentecostals practice "open" communion, i.e., anyone may participate in the Lord's Table provided that they acknowledge the Lordship of Christ and have examined their own dispositions (1 Cor 11:28). Roman Catholics, however, normally limit the receiving of communion to those who have the four requisites: 1) Baptism, 2) Roman Catholic faith, 3) full union with the Roman Catholic church, 4) are free from serious sin. This disciplinary ruling flows from and rests on the doctrine that the Eucharist, as the consummate expression of the church's total faith in Christ, should be received only by those who share fully in the life of the Church.

This separation at the Lord's Table is made more painful for Pentecostals by the fact that Roman Catholics whose lives do not conform to the Gospel are seen to receive the Eucharist simply on the basis of their supposed Roman Catholic faith. Though all Roman Catholics admit that this regrettable fact is contrary to Roman Catholic teaching and should be remedied; its reality and continuance does not change the reason why the Roman Catholic church cannot offer communion to non-members.

C. Membership of the Church

Pentecostals require of their members: personal conversion, regular attendance at worship, and participation in the life, leadership and responsibility of the Assembly. In many Pentecostal churches, membership is attributed to one's water baptism by immersion. For membership in the Roman Catholic church three basic elements are required: 1) Baptism, profession of Roman Catholic faith, 3) fellowship with the whole church involving acceptance of the authorities in the church.

Both among Pentecostals and Roman Catholics, members may lose their fellowship in the community. Both excommunicate or disfellowship for severe deviations in doctrine or practice. This penalty of severance from the church is remedial, a reminder of one's guilt before God and of the need for repentance.

D. Ecclesiology

Pentecostals insist on a personal experience with
Jesus Christ as central to their faith, rather than a
sacramental and ecclesial approach to the mediating work of
Christ. Roman Catholics also insist on conversion to the
living God and personal encounter with the living Christ.
For Roman Catholics, the church, its ministry and its
sacraments are acts of Christ which make present and active
the saving power of the Paschal mystery. The Pentecostals
agree that the presence of Christ in worship is assured in
every part of the worshiping community--singing, praying,
testimony, preaching, and the ordinance of baptism and holy
communion and also in all their life. The focus of the
Lord's Table is that of the sacrifice of Christ in His
trial, death, burial, resurrection, ascension, and return.

E. Body of Christ

The local Christian community is linked to other
communities in the Body of Christ. Both Pentecostals and
Roman Catholics agree that a common faith is the basis of
this communion. For Roman Catholics it also requires the
collegial unity of the heads of these communities: Bishops--
under the headship of the Bishop of Rome. Pentecostals
would not attach the same significance to the forms of
organization between churches, and will fellowship with
many autonomous churches. The Roman Catholic church recognizes the mediation of Christ at work in churches which are
not in communion with it--through the Word that is preached
and believed, the sacraments that are celebrated, and the

ministry that is exercised. If it considers that these
gifts are not found in their fullness in a particular church
it does not thereby make any judgement on the actual holiness of the members of that church. It described the members of these churches as brothers within a divided
fellowship.

II. TRADITION AND TRADITIONS

Our views concerning the sacredness and importance of
Holy Scripture allowed us to sense immediately that we had
much more to affirm in one another than to question. Both
sides of the dialogue agreed as to the inspired nature of
both the Old Testament and New Testament, thus giving
Scripture a privileged place in both churches.

The canonicity of the New Testament was agreed upon
in terms of selection and the process of its establishment
by the church. Both Roman Catholics and Pentecostals recognize the role of the church in the composition of the
books of the New Testament and in the formation of the canon
and both acknowledged that the church preceded the written
New Testament. The Pentecostal representatives pointed out
that the church itself was created by the "calling" (election)
of Christ, and formed both by the dominical sayings of Jesus,
and the Messianic interpretation of the "Scriptures of Jesus
Himself" (Lk 24:45 ff.). In this sense, according to Pentecostals, the church itself was formed by the "Word of God."
The church's role as author of the New Testament is then

essentially the transmission, interpretation and application of the salvific message of Jesus Christ Himself. The Catholics in addition emphasized the role of the church as having an authority to recognize and to enunciate doctrine.

Both sides recognized that Scripture is of necessity linked to interpretation. Both agreed that Scriptural content includes itself interpretation; that it requires interpretation; and thus an authentic interpreter. There was significant divergence as to the degree of interpretation within Scripture and the amount of interpretation by the church necessary in order to understand Scripture accurately. Disagreement centered around as to what or who is an authentic interpreter. To the Pentecostal it is the right of private interpretation under the illumination of the Holy Spirit leading to consensus. To the Roman Catholic, it is the church interpreting Scripture as understood by the people of God and discerned by the teaching office of the church. Both Roman Catholics and Pentecostals see interpretative authority as an expression of the activity of the Spirit in the church.

There was an encouraging consensus with regard to the process of discernment in the on-going life of the church. The Roman Catholics affirmed the ministry of discernment by the teaching office of the church and also recognized its existence outside the Roman Catholic church. The sharpest disagreement arose concerning the irreformable character of some of these discernments. The Roman Catholics

concluded that there can be no error when the authority
of the church is fully engaged in annunciating the faith.
The Pentecostals made no such claim.

At the same time there seemed to emerge out of our
differences a sense for the need among Pentecostals for
the strength of the Roman Catholic understanding of corporate and collegial interpretation of Scripture. The Pentecostals, for their part, would like to share with Roman
Catholics their characteristic experience of direct dependence upon the Holy Spirit for illumination and interpretation of Scripture.

A major difference was encountered in our understanding of tradition: by tradition (t1), the Roman Catholic
understands the whole of the Spirit-filled community's
response throughout history to the once-for-all revelation
made by God in Christ Jesus. As such t1 contains both an
active element of handing down by the church, and a passive
one of the material handed down. This material consists
of the varied responses of the believing community. In this
sense tradition (t1) is a continuous process. Within this
greater stream of tradition there can be discerned certain
moments: the first is the inspired Scripture--the New Testament; this is primary and normative. Secondly, and related
imprecisely to it, is tradition (t2). In its passive sense,
tradition (t2) clarifies those elements of Roman Catholic
faith, not clearly or explicitly or unambiguously found in
Scripture. For the Roman Catholics, among these traditions,
those relative to faith are normative, those related to

church practice and discipline are not necessarily normative. Pentecostals would not place the same value upon
tradition as Roman Catholics, unless grounded in the
express witness of Scripture. The Pentecostals, while
acknowledging the accumulation of tradition, would say
that tradition, apart from Scripture, has little authority
for the Church.

17 October 1980

ROMAN CATHOLIC/PENTECOSTAL DIALOGUE
13-17 October 1980 - Venice

Press Release

The 8th meeting of the Dialogue between the
Secretariat for Promoting Christian Unity of the Roman
Catholic Church and leading representatives of some of the
Classical Pentecostal Churches was conducted in Venice,
October 13th-17th, 1980. The subjects discussed were:
"The Church as Communion" and "Tradition and Traditions".

The delegates were welcomed by Pentecostal co-chairman,
Dr David du Plessis and the interactive process was set in
motion by Roman Catholic chairman, Rev Kilian McDonnell,
OSB.

The following papers were presented for discussion:
"The Church As a Worshiping Community" by Rev Richard B.
Foth, President of the Bethany Bible College, Santa Cruz,
California (USA); "The Church as Communion" by Rev Pierre
Duprey, WF, Under-Secretary of the Secretariat for
Promoting Christian Unity (Vatican City); "The Place of
Tradition in Scripture and in the Early Fathers" by Rev
Anthony Meredith, SJ, lecturer at Campion Hall, Oxford
University (England); "The Ties that Divide" by Dr Howard
Ervin, Professor of Old Testament, Oral Roberts University,
Tulsa, Oklahoma (USA).

Both sides endorsed the sentiments of Pope John Paul
II who stated at the ecumenical meeting in Trinity College,

Washington D.C. on October 7th, 1979: "Since the inception of my pontificate...I have endeavoured to devote
myself to the service of Christian unity...Jesus prays
that His followers may be one, 'so that the world may
believe' (Jn 17:21). That the credibility of evangelization should, by God's plan, depend on the unity of His
followers in a subject of inexhaustible meditation of all
of us."

The dialogue underscored many areas of concord as
well as distinctive areas of difference. Views concerning
the sacredness and importance of Scripture allowed delegates to sense that they had more to affirm in one another,
than to disaffirm. Both sides of the dialogue agreed as
to the inspired nature of both the Old and New Testaments,
thus giving Scripture a privileged place in both communions.

The celebration of the Eucharist was discussed at
length, with Catholics seeing the Eucharist as the central
act of worship. On the other hand most Pentecostals see
it as one part of a multi-faced worship process.
"Ecumenical pain" was mutually acknowledged over the fact
of separation at the Lord's Table.

Other matters of discussion included the criteria
for membership, canonicity of Scripture, traditions, and
the characteristic elements of Catholic and Pentecostal
fellowship.

The following persons were participants in the discussions:

[Roman Catholics:]

    Fr Kilian McDonnell, OSB
    Fr Jerome Vereb, CP (secretary)
    Fr Barnabas Ahern, CP
    Fr Pierre Duprey, WF
    Fr Anthony Meredith, SJ
    Fr Liam Walsh, OP
    Fr Robert Wister, of the Archdiocese of Newark,
        New Jersey, [USA]

From the Classical Pentecostals

    Dr David du Plessis
    Rev William L. Carmichael (secretary)
    Rev Justus du Plessis
    Dr Howard M. Ervin
    Rev Richard B. Foth
    Rev John L. Meares

Pentecostal Observers:

    Rev Desmond Evans
    Rev Ronald C. Haus
    Rev Terry Law
    Dr Ronald Douglas McConnell
    Rev Jerry L. Sandidge

The Cardinal Patriarch of Venice, His Eminence Cardinal
Marco Ce extended the hospitality of the diocese to the
participants of the dialogue in a written message. In his
absence greetings were offered on his behalf by Msgr.
Giuseppe Visentin, Vicar General of the Patriarchate, who
visited the members of the dialogue.

17th October, 1980

ROMAN CATHOLIC/PENTECOSTAL DIALOGUE
4–10 October 1981—Vienna

Dialogue Participants

1. Fr Robert J. Wister
2. Fr Pierre Duprey, WF
3. Fr Jerome Vereb, CP
4. Fr. William J. Dalton, SJ
5. Rev James H. Carmichael
6. Fr Kilian McDonnel, OSB
7. Rev William L. Carmichael
8. Fr Laurence R. Bronkiewicz
9. Rev Jerry L. Sandidge
10. Rev David J. du Plessis
11. Rev Howard M. Ervin
12. Rev Ronald McConnell
13. Miss Marigloria Iani
    (devoted secretary)
14. Rev Martin Robinson
15. Rev John L. Meares
16. Rev Justus T. du Plessis
17. The Very Rev Liam G. Walsh, OP
18. Rev H. David Edwards

<u>ROMAN CATHOLIC/PENTECOSTAL DIALOGUE</u>
4-10 October 1981 - Vienna

Schedule - Agenda

8:00 a.m.	Breakfast
9:00	Prayer in Chapel
9:15	Plenary
10:30	Coffee
10:45 - 12:30	Plenary
12:45 p.m.	Lunch
3:00	Plenary
4:15	Coffee
4:30 - 5:45	Plenary
6:00	Supper
7:30	Plenary
8:30	Prayer

Theological Paper

THE CATHOLIC VENERATION OF THE VIRGIN MARY,
MOTHER OF GOD AND OF OUR LORD AND SAVIOR,
JESUS CHRIST

by

Fr Laurence R. Bronkiewicz

INTRODUCTION

1. This paper is an attempt to present a brief and
hopefully clear summary of the Roman Catholic Church's
perspective on the veneration of Mary, which is rooted in
our faith and history. That faith is based on God's
revealing Word and the living Tradition of the Church under
the supervision of its teaching authority and guided by the
Holy Spirit. At the outset I should like to point out that
this is by no means an exhaustive treatment of the topic.
A fuller treatment of the topic would have to include, in
addition to the Scriptures and the official teachings of
the Church (teaching statements of the Church councils and
popes), Mary's place in liturgical and non-liturgical
prayer, art, architecture and music. This paper will deal
principally with the Scriptures and the official teachings
of the Church. It is written from the perspective of a
western, Roman Catholic while recognizing the rich tradition of Marian veneration in the Eastern churches and at

the same time the author's inability to give them adequate treatment here.

2. The Church's veneration of Mary is an essential piece of the rich fabric of Catholic Christian worship. Devotion to Mary, by the Church, from its earliest days, is rooted in God's Word and the teachings of the Church. It is based on Mary's special dignity as the Virgin Mother of God and of our Lord Jesus, her unique role in the mystery of salvation and her singular relationship to the Church and its members. However, who Mary is and what she does depend entirely upon Jesus Christ, her Son, her Redeemer and the Head of the Church of which she herself is the first member. The purpose of Marian veneration is not to honor Mary alone, but ultimately, as Pope Paul VI states in his apostolic exhortation, To Honor Mary: "to glorify God and to lead Christians to commit themselves to a life which is in absolute conformity with his will" (para 39). The format of this paper is: first, to examine Mary's relationship to Jesus, secondly, her relationship to her Son's work of salvation, thirdly, her relationship to the Church and finally to present some concluding remarks.

I. MARY'S RELATIONSHIP TO CHRIST

3. The basic fact on which the Catholic veneration of Mary is based is that she is the Mother of God and of our Lord Jesus Christ, perpetually a virgin, before as well as after the birth of her Son. This truth is the starting point for all of Catholic faith and theology about Mary and

is the basis for her role in the salvific work of her Son
and in the Church. In the letter of Pope John Paul II to
the Bishops of the Catholic Church for the 1600th Anniversary of the Council of Ephesus, which solemnly proclaimed
the truth of Mary's divine motherhood on June 22, 431,
the Pope states:

> His motherhood is not only the source and foundation
> of all her exceptional holiness and her very special
> participation in the whole plan of salvation; it
> also establishes a permanent maternal link with the
> Church, as a result of the fact that she was chosen
> by the Holy Trinity as the Mother of Christ who is
> "the head of the Body, the Church" (para 8).

4. The Word of God in the New Testament reveals Mary
as the Virgin Mother of Jesus. She appears principally in
the four Gospels and also the book of Acts, the letter to
the Galatians and the book of Revelation. It must be remembered that each Gospel writer's primary interest is the
person and work of Jesus. Like all the persons and events
in the New Testament, Mary has meaning and importance only
in relation to her Son.

5. In the Letter to the Galatians, Mary appears only
once, unnamed, but clearly as the Mother of Jesus (Gal 4:4).
In the opening chapters of the Gospels of Matthew and Luke,
the infancy narratives, which were composed in light of the
Easter faith, Mary is prominent. The Gospel of Matthew
begins with the geneology which ends with Joseph, the
husband of Mary: "It was of her that Jesus who is called
the Messiah was born" (Mt 1:16b)[1] In Mt 1:18-25, Mary,

---

[1]Quoted Bible passages are taken from the New
American Bible translation, 1970.

who is already clearly identified as Jesus' mother, is a virgin mother. The clear indication of Mary's virginal motherhood is reinforced by the Gospel's addition of a citation from Is 7:14: "Therefore the Lord himself will give you this sign: the virgin shall be with child, and bear a son, and shall name him Immanuel."

    6. In Luke's account (1:26-35), Mary's virginal conception of Jesus is announced. The role of the Holy Spirit is highlighted: "The Holy Spirit will come upon you and the power of the Most High will overshadow you. . ." (Lk 1:35). In Matthew's account (1:18,20), the Spirit's role is again emphasized: ". . .she was found with child through the power of the Holy Spirit. . .It is by the Holy Spirit that she has conceived this child". Mary's response to the angel's announcement is one of total obedience in faith: "I am the servant of the Lord. Let it be done to me as you say" (Lk 1:38). Mary is a "highly favored daughter" (Lk 1:28) who has "found favor with God" (Lk 1:30). Elizabeth, during Mary's visit, identifies Mary's blessedness: "Blest are you among women and blest is the fruit of your womb. But who am I that the mother of my Lord should come to me?" (Lk 1:42, 43). Mary is blessed because of what God Himself has done for her in inviting her to become the mother of His Son and because of her own faithfilled yes to that invitation. She had complete trust that the promise made to her would be fulfilled (Lk 1:45). Mary acknowledges her blessedness in the canticle of Lk 1: 46-53. Humbly-obedient to God and to His word the virgin mother of Jesus praises God for His goodness.

7. Mary is primarily the faithful, obedient hearer
of God's word in Luke's Gospel. Because she hears the word
of God and does it (Lk) and does the will of the heavenly
Father (Mt), she is a member of Jesus' eschatological family
(Mt 12:24-50; Lk 8:19-21). This is reinforced in Lk 2:27, 28
when Jesus responds to a woman who declares his mother
blessed, saying: "blest are they who hear the word of God
and keep it."

8. At the same time Luke suggests that Mary's faith
is a human faith which did not include a clear understanding
of all of the events in which she participated: "Mary
treasured all these things and reflected on them in her
heart" (Lk 2:19); "His mother, meanwhile, kept all these
things in memory" (Lk 2:51).

9. In the book of Acts, Mary is mentioned only once,
again living out her faith in prayer: "Together they devoted
themselves to constant prayer. There were some women in
their company, and Mary, the mother of Jesus, and his
brothers" (Ac 1:14). Mary is praying among the group of
post-Easter believers for the coming of the Holy Spirit at
Pentecost. So it appears that she shared the earliest
Christian community's faith in Jesus.

10. In the Gospel of John, Mary is a woman of growing
faith. In the account of the miracle of Cana (Jn 2:1,2) her
faith is imperfect, she misunderstands Jesus and does not
realize that the work given to her Son by His Father takes
precedence over the needs of the wedding event. Mary,
however, exhibits an unwavering faith in Jesus which is

expressed in her presence at the foot of the cross. There, according to Jn 19:25-27, she becomes the supreme model of Christian faith and discipleship.

11. The basic scriptural truth of Mary's divine mother-hood which forms the basis of the Catholic veneration of Mary is reaffirmed in the faith life and theological tradi-tion of the Church. In the post-apostolic Church Christian preachers and teachers continued to reflect on the divine maternity and often repeated it in their homilies and writings. In 431 it was solemnly and officially proclaimed by the Council of Ephesus. The significance of the Ephesus teaching about Mary is that it was used by Ephesus to defend and clarify the truth that Jesus is one divine per-son with two natures, divine and human. Mary is the *"Theotokos"*, the bearer or mother of the divine person, Jesus, who has both a divine nature and a human nature; she is not the mother merely of his human nature. Mary then is truly the Mother of God. So the council's teaching about Mary was in fact used to support its primary teaching about Jesus Christ. The teaching about Mary's divine motherhood is repeated again by the Council of Chalcedon in 451, once again in response to a christological controversy. It has been the constant teaching of the Church up to the present day.

12. Mary's virginity was a favorite theme of the patristic writers. Some described her as a virgin before Jesus' birth. Others taught that she remained a virgin after her Son's birth. Soon there appeared a growing

consensus that Mary was perpetually a virgin, and from the 4th century on her perpetual virginity is often mentioned. After the Council of the Lateran in 649, which taught the perpetual virginity of Mary, the formula that Mary was a virgin before, in, and after the birth of Jesus came unto use. Catholics venerate Mary as the ever virgin Mother of God.

13. Eventually, theological reflection about Mary shifted and Christian thinkers began reflecting on the implications of Mary's singular dignity as Mother of God for herself. These have been referred to as Mary's privileges, and the Catholic Church understands them as gifts given to Mary because she is the Mother of the Lord. The two major privileges granted to Mary, which are both solemnly defined truths of the Catholic faith, are the Immaculate Conception and the Assumption.

14. The Church's teaching about the Immaculate Conception, while not explicitly supported by the Scriptures, is based in the Church's continual reflection on Mary's holiness. According to Augustine, Mary was absolutely sinless. Soon, this belief in Mary's sinlessness extended to freedom from original sin. Theologians tried to reconcile the universal necessity of redemption with the possibility of Mary's freedom from original sin. Gradually there arose the general conviction among the faithful that Mary had been redeemed in a special way. The Council of Trento (16th century) stated that it was not its intention to include Mary in its teaching on the universality of

original sin. Finally, in the 19th century the general
Catholic conviction in Mary's freedom from original sin
was solemnly proclaimed by Pope Pius IX on December 8,
1854 in the dogma of the Immaculate Conception:

> . . .the most Blessed Virgin Mary was, from the first
> moment of her conception, by the singular grace and
> privilege of Almighty God and in view of the merits
> of Christ Jesus the Savior of the human race, pre-
> served immune from all stain of original sin. . .
> (from the Bull, Ineffabilis Deus, December 8, 1854).

15. The Church's teaching about the Assumption of
Mary, also not explicitly found in the Scriptures, is
rooted in the Church's reflection on Mary's unique dignity.
Patristic writings about the assumption begin in the 6th
century. The apostolic constitution: Munificentissimus
Deus, defined the assumption of Mary as a truth of the
Catholic faith; it was solemnly proclaimed by Pope Pius XII
on November 1, 1950. It contains a survey of the history
of belief in Mary's assumption, body and soul, into heavenly
glory, as expressed in previous Church teaching, popular
piety, and liturgy.

16. The teaching is, as stated in the constitution:
". . . the Immaculate Mother of God, Mary even Virgin, when
the course of her earthly life was finished, was taken up
body and soul into the glory of heaven" (from the apostolic
constitution, Munificentissimus Deus, November 1, 1950).

17. Catholic veneration of Mary today understands
both privileges of the Immaculate Conception and the Assumption as personal privileges, unique to the Mother of God
but also as having a wider importance in terms of Mary's
role in the mystery of salvation and in the Church.

II. <u>MARY'S</u> <u>RELATIONSHIP</u> <u>TO</u> <u>THE</u> <u>MYSTERY</u> <u>OF</u> <u>SALVATION</u>

18. Mary's relationship to the plan of salvation flows from her unique relationship to Christ. Because of her singular relationship to Jesus she has a unique role in the work of redemption.

19. Reflection on her special role in the work of Christ began during the patristic period. In the 9th century the title, "redemptrix," was applied to her. In the 15th century this was changed to "co-redemptrix." In the 19th century there was a concerted effort by some theologians to develop a theology of Mary focusing on her role in the redemptive work of her Son. There was a gradual shift away from a theology concerned primarily with Mary's personal privileges to a theology which attempted to understand her in the wider context of the whole plan of salvation and her role in the Church.

20. The first Church document to synthesize so extensively and profoundly this wider perspective on Mary was the Second Vatican Council's "Dogmatic Constitution on the Church" (LG), whose teaching about the Mother of God is marked by a christocentric and ecclesial emphasis. Pope Paul VI in his apostolic exhortation, <u>To</u> <u>Honor</u> <u>Mary</u>, addressed to all Catholic bishops, takes up the principles of the Vatican II teaching and develops them "for the right ordering and development of devotion to the Blessed Virgin Mary" (from the full title of the document). Both documents provide an excellent summary of the bases for the contemporary Catholic veneration of Mary.

21. Catholics venerate Mary as one who shares in the work of Christ to save mankind. Christ is the Redeemer, the one Savior, the one and only Mediator. This is the clear teaching of God's revelation in the Scriptures and reaffirmed by the living Tradition of the Church. Mary's role in the work of redemption is, of necessity, secondary to, dependent upon, and subordinate to the role of her Son. She is associated with Him in His work but not as an equal. (Please confer LG, para 60.)

22. Mary is venerated as one who was actively engaged in the work of redemption. The Council repeated the patristic teaching: "Rightly, therefore, the Fathers see Mary not merely as passively engaged by God, but as freely cooperating in the work of man's salvation through faith and obedience" (LG, para 56).

23. Mary is venerated as one who freely assented to and cooperated with the establishment of God's plan of salvation, that is, in becoming the virgin mother of His Son, through the power of the Holy Spirit.

24. She is venerated as one who enjoyed a lifelong union with her Son and His work of redemption from the moment of His conception, through His birth, childhood, public life, death on the cross and resurrection. We see Mary praying with the apostles for the coming of the Spirit at Pentecost. Her assumption, body and soul, into heaven, is the sign of her perfect union with her Son.

25. Catholics venerate Mary not only as one who was present at Christ's death on the cross, but as associated

with Him, in a secondary way, in His sacrifice itself and in His suffering.

26. Mary is venerated as a person who needed the grace of Christ in order to be saved: ". . .being of the race of Adam, she is at the same time also united to all those who are to be saved. . ." (LG, para 53). The Council also stated: "She stands out among the poor and humble of the Lord, who confidently hope for and receive salvation from him" (para 55). The Church's teaching about the immaculate conception explicitly states that the grace and merits of her Son preserved her from original sin.

27. The Church venerates Mary as one who enjoys a special relationship to the Holy Spirit as a result of the Spirit's role in the incarnation of Jesus. In his exhortation on Marian devotion, Pope Paul VI reminds the Church that the Spirit should be prominent in Marian devotion (To Honor Mary, para 26). He encourages more reflection on the role of the Spirit in the history of salvation and adds: "Such a study will bring out in particular the hidden relationship between the Spirit of God and the Virgin of Nazareth, and show the influence they exert on the Church" (para 27).

III. MARY'S RELATIONSHIP TO THE CHURCH

28. Mary's relationship to the Church is based on her relationship to Christ and her role in salvation. Because of her relationship to the Lord and God's plan of salvation, she has a special role in the Church.

29. She is venerated as the pre-eminent member of the Church: "It is also necessary that exercises of piety with which the faithful honor the Mother of the Lord should clearly show the place she occupied in the Church: 'the highest place and the closest to us after Christ'." (To Honor Mary, para 28).

30. Catholics venerate Mary as "a mother to us in the order of grace" (LG, para 61) because of her unique role in the life and work of her Son. Even after her death and assumption into heavenly glory, her involvement in God's saving plan continues through her role in the mediation of grace. The Council used the titles of Advocate, Helper, Benefactress and Mediatrix to describe Mary's role, but added: "This, however, is so understood that it neither takes away anything from nor adds anything to the dignity and efficacy of Christ the one Mediator " (LG, para 62).

31. The Council's teaching on Mary's role of mediation must be viewed especially against the background of the Church's understanding of the priesthood of all believers, in which Mary has a greater share than other human believers.

32. Mary is venerated as the type of model of the Church and of the individual Christian. Mary's faith, charity, hope, obedience, holiness, prayerfulness are models for the life of the Church as a whole and all of its members. She is the perfect example of what it means to be a member of Christ, totally dedicated to the Lord and His work. The Church reflects the virgin motherhood of Mary as "she keeps intact faith, firm hope and sincere charity"

(LG, para 64) and as she does God's will by proclaiming
the Word of God and baptizing new members of Christ's body,
giving them new life. Pope Paul VI in his document on
devotion to Mary, explains why Mary's life has permanent
and universal exemplary value:

> She is held up as an example to the faithful rather
> for the way in which, in her own particular life, she
> fully and responsibly accepted the will of God
> (cf. Lk 1:38), because she heard the word of God and
> acted on it and because charity and a spirit of ser-
> vice were the driving force of her actions. She is
> worthy of imitation because she was the first and
> the most perfect of Christ's disciples (To Honor
> Mary, para 35).

33. The Church venerates Mary under the titles of the
Immaculate Conception and the Assumption. These teachings
are not only statements about Mary herself but about her
relationship to the mystery of salvation and to the Church.
Mary's immaculate conception is a sign of "the beginning
of the Church, the spotless Bride of Christ" (To Honor Mary,
para 11), the first sign of God's will to save mankind, a
symbol of Christ's love for the Church which He makes holy
through the blood of His cross. Mary's Immaculate Conception becomes a symbol of the holiness and salvation to
which the whole Church is called. Mary's Assumption, body
and soul, into heavenly glory reminds the Church that what
has already begun, namely its union with Christ, must be
completed. In Mary's Assumption the pilgrim Church sees
the successful completion of its own journey, the fulfillment of Christ's promise to all who believe, perfect union
with the Lord to which all Christians aspire. The
"Constitution on the Sacred Liturgy" of the Second Vatican

Council, para 103, states that Mary is "the most excellent fruit of the redemption, the spotless model in whom the Church sees its own ideal".

IV. CONCLUDING REMARKS

34. Although certain forms of popular devotion in the past and incorrect attitudes on the part of the faithful reflected an unbalanced understanding of Mary, the Church, in its preaching and teaching, has always tried to encourage proper veneration of the Mother of God. Catholic veneration of Mary, properly understood and expressed, sees her always in relation to her Son, His saving work and the Church which is His Body. As Pope Paul VI stated in his letter on Marian devotion, in the introduction:

> The Development, desired by us, of devotion to the Blessed Virgin Mary is an indication of the Church's genuine piety. This devotion fits....into the only worship that is rightly called 'Christian', because it takes its origin and effectiveness from Christ, finds its complete expression in Christ, and leads through Christ in the Spirit to the Father. In the sphere of worship this devotion necessarily reflects God's redemptive plan, in which a special form of veneration is appropriate to the singular place which Mary occupies in that plan.

Bibliography

The New American Bible.

The Christian Faith in the Doctrinal Documents of the Catholic Church.

The Documents of the Second Vatican Council.

To Honor Mary, Apostolic Exhortation Marialis Cultus of His Holiness Paul VI to All Bishops in Peace and Communion with the Apostolic See for the Right Ordering and Development of Devotion to the Blessed Virgin Mary.

Letter of the Holy Father Pope John Paul II to the Bishops of the Catholic Church for the 1600th Anniversary of the First Council of Constantinople and the 1550th Anniversary of the Council of Ephesus.

Mary in the New Testament, ed. Raymond Brown, Karl Donfried, Joseph Fitzmyer and John Reumann.

Understanding the Mother of Jesus, Eamon Carroll, O. Carm.

Sacramentum Mundi, an Encyclopedia of Theology, pertinent articles.

The New Catholic Encyclopedia, pertinent articles.

ROMAN CATHOLIC/PENTECOSTAL DIALOGUE
4-10 October 1981 - Vienna

Theological Paper

A PENTECOSTAL PERSPECTIVE OF MARY,
THE MOTHER OF JESUS
by
Rev Jerry L. Sandidge

PREFACE

     1. The research for this paper has been conducted
under difficult circumstances. Between November 1980 and
April 1981, when research was done at all, it was carried
out while undergoing hospitalization and treatment for throat
cancer. Reading books about Mary while in the hospital or
in waiting rooms or in times of physical discomfort was not
easy. It was, however, a great help to have access to the
theology liberary of the Catholic University of Louvain in
Belgium.

Between May and August (1981) the research was pursued in Dallas, Texas, at a neighborhood library or at Dallas Theological Seminary in conjunction with further medical observation. This is in no way to make excuses, but simply to explain why my deadline was missed and why there may be small "gaps" in the flow of the paper or in the sources.

2. There were at least two surprises waiting for me at the time I began searching the sources on the subject of the Blessed Virgin Mary. First, there is a great dearth of material written by Pentecostals about Mary. Outside of some discussion centered around the Christmas story and the Virgin Birth of Jesus (Mt 1; Lk 1), and a few lines about Mary at the Wedding of Cana (Jn 2), there is practically nothing on the subject. I discovered a few remarks by Pentecostals criticizing the Roman Catholic view of Mary, written after the birth and spread of the charismatic renewal in the Catholic Church throughout the world. Thus, it could be said that Pentecostals, generally speaking, do not have a "theology of Mary." In fact, it could almost be said that we do not even have a "view" of Mary, unless it would be in negative terms, i.e., those things which we universally do not believe about her.

Since there is very little written about a "Pentecostal theology of Mary," and since I did not feel (literally) capable of writing such a theology, I decided to read up on the Catholic position concerning the Mother of Jesus and attempt to respond to those teachings as a Pentecostal.

By contrast, the subject of Mary in the Roman Catholic tradition has an unending supply of books and articles (whole libraries in fact), official statements, stories and legends, societies and study groups, liturgical practices, popular devotions, and long traditions reaching back to patristic times. Such as abundance of material was simply staggering to me. I had to face such important questions as: "What sources are the best?" "Which subjects should be omitted?" "What is the best way to arrange and present this material?" "How can I ever stop researching and start writing when I keep finding important, relevant information?"

3. In finding so much material on Our Lady in Catholic sources, I was faced with another two-fold problem that was also a bit overwhelming. First, I very soon discovered that a non-Catholic cannot fully appreciate nor understand the rich tradition and teaching concerning the role of Mary in the body of Catholic truth without examining a number of related theological subjects as well. There is harmony and applied consistency among dogmas which overlap and touch each other. It is difficult to isolate one topic and ignore the related topics. In compiling a list of such related subjects, I came up with the following. Though by no means exhaustive, it proved to be exhausting enough for me: 1) Scripture, exegesis, interpretation and biblical theology are important as they relate to texts in which Mary is mentioned or implied; 2) The history of dogma from the Protoevangelium of James at about the end of the second century to Pope Pius XII declaring *ex cathedra* the dogma of

the bodily Assumption of Mary in 1950; 3) Related to the history of dogma is the development and role of authentic tradition as viewed by the Catholic Church; 4) It is vital to know something about Catholic teaching concerning the Communion of the Saints to fully appreciate Mary's special and elevated position; 5) Of course, the Church and ecclesiology and the mediation of Christ in salvation and the answering of prayer are important related topics to a Catholic understanding of Mary; 6) The practice of "popular devotion" to Mary by faithful Catholics is a subject all its own; 7) Finally, the relationship of the work of the Holy Spirit and the role of Mary is a subject of great importance in the charismatic renewal today.

4. In order to keep from writing a book instead of a paper for the Dialogue, certain subjects had to be omitted. This is a matter of judgment in light of what is really pertinent to our objective in the Dialogue. I have tried to keep this in mind in this paper, but realize that certain significant items may be scarcely mentioned, or passed over entirely. Suggestions for improvement in this area will be especially welcome.

5. Being a non-Catholic seeking to understand the wealth of information about the Blessed Virgin, I was faced with a further problem. That was simply: "Which view of Mary do I pursue as best representing Catholicism?" For I discovered that not every Catholic agrees at every point about Mary. There are, first of all, official pronouncements such as papal documents and various Council statements

292

concerning Mary. Secondly, there are the books and articles by leading theologians which often are different from and disagree with the official ecclesiastical documents. Thirdly, there is the wide variety in practice of these Marian dogmas. Some Catholics exaggerate their devotion to Mary while others almost repudiate her role altogether. Finally, there seems to be a rather indefinite pattern within the Catholic charismatic renewal concerning Mary's proper place in the life of the Christian, the prayer group, the parish, and the Church at large. Indeed, it is true as Kilian McDonnell points out that as "the Second Vatican Council adequately demonstrated, there is room within the (Catholic) church for various theologies of Mary."[1]

6. Why such an abundance of lengthy footnotes? The paper can be read and understood with perhaps little reference to the footnotes. But my Pentecostal brethren, who may be as unfamiliar as I was with certain Catholic terms, teachings or practices, will find the explanatory footnotes invaluable. Catholics too will gain some insights into pentecostalism in many of the footnotes. It was simply for neatness of appearance and ease in typing that the footnotes are at the end of the paper and not at the bottom of each page (which is my first preference).

7. The proper role of Mary and the correct understanding of her function in the economy of salvation is a subject of great ecumenical significance today. In the summer of 1980 a six-day conference on ecumensim was held at Assumption College, Worcester, Massachusetts. A three-man panel--a

Catholic, a Lutheran, and a Presbyterian--told the 150
conference delegates that "Mary, once a seeming stumbling
block to church unity, might become the basis of ecumenical
unity."[2] I doubt if there would be widespread agreement
with such an idea. However, it does point out the importance and timeliness of discussing the doctrine of the
Virgin Mary at our Dialogue session for 1981.

INTRODUCTION

> *Hail Mary, full of grace,*
> *the Lord is with thee.*
> *Blessed art thou among women,*
> *and blessed is the fruit of they womb, Jesus.*
> *Holy Mary, Mother of God,*
> *pray for us sinners, now, and at the hour of our death.*
> *Amen.* [3]

This simple prayer seems to summarize for non-Catholics
"one of the most perplexing elements in the riddle of Roman
Catholicicm,"[4] i.e., the cult of Mary and her veneration.
As a child I recall seeing this prayer displayed along the
highway "Burma shave style," and thinking to myself, "Why
don't Catholics pray to Jesus, instead of to Mary?"

My childhood question has been answered, for I have
learned that Catholics <u>do</u> pray to Jesus, and do so with far
greater frequency than to Mary. But there is more to it.
For the Blessed Virgin Mary has, it seems, become synonymous
with Roman Catholicism. The veneration of Mary[5] is a
stumbling block for most Pentecostals. We do not understand
her role in Catholicism, nor have we taken the time to find
out. She appears to be a great obstacle in making ecumenical
progress possible today. And especially for Pentecostals,

it is extremely hard to accept the honor given her within the current charismatic renewal of the Catholic Church.

The *Ave Maria* embodies many of the questions and problems that Pentecostals would raise concerning the place of the Virgin Mary in the Christian faith. Half of this prayer comes directly from Scripture and half comes from later Church practice and tradition. So a proper scriptural view of Mary is necessary as well as insight into the development of certain dogmas of Mary within Roman Catholic Church tradition.

The "Hail Mary" is used extensively in various liturgies, feast days, and devotional practices of the Catholic Church. It is necessary to see the elevated position given to Our Lady in the life, theology, and practice of Catholicism in contrast to almost complete negligence of her in Pentecostal worship.

History has produced many miracle stories in which persons who called on Mary through repeating the *Ave* "knew no limitations of nature."[6] The addition of the last half of the prayer came about when a mere greeting or praise to her was not enough, but required some form of impetratory prayer. This raises the whole question of Mary's role as intercessor and Mediatrix, which is theologically unacceptable to Pentecostals.

Pope Urban VI (1261-1264), who is credited with adding the name "Jesus" to the prayer, "gave an indulgence of thirty days to all who prayed it. Pope John XXII (1316-1334) reportedly increased this to sixty days."[7] Although it is true that such forms are not so commonly practiced within Catholicism today, it is true that enough remains to be a source of irritation to Pentecostals.

Thus, the *Ave* provides at least three major areas of discussion for our Dialouge. 1) "Hail Mary, . . .the Lord is with thee; blessed art thou among women. . . ." This will be the biblical section in which we disucss the Annunciation; Magnificat; virginal conception, virgin birth, perpetual virginity; and role of Mary in the New Testament. 2) "Holy Mary, Mother of God. . . ." In this section various Roman Catholic dogmas concerning Mary will be examined, including: the title "Mother of God," the Immaculate Conception, and Assumption. This may be called the historical section. 3) "Pray for us sinners. . . ." The last major section will be theological in which we consider Christ and Mary, the Holy Spirit and Mary, the Church and Mary, the special veneration of Mary, and Catholic charismatics and Mary. The conclusion will contain suggestions for both sides in helping to resolve some of the current conflict and move a significant step closer toward full Christian understanding, ecumenical cooperation, spiritual harmony, and mutual acceptance. The paper ends with a personal reflection concerning the impact of the study on my own personal appreciation of Mary and her importance as the "first Christian."

I. *"Hail Mary. . .the Lord is with thee, Blessed art thou among women. . . ."*
BIBLICAL PERSPECTIVES ON MARY

There has been much ecumenical progress between Roman Catholics and those of other confessions since the Second Vatican Council. One Catholic writer lists "the role of Mary in man's salvation" and "the nature of ordained ministry" as two of the main theological differences to be worked out. On these points "there have been significant advances, as theologians in dialogue have been able to reach a consensus that was previously considered impossible."[8]

When it comes to Mary, Pentecostals do have a hard time. The reason for this difficulty can be seen clearly as two-fold: Catholic excesses and the Pentecostals' silence. Handel H. Brown, a Presbyterian, expresses it very well as follows:

> It is difficult, if not impossible, for us to form an unbiased estimate of Mary. As Protestants, we are conditioned against her by what we consider to be the excesses of Rome. This does not, however, justify us in going to the other extreme. We cannot lightly dismiss her as "just another woman." She was the Mother of our Lord....If we put the prejudices out of our minds, along with what we consider to be the extravagances of others, it may be that we shall come to regard her as the most beautiful character in the Bible.[9]

A. The Annunciation (Lk 1:26-38)

There is a fundamental difference, I think, in the way a Pentecostal and a Catholic would approach this event in the life of Mary. A Pentecostal would view this experience by emphasizing Mary's example of humility, faith and obedience. Catholics, on the other hand, without denying or rejecting this approach, would also emphasize the role of Mary in the economy of man's salvation.

One Pentecostal minister cites Mary, along with many others (Eve, Sarah, Miriam, Deborah, Hannah, Huldah, Elizabeth, Anna, Phoebe, Priscilla) to show how the Holy Spirit uses women in important ways. He draws a strong comparison between Mary and Hannah (1 Sam 1:2).[10] The Pentecostal emphasis is clearly not on Mary's uniqueness, not on her total cooperation, nor on her special function. She is a young Jewish "handmaid" who, for some reason known only to God, was the channel or means for the Messiah's birth.

For the Catholic, there must be a distinction between example (model) and role of Mary. Yes, she is an example of faith, but more than that; her role in the incarnation and plan of redemption is of greater importance. "Mary is not an accessory to Christianity. Without her role Christianity would no longer be itself."[11] Her role is absolutely necessary to Christianity.

Catholics see Mary as the New Eve. Adam and Eve were also an example and fulfilled a role. Their role was all important to God's divine plan but their example was not so good. Jesus became the New Adam and Mary became the New Eve. In both cases the example was flawless, but more importantly the role was fulfilled and completed. The Annunciation passage clothes Mary in a rich theology of holiness. No one in Scripture, aside from God, receives "such beautiful salutations as Mary."[12] (See Lk 1:28, 30, 35, 45 as well as 2:19, 34.) Her holiness is essential to her unique role. "Because of God's generosity in her regard she already possesses what the rest of the world still anticipates. She receives in advance what other men will be given after the death and Resurrection of Jesus."[13] Here we find a hint of the doctrinal developments to come later, i.e., her Immaculate Conception, lack of original sin and her Assumption.

B. The Magnificat (Lk 1:46-55)

In the Annunciation, God, through Gabriel, asks permission of Mary to allow the Holy Spirit to conceive in her womb, Jesus. By faith she accepts the challenge. Thus, the Annunciation was first necessary to obtain her cooperation in God's plan. "Here was the one heart in all the world to whose love, authority and strength God was willing to entrust His only begotten Son."[14] Mary, by her full and eager acceptance of God's eternal purpose for her, entered into "the joy of the Lord" and sang the "Song of Mary" as Pentecostals would call it. "She recognized that although she was privileged to be the human agent for the accomplishment of God's purpose, all honor and glory must belong to Him. So she praises Him with her whole personality."[15]

Catholic theologians would give the same emphasis to the Magnificat but would also add other elements. There is an emphasis upon Mary as the "highest and most perfect personification of Israel." She is the "Virgin Daughter of Zion" and the "ultimate achievement of the history of the preparation of Israel, the last and summit of the many elections made by Yahweh."[16] Mary's predestination and high position are clearly seen here in her very special role in man"s salvation.

Another emphasis is that Mary is characterized "as
the perfect representative of the ánáwîm (lowly, humble,
poor), the spiritual community of the poor, the remnant,
whom God was to prepare to receive His expected salvation."[17]
God has taken into account her humble station in life (Lk
1:48) and is favorable to her longing for deliverance as
was promised to Abraham (Lk 1:55).

There is also a strong contrast drawn between the
Magnificat and the Canticle of Hannah (1 Sam 2:1-10). These
two songs have a similar content; in fact, most scholars
claim that the Magnificat is built from the Song of Hannah.
In both the Lord is the God of all the world, not just
Israel. So there is a universal, redemptive theme.[18]

The first two chapters of Luke are called "Our Lady's
Gospel" by some Catholic scholars. The reason is not only
that Mary is the subject, but some feel these chapters may
have been "virtually dictated by Our Lady herself." Mary
may well have been one of Luke's "eye-witnesses" (1:2) in
compiling and writing his Gospel.[19]

So basically, the Magnificat does not contain any
major ecumenical problems with regard to Mary. Once again,
Catholics would accept the Pentecostal view of this text,
but Catholics would elaborate further to bring in symbolic
elements from the Old Testament and underscore Mary's
"chosenness," her "fulfillment of God's plan," and thus her
special role in God's economy for man's redemption.

C. The Virginity of Mary

By Mary accepting to be the bearer of Jesus' humanity

and accepting the divine plan for her, "she is an example
to all the children of God to obey His will at all costs and
leave the future in His loving hands."[20] Throughout her
life, Mary was a model of faith and devotion and reliance
upon the Holy Spirit.

Pentecostals would view the virgin birth (more
accurately, the virginal conception) as a divine act on the
part of God and as an act of obedience on the part of Mary.
Again, Mary would be revered for her faith, her submission,
and her courage. In this sense, she is regarded as an
example for all Christians. Pentecostals also accept with
no difficulty the miraculous nature of the conception of
Jesus. To debate this point with liberal Protestant and
Catholic scholars would largely be a futile effort, since
there would seem to be no "middle-ground" or meeting point.
There would be no compromise because of the Pentecostal's
respect for the integrity of the Bible and a desire to
preserve the divine nature of Christ.[21]

Roman Catholic teaching concerning the virginity of
Mary falls into three parts:

> the virginal conception of Jesus by Mary without any
> human father, the virginal birth of the child from
> the womb of his mother without injury to the bodily
> integrity of Mary, and Mary's observance of
> virginity afterward throughout her earthly life.[22]

Hans Küng elaborates further on these three aspects
of Mary's virginity. The first (virginal conception) was,
"taken in a strictly Christological sense, as in Matthew
and Luke, as virginity before the birth." But from the
fourth or fifth century, under the influence of the

301

<u>Protoevangelium</u> <u>of</u> <u>James</u> and a strong ascetic movement, "it was given a broader meaning to include virginity <u>in</u> the birth. . . .Finally, it came to be understood as virginity--likewise not attested in the New Testament-- <u>after</u> the birth."[23] So as time passes there is a shift from the Christological approach to the Mariological approach, which becomes increasingly prominent.

On the first point there is no argument. But for Pentecostals to appreciate the teaching of Mary's virginity <u>in</u> and <u>after</u> Jesus' birth is a problem.

Mary's virginity in parturition (childbirth) certainly was possible, since God is a God of miracles. How the event took place "remains a mystery that God has not deigned to reveal."[24] Catholics admit that there is "no clear text of Sacred Scripture concerning Mary's virginity in childbirth."[25] Such a dogma, for Pentecostals, appears unbiblical and indicates yet another unnecessary "embellishment" upon events in the life of Mary. At the same time, however, it need not be an obstacle to ecumenical progress.

But, the dogma of Mary's perpetual virginity does contain elements which bother Pentecostals and is a source of irritation and strong disagreement. To accept the perpetual virginity of Mary raises, to my mind at least, more questions than it solves. Can Lk 1:34 be interpreted to mean that Mary agreed to remain a virgin when she accepted to be the mother of the Messiah? Why, then, did she agree to marry Joseph? Was there a mutual agreement between Joseph and Mary <u>never</u> to consumate their marriage? Does not Mt 1:25 weigh against perpetual virginity, since a marriage is hardly a marriage without conjugal relationships? How could they be considered truly as "one flesh" if there was never sexual union?

For me, the problem is not the question of whether or not Mary had other children. A recent study on Mary concludes that the "brothers" and "sisters" of Jesus cannot be identified <u>without</u> <u>doubt</u> as being blood relatives of Jesus and children of Mary.[26] I accept that inconclusion. The big difficulty, it seems, is that by having a marriage which is not, in fact, a marriage, Mary is cast into a mold of strangeness. Marriage is divinely ordained (and a sacrament in the Catholic Church), including the physical union, so there should be nothing wrong in the idea that Joseph and Mary <u>could</u> have had other children or certainly have experienced sexual union in their marriage.[27] It seems to make more sense and to be more meaningful to the Church to have her as a model wife (and parent) than as a model virgin. To do this would not necessarily diminish her theological significance for her role in the Incarnation, her role as the New Eve (Eve had sexual union and more than one birth), and her being the handmaid of the Lord chosen for a special place of reverence and honor.

The Pentecostal objection to Mary's perpetual virginity comes to the surface with such Roman Catholic statements as those of Msgr Conway:

> To Catholics, this idea (i.e., that Mary had other children) is impious and defamatory. . . .We consider it incongruous that other children, thoroughly human,

should share the womb and love which were given first
to God's own eternal Son. We sense that those who
hold otherwise are well on the way to denying the
divinity of Christ.[28]

D. <u>Mary in the rest of the New Testament</u>

In the miracle at Cana (Jn 2:1-11) Jesus said to His

mother, "My hour has not yet come" (v 4). But later in

chap 19 His "hour" has come and Mary is there.

> At the moment she said yes to the way of the cross,
> yes to the falling and spitting and beating, at the
> moment she said, "Father, may your will be done--I
> accept this hour," at that moment Mary became the
> mother of mankind. She agreed to the redemption.
> She gave her Son. . . .Mary, the mother of the
> Redeemer, became the mother of the redeemed.[29]

This theme in Catholicism is called *mater dolorosa* ("Mother

of Sorrows") and finds expression in various forms. This

sorrowful description of Mary at the foot of the cross is

conjecture. There is no biblical support for such a view

of Mary. The text simply says she "stood" at the cross

(Jn 19:25).

No doubt at the foot of the cross she recalls the

prophecy of Simeon (Lk 2:35) and experienced the "piercing

of the heart" of which he spoke. Yet, "there is no record

of her lamenting, wringing her hands, rending her clothing,

or even making an outcry."[30] The focus is clearly on Jesus

and not on Mary.

In Ap 2:1 it speaks of "a woman robed with the sun."

Some Catholic scholars see in this an allusion (at least)

to the Virgin Mary. Some use this text to see Mary's role

as Mother of the Church. At first she was all the Church

there was when she consented to the virginal conception.

But then she also became the spiritual mother of all

Christians.[31]

The Catholic titles given to Mary of "Mother of
Mankind," "Mother of the Redeemed," and "Mother of the
Church" will come up again. But for the Pentecostal there
is insufficient biblical evidence to warrant such titles
for her. Certainly she is to be honored and loved, but
these honors seem to elevate her beyond the position
intended by the biblical writers.

Perhaps to end this section (so much more could be and
needs to be said) two points of ecumenical satisfaction
could be made. First, Küng sees two features of Mary that
are solidly founded in Scripture and must be proclaimed.
1) She is the mother of Jesus. She is human and not a
heavenly being. She is a witness to Jesus' true humanity
and of His divine origin. 2) She is the model and example
of Christian faith. There is nothing unique about her faith,
nor does she have any special insights into the mysteries
of God. Her faith has a history and is a pattern of
Christian faith as a whole. Hence, she is seen as the first
(Mother?) of believers and is an _image_ of the Church.[32]

Second, Pentecostals must remember that in Catholicism,
Mary fills a "secondary truth in a hierarchy of New Testament
truths." At the top is the Fatherhood of God, the death and
resurrection of Jesus, the power and works of the Spirit,
forgiveness of sin, and the promise of eternal life. "Mary's
role does not have the same 'weight' in the New Testament
witness as these truths and events." Yet, we are warned,
Mary should not be thought of merely as "Roman Catholic

denominational baggage." It is not acceptable to Catholics
to use Mary to show a distinction between a Catholic truth
and a Christian truth. "The role of Mary, it is our
[Catholic] contention, is specifically a Christian truth."[33]

II. *"Holy Mary, Mother of God. . . ."*
HISTORICAL PERSPECTIVES ON MARY

Very little, if any, ecumenical progress can be made
at certain points unless Pentecostals work overtime to understand something about the Roman Catholic view of the development of doctrine, the "deposit of faith," and the important role of tradition. When it comes to the Marian dogmas
of the Mother of God, the Immaculate Conception, and the
Assumption, much study, insight, and understanding are
needed.

The reality of doctrinal development contains three
elements, which is explained by Jan Walgrave as follows:

> (1) The objective correlative of faith. . .is under-
> standable truth, which can be communicated in human
> language. (2) The historical revelation of that truth
> was given in a definite epoch, closed, as is generally
> admitted by orthodox Christianity, at the end of the
> apostolic generation. (3) Since that moment points
> of doctrine that were not explicit in the primitive
> deposit of faith have, nevertheless, emerged in dog-
> matic tradition.[34]

Thus, it is possible that in the Church creeds "there
may be points of doctrine which, although agreeing with
Scripture, are not explicit in it."[35]

> Doctrinal development, then, is a process of explication,
> historically conditioned but guided by the light of the
> Spirit. In that process new aspects emerge from the
> depths of the mystery into the consciousness of the
> Church, but always in connection with what is explicitly
> believed. The Church, consulting that ripening

consciousness, declares from time to time, under the pressure of circumstances, that some point or other, which formerly was not explicitly believed, belongs to the original treasure of revelation.[36]

The Pentecostal churches do not have such a refined system to handle theological development. Their appeal returns exclusively to the Scriptures. There is no official procedure to deal with doctrinal change and situations which did not come up or did not exist in biblical days.[37] Therefore, it is difficult for Pentecostals to feel comfortable with Catholic dogmas that are not explicitly taught in Scripture, and dogmas that are proclaimed by Church Councils and papal decree. Our first reaction is simply flat rejection--no discussion, no compromise, no meeting of the minds. Such an approach is unproductive. As C. H. Jung, the Swiss psychiatrist has said: "Nothing is achieved by merely negative criticism. It is justified only to the degree that it is creative."[38]

A. Mary Mother of God (431)

The earlist known Marian prayer, which comes from the fourth century begins with: "We fly to thy patronage, holy Mother of God."[39] This was years before the Nestorian controversy which caused the Council of Ephesus (431) to take place.

Nestorius, a monk of Antioch and patriarch of Constantinople, taught that "the most accurate way of speaking about the Holy Virgin is Christ-bearer, not God-bearer."[40] St Cyril of Alexandria argued that Mary was *theotokos* ("God-bearer") and not *christokos* ("Christ-bearer"). Jesus received His human nature from His human mother, thus Son of

Mary (Son of Man). He received His divine nature eternally
from the Father, thus Son of God. The Council of Ephesus
"ruled against the Nestorian position and in favor of the
term *theotokos*. Mary is indeed the 'Mother of God' for
there is only one Person in Jesus Christ, not two, and that
Person is the very Word of God."[41]

In reviewing the events of the Council of Ephesus
four points can be made. 1) The title "Mother of God" was
a way of speaking about Christ. The definition was not a
Marian definition but a Christological one. Nearly all
scholars would agree on this point.[42] 2) Yet, the decision
at Ephesus provided a major thrust to Marian devotion. "The
use of this title by the Church was undoubtedly decisive for
the growth in later centuries of Marian doctrine and devotion."[43] 3) In a way it is unfortunate that the title
"Mother of God" was proclaimed in Ephesus, the city where
the people cried "Great is Diana," the temple goddess (Ac
19:23-41). "The worship of the divine mother, which Christian monotheism had thrown out headlong through the front
door, now crept back in through the back door."[44] 4) Although the term "Mother of God" may not be so offensive to
Pentecostals, it is one which is never used. "Mother of
Jesus" seems to be the common expression; thus, the term
sounds strange, maybe uncomfortable. But theologically, it
should not cause strong objections since Pentecostals believe that Christ was God "in the flesh" (Jn 1:14).[45]

B. <u>The</u> <u>Immaculate</u> <u>Conception</u> <u>of</u> <u>Mary</u> (1854)

The doctrine of the Immaculate Conception developed through many centuries. Finally, the definition by Pope Pius IX in 1854 (<u>Ineffabilis</u> <u>Deus</u>) raised to a dogma of faith a doctrine that had a long tradition behind it:

> the doctrine which holds that the most blessed Virgin Mary was, from the first moment of her conception, by the singular grace and privilege of almighty God. . . preserved immune from all stain of original sin, is revealed by God and, therefore, firmly, and constantly to be believed by all the faithful.[46]

Since Jesus was God and pre-existent, He could give Mary His mother (to be) gifts not only before He was born of her, but also before <u>she</u> was born. This is the meaning of the Immaculate Conception--a mother gift given by the Lord to Mary at the time of <u>her</u> conception. This does not mean she was virginally conceived: she had earthly parents. It means that "she whom God chose to be His mother never existed for an instant without sanctifying grace in her soul."[47]

This doctrine was a part of the deposit of faith, i.e., it "was included in the body of doctrine originally entrusted to the Apostles and transmitted by them to the Church; otherwise it could not now be made a matter of faith."[48] The doctrine was questioned by Bernard of Clairvaux (1090-1153) and Thomas Aquinas (c. 1225-1274). It was, according to Küng, "explicitly formulated only in the twelfth century and disputed up to the sixteenth, but taught with increasing clarity at the time of the Counter-Reformation and infallibly defined by Pius IX in 1854."[49]

In evaluating the dogma of the Immaculate Conception there are at least five points I would like to make. 1) The doctrine is not explicitly taught in Scripture. Therefore, Catholic theologians must find it implicitly taught, and in doing so cite biblical texts (Gn 3:15; Lk 1:28,41)[50] which are open to differing (and I think, better) interpretation. 2) Another problem is that the dogma not only is not taught in Scripture, but to many it seems contrary "to the biblical and traditional doctrine of original sin."[51] This is the basis upon which St Thomas criticized the teaching:

> Thus in whatever way the blessed Virgin would have been sanctified before animation she never could have incurred the blemish of original sin. She would not then have needed the redemption and salvation which is through Christ. . . .Now it is simply not fitting that Christ should not be saviour of the whole human race. Hence it follows that the sanctification of the blessed Virgin was after animation.[52]

3) This issue (as with Mary's Assumption) is not as easy to discuss and dialogue as some other subjects. The reason for this is that they are not matters of theological opinion and therefore cannot be treated with flexibility. For Catholics it is *de fide*, i.e., a dogma essential to salvation. Further, since this dogma was defined *ex catherda*[53] there seems to be no point in discussing the ramifications of the dogma. Such themes as this and the Assumption of Mary are issues which tend to polarize theological thinking and make it difficult to build bridges of understanding. These dogmas rouse all the non-Catholic suspicions of Mariolatry and fears that the specialness of Jesus Christ is being diminished.[54] 4) The dogma seems to give the impression that both Jesus and Mary

must be spared any connection to or identification with sex.
As Küng says, "the sanctity (understood in a moral sense)
of Jesus and Mary had to be protected from the evil influence
of sex."[55] 5) Finally, it is somewhat distressing, in this
ecumenical age, to face this dogma and realize it is yet
another "Marian riddle" and has further encouraged an already exaggerated devotion to the Blessed Virgin. One is
in sympathy with Walter J. Hollenweger's question and with
its implication of mild despair: ". . .one would ask where
is the need for the doctrine of the immaculate conception?"[56]

C. The Assumption of Mary (1950)

The peak of the "Marian Age" came in 1950 when Pope
Pius XII defined the dogma of Mary's Assumption over the
misgivings of Protestants, Orthodox, and Catholics alike.
The definition reads, in part, as follows:

> . . .by the authority of our Lord Jesus Christ, of the
> blessed apostles Peter and Paul, and by our own au-
> thority, we proclaim, declare and define as a dogma
> revealed by God: the Immaculate Mother of God, Mary
> ever Virgin, when the course of her earthly life was
> finished, was taken up body and soul into the glory
> of heaven.[57]

The promulgation of this dogma was "the final chapter
of the long tradition of belief in this mystery."[58] The
early Church celebrated a feast on August 15 honoring Mary.
It was a memorial service commenorating her death and was
called the "Dormition (falling asleep) of the Virgin."
This practice was "vigorously present" in both religious
literature and sacred liturgy by the end of the fifth century. Rome adopted the feast in the seventh century and by
the end of the eighth century theologians had changed

dormitio (sleeping) to *assumptio*, thus, the Feast of
Assumption.

> Christian intuition, guided by the Holy Spirit,
> gradually came to see that Mary's share in Christ's
> victory over sin began with her conception in a state
> free from all sin (the state in which Eve was created),
> and ended with her miraculous Assumption (an immunity
> from death and corruption which Eve enjoyed until
> the fall).[60]

Pope Pius XII repeated often the theological reason for
Mary's Assumption was that she was the Mother of God. Mary
was, according to Pius XII, "united to all three Persons of
the Blessed Trinity in a unique relationship--as privileged
daughter, mother and spouse, privileges that involved her
body and soul, that implicated her in extraordinary suffering and joys."[61] From this flows such titles as "Queen of
Heaven," "Mother of the Faithful," and "Mediatrix," as
well as others.

It is difficult to calculate the impact of the promulgation of this dogma upon the non-Catholic world. German
evangelicals expressed that "no event in the history of
doctrine since the Reformation has equalled in significance"
the proclamation of the Assumption of Mary.[62] C. G. Jung
calls it "the most important religious event since the
Reformation."[63] Barry Till echos a familiar refrain: "Once
again Protestants could only see this as Mariolatry, while
for those who were concerned with the future of the whole
ecumenical movement the step could not but be seen as one
which deliberately put further obstacles in the way of
progress."[64] Even Catholic scholars admit this subject is
one of controversy among themselves.[65]

Comments above concerning the Immaculate Conception
of Mary could also be applied here. (See numbers 1, 3, 5
of the preceding section.)

C. G. Jung, a noted psychiatrist and lay theologian,
describes "the dogma of the assumption as a timely response to contemporary yearning for a sense of incarnation
in an apocalyptic world situation." Protestants are
warned that "much of their criticism of Marian dogma con-
fuses psychic with physical truths and judges the former by
criteria appropriate to the latter."[66] Jung himself explains: "Physical is not the only criterion of truth: there
are also _psychic_ truths which can neither be explained nor
proved nor contested in any physical way."[67] As examples
he uses the virgin birth of Christ and the Assumption of
Mary. He says none of the journalists in either the
Catholic or Protestant press said anything about what was
to him the "most powerful motive: namely, the popular movement and psychological need behind it."[68] He points to the
increase of apparitions of Mary and especially to children
and the pope himself as indications "that there was a deep
longing in the masses for an intercessor and mediatrix who
who would at last take her place alongside the Holy Trinity
and be received as the 'Queen of Heaven and Bride of the
heavenly court.'"[69]

Arugments, therefore, "based on historical criticism
will never do justice to the new dogma." First, because the
declaration has not changed anything in Catholic thought
that has not been there already for a thousand years.

Second, Protestants have not understood the signs of the time and they are out of touch with psychic reality.[70]

Finally, Jung appeals to Protestants to remember. . .

> . . .how much it owes its very existence to the Catholic Church. . . .In view of the intellectual *skandalon* which the new dogma represents, he should remind himself of his Christian responsibility--"Am I my brother's (or in this case, my sister's) keeper?"--and examine in all seriousness the reasons, explicit or otherwise, that decided the declaration of the new dogma. In so doing, he should guard against casting cheap aspersions and should do well to assume that there is more in it than papal arbitrariness.[71]

I am not exactly sure what Jung is saying in all this. But of this I am sure, Catholicism will never rescind its dogmas on Mary's Immaculate Conception and Assumption. Pentecostals will probably never embrace them. Thus, the best we can hope for in this case is to seek for continual understanding--theological, historical, psychological, and personal. The charisms of grace and mutual acceptance and respect are called for in dialogue, in charismatic contacts, and in personal relationships. A part of Job's suffering (the theme of Jung's book) was the misunderstanding and confusion of his brethren about Job's "theology."

III. *"Pray for us sinners. . . ."*
      THEOLOGICAL PERSPECTIVES ON MARY

Up to now the contrasts drawn between Roman Catholics and Pentecostals concerning Mary may tend to leave the impression that ecumenical progress is virtually impossible. However, in my view, this is not the case. All the problems will not be solved in one dialogue exchange, but certainly each group will have benefited by discussing this important matter.

314

Part of our wide separation concerning Mary is the result of historical happenings. All of the early reformers honored Mary. But as Reformation theology developed, it did so along separate lines with regard to devotion to Mary. Protestants reduced Marian spirituality while Catholics strengthened it and introduced new dogmas which emphasized the difference.[72] Something was lost in the process. As the Reformation progressed, "Mary became a test of Catholic orthodoxy, an easily recognized symbol of the Catholic faith, and therefore obtrusively preserved or promptly ejected, according as one stood within or outside the work of reform."[73]

By the time of the twentieth century this separation, which began in the sixteenth, became almost total. The singing of the Magnificat was dropped. The Puritans stopped using the Apostles' and Nicene Creeds, which "may have been prompted as much by the mention of the Virgin as by the use of the increasingly offensive and polemical adjective 'catholic.'"[74] Pentecostals have, unwittingly perhaps, followed in this "tradition." Now we find ourselves in a new theological age: post-Vatican II, a world-wide charismatic renewal, fourth generation classical Pentecostals, and Roman Catholics and Pentecostals sitting together in dialogue. Pentecostals still do not sing the Magnificat nor say the Apostles' and Nicene Creeds in worship. But there is much "historical prejudice" to unload so we can return to a biblical, balanced, and spiritual understanding of Mary,[75] the Mother of Jesus.

A. Christ and Mary

The documents of Vatican II make it very clear that
there is but one Mediator and that is Jesus Christ (1 Tim
2:5,6). The role of Mary "in no way obscures or diminishes
this unique mediation of Christ. . . ."[76] Two paragraphs
further it says that the Blessed Virgin "is invoked by the
Church under the titles of Advocate, Auxiliatrix, Adjutrix,
and Mediatrix. These, however, are to be so understood
that they neither take away from nor add anything to the
dignity and efficacy of Christ the one Mediator."[77]

Pentecostals would say Christ is the only mediator
while Roman Catholics teach that Christ is the one mediator
and that Mary also has a strong mediation role as well. To
grasp the nuance of Mary's role here is difficult. One
Catholic writer helps some with this: "Our understanding
of our Blessed Lady depends totally upon our understanding
of her Son."[78] Or, to say it again in other words: "No one
who really understands Mary can misunderstand Jesus."[79]
This christological focus is good but Mary's participation
with Christ as Mediatrix and Coredeemer is still problematic
for non-Catholics.

Catholic dogma would say Mary is not the saviour;
Christ is that. But she is witness and interpreter of the
God to whom we have access in Christ. Christ, not Mary,
is preached. Yet, communion with her is also possible.
However, Giovanni Miegge has made the charge that Catholic
teaching and practice makes of Mary a copy of Christ "in
His life, His person and His work."[80]

316

Sometimes Mary's mediation and intercession for the faithful comes across to non-Catholics as bordering on divine maternalism. The stern (austere) justice of God is contrasted with the extreme mercy and gentleness of Mary. This implies that Mary is more full of love and softer hearted than God. The Blessed Virgin can get around her Son and drop a soothing word in His ear about someone in need.[81] It is something of the mentality of St Bernard who said, "let him who fears the Son take refuge in Mary." Certainly, this view of Mary seems to have changed in recent years with leaders and scholars of the Catholic Church, but the new approaches need to reach the grassroots, the faithful scattered throughout the world.[82]

Mary's role in coredemption consists of her becoming the Mother of the Redeemer and in her compassion and suffering at Calvary. But only Christ is the Redeemer and Mary is one (the first) of the redeemed. "Yet in redeeming men, He willed to associate Mary with Himself in such a way that together they would form the one total principle of man's salvation." Mary's coredemption is "immeasurably below Christ's Redemption in dignity and destiny, and proper to herself alone."[83] Although there are papal Encyclicals to support this role for Mary—Leo XIII, Octobri mense (1891); Pius XI, Ingravescentibus malis (1937); Pius XII, Mediator Dei (1947)—Ludwig Ott says: "Express scriptural proofs are lacking."[84] The constant cry here from Pentecostals would be to ever keep a christological focus and keep Christian theology centered squarely in Scripture. If this is done the role of Mary will find its proper place and not become

317

unduly "embellished."

B. The Holy Spirit and Mary

Heribert Mühlen says that "Western theology has not
adequately developed a doctrine of the Holy Spirit. As a
result, there is a danger of identifying Mary with the
function of the Spirit, since she stands in a unique relationship to him."[85] In 1955 the Presbyterian Church in the
USA issued a statement on "The Marian Cult." (This was one
year after Pius XII declared the year 1954 in honor of
Mary.) Catholic dogma was criticized in four broad areas.
One of them was that Mary had "become in the present age
the virtual incarnation of the Holy Ghost."[86] Pentecostals
have also expressed this danger within Catholicism of con-
fusing or exchanging the role of the Holy Spirit with that
of Mary.

It is satisfying, however, to see that this problem
is recognized by Catholics and hopefully steps are being
taken to rectify it.

> Many theologians have recognized that there is a
> theological stream in Catholicism which attributes to
> Mary the role that Protestants attribute to the Holy
> Spirit. This was more an attitude than a worked out
> theology. . . .At the level of popular piety there
> were real exaggerations. Many of these exaggerations
> were openly admitted at the Second Vatican Council
> . . . ."[87]

Further indications of this shift between Mary and the Holy
Spirit can be demonstrated from an encyclical of Pope Leo
XIII (1894): "Every grace which is given to this world is
dispensed in three ordered stages: from God to Christ,
from Christ to Mary, and from Mary to us."[88] Such a role
for Mary usurps the role of the Holy Spirit. The New

Testament process, on the other hand, is "in the one Holy
Spirit through Christ to the Father" (Eph 2:18; Gal 4:6;
1 Cor 12:4-6; Tit 3:6,7; Jn 14:16-26). The Holy Spirit,
in fact, mediated Himself to Mary just as He does to others.
Because of this it was possible for Mary to complete her
role in God's economy of salvation. "The prime mediator,
then, is the Holy Spirit."[89]

At Vatican II any tendencies toward a dogmatic formulation of the mediation of Mary *(Maria mediatrix gratiae)*
were halted. Instead, the mariological schema was included
into the "Dogmatic Constitution on the Church."[90] However,
Heribert Mühlen points out that even here "Mary is appealed
to under the title 'Mediatrix'" and "this title too is an
example of. . .deficient Pneumatology." For St John uses
the term "the paraclete" for the Holy Spirit which means
precisely Intercessor, Advocate, Helper (Jn 14:16,26; 15:26;
16:7.)[91]

In Ac 1:14 Mary is named along with the twelve disciples as being present in the upper room on the day of
Pentecost. The text mentions her specifically along with
"a group of women." Luke was explicit with regard to Mary.
René Laurentin makes three good points about Mary at
Pentecost. 1) "Mary is the model for the Church in her
receptivity to the Holy Spirit, who forms Christ in the
people of God." 2) "Mary is the model for Christians
baptized in the Spirit." 3) "Mary is also model of the
charismatic life." She is "the model not only for the
charismatics in general but specifically for the praying
in tongues that is characteristic of the Pentecostal

movement."[92] This is an example of a Catholic scholar
getting Mary in proper perspective, which, to the joy and
satisfaction of Pentecostals, is one important service of
the Catholic charismatic renewal.

C. The Church and Mary

Several images are used in Catholic literature to
describe the relationship of Mary to the Church. Some, but
not all, would seem to pose no difficulty for Pentecostals,
even though theologically, they may not use such images
themselves.

We have already seen the emphasis in which Mary is an
example or model of faith and piety. She is also an example
of and for the Church. From the time of her Fiat!, i.e.,
accepting God's proposal for her life, until the events of
Passion Week, Mary was involved with and cooperated with
her Son. In this respect she is an eminent (Catholics would
prefer to say pre-eminent) example for the whole Church of
obedience, identification in suffering, and faith.

Mary can also be seen as a symbol of the Church. She
was a pure virgin in body just as the Church should be in
piety and in practice. Mary is the physical mother of
Christ just as the Church is the spiritual mother of Christians. Mary, in all her chastity, charm, character, and
consecration surely symbolizes what the true nature of the
Church is to be. Such comparisons between Mary and the
Church do not step outside of scriptural tradition but provide deep insights into the divine, mystical reality of both.

Mary was a predecessor of the Church. Some Catholic

scholars call her the "first Christian," which if applied chronologically would be well received by Pentecostals. But if applied in terms of role, value, or position would be problematic. She preceded the Church by consenting to being the mother of our Lord. According to Catholic dogma, she also excels the Church by virtue of "her Immaculate Conception and by her progress in sanctity. . . ." Between Pentecost and her Assumption she preceded the Church, even though she was a part of that Church. "During this period she lived in the Church as its first and most important member. . . .Her hand did not hold the keys of the kingdom, but her prayers sustained the Apostle's hands that held them."[93]

In the Apocalypse is a text which says that in the heavens there appeard "a woman clothed with the sun, the moon under her feet, her head crowned with twelve stars" (12:1). This is a picture, an image of the victorious Church. But some scholars also see in this passage "the personification of the Church in Mary."[94] Here Mary is seen as a prototype of the believing Church in that she is already experiencing the glory that the total Church will some day share. Perhaps the symbolism of this verse could be applied to Mary, but if so only in a secondary way. Of course, Pentecostals would also say that Mary, like all the Apostles, saints, and faithful who have gone before, awaits the day of resurrection; so for us she has not yet entered into that full glory prepared for the Church Triumphant.

A final word on this matter of Mary and the Church.
After much debate the Second Vatican Council decided against
giving a separate treatise on Mary. Her role is included
in the statement about the Church. This decision "was the
closest of all the votes taken in St Peters."[95] This is
important, for in spite of her "unique prerogatives" she is
"still to be regarded as a fellow member of the Church and
not as some kind of semi-divine being exalted above the
Church."[96] This clarification, by a Catholic writer, is
appreciated by non-Catholics; but still in many Catholic
minds Mary remains in a dangerously high exalted position
with her on one side and the rest of the Church on the
other. But to do this distorts the role of Mary and minimizes
the Church.

D. The Special Veneration of Mary

It is necessary to understand something about Catholic
teaching on the communion of saints before discussing the
special veneration of the Blessed Virgin. The phrase, "I
believe in. . .the communion of saints" is one line of the
Apostles' Creed. This idea is central to the life of the
Church. The communion of saints is comprised of all the
faithful regardless of on which side of death they are.
There is, therefore, "the mutual interchange and interplay
of supernatural energies" among the members of the tripartite
Church which is "triumphant in heaven, expectant in purgatory,
and militant on earth." Leo XIII in Mirae caritatis (May 28,
1902), speaking of the communion of the saints, spoke of it
as a "mutual communicaton" on all three levels. It is an

incarnational unity dependent on Christ as the head.[97] All believers are thus united in the mystical body of Christ so there can be exchanges back and forth.

Mary is seen as an intercessor to whom petitions are addressed. Veneration belongs to both the saints and the angels, but she is the queen of them all. "As the saints hold a special place among men, so she holds a special place among the saints."[98] In fact, she is elevated to a position above the angels but below the Godhead. By virtue of Mary's position, prayer to her is considered especially effective. The Vatican II statement on Mary says that "she was, after the Son, exalted by divine grace above all angels and men. Hence, the Church appropriately honors her with special reverence." This reverence, however, is not on the same level as that offered to God. Warnings are given about exaggerations in this regard.[99]

The whole idea of petitioning Mary for some personal need is repugnant to Pentecostals. It does help some, however, to hear in return: "But a prayer to Mary (or one of the saints) is actually a prayer to Jesus." But if that is true, then why not direct prayers to Jesus in the first place? Also, it is a little more help to understand the three levels (see fn 5) of Catholic devotion.

The problem is, however, that much popular Catholic devotion seems to offer Mary a worship that is indistinguishable from that reserved for God alone. Besides, such distinctions are absent in Scripture and it is very difficult to maintain them in practice. "When the average Roman

Catholic invokes the aid of 'Jesus, Mary and Joseph,' it is hard to conceive that He distinguishes, in a split second, between *latria*, *hyperdulia*, and *dulia!*"[100]

No doubt many Pentecostals in southern Europe, Latin America and the Philippines regard all veneration of Mary as superstitious and idolatrous. The repeating of prayers, lighting candles, kneeling before images of Mary could recall to them the words of Jeremiah (albeit inappropriately) where the people say "'You are our father' to a block of wood and cry 'Mother' to a stone" (2:27). From my observation it appears that here is a point where Pentecostals view Catholic dogma and Catholic practice showing one of its greatest gulfs. If common Catholics would be more authentic in their own theology of Mary it would be a great ecumenical step forward and especially, I believe, Pentecostals would begin to respond more favorably.[101]

A few words should be said about the miracles of Mary. Certainly one thing Pentecostals and Catholics have in common is a belief in the supernatural and the reality of miracles taking place in our world. The problem comes, however, when Mary instead of Jesus is given the credit for such miracles. Pentecostals also believe in the appearance of angels, although it does not happen on a large scale. (However, it is true that in very recent years more and more angelic visitations are being reported and many books are now published about it.) But it disturbs Pentecostals to read about the many apparitions of <u>Mary</u>, instead of Jesus or an angel. Finally, various forms of religious paraphernalia

related to Mary is received with a degree of skepticism.
Indeed these matters are rather peripheral and are not at
the center of the theological issues concerning Mary. But
on a popular, pastoral level they are important. Because
often it is smaller, less significant things which cause
mistrust and criticism, especially at the level of ordinary
piety.[102]

It is true that the impact of Vatican II on Marian
devotion "has been enormous" as one Catholic historian put
it. He goes on to add: "There has been a great decline in
traditional forms of piety toward Mary: rosaries and medals
have been tossed away, statues of Mary have been removed,
hymns to Mary have faded out of memory, and May Day celebrations have disappeared."[103] On the other hand, scriptural
and historical foundations of Mariology are receiving much
attention by theologians and scholars. Certainly this change
is welcomed by Pentecostals with the hope that such emphasis
will continue.

E. Catholic Charismatics and Mary

Research seems to indicate that the Catholic charismatic response to devotion to the Blessed Virgin varies.[104]
René Laurentin reports that in France and Canada, Mary is
"enthusiastically invoked" in renewal prayer meetings. It
is usually simple, biblical and matter-of-fact. However,
some fervent persons may use "questionable formulas of the
preconciliar period." Such cases are a detriment to the
ecumenical spirit and to authenticity as well. In America
there is a "much greater reserve" in this area. Often the

prayer groups are interdenominational, so caution in devotion to Mary is shown. The Catholic renewal has seemingly "rediscovered Mary" and "now it must learn to express Mary's spirit-animated presence in the communion of saints in a way that is faithful to the spirit of the movement itself, which is so truly biblical and ecumenical and which will not be satisfied with more words."[105]

Perhaps Laurentin is right when he says that the Catholic renewal has rediscovered Mary. But if so, it is only incidental to the more important fact that charismatics have made a fresh and dynamic rediscovery of Jesus Christ as Lord, and of the person of the Holy Spirit. It is expected that for participants in the Catholic renewal, Mary will have a role. But this role seems to be rather balanced and biblically oriented in practice and expression. Dorothy Ranaghan seems to verify this when she says:

> Pruning superstitious and quasimagical accretions from true Marian devotion has been a healthy process. But we may see more, not less of Mary, and of Jesus whom she reveals, at the end of this process. Mary is eternally intertwined with the body, the people, and the church of Jesus Christ--essentially so.106

Yet, Pentecostals seem skeptical and unhappy at the attention Mary receives in the Catholic renewal. Many would agree with the charge of H. M. Carson (a Baptist) that the renewal is too strongly committed to Mary. To hear those who have experienced the release (or baptism) of the Holy Spirit profess a deeper devotion to Mary and the rosary is a stumbling block.[107]

Catholics are not unaware of this feeling on the part of Pentecostals.[108] The consternation expressed by

Pentecostals comes largely from two factors: 1) there is no emphasis given to Mary in our theology; and 2) in the "early days" when a Roman Catholic received the baptism in the Holy Spirit, it was expected that he would leave his Roman Catholic faith and embrace Pentecostal theology and practice, and attend a Pentecostal church. In order to illustrate this rather deep apprehension by Pentecostals, I have chosen four items from Catholic charismatic literature, probably all of which would be severely criticized by most Pentecostals.

1. ". . .Mary at Lourdes was the only Catholic charismatic of the last century with prophecy, healings and conversions; she was keeping the charismatic gifts alive."[109]

2. During the Catholic charismatic conference at the University of Notre Dame, South Bend, Indiana in 1973 there were three peaks of ovation. One was when Cardinal Suenens, in the closing homily, said the secret to finding "unity with the Holy Spirit in the best way is our unity with Mary, the Mother of God."[110]

3. St Patrick's parish, Providence, Rhode Island is a charismatic parish and Christian community. One of its members reports that "the Holy Spirit unmistakably pointed us along the pathway of devotion to Mary as the way He wanted us to go in order to bear rich fruit." And again, "Jesus has taught us over and over again to go to His mother, to learn from her."[111]

4. A message in tongues occured in a Catholic charismatic prayer group and the interpretation that came was

the first part of the *Ave Maria:* "Hail Mary, full of grace, the Lord is with thee."[112]

For Pentecostals, the first example is a problem of the special power and veneration of Mary; the second, of Mary almost superceding the Holy Spirit; the third, of the Holy Spirit and Jesus pointing to Mary, instead of the other way around; and the fourth, of what many would consider a misuse or inappropriate use of the spiritual gifts of utterance. It is not intended to discuss these examples one by one, but collectively they serve to show some of the concerns of Pentecostals when they see Marian devotion in the Catholic charismatic renewal.

On the one hand, Kilian McDonnell is correct when he advises Christians of all confessions not to neglect to proclaim the full gospel, which includes not neglecting texts of the New Testament which discuss Mary. For it is true that "over the centuries the experience of millions of Christians witness to the role of Mary." Should this whole historical reality now be dismissed?[113]

On the other hand, Pentecostals would plead for consideration of their complaints about the overemphasis, escalating theology, and exaggerations in popular devotion to the Blessed Virgin Mary. They would hope to see in the Catholic charismatic renewal a continued emphasis upon the Lordship of Christ and leadership of the Holy Spirit. Mary will have a place, but one that is biblical and is updated by the latest work of Catholic and Protestant biblical scholars alike. Also, charismatics can help the cause of ecumenism greatly by not allowing extremes in Marian devotion within their ranks and by speaking out against wrong and unwarranted practices, even by Roman Catholic standards, among the Catholic faithful.

CONCLUSION

Almost eighty years ago G. M. Grant wrote an article
entitled, "The Outlook of the Twentieth Century in Theology."
He said the only kind of theology worthy of this century
would be one produced by "the ecumenical reason and conscience, enlightened by the Holy Spirit 'which lighteth
every man who cometh into the world.'"[114] Indeed, in
ecumenical dialogue the two ingredients of reason and
enlightenment are absolutely necessary. An encouraging
factor in considering our different understandings of the
role of Mary in the Christian faith is that in the very
process of "reasoning together" the Holy Spirit is provided
an opportunity to enlighten both sides, strip away mis-
understandings, show the areas of consensus, pinpoint the
specific problems, and indicate the way ahead. This is why
such dialogue over knotty theological issues is so important.

It will not be easy to reach ecumenical agreement on
Mary. But a start has been made. To Roman Catholics I would
suggest several things:

*In Marian theology, put the stress on the biblical
evidence and continue to follow the openness expressed by
Vatican II.

*Do not feel attacked when there is critical examina-
tion by non-Catholics of some aspects of Marian theology
that is at best only implicitly to be found in Scripture,
though fully developed in Church tradition and by papal
decree.

*Realize the "excess baggage" that has accumulated

over the centuries--myths, legends, miracle stories, songs and poems--with regard to Mary, which works as a "log jam" for non-Catholics and prevents them from being fully objective.

*Continue to recognize and seek to rectify the exaggerations and excesses of Marian devotion by faithful Catholics so that at the grassroots level some barriers to ecumenical progress can be removed.

*Continue to seek for ways to bring understanding to the non-Catholic churches on the current status of Marian thought within the Roman Catholic Church.

Of course, dialogue is a two-way street and I have some recommendations for Pentecostals:

*Recognize that not only do we not have a theology or "view" of Mary, but we seem to go out of the way to avoid her. This is wrong. We need to examine not only her example, but also her role in the New Testament.

*In seeking to understand the Catholic position on Mary we must realize that simply taking the apologetical and polemical approach is not sufficient. We must admit our theological prejudice and maintain a conciliatory attitude.

*Time and diligence must be expended to understand Marian theology as it is today in the Catholic Church. We must not judge it based only on medieval evidence or even pre-Vatican II statements and practice.

*Accept the fact that Catholicism has always had a great emphasis upon the Blessed Virgin Mary. She is a part of their dogma, their history, their faith. Allow them that privilege. She deserves some recognition in and by the Church.

*In criticizing Catholic dogma on practices concerning Mary, do so objectively and only after research and "reasoning" and never fall into the trap of using emotional language, making unfair generalizations, or citing extreme cases.

Kilian McDonnell has expressed a positive hope about Mary in the charismatic perspective. Classical Pentecostals and Protestant charismatics are very diverse. But in two spiritual forces--presence (in the sense of God acting and revealing Himself as Person and One who cares) and praise-- they are together. These two characteristics are also found in Mary, the Mother of Jesus. Thus, perhaps "Mary can become an instrument of understanding between classical Pentecostals and Protestant charismatics on the one hand, and Roman Catholic charismatics on the other."[115]

To speak of a "balanced" view of Mary may be the same as speaking of an "ecumenical" view. In either case, I think René Laurentin gives us a fitting conclusion to this discussion of Mary, who was so singularly blessed of God and is the Mother of our Lord.

> . . .many theological or pious theories have proven untenable about Mary, many honorific titles have been forgotten, and many devotions have been jettisoned, sometimes hastily and in an excessively radical spirit; but amid this collapse of a "Mariology" and a "Marian" devotion that were marked by extremism and an inflated narrowness, something solid and inescapably true has been coming to the fore. It has

332

> become clear that Mary, as Mother of Jesus, is at the
> very heart of revelation and the Church life. It is
> essential that Christians make this rediscovery, for
> Mary's real place has often been mistaken; her true
> stature has been hidden by too many superstructures.[116]

A PERSONAL NOTE

This study has been both enjoyable and enlightening.
I accepted the assignment with some apprehension because I
felt I knew so very little Marian theology and because I had
never before written a paper for a theological dialogue.
My attitude, perspective, and appreciation concerning Mary's
role as the "first Christian" has been significantly clarified and enriched as a result of this study. Like so many
Pentecostals I have largely ignored Mary and her importance
in God's economy. On the other hand, I understood little
of Roman Catholic teaching concerning Mary. I rejected so
many Catholic aspects of her place and importance without
giving enough serious reflection and study into the subject.
I was guilty of "throwing the baby out with the bath."

What has happened to me ought to happen to everyone
on both sides of this Dialogue, i.e., we should change and
adjust our view as we become convinced and enlightened by
each other, by research, and by personal reflection.
Furthermore, any changes should be reflected in our attitudes, contacts, and writings. For only if we act in this
way can a dialogue pay ongoing dividends.

FOOTNOTES

[1] Kilian McDonnell, "Protestants, Pentecostals, and Mary," New Covenant 6, 9 (March 1977) p 29.

[2] Theodore P. Letis, "Mariology: The Answer for Catholic/Protestant Ecumenism?" Reformation Research Press 1, 1 (Spring 1981) p 3. This article was quoting from a Providence, Rhode Island newspaper The Providence Journal-Bulletin entitled "Scholarship on Mary May Lead to New Unity" (August 23, 1980).

[3] The Sunday Missal (Glasgow: Collins, 1975, revised edition July 1977), p 798. This prayer, known as the "Hail Mary," or "The Angelus," or "Ave Maria," or "the Angelic Salutation," is probably one of the most popular in the history of Christianity. Juniper Carol says it is "the treasured possession of the entire Christian West" (Vol 3, p 43).

There are three parts to this prayer: the greeting of the Archangel Gabriel in Lk 1:28; the words of Elizabeth in Lk 1:42; the last part is a petition added by the Church

The first two parts were "early used as a salutation, the (last) part was added in the eleventh century, and the prayer thus constituted became very popular. . . .The addition of the name of Jesus is commonly ascribed to Pope Urban IV (1261). The complete Ave as now used was printed in 1495 and approved in 1508" by Pope Pius V--Collier's Encyclopedia Vol 3 (New York: Macmillan, 1980), p 369.

For further discussion see Juniper B. Carol (ed.), Mariology Vol 3 (Milwaukee: Bruce Pub. Co., 1961), pp 68-73; New Catholic Encyclopedia Vol 6 (London: McGraw-Hill, 1967), p 898. (New Catholic Encyclopedia is hereafter condensed to NCE.)

[4] Jaroslav Pelikan, The Riddle of Roman Catholicism (London: Hodder & Stoughton, 1960), p 120. His chapter on Mary (pp 120-134) is entitled "Ave Maria." He opens the subject with the prayer and divides the chapter into subtitles, using the text of the "Hail Mary." I chose to adopt his schematic approach in this paper.

[5] It is important here to distinguish the three levels of worship in Catholic theology: 1) Latria--adoration and worship which is given only to God; 2) Hyperdulia--special veneration addressed to Mary, the Mother of God for her unique dignity and exalted privileges; 3) Dulia--veneration given to the saints as servants of God. (More will be said about this later in this paper.)

[6] Juniper Carol, Mariology Vol 3, p 69.

[7]Ibid., p 71. "Canonically, an indulgence is a remission in the sight of God of temporal punishment due to sin the guilt of which is already forgiven; it is granted from the treasury of the Church by ecclesiastical authority, in the manner of absolution in the case of the living, and in the manner of suffrage in the case of the dead"--J. J. Markham, "Indulgences, Canon Law of," NEC Vol 7, p 485.

[8]Thomas Bokenkotter, A Concise History of the Catholic Church (Garden City, NY: Doubleday, 1977), p 405. The other subjects he lists as being major issues "have involved the relation of Scripture to tradition, . . .the true meaning of the Lord's supper, . . .and papal primacy and infallibility" (p 405).

[9]Handel H. Brown, When Jesus Came (Grand Rapids, MI: Eerdmans, 1963), p 87.

One factor which helps close this chasm has been the recent emphasis in Catholic scholarship to use a more biblical approach to Mariology. An example of this is the reverent and humane study by Salvatore Garofalo, Mary in the Bible (Milwaukee: Bruce Pub. Co., 1961). He is a professor at the Pontifical Urban University of Rome. On almost every page there is Scripture and it is refreshing and unoffensive to non-Catholics.

In spite of the ecumenical importance of the role of Mary in salvation, there has not been, until very recently, a lot of dialogue on the subject. The 1976 Catholic Almanac (Huntington, ID: Our Sunday Visitor, 1975), pp 337-341, does not show a single conference held between US Catholics and Protestants over the previous ten year period. This is rather surprising since Vatican II "laid down the groundwork for a new approach that does much to meet traditional Protestant objections to the Catholic position on Mary" (cf. Bokenkotter, A Concise History, p 408).

[10]Francis P. Hoy, "Handmaiden of the Spirit," Paraclete 12, 3 (Summer 1978) pp 25-27.

[11]Gerry Rauch, "Mary's Role in the Incarnation and Redemption, No 1." A cassette tape of a talk given 29 March 1981 at a meeting of the Christian community "Jerusalem," Brussels, Belgium.

[12]C. Stuhlmueller, "Annunciation," NCE Vol 1, p 565.

[13]Ibid. Catholic theologians also present Mary as the new Temple, as well as the new Ark of the Covenant, for the Holy Spirit overshadows her (Lk 1:35) just as in the Tabernacle and Temple (Ex 40:35; 1 Kg 8:10,11). She also represents "God's people at prayer, in pilgrimage to the Temple, struggling with the evil one and witnessing the promised salvation" (Heb 1:35, 45-55; 2:21-50).

See also Kilian McDonnell, "Protestants, Pentecostals, and Mary," New Covenant (March 1977) pp 27-29.

[14] Handel H. Brown, When Jesus Came, p 90.

[15] Ibid., p 105.

[16] M. E. McIver, "Magnificat," NCE Vol 9, p 72.

[17] C. P. Ceroke, "Mary, Blessed Virgin, I (in the Bible)," NCE Vol 9, p 340.

[18] Ralph J. Woods (ed.), The Catholic Companion to the Bible (New York: J. B. Lippincott, 1956), pp 276-279.

[19] Ibid. Much more could be said about the Magnificat. The title "Magnificat" comes from the first word of its text in the Latin Vulgate. M. C. McIver outlines the Magnificat into three parts; vv 46-50 is Mary's praise, vv 51-53 Mary recalls God's acts, and vv 54,55 speak of God's divine plan being perfected in and through her. One Protestant author calls this the "Gospel According to Mary" and says it is a "manifesto of the Kingdom of God." He also quotes C. S. Lewis' description of the Magnificat as "a calm and terrible gladness." (cf. David H. C. Read, "The Gospel According to Mary," New Pulpit Digest 59, 410 (November-December 1974) pp 48-52.

There is a very fine discussion of Lk 1:46-55 by Robert C. Tannehill, "The Magnificat Poem," Journal of Biblical Literature 93, 2 (June 1074) pp 263-275. Here the author tries to show that the full meaning and significance of the text cannot be realized without taking its poetic structure into account.

By the way, it is interesting that Salvatore Garofalo in Mary in the Bible says that some Catholic scholars feel that Lk 1; 2 were written by John the disciple.

[20] Francis P. Hoy, "Mary's Experience with the Holy Spirit," Paraclete 12, 1 (Winter 1978) p 16.

[21] The denial of the virginal conception of Jesus by contemporary theologians is a subject related to the role of Mary outside our purpose here. Generally, Pentecostals and Catholics would agree on the divine participation in the conception of Jesus. Both Confessions would reject the modern position which says the virginal conception is not necessarily true from an historical standpoint. (cf. Elsie Gibson, "Mary and the Protestant Mind," Review for Religious 24, 3 (May 1975) pp 383-398, especially p 384.)

The virgin birth was part of the teaching and faith of the early Church. It was held by the giants of the patristic period and was not challenged by the Reformers. Until nineteenth century liberal Protestantism "it was the

universal belief of Christendom." All of the major creeds
confess it because two cardinal elements of the Christian
faith must be preserved; 1) Jesus was God in human form,
and 2) the real humanity of Jesus. "While we maintain that
the Virgin Birth is not 'contrary to nature,' we readily
admit that it transcends our knowledge of nature." (cf.
Handel H. Brown, When Jesus Came, pp 98-100.)

Bokenkotter, A Concise History, says the subject of
the virginal conception of Jesus is one, "that no Catholic
would have dreamed of debating a few years ago. . . ."
René Laurentin, a defender of the traditional position,
claims that the "symbolic interpretation of the virgin birth
is now the dominant one among continental European Catholic
theologians" (p 411).

On this question of the biological virginity of Mary,
the highly controversial and bestselling The New Dutch
Catechism, "purposely chose vague formulas which, though
compatible with orthodox interpretation, leave openings for
further doctrinal development"--John A. Coleman, The Evo-
lution of Dutch Catholicism, 1958-1974 (London: University
of California, 1978), p 248. The catechism sold more than
a million copies in six lnaguages--Dutch, English, German,
Spanish, French, Italian--and "became an international
Catholic best seller" (p 257).

[22]L. G. Owens, "Virgin Birth," NCE Vol 14, p 692.
(Italics mine.)

[23]Hans Küng, On Being a Christian (Garden City, NY:
Doubleday, 1976), p 453. The Latin scheme of things, as
it developed historically, would be:

virginitas ante partum = virginal conception ("before");

in partu = without birth pangs and/or rupture of the
hymen membrane ("in");

post partum = no sexual relations and no further
children ("after"), that is, *semper virgo*, for all time or
perpetual virginity.

[24]L. G. Owens, "Virgin Birth," p 693.

[25]Ibid., p 695. The purpose, or significance, of this
teaching for Catholics seems to be two-fold: 1) To emphasize
Jesus' "Ressurrection-freedom from subjection to the laws of
the corporate world." 2) To contrast Mary (Lk 1:28) with
Eve (Gen 3:16) who did suffer childbirth pangs. Thus, for
Christ, it is a reflection of the glory of His eteranal birth.
For Mary, it is "a privilege of her role as the new Eve, ex-
empt from the curse and sorrows of the first Eve" (p 695).

[26]Raymond E. Brown, Karl P. Donfried, Joseph A. Fitzmyer,
and John Reumann (eds.), Mary in the New Testament (New York:

Paulist Press, 1978), p 72. This is perhaps the best recent book on Mary. It is a united assessment by both Protestant and Roman Catholic scholars and is very sensitive to the ecumenical issues and the problems of biblical textual study.

[27] H. M. Carson, _Dawn or Twilight? A Study of Contemporary Roman Catholicism_ (Laicester, England: Inter-Varsity Press, 1976), pp 121,122.

[28] Msgr J. D. Conway, _What the Church Teaches_ (New York: Harper, 1962), p 88.

The whole question of how many there were in the "Holy Family" is a subject all its own. Scholarship is divided. Not all Protestants believe there were other children born of Mary. Not all Roman Catholics follow their Church's teaching that Jesus was the only birth of Mary. This is not the ecumenical question. The major issue is _perpetual virginity_, and here much dialogue is necessary.

[29] John Randall, Helen P. Hawkinson, and Sharyn Malloy, _Mary: Pathway to Fruitfulness_ (Locust Valley, NY: Living Flame Press, 1978), p 57.

[30] Frances P. Hoy, "Mary's Experience," p 19. A personal experience is relevent here. In May 1981 I was in Rome and had opportunity to view Michelangelo's magnificent _Pieta_ in St Peters'. This sculpture shows a rather young, sweetly serious Mary holding the broken, crucified body of Jesus. Any who view this masterpiece do so with awe, reverence and sympathy.

To me the bereaved mother does not appear to be overcome by the tragedy, but quietly trying to fully understannd it all. The face of Mary conveys a spiritual dignity that reveals a deep and enduring faith. Here, is clearly the focus of attention. It is her controlled grief and great loss that a viewer senses. You see her trust in God softly carved upon her face. Indeed, she is a model and example for every Christian.

[31] Gerry Rauch, "Mary's Role," cassette tape.

[32] Hans Küng, _On Being a Christian_, p 459.

[33] Kilian McDonnell, "Protestants, Pentecostals, and Mary," p 28.

[34] J. H. Walgrave, "Doctrine, Development of," _NCE_ Vol 4, p 940.

"Deposit of faith" became a theological term in the sixteenth century and at Vatican I (1869-1870) it was canonized and identified "with the revelation made known by God and handed down to the Church through the Apostles."

It "can be considered as an ensemble of truths entrusted by Christ to the Apostles and now guarded as a
sacred trust by the Church, which can neither substract nor
add to it." This means the Church "guards the deposit by
making it relevant to every age and mentality" and not by
keeping it rigid and immobile as a buried treasure." "The
deposit of faith includes all that God has entrusted to the
Church--His great acts in history. . ."--P. F. Chirico,
"Deposit of Faith," NCE Vol 4, p 780.

[35]Ibid. Vincent of Lerins (died before 450) spoke of
a triple test by which the Church could differentiate between true and false traditions: *quod ubique, quod semper,
quod ab omnibus creditum est*--"what has been believed everywhere, always, and by all." This is called the Vincentian
Rule. It has, however, since the Reformation been brought
into question and today has fallen into disuse. (cf.
Walgrave, p 940.)

[36]Ibid., p 942. Mystery is a very real part of Roman
Catholicism. Many of the dogmas relating to Mary are bound
up in mystery. Examples would be the birth of Jesus *in partu*
(fn. 23), the Immaculate Conception, and the Assumption, as
well as others. Avery Dulles, a prominent Catholic theologian defines mystery: "In the theology of Revelation, a
truth that man cannot discover except from revelation and
that, even after revelation exceeds human comprehension."
This is the primary meaning but it has two connected meanings: 1) in soteriology, i.e., "the great redemptive acts
of God in history," especially Jesus; 2) in the theology of
worship, i.e., "the sacramental reenactment of the redemptive
deeds of Christ"--A. Dulles, "Mystery (in Theology)," NCE
Vol 10, p 151.

[37]There are in Pentecostal denominations and independent churches unwritten procedures for dealing with doctrinal change. Current situations which are not explicitly
discussed in Scripture are interpreted and put into a traditional Pentecostal "deposit of faith." For example,
fashions for women, rejection of certain "worldly" practices
and modern forms of amusement, specific worship patterns,
and criticizing questionable social issues are just some of
the areas where Pentecostals decide ("pass" or "disapprove")
practice, attitudes, behaviour not explicitly taught in
Scripture. Though this procedure usually operates informally
and on a much less sophisticated scale than in Catholicism,
it exists nonetheless. In view of this, we Pentecostals
should be more prudent in expressing our disfavor with
official dogmas and decrees of Catholicism which come from
centuries of history, tradition, and theological reflection
and development.

[38]C. G. Jung, Answer to Job: The Problem of Evil, Its
Psychological and Religious Origins (New York: World Pub.
Co. 1960), p 195.

[39]P. C. Hoelle, "Mother of God," NCE Vol 10, p 22.

[40]J. M. Carmody, "Theotokos," NCE Vol 14, p 75.

[41]Richard P. McBrien, Catholicism Vol 2 (Minneapolis: Winston Press, 1980), p 872. Chapter XXIV entitled "Mary and the Church," pp 865-901 is a recent and excellent treatment. It contains the latest attitudes about Mary and is very ecumenically oriented.

[42]A very good discussion of *theotokos* is contained in Walter J. Burghardt and William F. Lynch (eds.), The Idea of Catholicism (New York: Meridian Books, 1960). The chapter, written by Walter J. Burghardt, entitled "Theotokos: The Mother of God," pages 166-183, is a discussion of the Council of Ephesus and its significance for today. The following remarks come from the opening paragraphs of this article:

"One of the most significant sermons of antiquity was delievered fifteen centuries ago" in the Church of St Mary at Ephesus by Cyril, Patriarch of Alexandria, to some 200 bishops of the East. He opened with an eulogy to Mary: "'Hail, from us, Mary, Mother of God, majestic treasure of the whole world. . .crown of virginity, sceptre of orthodoxy . . . .'" He closed with this remarkable sentence: "'May we. . .reverence the undiveded trinity, while we sing the praise of the ever-virgin Mary, that is to say, the holy Church, and of her spotless Son and Bridegroom.'"

Cyril dignified Mary as "Mother of God," and as "Mary, that is to say, the holy Church." In 431 the significane of the divine maternity "lay in its relationship to the physical Christ." Today its significance "lies in its relationship to the mystical Christ." The divine maternity, in 431, gave a "fresh insight into the person of Christ, into Christology." Today "it suggests a fresh insight into the work of Christ, into soteriology" (pp 166,167).

[43]J. M. Carmody, "Theotokos," p 75.

[44]Jaroslav Pelikan, Riddle of Catholicism, p 124. This is a harsh criticism by a Protestant scholar. However, it seems to have some justification as later centuries showed a proliferation of Marian devotion. McBrien (fn 41) points out that after Ephesus, Marian feasts began to multiply. Whereas before Ephesus there was only one (the feast of the Purification), by the "middle of the seventh century four separate Marian feasts were observed in Rome: the Annunciation, the Purification, the Assumption, and the Nativity of Mary" (p 873).

[45]In passing, it is interesting to point out that the Council of Ephesus was called to convene on Pentecost, 431. This year (1981) is the 1550th anniversary of the Council. Also, it is the sixteenth centenary of the Council of

Constantinople (381) to which we owe one of the great
Christian creeds and a special emphasis on the doctrine of
the Holy Spirit. Pope John Paul II, in a letter to Catholic
bishops said: "The anniversaries of the two great Councils
this year direct our thoughts and hearts in a special way
to the Holy Spirit and to Mary, the Mother of God." The
Pope called for a great ecumenical celebration in Rome on
Pentecost, June 7 (just as it did in 431). That great and
unusual meeting was held in the Marian Basilica of Rome,
in spite of the personal injury to the Pope. Indeed it
appears that the subject of the 1981 Roman Catholic/Pente-
costal Dialogue is most timely and important. (cf. "Letter
of the Holy Father Pope Jon Paul II to the Bishops of the
Catholic Church" (Rome: Vatican Polyglot Press, 1981).

[46]J. Neuner and J. Dupuis (eds.), The Christian Faith
(Bangalore, India: Theological Pub. in India, 1978), pp
196,197. This 687-page book contains doctrinal documents
of the Catholic Church. A British edition existed first as
The Teaching of the Catholic Church (Cork, Ireland: Mercien
Press, 1967). Among others, the book is based on the Latin
classic by Denzinger and Schönmetzer, Enchiridion Symbolorum,
Definitionum et Declarationum de Rebus Fidei et Morum, 1962.

[47]F. J. Sheed, Theology for Beginners (New York: Sheed
and Ward, 1957), pp 165-167. (Chap XV "The Mother of
God," pp 161-170.)

[48]E. O. O'Connor, "Immaculate Conception," NCE Vol 7,
p 378.

[49]Küng, On Being a Christian, p 454.

[50]Ludwig Ott, Fundamentals of Catholic Dogma (Rockford,
IL: Tan Books, 1974), p 200. The same criticism is brought
by the Orthodox theologian, John Meyendorff (see fn 51).

[51]John Meyendorff, "The Meaning of Tradition," in
Scripture and Ecumenism (Louvain: Editions E. Nauwelaerts,
1965), pp 48,49.

[52]Thomas R. Heath (ed.), St Thomas Aquinas, Our Lady,
Summa Theologiae Vol 51 (London: Eyre and Spothiswoode,
1979), pp 11,13. There is an interesting footnote by
Heath, which reads in part: "After the dogmatic definition
of the Immaculate Conception the *magisterium* no longer fav-
ors the doctrine of this article" (pp 10,11). He goes on
in the footnote to improve the sentence I quoted in the paper as follows: '"in whatever way the blessed Virgin would
have been sanctified before animation she would never have
been subject to the common law of original sin,' namely,
she never would have been in danger of having sin" (p 11).

Duns Scotus (c. 1264-1308) a Franciscan from Oxford
provided the answer for Catholics to solve the dilemma of

harmonizing Mary's Immaculate Conception with the dogma of original sin. He argued: "'. . .Mary more than anyone else would have needed Christ as her Redeemer, since she would have contracted original sin. . .if the grace of the Mediator had not prevented this. Thus, as others needed Christ so that the sin already contracted should be remitted for them through His merit, so Mary had even greater need of a prevenient Mediator lest there be sin to be contracted and lest she contract it'"--E. E. O'Connor, "Immaculate Conception," p 381.

[53]It is my experience that most Pentecostals do not properly understand the meaning of *ex cathedra*. The term *ex cathedra* "symbolizes the Roman pontiff's title to that supreme authority and to the charism of infallibility that accompanies it: because he is the successor of Peter, head of the college of Apostles. . . .Through succession to his chair, or supreme office, in the Church, the authority and infallibility of Peter lives on in the Roman pontiff"-- E. G. Hardwick, "Ex Cathedra," NCE Vol 5, p 699.

The "Chair of Peter" is a theological term which signifies the teaching authority of the pope. "The chair in which a bishop presides over his people was from early times regarded with respect as symbolizing his authority, since it was from his official chair. . .that he gave the homilies by which he instructed his flock in the Word of God." The chair of Peter indicates the pope's authoritative power in matters of doctrine, which is the origin of the expression, *ex cathedra*. "Such a papal pronouncement (very rarely made) is one in which the pope's infallibility defines a doctrine that is irrevocably binding on all the faithful"--B. Forshaw, "Chair of Peter," NCE Vol 3, p 422.

It was not until the First Vatican Council that the dogma of the infallibility of the pope was defined. To the best of my research, I only find twice when the pope spoke *ex cathedra*, i.e., infallibly; in 1854 (15 years before Vatican I) when the dogma of Mary's Immaculate Conception was defined, and in 1950 (12 years before Vatican II opened) when the dogma of the Assumption of Mary was defined.

[54]Barry Till, The Churches Search for Unity (London: Penquin Books, 1972), pp 432,433.

[55]Küng, On Being a Christian, p 454. This problem is reflected in the book about Mary by Marina Warner entitled Alone of all Her Sex: The Myth and the Cult of the Virgin Mary (New York: Alfred A. Knopf, 1976). Another helpful book in this regard is Power and Sexuality by Samuel Laeuchli (Philadelphia: Temple Univ. Press, 1972). It helps a person to understand the early Catholic attitude toward sex.

[56]Walter J. Hollenweger, "Ave Maria: Mary, the Reformers and the Protestants," One in Christ 13, 4 (1977) p 287.

[57]Neuner and Dupuis, The Christian Faith, p 200.
The statement ends with a rather solemn warning (as did also
the definition of the Immaculate Conception of Pius IX, p
197): "Wherefore, if anyone--which God forbid--should wil-
fully dare to deny or call in doubt what has been defined
by us, let him know that he certainly has abandoned the
divine and catholic faith" (p 200).

[58]J. W. Langlinais, "Assumption," NCE Vol 1, p 971.

[59]D. F. Hickey, "Dormition of the Virgin," NCE Vol 4,
p 1017.

[60]J. W. Langlinais, "Assumption," pp 972,973.

[61]Ibid., p 973.

[62]Edmund Schlink (et. al.), "An Evangelical Opinion
on the Proclamation of the Dogma of the Bodily Assumption
of Mary," The Luthern Quarterly 3, 2 (May 1951) p 123.

[63]C. G. Jung, Answer to Job, pp 191,192.

[64]Berry Till, The Churches Search for Unity, p 182.

[65]Küng, On Being a Christian, p 457, and J. W.
Langlinais, "Assumption," pp 971-975.

[66]Samuel C. Pearson, "Ecumenism, Feminism, and the
Reconstruction of Marian Theology," Mid-Stream 19, 4
(October 1980) p 446. (In this article the author is
discussing Jung's Answer to Job.)

[67]C. G. Jung, Answer to Job, pp 13,14.

[68]Ibid., p 187. "When the immaculate conception was
promulgated, petitions began coming to the Vatican for a
definition regarding the assumption of the Virgin into heaven, . . .During the century that followed, more than 8,000,
000 persons signed petitions; yet Rome hesitated, the doctrine being difficult to define on the basis of Scripture
and early witnesses to Christian faith"--Jaroslav Pelikan,
"Mary," Encyclopedia Britannica, 1958, p 1000. This
quote seems to lend some support to Jung's idea that the
dogma of the Assumption of Mary met a psychological need
for many Catholics.

[69]Ibid., p 188.

[70]Ibid., pp 189,190. (The "new" dogma makes sense
when it is known that this book was first published in 1952
as Antwort auf Hiob. Jung was about 75 when he wrote it.)

[71]Ibid., pp 195,196.

[72]Walter J. Hollenweger, "Ave Maria," p 289.

[73]Ross Mackenzie, "Calvin and the Calvinists on Mary,"
One in Christ 16, 1-2 (1980) p 73.

[74]Ibid., p 72.

[75]Samuel C. Pearson (see fn 66) discusses several
factors that have helped to radically reshape Marian thought
and interest since mid-century. They are: 1) the "resur-
gence of biblical studies within Catholicism;" 2) ecumenism;
3) an "increasing sensitivity to feminist issues"; 4) the
"rediscovery of myth as a potent force and a growing recognition of the dependence of all religious explanation and
religious language on Myth. . ." (pp 430,431). (Here myth
may have about the same definition as Jung's psychic truth
discussed earlier.)

[76]Walter M. Abbott (gen. ed.), The Documents of
Vatican II (New York: Guild Press, 1969), p 90.

[77]Ibid., pp 91,92.

[78]F. J. Sheed, Theology for Beginners, p 163.

[79]Msgr J. D. Conway, What the Church Teaches, p 212.

[80]Giovanni Miegge, The Virgin Mary (Philadelphia:
Westminster Press, 1955), p 178.

[81]Magdalen Goffin, "Some Reflections on Superstition
and Credulity," in Objections to Roman Catholicism (London:
Constable, 1964), pp 36,37.

[82]Three points of St Bernard's Mariology have been
often commented upon. 1) His rejection of the Immaculate
Conception. 2) His leaning toward affirming the dogma of
Mary's Assumption. 3) His insistence upon the mediation of
Mary. It is probably from his well-known Sermo de aquaeductu;
Patrologia Latina Vol 183, pp 437-448 that the famous
"refuge" quote comes. (cf. P. Zerbi, "Bernard of Clairvaux,
St," NCE Vol 2, p 337.)

There is sociological evidence to show this overemphasis
on Mary interferes with the image of God and of Christ.
Professor William McCready and a team of associates led a
study of Catholic young adults. The program was sponsored
by the Knights of Columbus and the research was conducted in
the spring and winter of 1979 in the USA and Canada involving a total of 2,504 respondents.

A number of questions and subjects were used in the
study. The full report of the Knights of Columbus is published as The Young Catholic Adult. One question, however,
dealt with Mary and this information indicates that "the

344

Mary image proved to be stronger than either the Jesus image or the God image. As Professor Sullivan remarked: 'Bernard of Clairvaux was right: "If you fear the Father, go to the Son. If you fear the Son, go to the Mother."'" The article dealing just with the Marian aspects of the study and containing this quote (p 135) is: Andrew M. Greeley, William McCready, Teresa Sullivan, and Joan Fee, "Mary Survives," _America_ 142, 7 (February 23, 1980) pp 135-137.

[83]M. J. Horak, "Coredemption," _NCE_ Vol 4, pp 323-324.

[84]Ludwig Ott, _Fundamentals of Catholic Dogma_, pp 213-214.

[85]Heribert Mühlen, "New Directions in Mariology," _Theology Digest_ 24, 3 (Fall 1976) p 287.

[86]"The Marian Cult: Statement by the Permanent Commission on Inter-church Relations of the Presbyterian Church in the U.S.A., approved by the recent Los Angeles General Assembly of that Church," _The Christian Century_ 72, 26 (June 29, 1955) pp 756-758.

The other three points in the statement are: 1) In the course of Christian history, honor given to Mary has closely paralleled or duplicated honors paid to Jesus. (This has been discussed above and in fn 80.) 2) Mariology today is the result of "a craving which has been keenly felt in Roman Catholic circles" following the post-Reformation vacuum when "Christ was removed further. . .away from direct contact with human life." (This takes us back again to Jung's discussion on psychic truth.) 3) A growing Marian cult "has widened the breach between the Roman Catholic Church and all other Christian communions." (This point too has already been discussed under the section on the Immaculate Conception.)

[87]Kilian McDonnell, "Protestants, Pentecostals, and Mary," p 27. I am aware that Cardinal Suenens does not agree with the criticism that Mary has often taken the place of the Holy Spirit in the Church. Yet, he does seem to confuse the issue when he says: "to breathe Mary is to breathe the Holy Spirit." (cf. Leon Joseph Cardinal Suenens, _A New Pentecost_? (New York: The Seabury Press, 1975) "The Holy Spirit and Mary," pp 196-211.)

[88]Heribert Mühlen, "New Directions," p 287.

[89]Ibid., p 288.

[90]Bernard C. Pawley (ed.), _The Second Vatican Council, Studies by Eight Anglican Observers_ (London: Oxford, 1967), pp 19,20. Another Marian doctrine that some bishops wanted promulgated was the Coredemption of Mary (_Maria Coredemptrix_). In fact, the term was eventually dropped by Vatican II.

[91]Heribert Mühlen, Ibid.

[92]René Laurentin, <u>Catholic Pentecostalism</u> (Garden City, NY: Image Books, 1978), pp 222-225. The author considers his chapter on "Mary, Model of the Charismatic" to be "regarded as a basis for a constructive dialogue between Pentecostalism and the Catholic Pentecostal movement" (p 220). He says, in fact, that this chapter on Mary was well received in a Pentecostal periodical in France, <u>Experience</u>, (Vol 16, 1974) as being "quite acceptable to an evangelical Christian" (p 219).

[93]C. O. Vollert, "Mary and the Church," <u>NCE</u> Vol 9, p 356. (Vollert discusses at length Mary and the Church in his excellent book, <u>A Theology of Mary</u> (New York: Herder and Herder, 1965).)

[94]J. W. Langlinais, "Assumption of Mary," p 972. The book, <u>Mary in the New Testament</u> (see fn 26) contains a chapter entitled "The Woman in Revelation 12," which gives a thorough discussion of this text. It too concludes that a secondary reference to Mary "remains possible but uncertain" but also admits that the passage "might well lend itself to Marian interpretation" (p 239).

[95]Walter M. Abbott, <u>Documents of Vatican II</u>, p 103. (Pages 102-106 is "A Response" written by Albert C. Cutler, a Methodist and professor at Perkins School of Theology, Southern Methodist University, Dallas, and an official observer at the Council.)

Mary is hailed as "a pre-eminent and altogether singular member of the Church" in the Council treatise on Mary (p 86). A footnote, added by Avery Dulles, says: "The Council comes very close here to calling Mary 'Mother of the Church,' This title, while not bestowed by the Council itself, was actually conferred by Paul VI in his closing allocution at the end of the third session, November 21, 1964."

Don Sharkey, <u>The Woman Shall Conquer</u> (Libertyville, IL: Franciscan Marytown Press, 1976), pp x-xi, says: "On October 29, 1968, by the close vote of <u>1,114</u> to <u>1,024</u> the Council decided that the schema on Mary should be included in the schema on the Church instead of being a separate document" (italics mine).

[96]Thomas Bokenkotter, <u>A Concise History</u>, p 408.

[97]F. X. Lawler, "Communion of Saints," <u>NCE</u> Vol 4, pp 41-43. (This brings up other questions such as prayers for the dead, praying to the dead, Masses for the dead, purgatory, and veneration of the saints. These are worthy topics for discussion but which lay outside our concern in this paper. The communion of the saints is brought up here only to introduce the matter of the special veneration of

Mary.)

[98] Jaroslav Pelikan, <u>Riddle of Roman Catholicism</u>, p. 127.

"One common misconception of non-Catholics is that in praying to Mary, Catholics show a lack of confidence in Christ or even worse they exalt the mother of Jesus to a divine position. This is not an uncommon misconception and is very widespread. . . .I believe there are many Protestants who feel that Catholics do this, and consequently, rightly reject it. Even when the misconceptions have been cleared up and all the explanations have been made we still have differences with Protestants in our attitude toward Mary. . . .

"Our beliefs as Catholics involve an acceptance of tradition. The very early Christians did not pray to the saints. The first veneration of the saints was of the martyrs, with the sense that they hadn't died forever. They were born into heaven and are still concerned with us. We can ask for their assistance because they are close to Christ for whom they died. The other saints, including the mother of Jesus, came to be included in this conviction of the communion of saints. This took a while to develop. Many Protestants would say that if it wasn't a bad development, it certainly wasn't a scriptural development.

". . .It is a traditional matter. If one does not accept the legitimacy of traditional development, one will not accept what falls under that tradition. It can be demonstrated that it's not anti-biblical, but many a Protestant would want something more than that. . ."--Eaman R. Carroll, "Mary, the Mother of God," <u>The SCRC Vision</u> 7, 12 (December 1980) p 7.

[99] Walter M. Abbott, <u>Documents of Vatican II</u>, pp 94,95.

[100] H. M. Carson, <u>Dawn or Twilight?</u>, p 129.

[101] In all fairness to my Catholic friends, I must share an experience. Recently I was told this story: A Pentecostal woman in southern France, a former Catholic, was concerned about some needs in her life. In her church was no image of Mary nor any candles, of course. But she wrote out her prayer request on a piece of paper, folded it up, and stuck it in a crack of the communion table at the front of the church, and left. This kind of "popular devotion" borders on superstition just as it does in other forms in the Catholic Church. Other examples could be given but one is enough to illustrate: 1) that we Pentecostals do have the same problem, even if, by our judgement, on a smaller scale; 2) that charity is needed when we have a tendency to attack some exaggerations we may see in the Catholic Church.

Aloysius J. Burggraff, <u>Handbook for New Catholics</u> (Glen Rock, NJ Paulist Press, 1960): On page 115 of this book the author explains religious statues. "One prays before a statue not <u>to</u> a statue. The presence of statues

347

in church by no means invites idolatry because statues are not idols of things on earth but symbols of saints in heaven, the especially elect of God. To venerate, not adore, a statue brings one closer to God whose will the saints personified in human flesh and blood."

[102]I gathered much material on the apparitions and miracles of Mary, but after reflection decided not to include it because it would make the paper much too long and perhaps lose its major focus. Although I would like to say that Catholics generally believe and accept the miracles and cures which Mary performs but "only as the instrument of God; not through her own power"--Stanley J. Stuber, _Primer on Roman Catholicism for Protestants_ (New York: Association Press, 1960), p 124. (Chapter 11, "Veneration of the Virgin Mary," pp 119-131).

Listed below are the sources used in gathering material on various phases of the miracles of Mary.

New Catholic Encyclopedia

E. R. Carroll, "Mary, Blessed Virgin, Devotion to" Vol 9, pp 364-369.

M. S. Conlan, "Our Lady of the Snow," Vol 10, p 837.

J. D. Dirvin, "Miraculous Medal," Vol 9, pp 894-895.

A. J. Eunis, "Our Lady of Good Counsel," Vol 10, pp 833,834.

C. Henze, "Our Lady of Perpetual Help," Vol 10, pp 834,835.

Liturgy and Cultural Religious Traditions (New York: Seaburg Press 1979). Pages 25-33 has an article by Virgil Elizondo "Our Lady of Guadalupe as a Cultural Symbol."

Bernadette of Lourdes (London: Darton, Longman and Todd, 1979). Biography by René Laurentin and translated from the French by John Drury.

Our Lady of Fátima (New York: Macmillan, 1954). A factual account written by W. Thomas Walsh.

The Woman Shall Conquer (Libertyville, IL: Franciscan Marytown Press, 1975). Written by Ron Sharkey, a journalist and not a theologian, this book gives much attention to apparitions and other manifestations of Mary that have occured since 1830. He points out that since the approval of the Weeping Madonna of Sicily (1953), to his knowledge, no "manifestation" of Mary has received ecclesiastical approbation" (p ix).

[103]Thomas Bokenkotter, _A Concise History_, p 410.

[104]Jerry L. Sandidge, "The Origin and Development of
the Catholic Charismatic Movement in Belgium" Louvain,
Belgium: Catholic University of Louvain, Unpublished
M.M.R.Sc. thesis, 1976, pp 132,133.

Some Catholics testify of a greater devotion to Mary
after becoming involved in the charismatic renewal. Others
speak of learning from Mary's example "under the guidance
of the Spirit." Still others give a different slant, for
just after coming into the renewal Marian devotion
increased: "But after a time this devotion. . .shifted away
from Mary and the saints to Christ and the Holy Spirit."
(Ibid.)

[105]René Laurentin, Catholic Pentecostalism, pp 220,221.

[106]Dorothy Ranaghan, "Mary," New Covenant 9,3 (October
1980) p 27. Two recent articles in New Covenant 10, 11
(May 1981) reflect this balanced and biblical view of Mary,
which is an aid, not a hindrance, to unity; George Montaque,
"Behold Your Mother" (pp 4-7) and Ann Thérèse Shields,
"Open to God's Word," (pp 8-11).

[107]H. M. Carson, Dawn or Twilight?, p 134. His Catholic
sources used to illustrate this point came from Kevin and
Dorothy Ranaghan, Catholic Pentecostals (Paulist Press, 1969),
pp 30, 68, 90, 178; and Thomas Flynn The Charismatic Renewal
and the Irish Experience (London: Hodder and Stoughton,
1974), p 171.

[108]"The role assigned the Virgin Mary in Catholic Neo-
Pentecostalism usually does not sit well with classical
Pentecostalsim"--René Laurentin, Catholic Pentecostals,
p 219.

"The role of Mary is a great stumbling block for many
within the classical Pentecostal and Protestant charismatic movements"--Kilian McDonnell, "Protestants,
Pentecostals and Mary," p 29.

"Of course I am often attacked by Pentecostals because
I speak of our Blessed Lady in the book" (A New Pentecost?)--
Cardinal Suenens in Jerry L. Sandidge's thesis "Catholic
Charismatic Movement in Belgium," p 132.

[109]John Randall, Fruitfulness, p 103.

[110]Germein Marc'hadur, "The Holy Spirit Over the New
World," The Clergy Review 59, 3 (March 1974) pp 184-200;
59, 4 (April 1974) pp 246-269; p 257.

(The other two ovations came when the American Bishops
were acknowledged as "our shepherds in the Lord" to whom
Catholics would pledge their obedience and desire their
guidance and discipline; and when Pope Paul VI was asked to

support the renewal: "We want your discernment. We are
founded on this rock and on this rock we stand.")

[111]John Randall, <u>Fruitfulness</u>, pp 9,10, 100. "This
ever-fresh Spirit taught us new approaches to an old devotion and then revitalized our lives." ". . .when we have
learned the wisdom of effectively going to his [Jesus')
mother, miracles have happened. . . ."

[112]This specific experience is a very famous one because
it happened very early in the Catholic charismatic
renewal and because it has been written up in the literature
(and rewritten, quoted, misquoted and misunderstood). I
learned that Gerry Rauch, living in Brussels, was in this
gathering and was, in fact, the leader of the meeting when
this event took place. I asked him to write the experience
out for me, which he did in a letter dated 1 May 1981.
Because of its importance to our dialogue I relate the whole
incident exactly as Gerry Rauch describes it in his letter.

"In March 1967, after a group of us who were students
and faculty at the University of Notre Dame were baptized
in the Spirit, we began to have charismatic prayer meetings.
The experience of charismatic gifts was totally new to us.
The Pentecostal literature we had read discussed tongues
and interpretation, and we had observed these gifts operating
when we had prayed with Pentecostal brothers. However, none
of us had yet given a message in tongues or an interpretation of tongues. This was still the very first weeks of
the Catholic Charismatic Renewal.

"One evening we gathered for a prayer meeting in someone's living room, and the others asked me to lead that
meeting. After we had been praying for a while, one of the
students began to make a funny kind of noise which I thought
was a message in tongues that the Holy Spirit wanted him to
give but he was afraid of. So I said something to encourage him to go ahead and speak out freely and not be afraid.
Then he relaxed and spoke out clearly a message, but it was
not in English and I did not recognize if it was a language.

"I had read in the Pentecostal literature that when a
message in tongues was given we ought to wait for an interpretation. So I reminded everyone of that, and a prayerful
silence followed. But no one gave an interpretation.

"After waiting a few minutes, I asked if anyone had
received an interpretation. One of the students said that,
while the first one was speaking in tongues, the phrase,
'Hail Mary, full of grace, the Lord is with thee,' was
coming over and over in his mind. But he didn't know if
he should give it as the interpretation. I asked again if
anyone else had received anything, but no one had. So we
accepted what this student said as the interpretation and
went on with the prayer meeting.

"At the end of the meeting, a priest who had come for the first time that night, came up to me very excited. He said that the first student had spoken in Greek, and that the words of the interpretation were exactly what he had said. Of course, we were all delighted to hear this.

"The next day several of the same people who had been at the prayer meeting were gathered at a mass together. And we were shocked when it turned out that it was the feast of the Annunciation, and the gospel reading contained the words, 'Hail Mary, full of grace, the Lord is with thee.' We were also surprised that this was not the ordinary date for the feast of the Annunciation. The ordinary date is March 25th, but the feast had been moved in 1967 because March 25 was Holy Saturday that year.

"The effect on us of what had happened was two-fold. First of all, we celebrated the feast of the Annunciation in a much more lively way because of the tongues and inter-pretation that had come the night before. But, secondly, we saw it as strong confirmation of the working of the Holy Spirit in the gift of tongues and interpretation."

There are five important observations I made about this experience: 1) the interpretation not only was the first part of the Ave but it was also the scriptural greet-ing of Gabriel (Lk 1:28); 2) it was verified both as to language (or "tongue") and to interpretation by one who knew (a priest); 3) it fit into the liturgical calendar per-fectly; 4) it was a learning and spiritual experience for those new to the operation of spiritual gifts; 5) it followed the classical Pentecostal understanding of how the gifts of tongues and interpretation operate within the group.

[113] Kilian McDonnell, "Protestants, Pentecostals, and Mary," p. 29.

[114] G. M. Grant, "The Outlook of the Twentieth Century in Theology," American Journal of Theology 6, 1 (January 1902) p 14.

[115] Kilian McDonnell, "Protestants, Pentecostals, and Mary," p 27. (It is interesting that the recent three volume work edited by Kilian McDonnell of about 80 official Church documents--Catholic, Protestant, Pentecostal--concern-ing the charismatic renewal and the Holy Spirit is given the title Presence, Praise, Power.)

[116] René Laurentin, Catholic Pentecostalism, p 227.

Agreed Account

Introduction

At the 1981 meeting of the Roman Catholic/Pentecostal
Dialogue, October 4-10, in Vienna, special attention was
given to two topics: Mary, the Mother of Jesus, and
Ministry in the Church.

The first topic on the Dialogue's Agenda was Mary.
Two papers were presented on Monday, October 4: the first
by Laurence R. Bronkiewicz, representing the Roman Catholics,
entitled; "The Catholic Veneration of the Virgin Mary, Mother
of God and of our Lord and Saviour, Jesus Christ"; the
second by Jerry L. Sandidge, representing the Classical
Pentecostals, entitled; "A Pentecostal Perspective of Mary,
the Mother of Jesus". The Roman Catholic paper discussed
Mary in terms of a threefold relationship: to Christ, to
the mystery of salvation, and to the Church. The Pentecostal paper discussed Mary from three perspectives: the
biblical, historical, and theological. Most of the dialogue
discussion was devoted to the topic of Mary.

On October 6, the second topic of the Dialogue's agenda
was introduced with the presentation of two papers: the first
by H. David Edwards, representing the Classical Pentecostals,
entitled; "A Pentecostal Perspective of the Church and its
Ministry"; the second by Liam G. Walsh, OP, representing
the Roman Catholics, entitled; "Ministry in the Church".

The Pentecostal paper dealt with Ministry in terms of its origins, the ministries themselves and apostolic succession. The Roman Catholic paper discussed Ministry from two perspectives: Ministry in the Roman Catholic Church today and the faith of the Roman Catholic Church about Ministry. The consensus of the Dialogue group was to complete discussion on this topic of Ministry at next year's meeting.

I. BIBLICAL PERSPECTIVES ON MARY

The chief biblical text offered and discussed was the Lukan infancy narrative. Mention was also made of Mt 1, Jn 2:1-11, and 19:25-27.

While both Pentecostals and Roman Catholics agree that these texts witness to the importance of Mary in the New Testament, our discussion centered around the possibility of a developing understanding of these texts in the Roman Catholic Church's life. The main problem was that of interpretation. Pentecostals insist that they cannot go beyond the clear meaning of the text as a criterion for all later religious doctrine and experience. On the other hand, Roman Catholics state that, while Scripture remains the basic criterion of development, the Church, guided by the Holy Spirit in praying and reflecting on the Scriptures, can rightly find in them a meaning which goes beyond the Pentecostal interpretation of these texts.

Behind the differences of interpretation between Pentecostals and Roman Catholics, lie doctrinal differences,

often implicit and unexpressed. Possibly the most important of these concern ecclesiology, and, in particular,
the Communion of Saints.

Areas of agreement were surprisingly large. First,
Roman Catholics discovered that Mary enters more than they
had expected into Pentecostal preaching and devotion.
Again, although we are far from a consensus, Pentecostals
do admit some form of development in the interpretation of
Scripture. Also Pentecostals have noted the concern of the
official Roman Catholic Church to be prudent in discerning
the developments of Scriptural meaning as a basis for Marian
doctrine. Finally, Pentecostals see that, the presentation
of Mary's intercession in official Roman Catholic teaching
does not undermine the one mediatorship of Jesus taught by
the Bible.

II. THE VENERATION OF MARY

A. Mary, the Mother of God

Both Roman Catholics and Classical Pentecostals recognize the historical origins of the term "Mother of God"
arising from the Christological disputes concerning the
two natures and one person of Jesus Christ. Both parties
recognize that the issue was resolved at the Council of
Ephesus (431). In order to preserve the deity of our Lord
in the womb of the Virgin the Council approved the title
" Theotokos" ("God Bearer" or "Mother of God"). Both Roman
Catholics and Pentecostals agree that Mary is the Mother of

Jesus Christ who is the Son of God and as such occupies a unique place. She is the Mother of God in His incarnation. She is not the Mother of God in His eternal triune existence.

B. The Veneration of Mary

Roman Catholics and Classical Pentecostals concur in the unique respect due to Mary as the mother of Jesus. We both view her as the special example or model of faith, humility and virtue. We both remember with reverence her life and words and praise God for what He has done in her. Both Roman Catholics and Pentecostals share a concern for the necessity of a correct perspective on Mary's place in the economy of salvation. However, there were significant differences in the understanding of the degree and type of veneration that should be given to Mary.

Pentecostals expressed concern about what they consider to be excesses in comtemporary veneration of Mary. For Pentecostals, certain practices of Marian veneration appear to be superstitious and idolatrus.

Roman Catholics, while admitting certain excesses in the veneration of Mary, were careful to point out that proper veneration of Mary is always Christological. In addition, Roman Catholics gave evidence that practical steps are being taken to correct excesses, according to the norms of the Second Vatican Council, "Constitution on the Church," Chap 8, and Pope Paul VI in his encyclical Marialis Cultus (1974), paras 29-36.

C. The Intercession of Mary

Both Roman Catholics and Pentecostals agree that Mary in no way substitutes for or replaces the one Saviour and Mediator Jesus Christ. Both believe in the direct immediate contact between the believer and God. Both pray to God, the Father, Son and Holy Spirit. Catholics believe that intercessory prayers directed to Mary do not end in Mary but in God Himself.

Because of different understanding of the Communion of Saints which touched on the question of the intercession of Mary, both Roman Catholic and Pentecostal members of the Dialogue agree in recommending that the topic of Communion of Saints be placed on the agenda of a future Dialogue.

Pentecostals would not invoke the interest or attention of Mary or other saints in heaven because it is not a valid biblical practice.

III. THE GRACES GIVEN TO MARY

Introduction

Catholics believe that Mary always remained a virgin, that she was conceived free from all stain of sin, and that at the end of her life she was assumed body and soul into heaven. Pentecostals reject these beliefs.

Pentecostals can find no warrant for these beliefs in Scripture. Catholics claim that they are found in Scripture implicitly but state that they are made explicit in the tradition of faith, which is the Church's ongoing

reflection and living of the Scriptures. As well as questioning the value of tradition as a basis for the doctrines
of faith, Pentecostals would suggest that these traditons
about Perpetual Virginity, Immaculate Conception, and
Assumption are, in varying degrees, lacking scriptural basis.

In the hierarchy of truths of faith held by the Roman Catholics these three doctrines are placed among the
truths that are integral to the Roman Catholic faith but
not essential for salvation for all Christians.

A. The Virginity of Mary

Both Pentecostals and Roman Catholics agree that Mary
was a virgin in the conception of Jesus and see in the
texts which state it an important affirmation of the deity
of Christ.

Roman Catholics believe that Mary remained a virgin
after the birth of Jesus and did not have other offspring.
Pentecostals commonly accept that Scripture records she did
have other offspring and lived as wife of Joseph in the
full sense.

Roman Catholics take the evidence of Scripture as
being indecisive and as being open to the interpretation
which they find expressed in the earliest Fathers of the
Church. Roman Catholics find in tradition (understood as
ongoing meditation on Scripture) evidence of Mary's continued virginity. This has encouraged a positive attitude to
celibacy in the Church's life otherwise witnessed to in the
New Testament. Pentecostals in principle admit the Gospel
value of celibacy, but traditional Pentecostal lifestyle
regards marriage as normative.

357

Roman Catholics also believe that Mary remained a virgin in the actual birth of Jesus, but admit too a diversity of theological explanations about the exact meaning of this phase of her virginity. Pentecostals have no difficulty in admitting the possibility of a miraculous delivery for Jesus, but see no special reason for affirming it.

Further discussion of the virginity of Mary will have to focus on the relationship of Mariology to Christology and the mystery of redemption.

B. Immaculate Conception

Roman Catholics hold the doctrine of the Immaculate Conception to be founded on the Church's reflection on the Bible, both Old and the New Testaments. This doctrine is seen to flow from the fact that she is the Mother of the Saviour, from her presentation as the perfect fulfillment of Old Testament types, e.g., "the virgin daughter of Sion" (Lk 1:26-38; cf., Zph 3:14-20; Zch 2:10; 9:9); "the woman" (Jn 2:1-11, 19:25-27; cf., Gn 3:15) and from other texts. All these texts form a biblical theology of Mary, which provides a basis for the development of the doctrine of the Immaculate Conception. The explicit development of the doctrine, which led to its definition by Pope Pius IX in 1854, comes in the tradition.

Pentecostals appreciate Catholic assurances that the special grace claimed for Mary is a redeeming grace that comes from Jesus. She stands among the redeemed and is a member of the Church. Pentecostals cannot find any basis for the doctrine of Mary's Immaculate Conception in

Scripture. Furthermore Pentecostals do not see any value
in this doctrine for salvation.

The ecumenical meeting point in our mutual discussion
of this doctrine will not be easy to work out. To do so
will require more than simply taking the doctrine in isolation. There must be consideration given to the concept
of the development of doctrine, diverse theological traditions, and a recognition of the inadequacy and limitations
inherent in doctrinal formulations within a given
historical moment.

C. The Assumption

Roman Catholics see the doctrine of the Assumption,
which was explicitly affirmed in the Fathers of the Church
as early as the sixth century, to be in accordance with
basic biblical doctrines. The Risen Christ is the beginning
of the new creation. He is the giver of the Holy Spirit
by whom we enter this new creation, being born from above
in the death and resurrection of Christ. In Mary, because
of her unique relationship with Christ, this new creation
by the Spirit was achieved to the point that the life of
the Spirit triumphed fully in her and that she is already
with her body in the glory of God, with her risen Son.

The Pentecostal difficulty rests in the absence of
sufficient biblical evidence. There is a generally accepted
view that Mary, as one of the faithful awaits the day of
resurrection when she, along with all Christians, will be
united bodily with her Son in glory. Pentecostals see a
useful parallel in Mary's Assumption and the Pentecostal

understanding of the "bodily resurrection in the Rapture of the Church" (1 Thes 4:13-18; cf., especially verse 17), but differ only as to when this will take place for Mary.

Further discussion on the question will have to follow similar lines to that about Mary's Immaculate Conception.

Conclusion

The *charism* of grace, mutual acceptance, and respect have been experienced in our Dialogue, in charismatic contacts, and in personal relationships. There is a new appreciation for our common faith in Jesus Christ and Mary's relationship to the mystery of our salvation. It is our Christian hope that what appear to be major points of difference will, through continued discussion, produce greater clarity and understanding of our respective ecclesial traditions.

27 October 1981

ROMAN CATHOLIC/PENTECOSTAL DIALOGUE
4-10 October 1981 - Vienna

Press Release

The ninth meeting of the Dialogue between the
Secretariat for Promoting Christian Unity of the Roman
Catholic Church and leading representatives of some of the
Classical Pentecostal Churches was conducted in Vienna,
October 4-10, 1981. The subjects covered were "The
Doctrine of Mary" as well as an initial conversation on
the role of "Ministry in the Church".

The delegates were welcomed to the meeting by the
Pentecostal co-chairman, Dr David du Plessis, and the
interactive process was set in motion by the Roman
Catholic co-chairman, the Rev Kilian McDonnell, OSB.

The Cardinal Archbishop of Vienna, His Eminence
Cardinal Franz Koenig extended the hospitality of the
archdiocese to participants of the dialogue. His welcome
was expressed by the Very Rev Josez Zeininger, OSFS, Vicar
of the Archbishop for the city of Vienna, who met one
morning with the members of the dialogue.

Several of the participants expressed their delight
in the quality and intensity of the shared prayer among
the members during the services which opened and closed
each daily session.

On the first topic, the following papers were presented for discussion: "The Catholic Veneration of the

Virgin Mary, Mother of God and of Our Lord and Saviour, Jesus Christ" by the Rev Laurence R. Bronkiewicz, the Academic Dean of the North American College, Rome; and, "A Pentecostal Perspective of Mary, the Mother of Jesus," by the Rev Jerry L. Sandidge of the Institute of University Ministry, Louvain, Belgium. The Roman Catholic paper discussed Mary in terms of a three-fold relationship to Christ, to the mystery of salvation, and to the Church. The Pentecostal paper likewise discussed Mary from three perspectives: the biblical, historical, and theological. The discussions of the doctrine of Mary elucidated areas of agreement and difference. Both sides sought to focus on the relationship of Mary to the Church in a Christological context.

The topic which was anticipated to be extremely controversial ended with deeper consensus than anticipated.

The drafted expression of consensus reflected that: "Roman Catholics discovered that Mary enters [more than they had expected] into Pentecostal preaching and devotion.... The Pentecostals see that the presentation of Mary's intercession in official Roman Catholic teaching does not undermine the one mediatorship of Jesus taught by the Bible."

On the second topic, the following papers were presented: "A Pentecostal Perspective of the Church and its Ministry" by Rev H. David Edwards of Elim Bible Institute, Lima, New York [USA]: "Ministry in the Church" by Rev Liam G. Walsh, OP, of the Dominican Generalate, Rome. The

Pentecostal paper dealt with Ministry in terms of its origins, the ministries themselves and the apostolic succession. The Roman Catholic paper discussed Ministry from two perspectives: Ministry in the Roman Catholic Church today and the faith of the Roman Catholic Church about Ministry. The consensus of the dialogue group was to complete discussion of this topic of Ministry at next year's meeting, which is planned to take place in June, 1982 at St John's Abbey University, Collegeville, Minnesota, USA.

The next meeting will be the last meeting of the five-year period of dialogue. During this mext meeting a synthesis of the documents produced during the past five years will be published. These will include working papers and expressions of consensus, of convergence. The scope of the Dialogue involves a process of mutual, spiritual, and theological understanding. The next session of the Dialogue will mark an important step in that process.

The following persons were participants in the discussions.

From the Catholic side:

  co-chairman: Rev Kilian McDonnell, OSB - President, Ecumenical Institute, St John's Abbey, Collegeville
  co-secretary: Rev Jerome Vereb, CP - of the staff of the Secretariat for Promoting Christian Unity
  Rev Laurence R. Bronkiewicz - Academic Dean of the North American College, Rome
  Rev William Dalton, SJ - Director, Pontifical Biblical Institute, Jerusalem
  Rev Pierre Duprey, WF - Under Secretary, Secretariat for Promoting Christian Unity

The Very Rev Liam G. Walsh, OP - Assistant to the
Master General of the Dominican Order
Rev Robert J. Wister, Professor of Church History,
Darlington Seminary of the Archdiocese of Newark,
New Jersey.

From the Pentecostal side:

co-chairman: The Rev David du Plessis, known as
"Mr Pentecost"
co-secretary: The Rev William Carmichael, President,
Virtue Ministries Inc., Sisters, Oregon
The Rev Justus T. du Plessis, General Secretary,
Apostolic Faith Mission, South Africa
The Rev H. David Edwards, Executive Vice-President,
Elim Bible Institute, Lima, New York
The Rev Howard M. Ervin, Professor of Old Testament,
Oral Roberts University, Tulsa, Oklahoma
The Rev John L. Meares, Pastor, Evangel Temple,
Washington, DC
The Rev Jerry L. Sandidge, director of University
Action, Leuven, Belgium.

Observers were:

The Rev Ronald Douglas McConnell, Executive Vice-
President, 1st Century Broadcasting Company,
Benicia, California
The Rev James H. Carmichael, Pastor, Foothill
Christian Center, Los Altos, California
The Rev Martin Robinson, Secretary Churches of
Christ, England.

October 10, 1981

ROMAN CATHOLIC/PENTECOSTAL DIALOGUE
25–29 October 1982—Collegeville, Minnesota, USA

Dialogue Participants

1. Fr Michael Salvagna, CP
   (devoted secretary)
2. The Very Rev Liam G. Walsh, OP
3. Fr David N. Power
4. Rev Howard M. Ervin
5. Rev Jerry L. Sandidge
6. Br Columba Stewart, OSB
   (Dialogue host)
7. Bsp John L. Meares
8. Fr Joseph W. Witmer
9. Fr Robert J. Wister
10. Bsp W. Robert McAlister
11. Rev David P. Kast
12. Fr William J. Dalton, SJ
13. Rev H. David Edwards
14. Msgr Basil Meeking
15. Rev Justus T. du Plessis
16. Mrs Coleen Schoenleven
    (devoted secretary)
17. Fr Ivan Havener, OSB
18. Rev William L. Carmichael
19. Fr Kilian McDonnell, OSB
20. Rev David J. du Plessis
21. Fr Jerome Vereb, CP

ROMAN CATHOLIC/PENTECOSTAL DIALOGUE
25-30 October 1982
Collegeville, Minnesota USA

Schedule - Agenda

9:00 a.m.	Session in Alumni lounge
10:30	Coffee break
10:40 - 11:45	Session
12:00 - 12:12	Prayer in Abbey Church
12:25	Lunch
2:30	Session
4:00	Coffee break
4:20 - 5:40	Session
6:00	Supper
7:30 - 8:30	Session

Wednesday

4:20 - 5:30	Session
5:45	Meet in Great Hall (Meal with Monks)

Thursday

4:20 - 5:15	Session
5:30	Reception [with Catholic Bishop of St Cloud and local Pentecostal pastors.]
6:00	Festive Dinner [Honoring Kilian McDonnell and David J. du Plessis.]

Dialogue Schedule - Agenda 1982

Presentations and Discussions

Monday Evening (7:30-9:30)

> Worship
> Introductions and Greeting by Abbot Jerome Theisen
> Orientation by Bro Columba Stewart
> Paper on Ministry by Liam G. Walsh, OP
> Discussion

Tuesday Morning

> (Continuation of Discussion)
> Paper on Ministry by H. David Edwards
> Discussion

Tuesday Afternoon

> Continue Discussion of D. Edwards' Paper
> After Coffee - Reading of Final Report
> Discussion of General Character of the Report

Wednesday Morning

> Paragraph by Paragraph Discussion of Final
> Report in Plenary

Wednesday Afternoon

> Small Group Discussion of Final Report

Wednesday Evening

> Steering Committee Meeting and [Final Report]
> Small Group Discussions

Thursday Morning

> Final Report Small Group Discussions

Thursday Afternoon

> Drafting of Final Report

Friday Morning

> Reading of Amended [Final] Report [and Press
> Release] in Plenary

Theological Paper

MINISTRY IN THE CHURCH

by

Fr   Liam G. Walsh, OP

INTRODUCTORY

The term "ministry" translates the New Testament
greek word *diakonia*. As such it describes activities by
which members of the Christian community help others and
thus contribute to the common welfare; it expresses a certain style, which marks this activity, a quality of humility
and self-giving, a non-assertiveness by which the Christian
way of taking responsibility for others is contrasted with
the exercise of power in a worldly community; it expresses
a link with a modeling on the activity of Jesus who came
not to be ministered to but to minister (cf. Mk 10:42-45).

Many different kinds of activity are called ministry
in the New Testament. Some come in for more attention than
others because they seem to be more central to the building up of the community, more indispensable. Thus, for
example, in Eph 4:12, when describing the gifts given "for
the equipment of the saints, for the work of ministry"
Paul lists apostles, prophets, evangelists, shepherds and
teachers. These ministries are, like all activities that

contribute to the building up of the saints, gifts of the Spirit. They are charisms (cf. 1 Cor 12:4,5).

The ministries which found a church, which involve some kind of ultimate responsibility for its continuance, which have a role of coordination of all other ministries, which give leadership and direction to the community, have come to gain a certain distinctive right to the terms in the language of the church. All ministries are for the community. When one is talking about what is required for the very existence of the community, one is, no doubt, talking about ministry in a special sense. This discrimination within *diakonia* can be expressed in English with the help of a second word that translated the greek. The word "service" can express the broader sense of *diakonia*--the call given to every Christian to use the special gifts he has been given for the good of the community, and to do so in a humble, Christ-like spirit. This allows one to reserve "ministry" for those activities that seem more permanent and irreplaceable, more structurally essential in the building up of the Church.

However, not all churches restrict the word ministry to the same extent. The charismatic churches, I understand, give it a broader extention, to cover almost any activity that is recognized as being a charism for the building up of the community. We will, no doubt, have to discuss the pros and cons of the extention given to the word ministry in our different traditions. Nevertheless, we will also agree that there is need for particular discussion between

us about the foundational, institutional, leadership and
unifying functions that are exercised within our churches.
It is these functions that I take the word ministry to evoke.

I. MINISTRY IN THE ROMAN CATHOLIC CHURCH TODAY

In this section I want to describe how ministry, in
the sense explained, is received and structured in the
Roman Catholic Church. Here I am simply giving a factual
description of the way things are. Later, in section II,
I will be analysing how and why the Church believes that,
in this practice of ministry, it is being faithful to the
gift of God given to his church in Christ and the Spirit.

While my description will try to be factual, it will
inevitably be somewhat idealized. It will also involve
some theology of ministry and will therefore already open
up some areas of debate. I trust that what I have to say
is a reasonably faithful summary of what is taught and
ordained by the Second Vatical Council and subsequent
official documents of the church.

A. Bishops

First in ministry in the Roman Catholic Church is the
bishop. He is the pastor, the shepherd of his particular
church (which, as a territorial or jurisdictional unit is
called a diocese). Normally there is only one holder of
this ministry in each church. But when there are several,
one is the bishop and the others are his auxiliaries. His
ministry is basically to build up the church on the foundation of the apostles, and through his fidelity to them to

build it up in Christ. His ministry is derived from and
continues that of the apostles. It takes the form of ultimate responsibility for Word and Sacraments in the life of
the church.

The bishop is the first teacher of the faith in his
church. He has to ensure the effective preaching of the
Gospel in the area committed to his care, and the orthodoxy of faith and teaching among believers. He presides
over the worship of his church. In virtue of a unique sharing in the priesthood of Christ, which he is given at the
ordination, he has the fulness of priestly power to celebrate the sacraments or to authorize their celebration. He
is the first promotor of holiness among his flock, encouraging Christians to offer themselves as living sacrifices to
God in the Spirit and presenting their sacrifices in the
one sacrifice of Christ, when he presides over his church's
celebration of the eucharist.

The authority that goes with the bishop's ministry of
word and sacrament is extended to all that is required for
the building up of the community. The bishop is meant to
stimulate and co-ordinate all the other gifts, ministries
and services that the Spirit inspires in the members of his
church. He is responsible for the good order of the
community. All ministry in his church is eventually subject
to his authorization or commissioned by him. He works to
build a community of charity and sharing and he has a
special care for the poor.

1. <u>The College of Bishops</u>--A bishop is responsible for building up the church in unity. He exercises this ministry immediately in the church of which he is bishop. But the unity of the church is greater than the unity of a particular church. It is a universal communion. By the very fact of his ministry the bishop is responsible for building his church into communion with other churches, and of building other churches into communion with his church. He has a responsibility for the communion of all the churches. This ministry of catholic communion is exercised by the bishops as a body, which we call a college. They are all together, as a college, responsible for all the churches.

Bishops exercise their collegial responsibility in different ways. They may take part in an ecumenical council, which is made up of all the bishops of the church. Or they may be selected as members of the Synod of Bishops-- which is a representative body of the bishops that currently meets every three years to discuss matters of concern to the universal church. Some who are bishops of historically important churches have a traditional prestige, on which is based a certain primacy over neighboring churches, or churches that may have been founded from them. These are the bishops of the patriarchal sees and later on of metropolitan or primatial sees (Patriarchs, Primate, Archbishops). Among these there is one who is believed to hold a unique primacy, which entails responsibility for all the churches. This is the bishop of the church of Rome.

2. <u>The Pope</u>--The ministry of bishops is believed to be derived from the ministry that Christ gave to his apostles and that the Spirit confirmed at Pentecost. Among the apostles, Peter was given a special responsibility and authority for the entire church. The one who is bishop of Rome is believed to succeed to this special responsibility and authority within the college of bishops. While he is no more and no less bishop than any other bishop, and while his first responsibility is towards his own church in Rome, the Pope has a primacy of real authority over his fellow bishops in the exercise of their ministry, which allows him to be the ultimate minister and the ultimate guarantor of the building up of the church. This authority is believed to be reinforced and secured by his being able to personally count on having, in certain limited situations when the faith of the church and its unity is at stake, that charism of infallibility which the Spirit has given to the whole church.

3. <u>Ordination of Bishops</u>--The ministry of bishop, like all other ministry in the church, is given by God. God calls a man to this ministry and pours out his Spirit upon him for its acceptance and exercise. The call is heard by the individual within his own conscience. No one can be forced against this conscience to become a bishop. The call is also heard by the church, which has to discern and to decide about it. This is done in the Latin church by a process of consultation in the church to which the bishop has to be appointed, as well as in other churches of that

ecclesiastical area. The decision about the appointment
is made by the Pope, acting in virtue of the responsibility
and authority which he has over all the churches. Bishops
are normally selected from among those who are already
presbyters (commonly called priests). If the one selected
is not, in fact, a presbyter, he will be ordained to that
ministry before being ordained bishop.

The rite of ordination is a liturgical ceremony conducted by those who are already bishops--usually at least
three of them. In a prayer of thanks they call down the
Holy Spirit on the one to be ordained and they lay hands
on him in the traditional gesture of blessing and designation for ministry. This act is believed by the church to
be a sacrament, that is to say an action of the church that
makes visible and real the action of Christ, in this case
choosing and commissioning and sanctifying with the gift of
His Spirit this man for the ministry of bishop. By this
sacrament the man is made a member of the order or rank of
bishops. He is ordained.

By ordination the bishop is given power to represent
Christ in his leadership of the worship of the church. This
is a priestly power, because it makes it possible for the
unique priestly work of Christ to be made visible and present in the church. This sacramental power is found in its
fulness in the bishop. He has all the sacred power required
to build up the whole church as a priestly people of God.
He has this power forever. He may cease to exercise his
ministry or be forbidden to do so. But he always remains

marked by this gift of ministry and he will not need to be
re-ordained if he resumes his ministry after having laid
it aside.

4. Life-style of Bishops--Since bishops are called
to represent Christ in a particularly public way within the
community of the church, the call to discipleship and witness
given to every Christian is addressed to them with particular
urgency. The credibility of the church as the community of
those who make Christ and his Spirit present in the world
obviously depends very much on the Christian witness of its
public leaders--as of course does the credibility of these
ministers within the Christian community itself. Hence the
church requires a conspicuous practice of the evangelical
life from those called to the ministry of bishop. It
requires a following of Christ to the point of a readiness
to die for the flock. The bishop's total dedication to his
church, is expressed as a being wedded to the church. It
expresses itself too in voluntary celibacy for the sake of
the Kingdom.

B. Presbyters

In each church there is, as well as the bishop or
bishops, an order of ministers called presbyters. (In
English they are usually called priests. But since bishops
are also priests it is better to use the more specific term
presbyter to distinguish this second level of ministry from
that of bishops.) The ministry of presbyters is very similar to that of bishops. It is a pastoral responsibility
for Christian communities, involving a power of Word and

Sacrament, as well as a care for good order and welfare. Presbyters are meant to assist the bishop in his ministry. Their ministry is subordinate to his. It is exercised under his authority and by his commission. While a presbyter, or a group of presbyters may have responsibility for a local Christian community (a parish), they cannot provide all that is necessary to make that community a full, particular church. They cannot independently of their bishop guarantee the authenticity of its faith and the fulness of its life of worship. A presbyter cannot, for example, normally complete the process of Christian initiation, because he cannot perform that anointing of the Spirit that we call the sacrament of Confirmation. Nor can he ordain other priests. However, he can preside over the celebration of the Eucharist, exercising the same priestly power in that as does the bishop--although he normally needs the authorization of the bishop to do so. He can also reconcile Christians who have cut themselves off from the communion of grace by sin, in the sacrament of Penance. Presbyters ensure that the communities they serve are united together in the communion of the diocese or local church. The union they have among themselves in the order of presbyterate, and their collective subordination to their bishop serve to build up the unity of the local church.

The order of presbyterate is not restricted to those who are called to minister in a particular local church. Many men are ordained to the presbyterate for a wider

ministry in the universal church. They are at the service
of all the bishops and, especially, they come under the
obedience of the bishop of Rome. Generally they belong to
religious orders, societies or congregations that have been
approved by the Pope. He may authorize them directly for
some ministries that he considers to be for the good of the
whole church. But normally their ministry is exercised as
a service to a local church and under the authority of
local bishops. It is a sharing in the work of the local
presbyterate. On the other hand, because it is mobile and
non-local, this section of the presbyterate always has the
effect of opening up the local church to its communion with
the universal church.

1. Ordination of Presbyters--Presbyters are called
and ordained in somewhat the same way as bishops are. The
discernment of the call is made by the presbyterate into
whom the man is to be ordained and confirmed by the ordain-
ing bishop. At the ceremony of ordination the faithful are
asked to signify their approval or otherwise of the call.
The prayer of thanks in which the Holy Spirit is called
down is said by a bishop, who also lays on hands. He is
joined in the laying on of hands by presbyters. This
liturgical rite is also an act of the sacrament of Orders.

2. Life-style of Presbyters--In accordance with their
ministry, presbyters are also expected to live the evangelical life with special intensity. They are required to
be celibate in the Latin, though not in the Greek Catholic
church.

C. Deacons

The third grade of ministry in the Catholic Church
today is that of diaconate. The ministry confided to the
deacon is rather flexible. He generally functions along
with a bishop or presbyter as a kind of aide. There are
some functions which he can perform in his own right, when
specifically commissioned to do so. He can preach, preside
at the celebration of baptism, solemnize weddings, lead
liturgical prayer services, including distribution of the
eucharist. But he cannot preside at the celebration of the
eucharist or at the reconciliation of sinners. He cannot
therefore set up and maintain by his own ministry a
Christian community. That is the role of a bishop or at
least a presbyter.

In the Catholic Church the ministry of diaconate is
often a state in the training of presbyters. In recent
years diaconate has been re-introduced as a permanent
ministry. Married men are now ordained to the diaconate and
various pastoral as well as administrative responsibility
of the church are confided to them.

Ordination of Deacons--The call and ordination of
deacons follows the same pattern as that of bishops and
presbyters. The ministry is described in the prayer for
the sending of the Spirit in a way that makes it clear no
gift of independent priestly power is being asked for.

D. Other Ministries

Two other ministries are officially recognized in
the Catholic Church. These are *Acolyte*, which is a ministry

378

of assisting deacon and priest at liturgical celebrations, and *Reader*, which is for the public reading of Scripture in church. They are conferred by a liturgical rite, which, however is not a sacramental ordination.

Episcopal conferences may establish other ministries within the churches they represent. Considerable attention is being given in many parts of the church, especially where new churches are being founded, to the ministry of cathecist (cf. Ad Gentes, 15 and 17).

II. THE FAITH OF THE ROMAN CATHOLIC CHURCH ABOUT MINISTRY

The organization and understanding for ministry that I have been presenting is the outcome of a long historical process. The process has been determined by a number of concerns. Foremost among them is the concern of the church to accept and be faithful to the gift of God that has been given to it through Christ and in the Spirit. Secondly, there is a concern for effectiveness, and the adaptation of ministry to the needs of any given time and place and people. Thirdly, there is the consciousness that ministry in the church is prone to sinfulness and therefore in con-stant need of repentance and renewal. Apart from being beset by all the normal human frailties, ministry is particularly vulnerable to the contamination of worldly models of authority which can destroy the evangelical model given by Jesus.

The crucial question about the practice of ministry in the church at any point in time is, then, how much of

what it does is the gift of God and how much is the making
of man? That which is of God must be received with total
fidelity. That which is of man can be examined in terms
of effectiveness but always with a consciousness of the
issue of grace and sin.

And this, of course, is also the critical ecumenical
question. We want to be united in the gift of God. We can
agree to differ about all that is of man, as long as it is
not sinful.

What I want to present to you in this section is how
the Roman Catholic Church sees its practice of ministry in
these terms. I want to look at the church's professions
of faith that certain realities of ministry are the gift of
God, or in more technical language, are of divine not
ecclesiastical institution. Concomitantly, this should
allow us to see the aspects of ministry that are subject to
reform and renewal and do not have to be an obstacle to
communion between different churches.

A. Ministry in the Scripture

The church finds its faith in the Scriptures. But
its way of reading the Scriptures is already a profession
of its faith. Here is how I see the Catholic reading of
Scripture on ministry.

1. Apostles--Ministry, and the variety of ministries,
is a first fundamental reality of the church in the New
Testament. First among ministries is that of apostles
(1 Cor 12:28; Eph 4:11). Among the apostles there are the
Twelve, the chosen group of disciples to whom Jesus gave

380

fundamental responsibility for the church (Mt 10:2; Ap 21:14).
There is Paul, the apostle of the Gentiles (Rom 11:13).
And there are others who are given this title in the New
Testament (cf. 1 Cor 9:5; Ac 14:14). The ministry of the
apostles was to go out announcing in the name of Jesus that
the Kingdom of God had come in him and to gather together
those who believed into the community of the saved.   The
apostles made churches, by founding them but also by look-
ing after them, whether they had founded them or not.   We
know little of the ministry of the Twelve outside Jerusalem.
But they had a central role in the two major decisions
concerning all the churches that are recorded in the Acts:
the decision to give hellenist Christians in Jerusalem their
own leadership, the seven "deacons" (Ac 6:1-6); and the
decision that gentile Christians did not have to obey the
mosaic law (Ac 15:1-12). The apostle Paul founded many
churches and cared for them constantly by his visits and
his letters. He cared too for the churches he did not
found, for example for the church in Rome. There is no
special evidence that the apostles exercised special functions in the worship of the church. However, given the
leadership which they exercised in the community, it is hard
to exclude that they would have presided over the breaking
of bread (cf. Ac 2:42 "they devoted themselves to the
apostles' teaching and fellowship, to the breaking of bread
and the prayers").

   2.   Presbyters and Bishops--The relationship between
apostles and other leadership figures that emerge in the

New Testament is of particular concern to Catholic faith.
Specifically our faith affirms continuity between the
ministry of the apostles and the ministry of those called
bishops, presbyters and deacons.

People bearing these titles appear in New Testament
descriptions of the church. Their role can be divided from
the meaning and current usage of those titles, as well as
from the functions assigned to them in the texts.

What we translate presbyter comes from a greek word
meaning elder. Such presbyters already existed in Jewish
communities of worship. The synagogue had its group of
elders who advised and took a sort of collective responsibility for the life and worship of the community. It is
not surprising that in Christian churches that came out of
the Jewish tradition, a group of presbyters should have
been formed to look after its life and worship. There were
presbyters in Jerusalem (Ac 15:2,4,6,22; 16:4; 21:18), at
Ephesus (Ac 20:17), in the churches founded by Barnabas and
Paul (Ac 14:23), and by Titus (Ti 1:5). Timothy is ordered
to be concerned about them (1 Tim 5:17), and the writer of
1 Peter presents himself as a presbyter addressing his
fellowship presbyter (1 Pe 5:1).

The greek word *episcopos*, which we translate as
bishop, means something like "overseer". It seems to come
out of the hellenistic rather than the Jewish tradition--
although recent research has shown now a ministry of supervision or overseeing is recognized in the non-conformist
communities associated with Qumran. The role of bishops

382

within the Christian communion appears more clearly in the
later pastoral epistles, which give grounds for thinking
that there might have been at that time just one bishop
in each church (Ti 1:5; 1 Tim 3:1-7). However, in
earlier writings they are referred to in the plural
(Phil 1:1), and as a group they seem to be indistinguishable from the presbyters (Ac 20:28; 1 Pe 5:2; Ti 1:5-9).

It must be admitted that the presbyters and bishops
remain discreet, almost shadowy figures in the New Testament.
They could easily have been outshone by the holders of the
spiritual gifts listed by Paul. In the church of Corinth,
which seems to have been the most spiritually gifted of the
churches, there is no mention of them. It has been suggested that it took all the genius and personal authority
of Paul himself to provide the kind of ministry of overseeing and peace-making and unifying in that particular church
that presbyters and bishops were providing in other churches.
But the presbyters and bishops were overshadowed, above all,
by the apostles, who were the primary pastors and active
overseer of all the churches. They were also subject to men
whom the apostles appointed as their representatives, men
such as Timothy and Titus who shared the apostolic function
and authority.

But there is no doubt that presbyters and bishops had
real responsibility and some form of overall authority in
their churches. Paul tells the presbyters of Ephesus: "Take
heed to yourselves and to all the flock, in which the Holy
Spirit has made you guardians *(episkopous)*, to feed the

church of the Lord. . .fierce wolves will come in among
you. . . . Therefore be alert. . . ." This command is
echoed in 1 Pe 5:1-4. They are qualified as "presiding"
in 1 Tim 5:17, and said to be worthy of praise when they
labour in preaching and teaching. The qualities required
of the prospective bishop in 1 Tim 3:1-7 indicate something of the responsibility he will be expected to assume
in the church. And these texts make it clear that their
ministry comes to them from the Holy Spirit.

The tasks assigned to presbyters and bishops in the
New Testament deal primarily with preaching and teaching.
There is no explicit evidence of a special role in the
worship of the community. It is not unreasonable to assume
that they would have had a prominent role in guiding the
prayer of the community and that they could have presided
at the eucharistic breaking of bread. No one else is
assigned these functions in the New Testament. However,
there is nothing liturgical or cultic about the titles
presbyter or bishop. In the New Testament only Jesus is
called priest or high priest. A priestly quality is
attributed to the whole Christian community in 1 Pe 2:5,
but not to any individual within it. Catholic faith does
not believe that the New Testament excludes forever the
recognition of a priestly quality in the ministry of presbyters and bishops. But it must take account of the
reserve of the New Testament and admit that any subsequent
denomination of these ministries as priestly must not compromise the uniqueness of the priesthood of Christ, and the

claim of the whole Christian community to priestly status.

The New Testament is not very explicit about how the ministry of bishop and presbyter was conferred. Some, at least, were appointed by the apostles or their representatives. In the Jewish religious tradition, it was normal that those who were being given a mission of ministry were prayed over by the leaders of the community, who then laid hands on them in blessing. The Christian church adopted this practice (Ac 6:6; 2 Tim 1:6). But now it was a calling down of the power of the Holy Spirit, source of every gift and ministry. It is not impossible that it was part of the normal process of appointing bishops and priests, but one cannot say that the Scriptures absolutely require it.

The Catholic Church believes that the ministry of priests and bishops that I have been describing continues the ministry of the apostles. The apostles built up the churches and laboured to keep them united in fidelity to the Gospel of Christ. They themselves were the uniquely authorized witnesses to the Gospel, so they did not have to appeal to anyone else's testimony to justify their message and decisions. That qualification could never be communicated to anyone else. But the ministry of keeping the church united in fidelity to the Gospel had to continue. The point of reference would no longer be the personal experience of the minister but the witness given once and for all by the apostles.

All the members of a church would be responsible for its fidelity to the gospel preached by the apostles. The

continuity of the church is a lived continuity of grace and
spiritual gifts. In the New Testament, churches are judged
by the vitality and abundance of their grace and gifts, not
by the legitimacy of their ministries. However, bearing in
mind the responsibilities assigned by the New Testament to
presbyters and bishops, and remembering that this was often
by explicit arrangement of the apostles themselves, one can
begin to understand how these ministers of the church came
to continue that special responsibility for the churches
that marked the apostolic ministry. This role obviously
emerged more prominently as the apostolic generation of
church leaders passed away. One can sense Paul preparing
for this in his discourse to the presbyters of Ephesus,
and in the Pastoral Epistles. Presbyters and bishops would
become the recognized guarantors of the apostolic authenticity of their churches. And they would also become the
contact people between the churches, maintaining that communion of faith and love between the churches that
originated with the apostles.

3. Deacons--At the beginning of his letter to the
Philippians, Paul greets all "the saints in Christ Jesus
who are at Philippi, with the bishops and deacons".
1 Tim 2:8-13 follows up the instruction on bishops with an
instruction on the kind of people who should be called to
serve as deacons. And in Rom 16:1,2 Paul commends "our
sister Phoebe, a deaconess (diakonon) of the church at
Cenchreae. . .for she has been a helper of many and of
myself as well".

The title deacon is also given to the seven men selected from among the Hellenists to relieve the apostles of responsibility for the "daily distribution" (Ac 6:1-6). Many exegetes today think that these seven men were called to a much more comprehensive and foundational ministry than that referred to by Paul. The text is no longer used by the latest official Catholic document on diaconate.

However, it seems to me that the idea of assisting someone else in their ministry, of relieving them of burdensome responsibilities that their ministry entails so that they can be free to concentrate on essentials, gives the basic New Testament sense of the ministry of deacon. The deacon stands with another--apostle or bishop--to help him in ministry. He does not have a distinctive, independent set of functions. He is competent to help with anything from the ministry of the word to serving at table. I do not think one can find anything more specific than that about the ministry of the deacon in the New Testament.

B. Ministry in the Tradition of the Church

The Catholic Church finds its faith nourished and expressed in the ongoing tradition that is recorded in its historical documents subsequent to the New Testament. When it finds a consensus about basic issues of doctrine in the documents of the tradition, and when that consensus can stand up to the testing of the Scriptures, it regards it as binding on its faith and practice. When this consensus is expressed in formal definitions of church doctrine, it is considered to be still more explicitly binding.

I want to look briefly at some of the major moments
in which the church has expressed itself about ministry.
That should allow us to determine more exactly what in our
present practice of ministry we believe to be the gift of
God. At the same time it will allow us to see something
of how historical, human, and at times sinful factors have
influenced developments in ministry, without however, we
would hope, being accepted as belonging to the essence of
ministry.

1. The Apostolic Fathers--We have three writings
that show the structuring, functioning and understanding
of ministry in the church before the year 120. In the
Didache prophets and teachers are still given something of
the pre-eminence they have in the New Testament. But
bishops and deacons have emerged as the regular leaders of
the church. It is they who normally preside over the
eucharist. In his Letter to the Church at Corinth, St
Clement gives his solution to the problems still besetting
the church that had given Paul so much trouble. A key
element is submission to the presbyters and bishops who,
along with deacons, have been appointed by the apostles to
minister in the church (para 57; cf. para 42 sq). The
churches to which St Ignatius of Antioch writes his Letters
have a strongly structured ministry. There is one bishop
ruling each church. He presides over its eucharist. He is
surrounded by a college of presbyters who advise and assist
him. He may delegate one of them to preside at the
eucharist. And there are deacons.

The threefold pattern of ministry seems to have become
universal and unchallenged in the church of the apostolic
fathers. It is seen as the guarantee that the church remains
faithful to the apostolic tradition. The ministers, and
specifically the bishops continue the ministry of the
apostles. The apostolic succession of the church is
guaranteed by the derivation of their office from that of
the apostles.

The rite by which bishops, presbyters and deacons are
appointed to ministry is described in considerable detail
in documents that date from as early as the third century.
There is a process of discernment and call by the community.
There is the laying on of hands with a prayer for the coming
down of the Holy Spirit. For presbyters and deacons the
rite is conducted by the bishop. For bishops it is conducted by those who are already bishops. The substance of
the rite is the same in all the earliest records and has
been considered as binding on the church in the major
Christian traditions.

It is noteworthy that already during these early centuries the terminology of priesthood begins to be applied
to the ministry of bishops and presbyters. Parallels are
drawn between them and the priests of the Old Testament.
But it is especially from the role they have in the celebration of the eucharist that they come to be called priests.
As the eucharist comes to be explicitly recognized as the
representation of the sacrifice of Christ, the act of presiding at it comes to be seen as a special representation
of his priesthood. As the eucharist comes to be called a

sacrifice those who lead its celebration come to be called priests.

2. <u>Patristic Developments</u>--The major Fathers of the church and the early ecumenical councils develop the tradition about ministry in two major areas. They develop a spirituality of ministry and they develop the canonical discipline that regulates the practice of ministry. While the faith of the church about ministry obviously influences and is influenced by both these areas, one does not find major new declarations of faith about ministry, of the type we are examining, during this period. It is important to note this. Many of the features of ministry which are often regarded as typical of and integral to its practice in the historical churches of east and west have their origin during the patristic period. They are matters of discipline and spirituality rather than tenets of faith. Special forms of dress, titles, a certain apartness from other members of the community and not just from the world, celibacy, procedures for the discernment of vocation and special education for ministry, comprehensive subjection of almost every area of life of ministers to ecclesiastical authority and law, special prayer obligations--all these are disciplinary developments. They are the response of the church to a particular phase of its historical existence--even if it is a classical phase that will always be profoundly influential.

These disciplinary measures were developed and presented in a Gospel spirit. A'powerful spirituality of ministry emerges among the Fathers (Chrysostom, Augustine, Gregory the Great, for example). It celebrates the sense of dedication associated with ministry, the apartness of those who are called and the sacredness of their office. It is a spirituality which profoundly influenced what came to be called the clerical state. At the same time, many of the disciplinary developments were modelled on secular patterns. They undoubtedly helped the exercise of ministry in the church to be more effective, but they stand under the permanent judgement of the New Testament as a compromise that can corrupt. In the spirituality of the period the vices of pastors are ruthlessly identified: failure to guide the flock, pride and abuse of authority, venality and worldliness.

The hierarchical organization of ministry develops considerably during the patristic period. Churches become territorial units, eventually called dioceses. The bishop is responsible for a geographical area. As other communities were founded within cities or surrounding countryside they were given into care of one or more presbyters, and became parishes. For the service of each community, especially to meet its progressively more elaborate liturgical needs, further ministries were added to that of deacon--subdeacons, acolytes, exorcists, readers, doorkeepers. All the communities within a diocese, and their ministers, were ruled by the bishop. Bishops became organized among themselves. A certain primacy had always been recognized for bishops of churches that could claim

apostolic foundation, or special antiquity. Around these
were grouped ecclesiastical provinces. This is the period
when the primacy of the Bishop of Rome takes institutional
shape. All this ordered array of ministry, with its gradations of sacred power and authority, came to be called
hierarchy. In the theology of the age it was likened to the
celestial hierarchy of the angels, as the church on earth
was seen to be a reflection of the church in heaven.

3. <u>Middle Ages, Reformation, Council of Trent</u>--All
that I can do under this wide title is to situate and present the doctrine of the Council of Trent about ministry.

The scholastic theologians of the Middle Ages
developed their analysis of ministry primarily in terms of
the eucharist. They saw ministry as authority or power in
the Christian community. There is profound correspondance
between the sacramental body of Christ, which is the
eucharist, and the mystical body of Christ, which is the
church. This correspondence explains why ministry in the
church can be defined in terms of the sacred power to
realize the eucharist. And since the sacramental system
is built around the eucharist the grades of ministry can be
distinguished by degrees of power within the sacramental
system. Bishops have the fulness of priestly power and
so can celebrate all the sacraments. Presbyters have
power to do all that the bishop does except to ordain other
ministers and complete Christian initiation by the sacrament
of confirmation. Deacons can have a part in all the sacraments, but can act alone only in Baptism and matrimony.

Lesser ministers have an increasingly diminished participation in the sacramental activity that builds up the church.

At its best this scholastic theology of ministry can be rich and enlightening, especially when set in the context of a comprehensive understanding of the relationship between eucharist and church, and between faith and sacrament. But at its worst it can, and did, lead to a purely cultic conception of ministry. The minister is one who has power to do sacred actions. And what he does is holy just because it is he who does it and because he does it according to the rules. The temptation is to exploit this power, without paying much attention to how or whether the people for whom the sacred action is being done see or experience it, without seeking to call forth in them that living faith in which salvation comes. Ministers were very busy about the celebration of sacraments, especially of Masses, in the late Middle Ages, but they did very little preaching or pastoral care.

The protest of the Reformers was very much about this. Justification by faith meant the primacy of word over sacramental ritualism. If ministers of the church were to be anything they were to be preachers. And some would even say that if they did not preach they lost their title to ministry. The permanent sacred power that had been the justification for so many abuses had to be discounted. Priesthood in that sense had to be rejected. The ministry of sacraments was regulated by disciplinary arrangement of the church, not by the gift and command of God. Ordination to ministry was not a sacrament. The community had to be involved in the call and designation of ministers.

These shorthand statements are less than fair to the theology of Reformers. But I think they represent the issues, at least as the Council of Trent saw them. They are the background against which one has to read the definitions of the council about ministry. These express, with the authority which the council has for the church, the belief of the Roman Catholic Church about certain aspects of ministry that had been called into question by the Reformers. The Council does not provide a full dogmatic statement of the church's beliefs about ministry. But it does express certain fundamental beliefs about the gift of God in ministry.

Firstly, there is the belief that ministry involves priestly power, exercised in the celebration of the eucharist and in the forgiveness of sins. It is not simply the office of preaching.

Secondly, there is the belief that ministry as priesthood is the gift of God to the church, not merely a human institution. Ministry in its hierarchy of bishop, presbyter and ministers is set up in the church by divine arrangement. And it is conferred on individuals by a sacrament, that is by an act of God mediated by the church in which the Holy Spirit is given and a permanent character is imprinted that marks the minister forever. This ordination does not depend for its validity on the consent of the faithful, nor on that of secular authorities. Without it there is no ministry.

394

Thirdly, Trent affirms the preeminence of bishops in ministry. They are the successors of the apostles. They are superior in sacramental power to presbyters. And they are legitimately appointed by the Roman Pontiff.

4. <u>Second Vatican Council</u>--The teaching of Trent on priesthood and the sacrament of orders dominated the practice and understanding of ministry in the Roman Catholic Church until quite recent times. The disciplinary reforms of the Council, which put much more emphasis on preaching and pastoral care than the doctrinal statements of the council might have led one to expect, seem to have had less influence. The experience of ministry, and especially the training of candidates for ministry in seminaries, gave rise to a strong spirituality of ministry. This had genuine evangelical roots, as well as being marked by the social and religious situation of the times. It was a spirituality that made little concession to the reform tradition of the Protestants. Protestants, for their part, seem to have found little that was acceptable in the Council of Trent. They developed their own patterns of ministry in their own areas of influence.

While the teaching of Vatican II is primarily intended to restore Gospel sense to the meaning and practice of ministry in the church, it is also influenced by the religious and social preoccupations of today. A Church that is to be the sacrament of salvation in the world of today has to be fully missionary, actively evangelizing on every front. To be effective in its mission it has to

recover communion with all Christian churches in the one
church of Christ. And this Church--and the Roman Catholic
Church dared to speak for it at Vatican II--would have to
be a community in which all the gifts of the Holy Spirit
could be fully activated. The teaching of Vatican II on
ministry flows from this missionary and ecumenical concern for the world of our day.

The first thing the council did was to put ministers
in their place! The "Dogmatic Constitution on the Church"
deals first with The People of God--(<u>Lumen</u> <u>Gentium</u>, chap 2)--
with all the gifts of holiness, priestliness, prophecy,
charism, fraternity and missionary power which the Holy
Spirit pours out on all who are members of the Christian
community. Only then does it go on in chap. 3 to discuss
ministers, in the sense we have been taking the term, under
the heading "On the hierarchical constitution of the
church, and specially on the episcopate". There is no
going back on anything that has been defined by Trent or
Vatican I, or handed on in the mainstream tradition. But
there is a change of prospective in relation to Trent. The
first have been put last, which is where, according to the
Gospel, they belong. There is also a certain toning down
of some of the formulas in which Trent condemned protestant
ideas about the hierarchy. This represents a certain
openess towards the possibility of accepting ways of
structuring ministry other than that which is standard in
the Roman Catholic Church. It is dictated also by fuller
historical information than was available at Trent on the

variants there are in the structuring of ministry in the early church. Thus, the formulation of the church's belief in the divine origin of ministry is more nuanced than that of Trent. Whereas Trent says that the hierarchy made up of bishops, presbyters and ministers is of "divine ordinance", Vatican II says: "the divinely instituted ecclesiastical ministry is exercised in different degrees by those who even from ancient times have been called bishops, presbyters and deacons" (Lumen Gentium, para 28).

A second characteristic of Vatican II teaching on ministry is the importance given to preaching. "Among the more important duties of bishops, that of preaching the Gospel has pride of place" says Lumen Gentium, para 25. The same emphasis is repeated for presbyters in Presbyterorum Ordinis (para 4). Ministry is prophetic as well as being priestly. The restoration of emphasis on preaching is, of course, fully in line with the missionary and ecumenical concerns of the council.

A third characteristic that marks the documents of Vatican II is the wish to restore a certain authonomy to the ministers of local churches and communities. The centralization of ministerial authority remains strong in the Roman Catholic Church, both on the universal and on the local level. But Vatican II would want to make it less than it used to be. And this not just for "political" reasons. It recognizes that ministerial authority is not just delegated from higher levels of the hierarchy to the lower, but is inherent in the gift of ministry itself at every level. A bishop does not get his ministry from the Pope but from his ordination--although he may be nominated by the Pope and is subject to him for the lawful exercise of his authority. This recognition of the autonomy of local churches through the legitimate autonomy of their ministers, is of considerable importance for realizing the ecumenical goals of the council. And to the extent that it allows local churches to adjust to local situations it can strengthen the missionary potential of the church enormously. However, it is not being realized in the church without a certain amount of tension. Ideally the fears of decentralization should be set at rest by the hopes inherent in collegiality. Local autonomy should be counterbalanced by the drawing together of all the churches and of their ministers, in a spirit of responsibility for each other and for the whole church. However, the institutions of collegiality, such as the Synod of Bishops, are still at a very early stage of development.

CONCLUSION

I trust that what I have said about the faith of the church in section II of my paper has thrown some light on the sense we Roman Catholics give our practice of ministry, and why we organize it the way we do. Vatican II brought us to an important growth-point in our development of ministry. The council, and subsequent official documents, gave us a teaching and a certain amount of disciplinary orientation. There are many disciplinary questions that have been raised and not settled in the post-conciliar church. Some of them are fringe issues of the life-style, such as dress; other, such as those raised in a recent book on ministry by Edward Schillebeeckx, touch the very nature of the gift of God. A working solution to these problems depends on a good theology of ministry, which can be very much aided by good social and psychological analysis of contemporary human realities. But it is above all on the level of spirituality that they must be resolved. Ministry is a gift of God, to be experienced in His Spirit by those to whom it is given, as well as by those who have received other gifts. The basic rules for its exercise were laid down by Jesus and will be lived by those who are in Him. Being in Christ and in His Spirit is not, of course, an escape from human searching and institutional dilemnas. But it is the only ultimate verification of everything that is thought and that is done about ministry by men and women in the church.

NOTES

[1] VATICAN II: "Dogmatic Constitution on the Church" (<u>Lumen</u> <u>Gentium</u>) chap III, para 18-27.

"Decree on the Pastoral Office of Bishops in the Church" (<u>Christus</u> <u>Dominus</u>).

PAUL VI: Apostolic Letter (<u>Ecclesiae</u> <u>Sanctae</u>) 6 August 1966.

[2] VATICAN II: "Dogmatic Constitution on the Church" (<u>Lumen</u> <u>Gentium</u>) chap III, para 28.

"Decree on the Ministry and Life of Priests" (<u>Presbyterorum</u> <u>Ordinis</u>).

"Decree on the Training of Priests" (<u>Optatam</u> <u>Totius</u>).

PAUL VI: Apostolic Letter (<u>Ecclesiae</u> <u>Sanctae</u>) 6 August 1966.

SYNOD OF BISHOPS: "The Ministerial Priesthood," 1971.

[3] VATICAN III: "Dogmatic Constitution on the Church" (<u>Lumen</u> <u>Gentium</u>) chap III, para 29.

PAUL VI: Apostolic Letter containing norms for the Order of Diaconate (<u>Ad</u> <u>pascendum</u>) 15 August 1972.

[4] PAUL VI: Apostolic Letter on First Tonsure, Minor Orders and the Subdiaconate (<u>Ministeria</u> <u>Quaedam</u>) 15 August 1972.

[5] Council of Trent: Doctrine on the Sacraments of Orders Session XXIII, 15 July 1563 (Denz 1763-1778).

Theological Paper

A PENTECOSTAL PERSPECTIVE OF THE CHURCH
AND ITS MINISTRY
by
Rev H. David Edwards

I.   Origins of Ministry - Jesus and the Apostles

II.   Ordination and the Priestly Quality of Ministry

III. Bishops, Elders, Presbytery, and Other Offices

IV.   Priests and Other Clergy

V.   Priesthood of the Believers

VI.   Apostolic Succession

I understand that my assignment is to consider the above-mentioned issues from within a Pentecostal framework and from a Pentecostal point of view. I find those parameters somewhat difficult, not because of the inadequacy of my Pentecostal experience or tradition, but because, as has often been remarked, Pentecostal theology is still to be considered inadequate in some areas. Whether or not this is due to the fact that enough time has not yet passed to provide for the ordering of Pentecostal theology or whether or not it is because the contribution that the Pentecostal tradition is to make to the Church is one of revitalizing all other theologies by virtue of its dynamic and experience is an issue that must be left for others to determine. It is possible that Pentecostal theology is currently at the state of "oral tradition".

I come from a British Pentecostal background which must be borne in mind and also from a minor stream of the British Pentecostal tradition, which undoubtedly will color and influence my thought and interpretation in this perspective. Although minor, it is not without its own significant contribution to make. The denomination of which I was a part is the only Pentecostal group that I am aware of that includes in its statement of fundamental beliefs the clause "We believe in church government by apostles, prophets, evangelists, pastors, teachers, elders, and deacons."

It is probably held universally by Pentecostals as evangelicals that the ministry of our Lord begins with His dual-baptism, i.e., that at the hands of John the Baptist and the baptism of the Spirit by His Father. It would seem to me that there are two elements involved in this beginning of our Lord's ministry, inasmuch as I see that possibly His baptism at the hands of John is to be taken as the equivalent of the priestly bath that was necessary before a priest could enter on his ministry. Even though our Lord was not of the tribe of Levi but of Judah, it might well have been that this is what He had in mind in His response to John, "Suffer it to be so now: for thus it becometh us to fulfill all righteousness" (Mt 3:15). If this is so, it might well be that this establishes a pattern for all other ordinations in the ministry inasmuch as it should embody two elements, one human, the other divine. The one recognition, the other impartation. One possibly institutional or structural and one pneumatic or charismatic. A continuing misplaced emphasis on one or the other might be equally damaging--emphasis on the institutional character of the act leading to ritualism and an unbalanced approach to the supernatural expectation to be associated with it tending to fanaticism.

Following the trial in the wilderness our Lord now engages on the commencement of His ministry with His significant declaration in the synagogue, "The Spirit of the Lord is upon me, because He hath anointed me to preach the Gospel to the poor; He hath sent me to heal the brokenhearted, to preach deliverance to the captives, and recovering of sight to the blind, to set at liberty them that are bruised, to preach the acceptable year of the Lord" (Lk 4:18, 19). (In common with other evangelicals, Pentecostals reject the alleged childhood miracles of our Lord as recorded in the Pseudepigraphical "Gospel of Thomas".)

Our Lord's ministry of preaching, teaching and healing (including exorcism) might perhaps be understood as announcing, explaining, and demonstrating the Kingdom. The difference between preaching and teaching being a difference of sequence rather than the difference of method. In all of this His motivation appears to have been neither simply benevolent or compassionate, but rather "doing the will of

the Father". "The Son can do nothing of Himself. I do
only those things that please My Father. I do those things
I see My Father doing."

I. APOSTLES

From the disciples who followed Him early in our
Lord's ministry He selected twelve whom He named apostles.
Their selection as apostles did not mean that they lost
their relationship as disciples, as is obvious from a consideration of Mt 10:1,2; Mk 3:13-19; Lk 6:12-19; Mt 11:1.
It would appear that their apostleship, although intended
to be permanent, functioned in a temporary manner only as
long as our Lord was with them. When they were sent from
Him they became apostles. When they returned to Him they
resumed their former role as disciples until the Ascension
and descent of the Holy Spirit, for these same men are never
called "disciples" in Acts, but only "apostles".

Pentecostals in common with other evangelicals would
regard their ministry as foundational (Eph 2:20[1]).

The choice of Matthias as a replacement for Judas
would not be regarded as premature and in fact such scholastic assessment would be seen not necessarily as an
indictment of the wisdom of Peter and the others, but rather
a possible indictment against the wisdom of the Lord whose
name and intervention was invoked by the apostolic prayer

---

[1]Some Pentecostals would probably regard the prophets
of this verse as being Old Testament prophets, whereas others
would consider that their association with apostles in this
way could possibly identify them as charismatic prophets of
New Testament times.

concerning the choice, as seen in Ac 1:24.

Paul, in Pentecostal estimation, enjoys as significant a function as any of the twelve, except for whatever might be meant by our Lord's promise in Mt 19:28, "Verily I say unto you, that ye which have followed Me, in the regeneration when the Son of man shall sit in the throne of His glory, ye also shall sit upon twelve thrones, judging the twelve tribes of Israel." And also the inclusion of their names in the twelve foundations of the heavenly city as recorded in Ap 21:14. While Paul's call to apostleship might be identified with his encounter with our Lord on the road to Damascus (Ac 9:1-8; 26:14-18), the recognition of that ministry is probably to be found in Ac 13:1,2. No earlier references to either Paul or Barnabas as apostles are to be found, whereas they are clearly identified as such from this time on. The fact that frequently, at least in the earlier record, Barnabas appears to take precedence over Paul and that Paul appears to identify him as a fellow apostle (1 Cor 9:6) would lead me to believe that, at least in Paul's eyes, Barnabas shared equal authority and is not to be regarded as inferior in status or simply as an "apostle of the churches". Others, apart from the twelve and Paul, Barnabas and Matthias, are identified as apostles, as Silas and Timothy (1 Thes 1:1; 2:6), Epaphroditus (Phil 2:25), Titus and two unnamed brethren (2 Cor 8:16-23), possibly these latter to be understood as apostles in a somewhat different sense from the twelve or the others. James, the Lord's brother (Gal 1:19) and Andronicus and

Junia (Rom 16:17). It might be that Paul means that they
are known by the apostles rather than being recognized as
part of their number.

The words of Paul in his reference to what Pentecostals
understand as the continuing ministry and need of apostles
(Eph 4:11-16) would appear to suggest that until such time
as the whole body of Christ arrives at "the unity of the
faith and in the knowledge of the Son of God unto a perfect
man", the ministry of apostles will continue to be needed.

Pentecostals generally find it difficult to identify
apostles as long as they are alive, possibly out of fear
and concern lest unwarranted "apostolic" authority should
be exercised, or else in reaction to excesses which have
been seen in this connection. They do not find it as difficult to identify their dead or the dead of earlier generations as having possessed an apostolic ministry.

Where recognized, the authority of current apostles
is legitimately held to be subordinate to that of the
authority of the Scriptures. No current or New Testament
apostle, for that matter, used words similar to those of
our Lord, "Ye have heard that it was said by them of old
times. . .but I say unto you. . ." (Mt 5); nor did any
New Testament apostle introduce his preaching with "Verily,
verily. . ." or use the prophetic formula, "thus sayeth the
Lord." Where contemporary apostleship is legitimately
recognized it is not held to add to Scripture but certainly
might be considered as illuminating Scripture. Our Lord
could, and did, add to and advance on the revelation of the

Old Testament, but neither New Testament apostles or their successors are expected to. They might use Old or New Testament for illustration and foundation, as for example 1 Cor 10; Ac 26:22; Rom 15:26, but never to modify, advance, or correct the biblical statements set forth. Provided the apostle acts within the guidelines prescribed by the Scripture, he might expect God as He pleases to endorse and confirm his message and authority. For when he acts in accordance with his commission it is not his authority that is exercised, but rather that of the Lord whom he represents. I consider that the authority that the apostle exercises is God's delegated authority which might be considered to be different from transferred authority. If transferred, can it be recalled? If delegated, obviously it might, unless the terms of the original commission are honored. This probably requires that those who choose to submit to apostolic authority consider whether or not that which they are required to submit to is the truth. If it is the truth that is spoken, then submission is obligatory and without limit. Is this the two-fold lesson of Heb 13:7 and 13:17, that there are those who have the rule, whose responsibility it is to speak the word of God, that those who hear the word of God have the responsibility to obey as long as it is the word of God that is spoken?

The apostle is seen as both servant and authority, which is a difficult concept for us to hold with our hier-archial approaches. It might be explained by an analogy which would compare the apostle and the believer to that of the role of the physician and his patient. The physician is a servant inasmuch as his patient pays his fees, but he is also the authority whose direction must be heeded and obeyed if the patient is to benefit from his counsel.

II. ORDINATION

Pentecostal material on ordination is not extensive. The Ministers' Service Book, compiled by Myer Pearlman and published by Gospel Publishing House, Springfield, Missouri, but undated, on page 105 indicates that at the time of ordination the following charge is to be made:

> Brother Jones, we the presbytery of the Assemblies of God do now lay hands upon you, setting you apart for the ministry whereunto God has called you and pray the Lord may impart to you the gifts and graces of the Holy Spirit that will make you effective in this holy ministry.

Whether or not those gifts and graces are expected to be imparted at the time of ordination is not clear, although reference is made to Scriptures like 1 Tim 4:14 and Ac 13, 2 Tim 1:6, which appear to suggest that at least in biblical times there was an element of impartation which is not always recognized or obvious in our contemporary practices.

For Pentecostals, Moses and Joshua, Saul and David, Elijah and Elisha illustrate, if not determine, the principle of succession, i.e., that it is a "spirit" matter, sometimes accompanied by structure--laying on of hands--but not always. In fact, they would probably say that to insist always on the laying on of hands is to "limit the Spirit" and by way of analogy and illustration would refer to the

408

experience of the apostles in Acts, that whereas in Samaria and Ephesus the apostles laid hands on Christians that they might receive the Spirit, in the house of Cornelius the Spirit fell on them while Peter was speaking, without his laying hands on them (they would probably also add that this might have been occasioned by Peter's unbelief!--as is perhaps to be understood from Peter's own report in Ac 11).

Ordination for the most part is seen as a recognition of spiritual gifts already imparted, inasmuch as for Pentecostals ministry is always initiated with a divine call which at some time or other must be attended by impartation of necessary graces and some kind of authentication. Such authentication might be in the nature of supernatural miracle, as Saul's prophesying was a sign to him and to those who were with him that the Lord was with him (1 Sm 9, 10), and the comment of Nicodemus to our Lord, "No man can do these miracles save God be with him" as well as our Lord's response to others, "Believe me for the very work's sake."

The reconciliation of my comment that for the most part Pentecostals regard ordination as confirmation and the prayer or statement taken from Myer Pearlman's Minister's Service Book, together with references to relevant scriptures, might be that the prophesy referred to in those Scriptures is seen as proof of a divine call which is then recognized by the laying on of hands of those associated with the individual call and who might already be regarded as "clergy".

It has not been uncommon for Pentecostals to make use

of phrases like "the ordination of the pierced hands is the only ordination that counts or is significant" and to refer somewhat derogatorily to other ordinations as being "empty hands on empty heads".

For the most part, Pentecostals would regard the movement from the supernatural, pneumatic and charismatic to the structural and institutional as deterioration. If, as is sometimes suggested and apparently borne out by history, that the charismatic inevitably becomes institutional after a period of about twenty-five to forty years, even when such movement appears reasonable and acceptable to leadership, there are radical Pentecostals who would point to the experience of Aaron in his manufacture of the golden calf and his obviously blatant excuse, "I put it into the fire and this is what came out" (Ex 32:24) in contrast to the previous effort he had made to manufacture, as being an explanation of succumbing to demonic and carnal forces in the change from the charismatic and pneumatic to the institutional and structural.

Pentecostals would make a distinction between the general ministry of the Church, which is sometimes referred to as "body ministry", and the special ministries which are provided in order to secure the effective function of such "body ministries". For both styles of ministry they would insist that the source must be the Lord, the Spirit, and for the second and restricted class would insist that there must be proof and commission for its effectiveness.

I have not been able to locate any Pentecostal source

dealing with the issue of the priestly ministry of the "clergy". The question is dealt with very finely however, by W. H. Griffith Thomas in The Principles of Theology and although not written by a Pentecostal the ideas expressed would be endorsed by them and the truths are presented as clearly as they would wish. It might also be of interest to note that the author was an Anglican and the book is a defense of a commentary of the thirty-nine articles of the Church of England. I have taken the liberty of including his exposition on the point at issue as Appendix I.

III. BISHOPS, ELDERS, PRESBYTERY, AND OTHER MINISTRIES

If the question of bishops, elders, presbytery, and other ministries is intended to be related to the larger question of church polity, it might be well for a brief, general comment to be made initially.

At least a part of the strength of Pentecostalism is its ability to provide for a variety of forms of denominational administration without obviously surrendering any of its distinctives. Forms of church denominational administration, ranging from congregational through presbyterian to episcopal can be identified in its world-wide family. Some of these forms have been carried over from the roots of the fathers and others, knowing adaptation during years of development, so that no one form of denominational polity can be identified as being peculiarly Pentecostal.

Some of this variety might, as previously indicated, be due to the inherited traditions of Pentecostal pioneers, but some of it might also be due to: 1) the inability to identify any of the major systems of administration as having a broader biblical base than another, 2) the ability of the Holy Spirit to freely relate to any system of administration which provides for such liberty.

I do not regard the Church as a free association, able at whim to establish its own ecclesiastical Robert's Rules of Order and Procedure and solicit her own offices. The Church is not a voluntary organization. She is more than a voluntary organization of the recognizably disobedient who are anticipating heaven. Biblically she is more than that. The Church is bound not by legislation but by life to her own head without whose breath she not only has no beginning but no continuance and no guaranteed end.

The Church is the Church of God, purchase of His own blood, work of His own hands, vehicle of His own purpose, and is no more capable of self-sustenance than we are capable of unaided flight.

The Church is under necessity, if not under oath of fidelity, to submit herself to her Master's hand and provision for her well-being. She is under obligation to His holy law, not only to refrain from what it forbids, but to implement what it requires. It is not sufficient for us to anticipate an ideal Church in some far-off eternity, nor is it reasonable for us to say our perfections are spiritual, or heavenly, or imputed.

It is my opinion that as in that glorious day of His incarnation there was a remarkable blending of divine and human, so that the human remained real and the divine was not robbed of its deity, so the Church is intended to be visible, having a unity and a glory, a power and an authority which might be seen by unregenerate eyes, even if it is not always recognized, yet be manifestly human with powers and graces that bespeak of supernatural origins and continuing support. It is not our Church. We are not at liberty to choose the way in which we will be administered. Nor are we at liberty to choose our own administrators. The kind of relationship we have with our Head, if it is to be sustained, requires that we submit ourselves to that headship and allow Him to provide for His administration in what we confess to be His body.

Does she always have the same administrative patterns? Is there some essential element without which she is no longer the Church? Is there equally any pattern or procedure which, if persisted in, so nullifies this essence as to negate her existence? Is there something which is an imperative? Is there anything which if present means the absence of that imperative?

That God can and does take advantage of a variety of administrative patterns seems to me to be clear both from Scripture and from history. Does that mean that He is indifferent or that there is no pattern or ideal? That the scriptural variety arises from development the difference being only varying stages? Or does God accommodate Himself

to whatever ecclesiastical pattern is best suited to the
cultural needs of the moment?

I am of the opinion that the ambiguity, if there be
any, serves two not unrelated ends. Not all the "t's"
are crossed and not all the "i's" are dotted, lest we
should become so sure of precipitating God's presence, both
dramatic and continual, as we are sure of the outcome of
the chemical experiment which carefully follows previously
discovered and determined laws. Such a situation would
leave little place for faith and no room for His sovereign
intervention. There is an ambiguity which surrounds the
question of church structure and administration, which is,
in my opinion, not accidental. On the one hand the
ambiguity means that we cannot claim biblical warrant for
a particular system, so as to ensure God's endorsement of
it nor that it will provide in itself the imperative that
the Church needs before she can be recognized as the Church.
Conversely, however, sufficient is known for us to discover
to our mutual awareness whether or not we are prepared to
submit ourselves to His provision.

It seems to me that not only has He and does He wink
at our ignorance, how much out of mercy and how much out of
amusement we do not know, but also that the flexibility
within limits that seems to be indicated in His word provides both for His grace and intervention and for our faith.
Now where the boundaries of this flexibility lie, I am not
sure, except that in my opinion any situation which denies
the real expression of the Spirit of God in another, however

414

that is done, if persisted in, eventually so hurts the relationship as to make it non-Christian.

I consider that the major witness that the Pentecostal "Church" is intended to bear to the whole "Church" is that the dynamic of the Church is not preserved by the institution, but that the institution of the Church is preserved by its dynamic.

Because the terms bishop, elder, presbyter are biblical and Pentecostals generally have an interest in giving expression to their dependence upon biblical authority it will not surprise us that these terms occur frequently in Pentecostal circles. However, there is a variety of status and authority attaching to office bearers who carry the same title which varies, dependent upon the emphasis and interpretation given by that particular denomination. In the Pentecostal Holiness Church of North America the term "bishop" is reserved for the General Superintendent and is purely an honorary title.

As far as the Church of God is concerned, "the terms bishop, elder, presbyter are interchangeably used in the New Testament. It is quite difficult, if possible at all, to show the difference between these. If there is a difference it may be that the elder refers to the person, while the bishop refers to the office" (Your Pentecostal Neighbor, Earl P. Paulk, Jr.) In some Pentecostal denominations the elder is clearly a local official whilst in others the presbyter is an official having more than local authority, dignity, and status.

As far as the American Assemblies of God is concerned, it has identified the office of pastor and elder as can be seen from page 55, para D-2, the Minutes of the Thirty-Fifth General Council of 1973, "The office of elder (corresponding to pastor)".

The Apostolic Church of Great Britain, although placing great emphasis on the continuing nature of apostolic, prophetic, pastoral, evangelistic, and teaching ministry consistently addresses all their ordained "clergy" as "pastor".

The Church of God, as can be seen from their regular publication Evangel of the twenty-second of April, 1974 assumes the "angels" Ap 1:1 to be pastors and speaks of Paul as pastor in Philippi and Timothy as pastor in Ephesus.

I am of the opinion that a reasonable case might be made for affirming that on the basis of New Testament evidence alone a bishop is an ordained elder, i.e., not all elders are bishops, but all bishops are elders, with the added understanding that an elder is primarily "an older man". I would then speak of them as being our contemporary "cloud of witnesses". They are not spectators, but evidences not only of the validity of the life that we share, but of the real possibility of attaining the goals that we, together, pursue. They are those in whom time and the grace of God by His Spirit, through His word, have had an opportunity of so relating as to produce manifest evidences of that holy character and disposition which it is His expectation that all His children will ultimately share.

416

They are genuinely our superiors--better than we are. Our
superiors not in the sense of being our supervisors solely,
nor simply, but those who have made more progress in the
spiritual life so that they are not only a source of challenge but also an occasion of encouragement. The requirements, as defined in the pastoral epistles, are with one
exception exclusively character qualifications--not pneumatic
or charismatic. I consider it significant that if the
"faithful sayings" of the pastoral epistles are remnants of
an early creed or catechism one of them should say, "If a
man desire the office of a bishop he desireth a good work"
(1 Tim 3:1). I consider this significant because in spite
of the poverty of references to the office of bishop in
Paul's letters, it has never-the-less attained such a status
that by the time of the pastoral epistles, whether genuinely
Pauline or not, it is so widely known as to be incorporated
in a "faithful saying".

Paul speaks here of a singular bishop, but this should
not be interpreted to mean a representative of the modern
episcopacy because in the same letter he speaks of a widow
in the singular number. That would surely not be taken to
mean that the church should support only one widow.

IV. PRIESTHOOD OF ALL BELIEVERS

Of necessity the order and thought of this latter presentation must be even more disjointed and less coherent
than my opening pages.

Pentecostals would say that to restrict priesthood to clergy would appear to be an endeavor to either recognize the institutionalization or else to institutionalize the presence of Jesus, and that from their perspective the dynamic and vitality of the Holy Spirit needs no institutionalization and that institutionalization would and does, in fact, mitigate against such dynamic and vital recognition.

Would there be any reason to consider the minister a priest as a special case if he did not have the "mass"? Would he not then be placed in a position of nothing to offer than that which is required of all believers to offer?

None of the converted Jewish priests are recorded as enjoying or exercising any of their priestly rights or privileges when they entered into the status of believers-- does this say anything about priestly ministry?

The objection of Pentecostals to the "priestly" idea of ministry is twofold. They would say that it gives to many what belongs to one, i.e., the right of mediation which is peculiar to Christ and it restricts to few what belongs to all, i.e., the right of access.

In a community where there is neither Jew nor Gentile, are any to be recognized as Levites?

The scriptures which appear to be relevant to the question are Heb 4:14-16; 9:11,12; 10:19-23; 1 Pe 2:5; Ap 1:6, 5:10, 20:6; Rom 15:16.

The last chapter of Hebrews, in its injunctions concerning obedience and respect for leaders, makes it clear that universal priesthood does not invalidate special ministries.

418

V. APOSTOLIC SUCCESSION

Apostolic succession is defined by the Modern Catholic Dictionary (John A. Harden, SJ, Doubleday, 1980) as:

> The method by which the episcopacy has been derived from the apostles to the present day. Succession means successive consecration by the laying on of hands, performing the functions of the apostles, receiving their commission in a lineal sequence from the apostles, succession in episcopal sees traced back to the apostles, and successive communion with the apostolic see, the bishop of Rome.

Pentecostals would unhesitatingly affirm that they are both apostolic and in succession. The joint designation, if understood to affirm episcopacy as being the only method of guaranteeing authenticity and a wholly genuine expression of Christian continuity, they would unhesitatingly deny.

For Pentecostals to admit to the necessity of apostolic succession as held by the Roman Catholic Church would not simply be to deny their faith as doctrine, but it would be to call in question the whole validity of their spiritual experience and encounter with God, inasmuch as it has occurred outside the framework and the security allegedly guaranteed by apostolic succession.

Is the apostolic succession of the Church only secured by the succession of its bishops? Does it mean to affirm that only "apostolic" churches are Christian?

If apostolic succession is held to be the truth that Peter's successors--if so they be--will not fall away, that would appear to be at odds with the experience of Peter himself--an eventuality which he neither recognized nor provided for--possibly his successors are equally blind

to their own frailty. His restoration was dependent upon
the prayer of our Lord which might be held to secure the
restoration of Peter's successors, but it would also suggest that they might be excluded from its efficacy except
on the grounds of repentance, which would surely include
the admission of fault and guilt.

If Peter could err so soon after his great confession,
what guarantees are there that his successors may not?
Peter's continuing use of the keys after his failure is an
indication of God's persevering grace, but no guarantee of
infallibility on his part.

Did Paul's contention with Peter include a question
of both faith and practice? Is similar confrontation with
Peter's successors by those who might be equally held to
be "born out of due time" warranted and necessary?

Is succession a matter of faith or the faith? Is it
a matter of spirit and Spirit? Is it a matter of persons?
How is continuity assured? Is continuity assured on any
basis other than His promise?

Pentecostals would affirm that His promise of security,
"I will not leave you orphans. . ." is not fulfilled in the
ascent of the papacy, but in the descent of the Holy Spirit.
They would also say that they believe passionately in a
"vicar of Christ", who for them is the Holy Spirit, distinct
from the common subjective experience of the Church or any
part thereof. As we have an advocate "there", He has an
advocate "here". Pentecostals would recognize that the
Church is both dynamic and institutional, but affirm

positively that it is the dynamic that preserves the institution, not the institution that preserves the dynamic. He who guarantees succession by virtue of His presence can only fulfill His promise if He be seen also to have the freedom to remove the candlestick.

VI. ELDERSHIP

Is eldership an essential to the Church? Can a church-congregation be genuinely, authentically Christian without being wholly Christian? Is eldership in its traditional Pentecostal sense or in its traditional Catholic sense an imperative for a Christian church-congregation? I must say no, as a kind of "primitive" response, but also admit that eldership or something akin to it will, and I believe must, inevitably develop if that church-congregation is to mature, but that eldership or whatever it is that is akin to it, needs to be and must be always reminded that it is His presence, not their presence, that guarantees both the presence and the preservation of the Church. His presence authenticated not by tradition, but validated as was His personal physical presence by reference and cross-reference to both Word and Spirit, i.e., Holy Scriptures and Holy Spirit.

The fact that Paul ordained elders in the churches could be held to mean that they were valid churches without elders or possibly equally validly held that he saw that they were not authentic expressions without elders or else that there was no guarantee that they would persevere or be preserved without them.

Are elders a theological or a sociological imperative?
If sociologically necessary are they theologically irrelevant? Are they a theological/sociological necessity or a
sociological/theological imperative? Are they needed
because of the nature of the relationship or are they part
of the design? Are elders a sociological necessity with
biblical sanction and the papacy a sociological necessity
without biblical sanction?

3. Nor is mediation any proper part of the purpose
of the Christian ministry. The New Testament never uses
the word "priest" to describe the minister. Indeed, in the
singular number it is only found of Christ, and His Priesthood is said to be "undelegated" or "intransmissible"
(Heb vii. 24). When it is used of the Church it is always
in the plural, "priests" (Rev i. 6), or collectively,
"priesthood" (I Pet ii. 5). The truth, therefore, is that
Christianity is, not has, a priesthood. The silence of the
New Testament on this point is a simple and yet significant
fact. It is what Bishop Lightfoot calls "the eloquent
silence of the Apostolic writings." And if it be said that
the question is not one of words, but of things, Bishop
Lightfoot may again be quoted: "This is undeniable, but
words express things, and the silence of the Apostles still
requires an explanation." Neither the name nor the thing
is found in the New Testament idea of the Christian ministry,
and the reason is that it is irreconcilable with the letter
and spirit of Apostolic Christianity. In regard to the
priesthood "Christianity stands apart from all the older
religions," for it is "the characteristic distinction of
Christiantiy" to have no such provision. Three things
invariably go together; priest, altar, and sacrifice, and
where there is no offering there is no need of an altar;
where there is no altar there is no sacrifice; and where
there is no sacrifice there is no priest. As Hooker says:
"Sacrifice is no part of the Christian ministry." The New
Testament is clear as to the absence of sacrifice and in
regard to the absence of an altar, Bishop Westcott points
out that the term "altar" in Heb xiii. 10 is inapplicable
to the Lord's Table, and, indeed, incongruous. He remarks
that any such application to a material object would have
been impossible in the early days. To the same effect,
Lightfoot points out that St Paul had a special opportunity of using the word "altar" in connection with the Lord's
Supper (I Cor x), but that he quite evidently avoided it.

It is sometimes said, however, that our Lord's words
in St John xx. 19-23 constituted the ministry a priesthood. First of all, it is now generally recognised that
these words were spoken not to the ministry only, but to
the whole Church as there represented. Then the question
arises as to whether in any case the words can possibly be
made to mean a sacerdotal priesthood. There seems to be
some confusion in such an interpretation. A priest is one
who represents man to God (Heb v. 1), just as a
prophet is one who represents God to man (Exod vii. 1).
The passage is clearly to be understood of a messenger
from God to man, and this is the function of a prophet, not
a priest. So that to speak of priestly absolution

is really a contradiciton, since the Old Testament priest
never absolved, and absolution as a message from God to
man is the word of a prophet, not of a priest. The title
of a modern book, Ministerial Priesthood, is therefore
strictly a contradiction in terms, because a ministry is
not necessarily a priesthood; indeed, the representative
character of the Christian ministry is not a priesthood at
all. It is a beautiful and ingenious theory that the
Church, like Christ, is priestly and that therefore its
ministers are the organs of the Church's priesthood, but
this is really illusive, because it contains the doctrine
of a special and specialised priesthood which is subversive
of the New Testament priesthood of believers. Lightfoot
explains the silence of the New Testament by pointing out
that as there were no more sacrifices there were no more
priests. It is only too easy to fall into fallacy and confusion by noticing how a view of ministerial priesthood
develops from simple representation into substitution.

The only passage approaching the idea of priestliness
in ministerial functions is found in St Paul's words concerning his own ministry (Rom xv. 16). But the passage is
quite evidently metaphorical, with preaching as the function and the Gentiles as the offering. On any showing the
passage has no connection whatever with a "priest" offering
or sacrificing the Holy Eucharist.

We, therefore, return to the New Testament view of
the ministry, and call renewed attention to the striking
fact of its absolute silence as to any special order of
priests. The evidence taken separately in its parts is
striking, but as a whole it is cumulative and overwhelming.
There is no function of the Christian priesthood which
cannot be exercised by every individual believer at all
times. Differences of function in the ministry exist, but
none in the priesthood. It is almost impossible to
exaggerate the importance of this simple, striking, and
significant silence of the New Testament, that priestly
mediation is no part of the purpose of the Christian ministry.

In view of the foregoing it is sometimes asked why the
term "priest" should have been retained in the Prayer Book,
especially as it is well known that the word "altar" has
been omitted since the Prayer Book of 1552. The question
is one of history, and calls for the careful attention of
all pertinent facts of the case. The English word "priest"
has to do duty for two quite different sets of ideas and
terms; πρεσβύτεροσ "elder" and ἱερέυσ, "priest."
Lightfoot points out that it is a significant fact that in
those languages which have only one word to express the two
ideas, this word etymologically represent the word
"presbyter," and not sacerdos; French, prêtre; German,
priester; English, priest; thus showing that the sacerdotal
ideas was imported, not original. The question at once
arises, which of these two ideas was intended by the Prayer

Book? It is a question of fact and must be tested by all the available information.

1. Significant changes were made in the Holy Communion Service of 1552, showing an entire absence of anything sacerdotal and sacrificial.

2. The Ordinal of 1662 is described as "The Form and Manner of Ordering of Bishops, Presbyters, and Deacons." To the same effect are the words of Hooker: "Whether we call it a priesthood, a presbytership, or a ministry, it skilleth not."

3. In harmony with this the Latin Version of the Prayer Book, by Dean Durel, 1670, a few years after 1662, an almost official production, renders the term by *presbyterus*.

4. The word "priest" is frequently interchanged with "minister," as may be seen from the rubric before and after the Absolution at Morning Prayer, after the Creed, and before and after the Consecration Prayer in Holy Communion.

5. Nor is it without point that priests are entirely omitted from the *Te Deum*, which Blunt, in this annotated edition of the Prayer Book, regards as an argument for the extreme antiquity of that Song of Praise.

6. In Article XXXII, while the title speaks of "The Marriage of Priests" (*Sacerdotum*), doubtless referring to the Roman Catholic custom of celibacy, the Article itself refers to the three Orders, and describes them as "Bishops, Presbyters, and Deacons."

7. It is scarcely possible to overlook the significance of the change of usage in the versicle from Psa cxxxii. 16 from "Let Thy priests be clothed with righteousness" to "Endue Thy ministers with righteousness."

8. The Roman Catholic Church gives her "priests" power to "offer sacrifices." But this is entirely absent from our Ordination Service.

In view of these considerations, together with the fact that there is nothing sacerdotal provided in the ministry of our Church, it seems clear that the word "priest" can only be equivalent to "presbyter", and, as such, expresses the evangelistic and pastoral ministry associated with the Presbyterate in the New Testament.

In spite of all this it is said that the use of St John xx. 22, 23 in the Ordinal carries with it sacerdotal authority and functions. Dr Pusey was accustomed to say that the Confessional is built up on these words. But, as we have seen, it is now admitted with practical unanimity that these words were spoken to the whole Church, as there represented, and form St John's account of the great commission found in all the Gospels. When we turn to the Book of Acts we find that this, and this alone, was the work done (chs. ii; viii; x; xiii). Further, private confession was unknown for centuries, and these very words were not in any Ordinal until the thirteenth century, and even then were no essential part of the words of ordination. This makes Cranmer's deliberate retention of them, while rejecting other words and customs, all the more significant, because of their close adherence to Scripture as part of Christ's commission. The Prayer Book "priest" is, therefore, "presbyter," and corresponds to the prophet declaring the will of God. As already noticed, absolution is the work of the prophet, not of the priest. Keble took a similar position to Pusey in saying that it is impossible to get on without confession, and it is on this ground that these words are associated with priesthood to-day.

But the action of our Church at the Reformation ought to be sufficient to show its mind. First, there is the public confession in Daily Prayer and at Holy Communion; then there is the provision for the special case of a burdened soul before Holy Communion, though the wording, as distinct from that of the Prayer Book of 1549, shows quite clearly that there was no intention of a detailed and regular confession of sins. The usage in the Visitation Office is on similar lines, for the clergyman prays for forgiveness, and (as based on St Matt. xviii. 18) pronounces the absolution in regard to sins against the community. The power was left to the Church, not to the Ministry. The prayer for forgiveness significantly follows the pronouncement of the absolution. All this is totally different from the teaching and practice of the Roman Church, which compels auricular confession as a practice flowing out of the Sacrament of Penance. In the Church of Rome absolution is described by the word *"judicium,"* while with us we have its equivalent in *"beneficium"* by the ministration of God's Word.

It is, therefore, impossible to uphold confession from St John xx, for if it means absolution after auricular confession, it must of necessity be connected with a spiritual discernment which enables a man either to "forgive" or "retain" sins. We know that the Apostles had spiritual perception to see the condition of people like Ananias, Sapphira, and Elymas, but no such discernment exists now. As the words are not found in any Greek Ordinal to-day it is clear that they are not essential to Holy Orders, and their meaning in our own Ordinal can be illustrated from representative Churchmen like Whitgift, Becon, Hooker, and Jewel. In modern days the testimonies of representative High Churchmen support the contention that auricular confession is no part of the English Church, and is not warranted by anything in our Ordination Service.

426

It is quite impossible to suppose, because our Church
has continued these three Orders of ministry, that therefore of necessity there must be the same sacerdotal functions as in the Middle Ages. We have Bishops, Priests, and
Deacons, but the Priests are *Presbyteri* not *Sacerdotes*.
Bishop Gore has admitted that sacerdotal terms are only
found connected with the ministry at the end of the second
century. And Bishop Morton in his reply to Bellarmine very
forcibly said that if the terms "priest," "sacrifice," and
"altar" had been essential to the Christian ministry they
could not and would not have been concealed by the Apostles.
This is a striking anticipation of the very argument
emphasised by Moberly's Ministerial Priesthood.

4. Returning to the study of the actual ministry, as
seen in the New Testament and the Prayer Book, it is
essentially pastoral, never mediatorial, but always concerned with the word of preaching, teaching, and guiding
the flock. The minister is a prophet from God to the people,
and not a sacrificing or mediating priest, either in the
old Jewish or in the medieval meaning of the term. Such
being the case, the ministry must never be considered apart
from the Church as a whole. While there is a general service of the entire Church there is also a specific ministry
for the purpose of order and progress, but in all this the
minister is a medium, not a mediator; a mouthpiece, not a
substitute; a leader, not a director. The idea of the
Church always determines the form of the ministry, for the
Church as a whole was prior to the ministry, and the minister was intended to serve the entire community. We must,
therefore, take the greatest possible care not to exalt
the ministry above the community, for no ministry can fulfill its mission if it claims to control the Church. The
New Testament exalts the Body of Christ, and no trace can
be found of any direct Divine determination of the precise
development of the ministry. Any isolation of the ministry,
of whatever Order, is spiritually harmful as tending to make
them unrepresentative of the Church. The ministry only
exercises its functions in connection with the Church.

III.--THE FORM OF THE MINISTRY

1. This was gradually developed as it was needed.
At first there were Apostles only; then came Deacons (Acts vi.),
Evangelists (Acts viii.), and Elders (Acts xi. 30). Everything was adapted to the needs of a growing body. This is
further seen in the difference between the lists of ministries in I Cor xii. 28 and Eph iv. 11. The ministry is
thereby shown to be one of gifts rather than of offices.
With regard to the origin of elders, there is now a general
agreement "that this is nothing else than the standing
office of the Jewish synagogue transferred to the Christian
Church." There are no indications in the New Testament of

any direct Divine guidance of the development of the ministry. The suggestion that this was the subject of our Lord's instructions during the Great Forty Days after His Resurrection is, of course, a mere hypothesis and is wholly unsupported by evidence. It is impossible to explain the origin of the organisation of the ministry or, indeed, anything else in this way.

2. In time, however, the ministry naturally settled down into two main forms, evangelistic and pastoral, with something like an oversight in connection with the position of St James in Jerusalem (Acts xv.). But the pastoral ministry was concerned throughout with spiritual provision and organisation, and possessing nothing sacerdotal in its functions.

3. Yet the terms "Presbyter" and "Bishop" are always interchangeable in the New Testament (Acts xx. 17,28; Phil i. 1; I Tim iii. 1), and the term "Apostle" is applied not only to the Twelve, but also to St Paul, St Barnabas, and others.

"The absence of any sharp boundary between the Twelve and the larger class who bore the same name involves the exclusive claim which is made for the Twelve in serious difficulties."

Timothy and Titus evidently fulfilled temporary offices only, and are perhaps best regarded as Apostolic Delegates. At most they represent "a movable episcopate." There is no evidence that the Twelve received a commission to govern the Church, and in any case the appointment of elders later on shows the association of these with the Apostles (Acts xv. 6; xxi, 18).

4. The New Testament teaches a threefold function of ministry, not three distinct offices. This is really all that can be derived from the New Testament as essential, as distinct from what may be regarded as advisable. The term "Bishop" was therefore, first of all descriptive of a function not an office. "The ἐπίσκοποι of the New Testament have officially nothing in common with our Bishops."

5. There does not seem to be much doubt that the Christian ministry followed closely the analogy of the synagogue with its deacon, elder, and president. But whether this is so or not, there is no trace of any historical connection, or even ecclesiastical analogy between the Christian ministry and the Levitical priesthood. It is sometimes said that the priesthood offers an exact parallel, and is therefore typical of the ministry. But first of all there is no real parallel, because the High Priest was really only *primus inter pares*. Besides, the Levitical priesthood was typical of Christ, not of the

428

ministry, and the New Testament teaches that this priesthood is entirely abolished because fulfilled in Him
(Heb viii. 8, 9; 2 Cor iii. 6-16). Christ's work was to
bring us to God, and everything in the Old Testament was
fulfilled so completely in Him that there is no room and
no need for more. The question is not whether the powers
of the ministry come short of those of the Old Testament
priesthood, but whether they include them. This is not
only devoid of proof, but is absolutely opposed to the
very genius of the Christian religion. The first definite
connection of the Christian ministry with the Levitical
priesthood is seen in Cyprian, just as he is responsible
for the first definite use of "altar" to describe the Holy
Table. When episcopacy is seen in Ignatius there is nothing
sacerdotal in it.

Griffith Thomas,
The Principles of Theology,
London: Church Bookroom Press,
1945, pp 316-323.

APPENDIX II

EXTRACTS FROM DOCTRINAL STATEMENTS OF
REPRESENTATIVE PENTECOSTAL CHURCHES

ASSEMBLIES OF GOD (Great Britain)

We believe in the gifts of the Holy Spirit and the
offices set by God in the church as recorded in the New
Testament.

ASSEMBLIES OF GOD (U.S.A.)

A divinely called and scripturally ordained ministry
has been provided by our Lord for the threefold purpose of
leading the church in 1) evangelization of the world
(Mark 16:15, 16), 2) worship of God (John 4:23,24),
3) building a body of saints being perfected in the image
of His Son (Ephesians 4:11-16).

ELIM (Great Britain)

We believe that God has given some apostles and some
prophets and some evangelists and some pastors and
teachers for the perfecting of the saints, for the work of
the ministry for the perfecting of the saints, for the
edifying of the body of Chirst.

ELIM (U.S.A.)

We believe in the Baptism of the Holy Spirit according to Acts 2:4, 19:46, 19:6, and the present ministry of
the Spirit in and through the believer as manifest in the
five ministries as they are being restored in end-time
revival (Eph 4:11), the gifts of the Spirit (I Cor 12:
8-11), and the fruit of the Spirit (Gal 5:22,23).

SUGGESTED READING LIST

Bannerman, James. The Church of Christ. 2 vols London: The Banner of Truth Trust, 1960.

Berkouwer, G. C. The Church. Grand Rapids: William B. Eerdmans Publishing Company, 1976.

Bloesch, Donald G. The Reform of the Church. Grand Rapids: William B. Eerdmans Publishing Company.

Broadbent, E. H. The Pilgrim Church. London: Pickering and Inglis.

Bruce, F. F. Tradition: Old and New. Grand Rapids: Zondervan Publishing House, 1970.

Durnbaugh, Donald F. The Concept of the Believer's Church. New York: Macmillan.

Garrett. The Concept of the Believer's Church. Scottsdale: Herald Press.

Geldenhuys, Norbel. The Supreme Authority. London: Marshall, Morgan, and Scott.

Hollenweger, Walter J. The Pentecostals. Minneapolis: Augsburg Publishing House.

Hort, F. J. A. The Christian Ecclesia. London: Macmillan and Company, Ltd., 1914.

Leeming, Bernard. The Vatican Council and Christian Unity. Harper and Row, Publishers, 1966.

Lightfoot, J. B. St. Paul's Epistle to the Philippians. Grand Rapids: Zondervan Publishing House, 1970.

Lindsay, Thomas M. The Church and the Ministry in the Early Centuries. Minneapolis: James Family Publishing, 1977.

Murray, Iain, ed. The Reformation of the Church. London: The Banner of Truth Trust, 1965.

Newbiggin, Leslie. The Household of God. New York: Friendship Press.

Paulk, Earl P. Jr. Your Pentecostal Neighbor. Cleveland, TN: Hathaway Press, 1958.

Pieper, Francis. Christian Dogmatics, vol III. Saint Louis: Concordia Publishing House, 1953.

Robinson, William. The Biblical Doctrine of the Church. St Louis: Bethany Press.

Rowe, W. A. C. One Lord, One Faith. Bradford, Yorkshire: Puritan Press, Ltd.

Schaeffer, Francis. The Church at the End of the Twentieth Century. Downers Grove: Inter-Varsity Press.

Schlink, Edmund. The Coming Christ and the Coming Church. Philadelphia: Fortress Press, 1968.

Schmithals, Walter. The Office of Apostle in the Early Church. Nashville and New York: Abingdon Press, 1969.

Schnackenburg, Rudolph. The Church in the New Testament. New York: Seabury Press.

Schneider. Community of the King. Downers Grove: Inter-Varsity Press.

Thomas, Griffith. The Principles of Theology. London: Church Book Room Press Ltd, 1945.

Press Release

The tenth session of the dialogue between the
Secretariat for Promoting Christian Unity of the Roman
Catholic Church and representatives of Classical Pentecostal Churches took place at St John's Abbey,
Collegeville, Minnesota from October 25 through October
29. The meeting concluded the second Quinquennium, or
five-year term, of these conversations.

The session included the discussion of the topic of
ministry. This topic was discussed at the previous gathering of the dialogue in Vienna (1981) but it was felt that
the time alloted then was insufficient. The subject was
completed at this meeting and the final report of the
Quinquennium contains a summary of the discussions on
this matter. The papers on this topic were "A Pentecostal
Perspective of the Church and its Ministry" by H. David
Edwards, President of Elim Bible Institute, Lima, New
York and "Ministry in the Church" by Liam Walsh, OP,
Assistant to the Master General of the Dominican Order, Rome.

This meeting also drafted a second "Final Quinquennium
Report of the Dialogue between the Secretariat for Promoting
Christian Unity of the Roman Catholic Church and some
Classical Pentecostals, 1977-1982". The dialogue session
scheduled for 1978 was cancelled due to the death of Pope
John Paul I. This report synthesizes the topics discussed

during the meetings of the previous five years. These topics included faith and experience, speaking in tongues, healing, the inspiration of the Bible, Mary, tradition, worship, and ministry.

It is expected that the synthesized report will be published at a future date, sometime in 1983.

The participants included: Rev Kilian McDonnell, OSB, Collegeville, MN (Roman Catholic Co-Chairman); Rev David J. du Plessis, Oakland, CA (Pentecostal Co-Chairman); Rev Jerome M. Vereb, CP, Vatican City (Roman Catholic Secretary); Rev William L. Carmichael, Sisters, OR (Pentecostal Secretary); Rev William J. Dalton, SJ, Jerusalem, Israel; Rev H. David Edwards, New York, NY; Rev Howard M. Ervin, Tulsa, OK; Rev Ivan Havener, OSB, Collegeville, MN; Rev David P. Kast, Denver, CO; Bishop W. Robert McAlister, Rio de Janeiro, Brazil; Rev John L. Meares, Washington, D.C.; Msgr Basil Meeking, Vatican City; Rev David N. Power, OMI, Washington, D.C.; Rev Justus T. du Plessis, Lyndhurst, Republic of South Africa; Rev Jerry L. Sandidge, Houston, TX; Rev Liam G. Walsh, OP, Rome; Rev Robert J. Wister, Mahwah, NJ; and Rev Joseph W. Witmer, Washington, D.C.

At a dinner concluding the sessions, awards and mementos were presented to Rev David J. du Plessis and Rev Kilian McDonnell, OSB, who have co-chaired the dialogue since its beginning. The award to Dr du Plessis was presented by Rev Jerome Vereb, CP, of the Vatican Secretariat for Promoting Christian Unity in Rome. The award to Father

McDonnell was presented by Rev William L. Carmichael of Virtue Ministries Inc. of Sisters, Oregon. Speakers at the dinner included Bishop W. Robert McAlister, Pentecostal Bishop from Rio de Janeiro, Brazil and Msgr Basil Meeking of the Vatican Secretariat for Promoting Christian Unity in Rome, both of whom had previously served as co-secretaries of the dialogue.

Roman Catholic Bishop George Speltz of St Cloud [Minnesota, USA] and Abbot Jerome Theisen, OSB of St John's Abbey [Collegeville] greeted the participants at the dinner at which some representatives of local Pentecostal Churches were also present, including the Rev Herman Rohde, Superintendent of the Minnesota District of the Assemblies of God. At the dinner the participants in the Dialogue expressed their gratitude for the hospitality of the Benedictine monks of St John's Abbey.

ROMAN CATHOLIC/PENTECOSTAL DIALOGUE
25-30 October 1982
Collegeville, Minnesota, USA

Final Report of the Dialogue Between
the Secretariat for Promoting Christian
Unity of the Roman Catholic Church and
some Classical Pentecostals (1977-1982).

INTRODUCTION

1.   The following is a report of conversations at the international level which represent a second five-year series
that had its beginnings in informal talks in 1969 and 1970
between the Vatican Secretariat for Promoting Christian
Unity and some members of the classical Pentecostal churches.
The co-chairmen of this quinquennium were the Rev David
du Plessis of Oakland, California, USA, and the Rev Kilian
McDonnell, OSB, of Collegeville, Minnesota, USA. The conversations took place according to the indications agreed
to by the Secretariat for Promoting Christian Unity and the
Pentecostal representatives in 1970.

2.   This dialogue has its own specific quality. Growth
in mutual understanding of classical Pentecostal and Roman
Catholic theologies and spiritual practice rather than organic or structural unity is the special object of these bilateral conversations.

3.   It is a concern of the dialogue to seek out those
areas where classical Pentecostals and Roman Catholics represent divergent theological views and spiritual experiences,
and in this way to foster mutual understanding in what

distinguishes each partner, such as faith/experience and
its role in the Christian life. Without minimizing these
differences the dialogue also seeks common theological
ground where "the truth of the Gospel" is shared (Gal 2:14).

4.   The Roman Catholic participants were officially appointed by the Secretariat for Promoting Christian Unity.
There were various kinds of representation on the classical
Pentecostal side. Some were appointed by their individual
churches; a few were church officials; others were members
who came with the approbation of their churches; in still
other cases they came as members in good standing with their
churches.

5.   Besides the classical Pentecostals there were in the
first five-year series 1972-1976, participants from the
charismatic movement in various Protestant churches. These
were members of the Anglican or Protestant communions with
whom the Roman Catholic Church was already in formal contact through bilateral dialogues. These Anglican or
Protestant participants took part primarily because of
their involvement in the charismatic renewal rather than as
members of their own churches. The first five-year series
of conversations extended from 1972 through 1976. In those
meetings the following topics were discussed: "Baptism in
the Holy Spirit" in the New Testament and its relation to
repentance, sanctification, charisms, rites of initiation;
the historic background of the classical Pentecostal movement; the role of the Holy Spirit and the gifts of the

Spirit in the mystical tradition; the theology of the rites of initiation, the nature of sacramental activity; infant and adult baptism; public worship, with special attention given to eucharistic worship; discernment of spirits; and the human dimension in the exercise of the spiritual gifts; prayer and praise.

6.   In 1977 a second five-year series was initiated. This second series, 1977-1982 (no session was held in 1978 because of the death of the Pope), had a different character than the first series. In order to more clearly focus the conversations it was decided that this second series should be exclusively a conversation between the classical Pentecostals and the Roman Catholic Church. Therefore, participants in the charismatic renewal who were members of the Anglican and Protestant churches were not included in the dialogue in a systematic way.

7.   At the first meeting of the second series of talks, held in Rome, October 1977, the dialogue discussed speaking in tongues and the relation of experience to faith. The second meeting in Rome, October 1979, discussed the relation of Scripture and tradition, and the ministry of healing in the church. In Venice, October 1980, the meeting focused on church as a worshiping community and tradition and traditions. The meeting in Vienna in October, 1981, focused on the role of Mary. The last meeting of the series was held at Collegeville, Minnesota in October 1982, where Ministry was the area of concentration.

8.   A personal relationship with Jesus Christ belongs to
the definition of a Christian. Classical Pentecostals have
never accepted the position or taught that this relationship
must necessarily be expressed through speaking in tongues in
the sense that one could not be a Christian without speaking
in tongues.

9.   The manifestation of tongues was never entirely absent
in the history of the Church, and is found in a notable way
among Roman Catholics and other Christians involved in charismatic renewal, as well as among classical Pentecostals.

10.   It was agreed that every discussion about Christian
glossolalia should be founded on Scripture. That some New
Testament authors saw tongues as playing a role in the
Christian life is indicated in various books of the Bible.
(". . . and they were all filled with the Holy Spirit and
began to speak in other tongues as the Spirit gave them
utterance." Ac 2:4; Ac 10:46; 19:6; Mk 16:17; 1 Cor 12:4,
10, 18; 14:2, 5, 22; Rom 8:26.)

11.   The teaching of the classical Pentecostals on the
charisms seeks to be faithful to the picture of the New
Testament church as reflected in 1 Cor 12-14. Classical
Pentecostals have rendered a service by encouraging the
various communions to be open and receptive to those spiritual manifestations to which they claim to have been faithful.

12.　　By experience the dialogue understands the process or event by which one comes to a personal awareness of God. The experience of God's "presence" or "absence" can be a matter of conscious awareness. At the same time, and at a deeper level, there remains the constant abiding faith-conviction that God's loving presence is revealed in the person of his Son, through the Holy Spirit.

13.　　A Christian is one who experiences not only Easter and Pentecost, but also the Cross. The experience of God's "absence" can lead a Christian to a sense of being abandoned, as Jesus himself experienced on the Cross. The death of Christ is to be found at the heart of our Christian experience, and therefore we too experience a death: "I have been crucified with Christ; it is no longer I who live, but Christ who lives in me" (Gal 2:20).

14.　　There was no unanimity whether non-Christians may receive the life of the Holy Spirit. According to contemporary Roman Catholic understanding, to which Vatican II gives an authoritative expression, "All must be converted to Jesus Christ as he is made known by the Church's preaching" (Decree on the missionary activity of the Church, para 7). "The Church . . . is necessary for salvation" (Constitution on the Church, para 14). But Vatican II also says that all without exception are called by God to faith in Christ, and to salvation (Constitution on the Church, paras 1, 16; Declaration on the Relationship of the Church to Non-Christian

Religions, paras 1, 2). This is brought about "in an unseen way . . . known only to God" (Constitution on the Church in the Modern World, para 22; Decree on the missionary activity of the Church, para 7). This theology is seen as a legitimate development of the total New Testament teaching on God's saving love in Christ. The classical Pentecostal participants do not accept this development, but retain their interpretation of the Scripture that non-Christians are excluded from the life of the Spirit: "Truly, truly I say unto you, unless one is born anew, he cannot see the Kingdom of God" (Jn 3:3).

15.   In the immediacy of the Holy Spirit's manifestation in persons, he engages the natural faculties. In the exercise of the charisms, human faculties are not set aside, but used. The action of the Spirit is not identical with the forces inherent in nature.

16.   Individual spiritual experience is seen as part of the communitarian dimensions of the Gospel. Persons live in community, and the Church should be a lived-experience of community. There is rich history of community experience in the Church.

17.   No matter how vivid or powerful the individual's spiritual experience may be, it needs to be discerned and judged by the community. Love, which is the normative bond of community life, is the biblical criterion of all spiritual experience (cf. 1 Cor 13).

18.   Both Pentecostals and Roman Catholics hold that the
books of the Old Testament were accepted by the early
Church as inspired. The primitive Church existed for a
period without its own Christian Scriptures. Of the early
Christian writings, a certain number were accepted by the
Church, in the light of the Holy Spirit, as inspired.

19.   Roman Catholics believe that these Scriptures have
been handed down through the centuries in a tradition of
living faith, a tradition which has been experienced by the
whole Church, guided by Church leaders, operative in all
aspects of Christian life, and on occasion expressed in
written form in creeds, councils, etc. This tradition is
not a source of revelation separate from Scripture, but
Scripture responded to and actualized in the living tradition of the Church.

20.   Pentecostals maintain that there are not two authorities (i.e. Scripture plus Church tradition) but one
authority, that of Scripture. However, Scripture must be
read and understood with the illumination of the Holy Spirit.
Pentecostals believe that the interpretation of Scripture
can only be discerned through the Holy Spirit. In Pentecostal movements there is a broad consensus of what elements
are fundamental to the Christian faith. But there is a reluctance to give this consensus a status of tradition, because of a fear that religious tradition operates against
the Gospel.

442

21.   Pentecostals feel that further dialogue will be needed to discuss how the Roman Catholic Church can propose,
as a matter of faith, doctrines such as the assumption of
Mary which go beyond the letter of Scripture, and which
Pentecostals believe to be unacceptable tradition.

EXEGESIS

22.   In contemporary Roman Catholic scholarship the histo-
rial-critical method is the accepted framework within which
exegesis is done. In this method emphasis is given to understanding an ancient author in his own idiom, cultural context, and religious background.

23.   Pentecostals reject the philosophical and theological
principles of form and redaction criticism as militating
against the plenary inspiration of Scripture. They insist
on the necessity of the light given by the Holy Spirit if
the reader is to respond with faith and understanding to
the Word of God. It was a consensus of the participants
that this discussion was a valuable contribution to the dialogue.

24.   Roman Catholics believe that the light of the Holy
Spirit given in and through the Church is the ultimate
principle of interpretation of Scripture. They reject any
exegetical method that would deny this. However, they believe that critical methods are compatible with a Spirit-
inspired exegesis, and consider them necessary for a proper
understanding of the text.

25.   The Pentecostal form of exegesis, while having its
roots in evangelicalism, is not specifically defined. It
is admittedly in a formative stage. Current exegesis would
tend to be a pneumatic literal interpretation.

BIBLICAL INTERPRETATION

26.   In the event of conflicting interpretation of Scripture texts, Roman Catholics accept the guidance of the
Spirit as manifested in the living tradition. While the
teaching of the Church stands under the Word of God, this
same teaching serves the authoritative and authentic communication of the Word of God to the people. (Dogmatic
Constitution on Divine Revelation, para 10). While Catholics
believe both Scripture and Tradition cohere in each other
and, thus, transmit the Word of God, they do accord a priority to Scripture.

27.   In the event of conflicting interpretation of Scripture texts, Pentecostals rely on the Holy Spirit's guidance,
without the developed dogmatic structure found in the Roman
Catholic Church. While there may be some danger of subjectivism, God is trusted to provide the guidance of the Spirit
within the local body of believers. (Jn 14:26; 15:26; 16:13;
2 Jn 2:27)

FAITH AND REASON

28.   In the determination of the limits and validation of
religious knowledge, it was agreed that faith and reason

cannot be polarized. However, Pentecostals place a greater
emphasis upon pneumatic inspiration and supernatural manifestations, than on reason, for determining the limits and
validity of religious knowledge.

29.   In spite of the differences mentioned above, it is
seen that classical Pentecostals and Roman Catholics agree
on the basic elements of the Christian faith, e.g., Trinity,
incarnation, resurrection, inspiration of Scripture, the
preaching of the Gospel as an integral part of the ministry
of the Church, and the guidance of the Body of Christ by the
Holy Spirit.

30.   Still needing clarification in this dialogue is the
relation between Scripture and tradition. In this relationship, Roman Catholics do grant a priority to Scripture. But
according to Vatican Council II, (Decree on Revelation,
para 10): "Sacred tradition and sacred Scripture make up a
single sacred deposit of the Word of God. Hence both Scripture and tradition must be accepted and honored with equal
feelings of devotion and reverence." Also in need of further discussion is whether the various methods of exegesis,
for example the form-critical method which most Catholic
exegetes use, are compatible with classical Pentecostal
principles.

HEALING IN THE CHURCH

31.   The ministry of healing in the Church is practiced in
both the Roman Catholic Church and the Pentecostal churches

as part of their total ministry. Both Pentecostals and
Roman Catholics agree that through prayerful petition they
seek the healing of the whole person's physical, spiritual
and emotional needs. Catholics consider the "anointing of
the sick" a sacrament. Pentecostals accept anointing with
oil as a part of the commission to minister healing with
the preaching of the Gospel. (In the Roman Catholic Church
the sacrament of anointing of the sick was formerly named
"extreme unction.")

32.   In the life of the Roman Catholic Church there have
been, and are, those who dedicate their lives to the care of
and ministry to the sick. Pentecostals are becoming increasingly involved in this important aspect of ministry to the
sick and suffering.

33.   There are attitudinal differences with regard to healing. Roman Catholic practice regards healing of the body as
one outcome of the ministry to the sick in the church. Pentecostals place more emphasis on the expectation of healing
in the afflicted through preaching and praying. There is a
basic difference in each approach to healing. Roman Catholics may seek healing in sacramental rites, in healing services, novenas and similar forms of devotion. They also go
on pilgrimage to shrines where healing may take place. At
these places many seek and experience a deepening of faith
and a spiritual healing. Pentecostals teach people to expect healing anywhere at any time.

34.   Both in their official teaching, recognize and accept
that Jesus is the Healer and that faith looks to Jesus for
this grace. Pentecostals as well as Roman Catholics exercise reserve in making judgments about miraculous manifestations and healings.

35.   There is a difference in expectation--that of Catholics
being more passive while that of Pentecostals being more
aggressive. There is admittedly a new awareness of the
reality of the healing in the Roman Catholic Church, both
within and outside the sacramental order. On the other hand,
the dialogue is aware of the existence of some popular religious expressions that may lack sufficient theological understanding.

36.   The place of suffering in this life is looked upon by
Roman Catholics and some Pentecostals as a means of grace,
as a purifying of the soul, and as an instrument for opening
one to God's spiritual strength which sustains one and
causes one to rejoice in affliction. Both Roman Catholics
and Pentecostals believe that suffering may lead one to
understand and be conformed (Phil 3:10) to the redemptive
suffering of Jesus. However, Pentecostals continue to expect healing unless there is a special revelation that God
has some other purpose. Both Roman Catholics and Pentecostals accept that the will of God is preeminent in the whole
matter of healing.

37.   Although there appears to be some similarity in lay
participation in the ministry of healing, the discussions

revealed that there is still a wide gap between Catholics and Pentecostals. Catholics, singly and in community, pray for the sick and with the sick. However only the priest may administer the "Anointing of the Sick" which is a sacrament. Pentecostals anoint with oil (Js 5:14-15) but do not confine the anointing with oil to the ordained ministry. The ministry to the sick, with the laying on of hands by all believers (Mk 16:17-18), is commonly practiced.

38.   In contemporary Roman Catholic theology the necessity for healing is applied to a broader spectrum of social ills. In this application of healing to problems of social injustice Roman Catholics and classical Pentecostals have widely divergent views. Because of economic and cultural exploitation, many people live in subhuman economic disease. Roman Catholics and Pentecostals have different approaches to the mandate to heal the social conditions which hinder good health.

39.   Classical Pentecostals are reluctant to apply divine healing to such a broad range of social injustices. Though they believe exploitative conditions should be rectified they would emphasize the priority of direct evangelism, as the best means of effecting social change.

40.   There are a number of areas where there is agreement between Roman Catholics and Pentecostals: the necessity of the Cross, healing as a sign of the Kingdom, healing of the total person, the involvement of the laity in prayer for healing, the expectation of healing through the Eucharist/ Lord's Supper and, Christ as the Healer.

COMMUNITY, WORSHIP AND COMMUNION   [1980]

41.   Pentecostals insist on a personal confession of faith
in Jesus Christ as the basis of Christian community, rather
than on a sacramental and ecclesial approach to the mediating work of Christ. They hold that the believer experiences Christ in every aspect of the worshiping community:
singing, praying, testimony, preaching, the ordinance of
Baptism, the celebration of Holy Communion, and also in
daily living.

42.   Roman Catholics insist on conversion to the living
God by personal encounter with the living Christ. This
conversion often takes place gradually. For Roman Catholics,
the Church, its ministry and sacraments, are the normal instruments and manifestations of Christ's action and presence,
and of the gift of His Spirit. The sacraments are acts of
Christ which make present and active the saving power of
the Paschal Mystery.

43.   For membership in a Pentecostal church individuals are
expected to have experienced a personal confession of faith
in Jesus Christ; and then participate in the life, follow
the leadership and be willing to accept responsibility in
the church. In some Pentecostal churches, membership is
concurrent with one's water baptism by immersion. Membership in the Roman Catholic Church requires baptism, profession of Roman Catholic faith, and active communion with
the local community, the bishops and the successor of
St Peter.

44.   Both among Pentecostals and Roman Catholics, members
may lose their fellowship in the community for serious de-
viation in doctrine or practice. This penalty of severance
from the church is intended to be remedial, a reminder of
one's guilt before God and the need for repentance.

45.   Both Pentecostals and Roman Catholics celebrate the
Lord's Supper/Eucharist with notable difference in doctrine
and practice. Roman Catholics regard the Eucharist as a
sacramental memorial of Christ's sacrifice on Calvary in the
Biblical sense of the word *anamnesis*. By God's power, in
the Eucharistic celebration Jesus is present in His death
and resurrection. This sacred rite is for Roman Catholics
a privileged means of grace and the central act of worship.
It is celebrated frequently, even daily. Among Pentecostals,
the Lord's Supper does not hold an equally predominant place
in their life of worship. Most Pentecostals celebrate the
Lord's Supper as an ordinance in obedience to the command
of the Lord. Other Pentecostal churches believe this memorial to be more than a reminder of Jesus' death and resurrection, considering it a means of grace.

46.   Generally Pentecostals practice "open communion," that
is, anyone may participate in the Lord's Supper provided
they acknowledge the Lordship of Christ and have examined
their own dispositions (1 Cor 11:28). Except in certain
cases of spiritual necessity determined by the Church, the
Roman Church admits to communion only its own members provided they are free from serious sin. This is not meant to

be a refusal of fellowship with other Christians, but rather expresses the Roman Catholic Church's understanding of the relationship between the Church and the Eucharist.

47.   The justification for this practice by Catholics was contested by Pentecostals. This was found to be painful on both sides and the dialogue agrees that the subject with regard to admission to communion requires a great deal of further discussion.

48.   Both Pentecostals and Roman Catholics agree that a common faith is the basis of communion in the body of Christ. For Roman Catholics, full communion means the collegial unity of the heads of the local Churches; namely, the bishops, with the Bishop of Rome who exercises the primacy. Pentecostals would not attach the same significance to structural bonds between churches, and will welcome fellowship with many autonomous churches. The Roman Catholic church recognizes the mediation of Christ at work in churches which are not in full communion with it, through the Word that is preached and believed, the sacraments that are celebrated and the ministry that is exercised. If it considers that these gifts are not found in their fullness in a particular church it does not thereby make any judgment on the actual holiness of the members of that church. The Roman Catholic church describes the relationship of other Christians with Catholics as that of brothers and sisters in an incomplete communion (Decree on Ecumenism).

TRADITION AND TRADITIONS

49.   Our views concerning the sacredness and importance of
Holy Scripture allowed us to sense immediately that we had
much more to affirm in one another than to question. Both
sides of the dialogue agreed as to the inspired nature of
both the Old Testament and the New Testament, thus giving
Scripture a privileged place in both churches.

50.   The canonicity of the New Testament is agreed upon in
terms of selection and the process of its establishment by
the church. Both Pentecostals and Roman Catholics recognize
the role of the church in the composition of the books of
the New Testament and in the formation of the canon and both
acknowledge that the church preceeded the written New Testament.

51.   The Pentecostal representatives stress that the church
itself was created by the calling (election) of Christ, and
formed by the dominical sayings of Jesus, and the Messianic
interpretation of the Scriptures of Jesus Himself (Lk 24:45ff).
In this sense, according to Pentecostals, the church itself
was formed by the Word of God. The church's role in the
formation of the New Testament is then essentially that of
one who transmits, interprets and applies the salvific
message of Jesus Christ. Roman Catholics emphasize more
the role of the church as having an authority recognizing
and enunciating the truth of the Gospel in doctrinal pronouncements.

52.   Both sides recognize that Scripture is of necessity
linked to interpretation. Both agree that scriptural content itself includes interpretation; that it requires interpretation; and thus an authoritative interpreter. There is
significant divergence as to the degree of interpretation
within Scripture and the kind of interpretation by the
church necessary in order to understand Scripture accurately.
Disagreement centers around what or who is an authoritative
interpreter. To the Pentecostal it is the right interpretation under the illumination of the Holy Spirit leading to
consensus. To the Roman Catholic, it is the church interpreting Scripture as understood by the people of God and
discerned by the teaching office of the church. Both Pentecostals and Roman Catholics see interpretative authority as
an expression of the activity of the Spirit in the church.

53.   Both Roman Catholics and Pentecostals recognize the
existence of a process of theological discernment in the
on-going life of the church. The Roman Catholics affirm
the ministry of discernment by the teaching office of the
church and also recognize that a ministry of discernment
may exist outside the Roman Catholic church. The sharpest
disagreement arose concerning the irreformable character of
some of these discernments. Roman Catholics hold that the
faithful will not be led into error when the authority of
the church is fully engaged in enunciating the faith. Pentecostals make no such claim.

54.   Pentecostals recognize the strength of the Roman Catholic understanding of corporate and collegial interpretation
of Scripture. However, Pentecostals would like to share
with Roman Catholics their characteristic experience of
direct dependence upon the Holy Spirit for illumination and
interpretation of Scripture.

55.   A major difference was encountered in the understanding of the role of tradition. Roman Catholics in the dialogue explain tradition in a two-fold sense, each sense
related to the other. Tradition, here spelled with a capi-
tal T, stands for everything that is being and has been
handed down: the once for all revelation made by God in
Jesus Christ, the Word of God proclaimed in written and oral
form, and the whole of the Spirit-filled community's response to the truth of the Gospel. As such, Tradition contains both an active element of handing down by the church,
and a passive one of the material handed down. Within Tradition in this sense, the Word of God as Scripture has a
kind of primacy. In this understanding Tradition is a continuous process.

56.   Tradition in this sense is not to be confused with
traditions. These are various ways of practice and teaching whereby Tradition is transmitted. These traditions
become binding only when they are made the object of a
special decision of Church authority.

57.   Classical Pentecostals would not place the same value
upon Tradition (or tradition) as Roman Catholics, unless

grounded in the express witness of Scripture. The Pentecostals while acknowledging the accumulation of traditions in their own history would say that these traditions, apart from Scripture, have little authority in the Church.

PERSPECTIVES ON MARY [1981]

58.   Since Catholic doctrine concerning Mary was perceived as a point of divergence, it was important to classical Pentecostals to discuss this topic. Considerable time was needed to treat the various issues: the doctrine itself, the method by which the doctrine is justified, and the practical consequences at the popular level. The time devoted to the issues is reflected in the space given this topic in the report.

Perspectives on Mary

59.   Both classical Pentecostals and Roman Catholics agree that the various biblical texts which mention Mary witness to the importance of Mary in the New Testament. The point of divergence was the doctrinal development which took place on the basis of these texts. Classical Pentecostals insist that they cannot go beyond the clear meaning of the text which is normative for all doctrine and experience. Roman Catholics also maintain that Scripture is normative for any and all later doctrinal development. But they further hold that the church, praying and preaching the Scriptures, can, through guidance of the Holy Spirit who leads into all truth, find in the biblical texts and in

complete fidelity to them a meaning which goes beyond the classical Pentecostals' interpretation.

60.   Behind the differences between classical Pentecostals and Roman Catholics in interpretation of specific Marian texts in the Scriptures lie doctrinal differences, often implicit and unexpressed. Possibly the most important of these are in the area of Mary's relationship to the church and her role in the communion of saints.

61.   Both classical Pentecostals and Roman Catholics were surprised that they had entertained unreal perceptions of the others' views on Mary. Classical Pentecostals were pleased to learn of the concern of authorities in the Roman Catholic church to be prudent in appraising Marian doctrinal development which claims a biblical basis. Classical Pentecostals, while recognizing that doctrinal development that is clearly based on scriptural evidence is not entirely absent from Pentecostal history, admit no doctrinal development with regard to Mary.

The Motherhood of Mary

62.   Both Roman Catholics and Pentecostals agree that Mary is the Mother of Jesus Christ who is the Son of God and as such she occupies a unique place. Both Roman Catholics and classical Pentecostals recognize the historical origins of the title "Mother of God" (*Theotokos*), arising from the christological disputes at the Council of Ephesus (431 AD). In order to preserve the unity of the one person, having two natures, to which the Virgin gave birth, the council

approved the title "theotokos" ("God-bearer" or "Mother of God"). This was not a Marian definition, concerned to give Mary a new title, but a christological definition concerned with the identity of Jesus Christ. It is only at the moment of the Incarnation that she becomes the Mother of God. She is not the Mother of God in his eternal triune existence, but the Mother of God the Son in his Incarnation.

The Veneration of Mary

63.   Roman Catholics and classical Pentecostals concur in the special respect due to Mary as the mother of Jesus. Both view her as the outstanding example or model of faith, humility and virtue. Both Roman Catholics and Pentecostals share a concern for the necessity of a correct perspective on Mary. However, there are significant differences in the understanding of the veneration to be given to Mary.

64.   Pentecostals expressed concern about what they con-sider to be excesses in contemporary veneration of Mary. For Pentecostals, certain Roman Catholic practices of Marian veneration appear to be superstitious and idolatrous. For Roman Catholics there is an apparent failure among Pente-costals to take account of the place of Mary in God's design as indicated in Holy Scripture.

65.   Roman Catholics, while admitting the occurence of cer-tain excesses in the practice of veneration of Mary, were careful to point out that proper veneration of Mary is always christological. In addition, Roman Catholics gave evidence that practical steps are being taken to correct excesses

where they occur, in line with the norms of the Second
Vatican Council, "Constitution on the Church," Chapter 8,
and Pope Paul VI in his encyclical Marialis Cultus (1974),
paras 24-36.

The Intercession of Mary

66.   Both Pentecostals and Roman Catholics teach that Mary
in no way substitutes for, or replaces, the one Saviour and
Mediator Jesus Christ. Both believe in direct, immediate
contact between the believer and God. Both pray to God the
Father, through the Son, in the Holy Spirit. Catholics believe that intercessory prayers directed to Mary do not end
in Mary but in God Himself. Pentecostals would not invoke
the intercession of Mary or other saints in heaven because
they do not consider it a valid biblical practice.

Catholic Doctrine on the Graces Given to Mary

67.   Roman Catholics believe that Mary always remained a
virgin, that she was conceived free from all stain of sin,
and that at the end of her life she was assumed body and
soul into heaven. Pentecostals reject these beliefs.

68.   Roman Catholics claim that belief about these graces
given to Mary belongs to the tradition of the church in
which the Word of God is unfolded. Pentecostals can find
no warrant for these beliefs in Scripture. As well as
questioning the value of tradition as a basis for the doctrines of faith, Pentecostals would suggest that these traditions about perpetual virginity, immaculate conception,
and assumption, are without Scriptural basis.

69.   In the "hierarchy of truths" of faith held by the
Roman Catholics, these three doctrines are placed among
the truths that are integral to the Roman Catholic faith.
Roman Catholics do not believe that those outside the Roman
Catholic church who do not hold these truths are, on that
account, excluded from salvation.

The Virginity of Mary

70.   Both Pentecostals and Roman Catholics agree that Mary
was a virgin in the conception of Jesus and see in the texts
which state it an important affirmation of the divine Sonship of Christ. Roman Catholics believe that Mary remained
a virgin after the birth of Jesus and did not have other
offspring. Pentecostals commonly maintain that Scripture
records she had other offspring and lived as the wife of
Joseph in the full sense.

71.   Roman Catholics take the evidence of Scripture as
being open to the developments concerning the virginity of
Mary which they find expressed in the earliest Fathers of
the church. They found in Tradition (understood in the
total experience and response of the church as she prays
and preaches the Word of God) evidence of Mary's virginity.

The Immaculate Conception of Mary

72.   Roman Catholics hold the doctrine of the Immaculate
Conception to be founded on the church's reflection on the
Bible, both the Old and New Testaments. This doctrine is
seen to follow upon consideration of her role as the Mother
of the Savior and of texts which present her as the perfect

fulfillment of Old Testament types, e.g., "the virgin daughter of Sion" (Lk 1:26-38; cf. Zph 3:14-20; Zch 2:10; 9:9), the "woman" (Jn 2:1-11; 19:25-27; cf. Gn 3:15). These texts form a biblical theology of Mary, which provides a basis for the development of the doctrine of the Immaculate Conception. The explicit development of the doctrine in the life of the church led to its definition by Pope Pius IX in 1854.

73.   Pentecostals acknowledge Catholic assurances that the special grace claimed for Mary is a redeeming grace that comes from Jesus. She stands among the redeemed and is a member of the church. However, Pentecostals cannot find any basis for the doctrine of Mary's Immaculate Conception in Scripture. Furthermore, Pentecostals do not see any value for salvation in this doctrine. Roman Catholics see in the Pentecostal attitude a failure to appreciate fully the implications of the Incarnation and the power of Christ's saving and sanctifying grace.

74.   Further clarification of issues arising from this doctrine would entail a wider discussion by us of pneumatology, christology and ecclesiology. Roman Catholics believe a basic distortion takes place when this doctrine is considered in isolation.

The Assumption of Mary

75.   Roman Catholics see the doctrine of the Assumption, which was explicitly affirmed in the Fathers of the church as early as the sixth century, to be in accordance with basic biblical doctrines. The Risen Christ is the beginning

of the new creation, which is born from above in the death
and resurrection of Christ. In Mary, because of her unique
relationship with Christ, this new creation by the Spirit
was achieved to the point that the life of the Spirit triumphed fully in her. Consequently she is already with her
body in the glory of God, with her risen Son.

76.   The Pentecostal difficulty rests in the absence of
biblical evidence. There is a generally accepted view that
Mary, as one of the faithful, awaits the day of resurrection
when she, along with all Christians, will be united bodily
with her Son in glory. Pentecostals see a parallel between
Mary's "assumption" and the Pentecostal understanding of
the "bodily resurrection" or the "rapture of the church"
(1 Thes 4:13-18, cf esp. v 17), but differ as to when this
will take place for Mary.

MINISTRY IN THE CHURCH [1982]

77.   While it is recognized that the word ministry in the
New Testament covers many activities, the focus of the dialogue bears upon how ministry in the church continues the
ministry of the Apostles.

78.   Such ministry includes all that pertains to the
preaching and proclamation of God's Word on which the
churches are founded, and all that is required for the
building up of the church in Christ.

79.   For Roman Catholics, all ministries contribute to
these ends, but particular importance is attached to the
ministry of bishops, and to that of the presbyters and

deacons who collaborate with them. Classical Pentecostals find an exercise of apostolic ministry wherever through the preaching of God's Word churches are founded, persons and communities are converted to Jesus Christ, and manifestations of the Holy Spirit are in evidence. Within the variety of polity found in Pentecostal circles, biblical terms such as elder, deacon, bishop and pastor are used to designate a variety of offices and ministries, and are not always given the same meaning.

80.   It is agreed by both sides of the dialogue that order and structure are necessary to the exercise of ministry.

81.   In the development and structuring of ministry, there is no single New Testament pattern. The Spirit has many times led churches to adapt their ministries to the needs of place and time.

82.   Roman Catholics see evidence of ministerial office in the New Testament and find in such office part of God's design for the early church, but find in the gradual emergence of the three-fold ministry of bishop, presbyter and deacon the way in which God's design is fulfilled and structural and ministerial needs are met in the Church.

83.   The positions of Classical Pentecostals are more varied. Although there is reluctance in some Pentecostal circles to speak of the ministries of apostle and prophet because of the historical abuse sometimes associated with these ministries, they are recognized as existing and important to the life of the church. Even though there is no

uniformity in the way that the New Testament depicts ministry, it is the desire of Pentecostals to seek guidelines
for ministry and office in the New Testament.

84.   Pentecostals appeal primarily to the priesthood of
all believers, which connotes access to God and a participation in ministry on the part of all believers. Pentecostals
point to a problem of over-institutionalization of ministry.
They believe that they find evidence of this in the history
and practice of the Roman Catholic church.

85.   Roman Catholics place emphasis on the need for the
institution of ecclesial offices as part of the divine plan
for the church. They also see such institutions and ministries as related to and aiding the priesthood and ministry
of all within the one body. At the same time they are
aware of the dangers of institutionalism. In recent decades,
there has been a renewed concern in the Roman Catholic Church
for the development of the ministry of all believers. Roman
Catholics furthermore feel that Pentecostals fail to give
due acknowledgement to the visible aspect of the Church or
to the sacrament of order and the sacramental ministry.

Ordination

86.   Pentecostals see ordination as a recognition of spiritual gifts already imparted. For Pentecostals, ministry
is always initiated by a divine call and attended by evidence of reception of necessary gifts and graces. Ordination of one who has received appropriate gifts provides
denominational authority for his continuing function in the
ministry to which he has been called.

87.   For Roman Catholics, the ministry of ecclesial office
is given by God who calls a candidate and pours out his
Spirit upon him and gives him a special share in the priesthood of Christ. This gift must be discerned by the church,
in the form laid down by church discipline. Ordination is
considered a sacrament, which imparts grace, gifts and
authority for the ministry of the word, sacrament and pastoral office.

Apostolic Succession

88.   Both Roman Catholics and Pentecostals believe that
the church lives in continuity with the New Testament
apostles and their proclamation, and with the apostolic
church. A primary manifestation of this is to be found in
fidelity to the apostolic teaching.

89.   For Roman Catholics, the succession of bishops in an
orderly transmission of ministry through history is both
guarantee and manifestation of this fidelity.

90.   For Pentecostals, the current dynamic of the Spirit
is regarded as a more valid endorsement of apostolic faith
and ministry than an unbroken line of episcopal succession.
They look to apostolic life and to the power of preaching
which leads to conversions to Jesus Christ as an authentication of apostolic ministry. They question Roman Catholics
as to whether in their insistence on episcopal succession
they have at times ignored the requirements of apostolic
life. Roman Catholics held the necessity of apostolic life
for an effective ministry. However they maintain that the

sovereignty of God's act in the transmission of the Word
and the ministry of sacrament is not nullified by the personal infidelity of the minister.

91.   Both partners to the dialogue strongly assert that
holiness of life is essential to an effective ministry and
recognize that the quality of apostolic life of the minister
has an effect on the quality of his ministry. Both, by
their respective discipline and practice, seek to provide
seriously for the holiness of ministers. Both recognize
that at times, the power and sovereignty of God is operative in the ministry of a weak and sinful minister, although
the discipline of both Classical Pentecostals and Roman
Catholics provides for the removal from office of anyone
who is plainly unworthy.

Recognition of Ministries

92.   Each partner to the dialogue recognizes that God is
at work through the ministry of the other and recognizes
that the body of Christ is being built up through it.
(Decree on Ecumenism, paras 3 and 22) The issue of recognition depends on ecclesiological questions that still need
elucidation. However, serious disagreements still remain.

TOPICS FOR FURTHER DISCUSSION

93.   During our conversations we touched on a number of
topics which could not be discussed adequately and would
have to be taken up at a later date. Among them were the
following: a) the personal moment of faith, b) the

communion of saints in relation to mariology and the intercession of the saints, c) the development of doctrine in
its relation to Scripture and Tradition, d) the inadequacy
and limitation in doctrinal formulations marked with the
stamp of a certain historial moment, e) the binding force
of the Marian Doctrines which have been defined as they
relate to salvation, within the Roman Catholic church.

CHARACTER OF THE FINAL REPORT

94.   This international dialogue with representatives of
classical Pentecostals and Roman Catholics has been characterized by the seriousness of the exchange as participants
seek to reflect in all fidelity the doctrine of their
church and at the same time to learn from their opposite
partners in dialogue what their true faith stance is.
These responsibilities have been exercised with candor and
earnestness and have resulted in this final report. Clearly,
the report does not commit any church or tradition to any
theological position but is offered to them for their reflection and evaluation.

CONCLUSION

95.   The members of the dialogue have experienced mutual
respect and acceptance, hoping that the major points of
difference will provide an occasion for continuing dialogue
to our mutual enrichment.

96.   It is the consensus of the participants that the dialogue should continue in this same spirit. Every effort

will be made to encourage opportunities for similar bilateral theological conversation at the local level.

97.   To that end, the dialogue enters into a period of
assimilation to digest the results of the first two phases
of exchange and to give broader exposure to mutual efforts
undertaken to promote better understanding.

98.   Finally, the participants wish to affirm the dialogue
as an ongoing instrument of communication between the two
traditions.

May 9, 1984

STUDIEN ZUR INTERKULTURELLEN GESCHICHTE DES CHRISTENTUMS
ETUDES D'HISTOIRE INTERCULTURELLE DU CHRISTIANISME
STUDIES IN THE INTERCULTURAL HISTORY OF CHRISTIANITY

Begründet von/fondé par/founded by
Hans Jochen Margull † , Hamburg

Herausgegeben von/edité par/edited by

| Richard Friedli | Walter J. Hollenweger | Theo Sundermeier |
| Université de Fribourg | University of Birmingham | Universität Heidelberg |